£11.00

Climbers' Club Guides

Edited by John Willson

CW00421838

Swanage

(Reprint)

by

Nigel Coe

Maps and Diagrams by **Don Sargeant**

Front Cover: *Infinite Gravity*, Blackers Hole
Climber: Pete Oxley
Photo: Jon Cook

Rear Cover: *Skeleton Ridge*, Isle of Wight (first ascent)
Climber: Lorraine Smythe
Photo: Mick Fowler

Published by The Climbers' Club

Limestone Climbs on the Dorset Coast (Southampton UMC 1961)
by B Annette

Dorset Climbs (The Climbers' Club 1969)
by R C White

Dorset (Private publication 1977)
by R J Crewe

Swanage (The Climbers' Club 1986)
by G A Jenkin

Swanage and Portland (The Climbers' Club 1995)
by Nigel Coe

Swanage (The Climbers' Club – 1995 Edition Volume 2, reprinted 2002)
by Nigel Coe

© The Climbers' Club 1995
Coe, Nigel   Swanage and Portland   (Climbers' Club Guides)

British Library Cataloguing in Publication Data

A catalogue record for this book is available from the British Library

796.522

ISBN 0-901601-72-1

This volume is a reprint of *Swanage and Portland* 1995 (Book Two)

Some important additional and updated information is appended on page 304. The Historical printed in Book One in 1995 can be downloaded as a PDF file from www.climbers-club.co.uk

Prepared for printing by Parker Typesetting Services, Leicester
Produced by The Ernest Press, Glasgow G46 6AQ
Distributed by Cordee, 3a de Montfort Street, Leicester LE1 7HD

Contents

List of Maps and Diagrams

Introduction

This guidebook covers the climbing near Swanage in Dorset and on the Isle of Wight. The Dorset sea-cliffs are blessed with a mild climate and a low tidal range. During the winter months, and when the skies are clear, the area can be surprisingly warm and comfortable for climbing when other parts of the country might be considered out of the question. The location is further enhanced by the beauty of its setting within the serene Dorset countryside; whether for climbing, enjoying one of its many fine walks, or just exploring the coves and old quarries, it is an area that is a pleasure to visit time and time again.

THE ROCK

The limestone cliffs at Swanage were formed from the skeletal remains of marine organisms that lived in the warm Jurassic seas about 165 million years ago. Fossil remnants from this period are common throughout the area, with large ammonites occasionally providing a welcome jug. The upper section of the cliff yields the Purbeck/Portland building stone, known locally as 'cliffstone'. This is the youngest of the Jurassic limestone beds in Britain and requires a climbing approach that is quite different from the style demanded by the Carboniferous limestones of Derbyshire and Pembroke or the Devonian limestone at Torbay. The beds are almost horizontal and are set in massive rectangular blocks that jut further out above each other as height is gained, so that the top often overhangs the base. Consequently, the climbing is always steep, usually exposed, and invariably dramatic. Most of the climbs, although imposing, tend to be furnished with sizable holds and with good cracks for protection; the rock is rough and the friction excellent.

On the shorter sections of the cliff, where the sea has washed the surfaces clean, the rock is generally sound. However, the steepness of the climbing and the intimidating appearance of the routes are given added spice in the higher and more serious areas by a degree of loose rock that can be disconcerting when first encountered. The finish is often the most troublesome part of a Swanage climb irrespective of its grade, the insecure slope of earth and loose blocks at the top requiring great care for a safe exit to be ensured. This aspect of Swanage climbing needs a period of acclimatization, so that those situations which may initially be considered unnerving can later be enjoyed and savoured to the full.

APPROACH

While all the climbs in this book are on the Isle of Purbeck or the Isle of Wight, only the second is a true island. Swanage, on the Isle of Purbeck, is easily reached in just a few hours from either London or Bristol. However, in busy periods bottlenecks can occur on entering Purbeck; the journey around Poole Harbour and through Wareham is usually faster than the shorter route via the chain ferry at the harbour mouth. Durlston Country Park is the best parking spot for many of the Swanage cliffs. Cost-conscious regulars can save money with a season ticket; enquire at the Country Park information centre or ring 01929 424443 for details.

Two Ordnance Survey 1:50,000 maps are useful: Sheet 195 (Bournemouth and Purbeck) for Swanage and Sheet 196 (The Solent) for the Isle of Wight.

CRAG OVERVIEW
St Aldhelm's Head Far above the sea but exposed to the wind. Mainly for the loose-rock enthusiast.

Slippery Ledge A quieter alternative to Subluminal, although with slightly less sound rock. Many short Severes and Very Severes, for which calm seas are needed.

Winspit Away from the sea, Quarryman's Wall provides sport climbs which are usually sheltered from the wind.

Seacombe Low tide is required at Seacombe West, whereas only calm seas are necessary for The Gallery. There is a spread of grades but Very Severes predominate.

Hedbury Quarry This quarry, with its bolt-protected Extremes, provides a quieter alternative to Dancing Ledge.

Smokey Hole & Topmast Quarry Rarely climbed upon – so close to Dancing Ledge, yet a different world.

Dancing Ledge A popular venue also suffering from schizophrenia: a host of sport climbs on its quarried walls, and, down on the cliff below, the only spot in the area suitable for instructing groups of beginners.

Guillemot Ledge Excellent two-pitch climbs, safe tops, and protection from the sea ensure Guillemot's popularity.

Cormorant Ledge An area of adventure climbs, similar to Boulder Ruckle; sandwiched between a tidal base and relatively serious earth slopes.

Blackers Hole A multitude of overhang-laden, often bolt-protected Extremes, which include Dorset's hardest route!

The Cattle Troughs Area Calm seas are required throughout this varied area. Deep-water solos in Conner Cove, a sea of overhangs at Fisherman's Ledge, short vicious problems at The Promenade, and climbs to suit beginners at Cattle Troughs itself.

Boulder Ruckle The premier cliff of the region, where the accent is on adventure. There is something here to test your mettle, from Hard Severe to E6.

The Lighthouse Cliffs An easy approach helps make Subluminal, with its short, solid routes, the most popular cliff in this guidebook. Steep routes with hanging belays are the order of the day in the Black Zawn, and further east *Traverse of the Gods* is a must!

Old Harry Rocks The tidal considerations and problematic descents of these chalk sea-stacks add a certain something to their appeal.

The Agglestone Dorset's own little piece of The Peak! Although small, this ironstone boulder gives some of the best bouldering in the area.

Isle of Wight Impressive chalk expeditions made even more serious by their long approaches by abseil or boat.

SAFER CLIMBING

Swanage has had more than its fair share of accidents, so no apologies are made for offering the following recommendations.

Do not abseil into an area unless you are able and equipped to prusik out. When abseiling, ensure the rope is not laid over sharp edges or loose rock. Leave the abseil rope in place to aid retreat if necessary.

Consider wearing a helmet, but in any event choose belays protected from falling rock.

Always belay at the foot of sea-level cliffs.

Carry prusik loops on overhanging climbs.

Place extra runners before loose exits.

Make sure the rope stays out of the water: several ropes have been lost after being washed around submerged boulders.

On sea-level traverses carry gear on bandoliers, which, in the event of a fall, can be easily jettisoned before you reach Davy Jones's Locker!

For routes with lower-off points, ensure your second understands whether you are going to abseil or be lowered off.

THE SEA

The nominal tidal range is very small. The range of spring-tides, which coincide with a full moon, is about six feet, that of neaps only four feet. However, the actual range can be considerably greater in certain sea conditions. The flood tide flows to the east and the ebb tide to the west. Strong tidal races can be seen around the headlands and these areas are particularly dangerous. Swimming is not advised in the open sea in any but the calmest conditions, and then only for strong swimmers. Tide times can be obtained from local papers, the coastguard, or The Climbers' Club website (www.climbers-club.co.uk).

THE DESCRIPTIONS

All areas and route descriptions run in sequence from **left to right** (i.e. west to east). However, the introduction to each area describes the cliff in the direction of approach from the normal entry point.

Left and Right apply as the climber is facing the rock unless stated otherwise.

Read the full route description before embarking on a climb, as some climbs require pegs to be placed and a few need a fixed rope for a belay or to pull out on. Pitch lengths usually refer to the amount of actual climbing and do not necessarily include easy scrambling up grass and earth. Safe ground can always be reached with a 50-metre rope, however.

The symbol [R] is used to indicate routes which are affected by Nesting-Season Restrictions (See the Bird Restrictions section below).

Those routes not known to have had a second ascent are marked with a † symbol; their grades should be treated with caution. (The use of a dagger is an arbitrary choice but not totally inappropriate!) Routes marked †† have sustained a major rockfall, almost certainly resulting in significant but unassessed change to the climbing.

A few routes have suffered an ethical impropriety; these include bolted climbs on cliffs designated bolt-free and some with manufactured holds. As such impurities are likely to be (or to have been) purged, the descriptions and grades may well not stand. These route descriptions are marginally indented.

The *S* symbol indicates sport climbs, routes with good bolt protection; quick-draws only are required unless otherwise specified.

GRADES

The traditional adjectival grading-system is used throughout this guide: Difficult, Very Difficult, Severe, Hard Severe, Very Severe, Hard Very Severe, Extremely Severe. The latter is broken down into the open-ended E1, E2, E3... system. The old XS grade has been used for a small number of climbs in the Extremely Severe bracket where the first ascensionist has been unable to supply an E-grade, either because the climbs are on a marginal medium (chalk) or because they were soloed. Artificial climbs are graded A1, A2, A3. Numerical (technical) grades are provided for pitches of 4a and above.

Most climbers drop a grade or two when first climbing on a different type of rock because of the different skills required. The average gritstone climb needs a forceful approach coupled with competence in jamming or in handling rounded breaks, whereas a typical climb of the same grade in this guidebook demands greater proficiency in runner placement and dictates a more cautious climbing style. Similarly, if you are used to only one style of climb, whether it be nut- or bolt-protected, you may wish to lower your target grade when first sampling the other type. Nut-protected routes may feel bold to sport climbers and sport climbs may feel overly technical or fingery to those used to nut-protected routes.

Where bolted routes have been climbed without their fixed protection, two grades are given. The grade in brackets is that of the bolder style of ascent.

The routes are described in the freest manner in which they have been climbed. If any form of aid is required on a route, either for resting or to facilitate progress, then this is included in brackets after the grade as well as being mentioned in the text.

ROUTE QUALITY

The standard one-to-three star system is used to help indicate the respective quality of each climb. A single star indicates that a climb is of good quality, while three stars denote the very best. Many, many unstarred routes are worthy of attention, however. It must be stressed that the star ratings of unrepeated routes are based to a large extent on the opinions of the first ascensionist.

GEAR

It is assumed that *Friends*, wires, and microwires (*RPs*, etc.) are a standard part of a climber's rack of equipment. Sometimes the lack of a particular piece of gear may substantially increase the seriousness of a climb; these 'vital' placements are mentioned where known. They occur generally on the harder climbs. For climbs with bolt protection other than sport climbs a rack may be necessary.

There have been at least one death and one serious injury due to the failure of *in-situ* gear at Swanage. Fixed protection can deteriorate rapidly on sea-cliffs, so always treat it with caution. The author has removed several pegs where good natural placements existed close by. At a cursory glance these pegs appeared worth clipping, but they snapped under surprisingly little force, revealing cross-sections which were ninety-nine per cent rust.

Where pegs or bolts are mentioned without qualification they were in place at the time of writing (1995). The descriptions state explicitly where pegs need to be placed for protection and for belays. For threads, however, it is explicitly stated when they *are* in place. While modern-day wires and *Friends* have made pegs on a number of routes redundant, there nonetheless remain some climbs where pegs are essential. Legitimate *in-situ* pegs should therefore not be removed.

BIRD RESTRICTIONS

Certain parts of the cliff at Swanage are subject to restrictions during the bird nesting-season to protect species of sea-birds that are rare to this particular coastline. It is vitally important that climbers respect these restrictions since any disturbances could well have a serious effect upon these colonies. Those climbs which lie within a restricted area are denoted by [R] in the main text.

The original restrictions on Purbeck, introduced in 1976, remained unchanged for the following seventeen years and have in general worked well. However, it was thought that changes in the birds' habits necessitated (and the faster dissemination of information to climbers would allow) a more flexible and responsive approach. In future, an assessment will be made each year of nesting patterns, and as a result the seasonal restrictions may change. Any changes will be published in the climbing press and publicized on signs and in pamphlets available at the main access points to the cliffs.

The boundaries of the seasonally restricted areas are marked by red and green posts situated close to the cliff-top. Needless to say, the red side of a post indicates the restricted area, and the green the restriction-free side. (Note, though, that these marker-posts do not imply that permission to climb has necessarily been granted.)

The following areas are closed to climbing from **1st March to 31st July** inclusive (this list updated 2002).

Pier Bottom to **St Aldhelm's Head**   Pier Bottom is the valley to the north-west of St Aldhelm's Head. Restrictions apply from here to the eastern (right-hand) arête of The Yellow Wall.

St Aldhelm's Head to **Slippery Ledge**   Restrictions apply between Buttery Corner (the point at which the undercliff beneath St Aldhelm's Head gives way to sea cliff) and Slippery Ledge.

Winspit East End to **Halsewell Bars**   The wide quarryman's path that runs east from Winspit is in three sections separated by earth and rock buttresses. The westernmost buttress is pierced by a through-cave whilst the other is not. On the cliff-top path to the west of Seacombe are some old quarry workings set back from the cliff edge (Halsewell Bars). Restrictions here are from the easternmost buttress dividing the quarryman's path along to Halsewell Bars.

Hedbury Big Cove, Smokey Hole, and **Topmast Quarry**   Restrictions apply to the cliffs between Hedbury Quarry and Dancing Ledge.

Guillemot Ledge   Restrictions apply between *Sea of Holes* at Dancing Ledge and *Valkyrie Buttress Direct*, and to the east of *The Razor's Edge*.

Cormorant Ledge   Restrictions apply to the west of *Sea Cow* and to the east of *Oran*.

Blackers Hole   Restrictions apply to the left of *Frontiersman*, that is, the climbs to the west and north of it.

Boulder Ruckle   Restrictions apply between *Andycap* and *Raindrop*, between *Sardine Special* and *Hard Day's Night*, and between *Gimcrack* and *Airy Legs*. It is permitted to traverse along the base of the cliff beneath these sections, but take great care to avoid any disturbance.

The Lighthouse Cliffs   Restrictions apply east of *Scotsman Chimney* to the start of pitch 2 of *Traverse of the Gods*.

Tilly Whim Caves to **Durlston Head**   This section of cliff has been reserved as a bird sanctuary, the entire area being set aside for ornithological and ecological studies. Consequently **no climbing at any time** is allowed here. The walls both above and below the main ledge at Tilly Whim are included in this year-round restriction. It should be emphasized that any infringement of this ban could have serious repercussions in other equally sensitive areas where the buffer-space between climbers and the local wildlife is at an absolute minimum.

Isle of Wight   Restrictions apply to *Gateway to Heaven* at Sun Corner, the headland at the south-east end of Scratchell's Bay, and also to *Albatross* below and east of Sun Corner. Additionally, Highdown Cliffs (the cliffs to the east of Sun Corner) have been reserved as a sanctuary area by The National Trust. Consequently **no climbing at any time** is allowed here, apart from the aforementioned *Albatross* outside the nesting-season.

THE CLIFF ENVIRONMENT

The **Purbeck** coast is of international geological importance and has been studied for over 150 years. Partly as a result of its geological diversity, it offers a wide range of habitats which support several rare species of plants and animals.

One legacy of the stone trade is the large number of hibernation sites for bats. The quarry shafts and cliff workings mean that Purbeck has the widest range of bats in Southern England. Roe deer inhabit the woods between Tyneham and Swanage and are sometimes spotted by climbers on the undercliff at St Aldhelm's Head. Pilot whales together with bottle-nosed and common dolphins visit the waters off Durlston Head, which has the second highest number of dolphin sightings in the country.

The Swanage cliffs support Herring Gull, Kittiwake, Fulmar, Shag, and three Auks: Guillemot, Razorbill, and Puffin. Kittiwake numbers are higher and more stable than at Portland. Of the Auks, only the Guillemot is well represented. They choose nest sites above water, so that their fledglings have a watery landing on their first flight. Unfortunately, this means that the very cliffs which climbers would prefer to visit in summer, when the sea is generally calmer, are no-go zones because of nesting-restrictions. In the nesting season, Guillemots can be seen *inside* Durlston Country Park's information centre – via a cliff-mounted camera and television screen!

The Fulmar is a bird to admire from afar. Its name, said to mean 'foul gull', gives a clue to its means of defence; it vomits a rank, oily liquid over any creature unlucky enough to be considered threatening. An unexpected (and unfortunately unavoidable) encounter with a fulmar left the author with clothes and gear which still smelt strongly of fish after two washings! Most of the cliff-dwelling birds feed at sea, but Herring Gulls also flock to rubbish tips for easy pickings; the reason why chicken bones are sometimes found at the base of the cliffs or on the half-height ledges!

Peregrines in Dorset, in common with those in the rest of the country, were killed during World War II; they were seen as a threat to military communications as carrier pigeon formed part of their diet! Pesticides compounded the problem in the late 1960s. Their fortunes have now reversed, however; they are gradually re-establishing themselves along the coast and are breeding again after a gap of twenty years. A second fragile success is the return of the Raven, another bird which had failed to breed in the county for two decades.

The factors which affect the populations of the birds on the cliff are hard to establish with precision. Oil spills and pesticides have taken their toll in the past. Overfishing, the rise in numbers of a predator, or changes occurring in their winter haunts may be other influences. However, it is clear that disturbance by climbers can affect whether a pair of birds lay, whether the egg hatches, or whether the chick survives.

The remarkable flora and fauna are a result partly of the southern coastal location and partly of the geology of the region. Some of the plants here have quite specific soil preferences. Viper's Bugloss, for example, grows on the Portland stone at St Aldhelm's Head, but not on the Purbeck stone, another limestone, further to the east. Plants worthy of mention are the Early

Spider Orchid, Sea Cabbage, Sea Carrot, and, parasitic upon the latter, Carrot Broomrape – a rare plant dependent upon another rarity.

On the **Isle of Wight**, Annual Seablite, Sea Purslane, and Sea Heath – normally found only on shingle or in salt marshes – grow on the very thin layer of soil at the top of *Skeleton Ridge*. The sloping vegetated sections of the cliffs are known on the island as Greens; the Greens are home to the rare Ox-tongue Broomrape and other plants similarly adapted to mobile soil. Hoary Stock is another uncommon plant; this grows in cracks in the slabbier cliffs.

Herring Gulls nest in the *Wrinklie's Retreat* area, while Cormorants and Shags use The Needles for wing-drying. The cliff east of Sun Corner has the easternmost colonies of Guillemots and Razorbills on the south coast, as well as Peregrine and Raven nest sites. Kittiwakes, Shags, and Cormorants also nest hereabouts. Puffins, however, have not nested on the Isle since the 1970s.

The existence of rare plants on the cliffs lays a special responsibility on the climber. Many of them are very hard to distinguish from more common species, sometimes even for the experts, while others are inconspicuous and easily overlooked. Because of this the 'gardening' of new routes should be kept to a minimum.

ACCESS

Access to the cliffs depends on many factors, but one of the most important of these is the way climbers conduct themselves. The cliffs on which we climb are owned by a number of individuals and organizations who have one thing in common: climbing is not at the forefront of their priorities. As a result of their unspoilt nature as well as their flora and fauna, the cliffs are of immense worth; virtually all of them have been designated Areas of Outstanding Natural Beauty as well as Heritage Coast, and they are all Sites of Special Scientific Interest. With no rights, only privileges, we are on very delicate ground. A whole cliff could be lost to all climbers as the result of one thoughtless act by one person. Especially in the quarries, where the general public are nearest to us, the safety of non-climbers is of paramount importance. So, too, is minimizing disturbance, of whatever type. The cliffs, their environs, and their inhabitants deserve both our appreciation and our care.

Any incident concerning access should be reported to the British Mountaineering Council's Access Officer as quickly as possible to prevent deterioration of the situation (telephone number 0870 010 4878).

NEW ROUTES

As this reprint is published, work is well underway on new Portland and Swanage guidebooks. Please send details of any new routes as well as any comments regarding this guidebook to the guidebook team, either via The Climbers' Club website (www.climbers-club.co.uk) or to the club's co-ordinator for new-route information, Dave Viggers, at Windale, 64 Park Grove, Henleaze, Bristol BS9 4LQ.

Swanage

The Swanage coast is a place of great beauty and tranquillity. Unlike Portland, where both the quarrying and the insensitive development often jars, Swanage is unspoilt; even the quarries have mellowed over time as their harsh aspect has been softened somewhat by natural forces. In common with Portland, Swanage has a wealth of interest for birdwatchers and other naturalists. The Country Park and the suntrap coves draw a number of visitors, but these areas can be easily avoided. Once down below the brow of the cliff, climbers are in their own private world.

There are as many favourite climbs as there are climbers, but the concensus is that Guillemot Ledge, Fisherman's Ledge, Boulder Ruckle, and Subluminal are the cream of the cliffs.

The majority of the climbs added to the Swanage cliffs in the nine years since the last guidebook are on established cliffs. The only significant new areas are the cliff-top quarries at Winspit, Hedbury, and Dancing Ledge, where a number of sport climbs have been established. Although some of these are fine climbs, the definitive Swanage experience can be savoured only by getting to grips with one of the higher natural sea-cliffs, where commitment and ability, but also caution, are needed in equal measure.

APPROACH
The cliffs are reached from three main access points: south of the town at Durlston Country Park; south of Langton Matravers at the car-park near Spyway Barn; and at the old quarrymen's village of Worth Matravers.

WARNING
Unattended rucksacks have occasionally been stolen from the Boulder Ruckle area. Hide them below the bushes, out of sight of people on the cliff-top path.

St Aldhelm's Head   OS Ref 962 754

Surrounded by an enormous boulder-field and situated high up above the sea, the cliffs at St Aldhelm's Head can provide a useful option on a rough day. However, as they are never washed clean by the sea, the rock here can be rather loose. The unclimbed section of the cliff north-west of the coastguard station has a shale lower wall and a very shattered top section and is therefore not recommended.

Nesting-season restrictions apply on The Yellow Wall and the unclimbed cliff to the north-west as far as the valley of Pier Bottom (see Introduction).

Approach.

1. Follow the road from Langton Matravers through Worth Matravers passing by the *Square and Compass*. The tarmac road continues to Renscombe Farm where a track on the left leads to the Coastguard Station on the headland. Park by the chapel and walk 150 yards east to reach a set of concrete steps, just past an unusual pinnacle balancing a large block. At the foot of the steps, scramble down a short easy gully on the right for the Main Area and The Yellow Wall.

2. For Buttery Corner, go to the Main Area, descend further, and then trek eastwards to meet the sea at the end of the undercliff. Alternatively, follow the cliff-top path eastwards from the Coastguard Station until the fence makes a right-angle bend. Abseil from a stake down a west-facing wall to the undercliff.

THE YELLOW WALL

As one looks westwards past the main area from the descent gully, the cliff rapidly gains in height as the ground beneath it falls away. Beyond and out of sight is an impressive yellow wall which faces south and stands 140 feet high. It is split by several strong cracklines. The most distinctive of these are the Y-shaped crack of *Angel Pavement* and the chimney climbed by *Moebius* to its left.

Calamity Jane 140 feet Hard Very Severe 4c [R] †   (20.12.86)
Start in a bay opposite the western end of a ridge formed by huge flakes. Climb leftwards on shale for 20 feet to a wide crack. Continue up this and a short crack on the left to a ledge. Scramble up the gully on the right and belay a long way back with an extra rope.

Return of the Native

130 feet Hard Very Severe 5a [R] †   (20.12.86)
Start at a crack 10 feet left of the pinnacle flake on the left-hand side of The Yellow Wall. High in the grade.
Climb the crack to a grassy ledge and continue to the top. Belay a long way back with an extra rope.

Moebius 140 feet Very Severe 4b [R]   (9.1.77)
Start below a prominent cleft to the right of the pinnacle flake.
Climb the cleft to reach a flake at 40 feet. Continue to a chockstone and an earthy ledge, and finish up the gully on the left. Use an extra rope to belay.

Elm Street 140 feet E2 5b [R] †   (4.4.92)
Twenty feet right of *Moebius* a wide crack leans rightwards and outwards. Start here. Very strenuous, and with its fair share of dubious rock. Take

two sets of big nuts (*Hexes 9, 10, 11*)! Seekers after esoteric tactics may enjoy the simultaneous hand-jams either side of a loose block resting in the bottom of the wide crack.
Climb the crack (peg runner on the right), with a deviation right and back left around a triangular block. Follow the vague corner-line to the top. Extra rope needed to belay.

Angel Pavement   140 feet   E2 [R] †   (31.12.79)
Start 30 feet right of *Moebius* at the foot of a very loose shale corner topped by a Y-shaped crack. Easier than its neighbour.
1 50 feet 5a. Climb the loose corner to reach the top of a pedestal on the right. Follow the wide crack above to a jammed block and the slanting crack on the right to a small ledge.
2 90 feet 4c. Climb the crack at the right-hand end of the belay ledge to reach another ledge and finish up the corner above. Belay using an extra rope.

At the right-hand end of The Yellow Wall are two vertical cracks.

Mammotholian   120 feet   E1 [R] †   (25.2.95)
The left-hand crack requires large *Hexes* and *Friends* and has a poorly-protected start. Scramble precariously up 20 feet of steep scree to a peg belay at the base of the wall.
1 75 feet 5a. Climb the wide crack until it narrows and veers to the right. Traverse leftwards with difficulty for 10 feet and continue up to a layback flake, which is followed rightwards to the righthand end of a long grassy ledge.
2 45 feet 4b. Step up and right onto a pillar. Climb straight up the wall past a wide break and a strange pocket to the top. Nut belays.

MAIN AREA
Immediately west of the descent gully are the corners of *Loosestone Crack* and *Sigmoid Direct*. To the left, a small jutting buttress is home for *Claire's Brother*. The short, inset wall beyond is split by *One Nut Crack* and has an easy descent on its western side. After this, a cliff-top pinnacle conveniently marks the gully of the same name. Past an unappetizing wall, Block Wall Gully is a useful way down, provided the blocks stay in place. Further on the square-cut final overhang of *Battle of the Bulge* and the initial chimney of *Jim's Jam* are obvious reference points.

Jim's Jam   70 feet   Severe   (1971)
Start to the right of The Yellow Wall where a chimney on the right-hand side of a protruding nose leads to a ledge and a large, gaping chimney above.
1 40 feet. Climb the chimney, passing a chockstone near the top. Belay on a wide ledge.
2 30 feet 4a. Follow the corner to the right of the big chimney, with a difficult start. The upper chimney is an easier alternative (Difficult).

The obvious wide chimney to the right provides a small amount of climbing at Moderate standard.

Slimline   60 feet   Hard Severe 4b †   (27.4.86)
Climb the chimney and crack 6 feet left of *Battle of the Bulge*.

Battle of the Bulge   50 feet   Very Severe 4b   (26.1.86)
A route with good protection once the chimney is entered, and an interesting finish. Start beneath a wide chimney capped by blocky roofs. Climb the subsidiary rib below the chimney with care and follow the chimney itself to the roof. Step right (good thread runner) and exit using the right-hand crack. Belay on large blocks.
Variation
Weight Watchers Finish   60 feet   Hard Very Severe 5a † (27.4.86)
A direct finish via the left-hand roof-crack. Large hands required - or boxing gloves!

Internal Exile   50 feet   Hard Very Severe 5a †   (11.1.92)
An unpleasant finish.
Climb the second groove right of *Battle of the Bulge*. Continue straight up where the crack divides and grab the top. Now reach left and pull over. Belay on large concrete blocks.

Rescue Corner   50 feet   Severe 4a †   (9.6.91)
A loose and unsatisfying route up a large corner. Belay on a tangle of reinforcing rods.

Immediately right of *Rescue Corner* is a gully choked by a wall of blocks; Block Wall Gully provides a useful descent route, although care is required.

Every Whichway...   60 feet   Very Severe 4c †   (7.5.90)
On the wall immediately east of Block Wall Gully is a crackline with a small pinnacle midway. Loose.
Climb the lower crack (crux) to reach a ledge. Follow flake cracks to the pinnacle and continue left of this to the top. Belay on the back wall.

Spider Ledge   70 feet   Hard Very Severe 5b †   (9.6.91)
Start at the lowest point of the east wall of Block Wall Gully. A projecting foot-ledge at 8 feet marks the spot.
Climb to the foot-ledge and up the facet above. Step left to a corner. Climb this and follow the rightward-leaning groove to the top.

The Other Gully   60 feet   Severe †   (10.3.90)
Start beneath the conspicuous poised pinnacle on the cliff-top.
Climb the corner which finishes on the left-hand side of the pinnacle.

Pinnacle Gully   60 feet   Very Difficult
This also starts beneath the pinnacle.

Follow a crack to the terrace at 20 feet, and climb the wall on the right to finish on the pinnacle's right-hand side. Thread belay as for *Other Times*.

To the right of *Pinnacle Gully* is an obvious wide crackline upon which two climbs are based.

Other Times   60 feet   E1 5b †   (29.2.92)
This route climbs the corner-crack and the groove directly above.
Shoulder the ivy aside and climb a crack to a roof. Crawl left and follow a corner-crack to another roof. Cross this and step out left to a ledge and runners. Move back right and climb the groove to the top. Thread belay in large blocks right of the rock buttress.

Other Places   50 feet   E2 5c †   (4.4.92)
Some push is required for this punchy problem, which proves surprisingly steep and surprisingly good.
Follow the ivy-enveloped crack as for *Other Times*. Surmount the roof and follow the crack to a second roof. Pull over this and move slightly leftwards to finish up a short corner. Thread belay as above.

The Last Corner   45 feet   Severe 4a †   (10.3.90)
Climb the corner 30 feet right of *Pinnacle Gully*. Solid for the area and with good protection. Belay as for *Other Times*.

Northern Sky   45 feet   Very Severe 4b   (14.4.87)
To the right of *The Last Corner* is an overhang. Start on its right-hand side. An unpleasant route with poor protection.
Climb a short crack, traverse left to the arête, and follow the vague groove above. Belay as for *Other Times*.

Quick Chimney   35 feet   Severe   (26.1.86)
The loose chimney right of *Northern Sky*, just before an easy way down.

* **Seriously Short**   30 feet   E2 6a †   (11.1.92)
A strenuous exercise of sedimentary solidity on which the sequence is all-important. A good peg provides half of the protection.
Climb the arête immediately right of the easy way down, artificially avoiding *Little Corner* for the first few moves.

Little Corner   30 feet   Severe 4a   (26.1.86)
Climb the corner near the left-hand side of the short recessed wall. Exit to the right of the capping block.

One Nut Crack   30 feet   Hard Severe 5a   (27.4.86)
Popular with 'first ascensionists', all of whom gave a different grade! Solid and well protected.
Climb the crack in the middle of the short recessed wall.

Pineapple Edge   30 feet   Hard Very Severe 5b †   (3.12.89)
A sustained and poorly-protected route.
Climb the right edge of the short recessed wall straight to the top.

Difficult Descent   35 feet   Difficult   (26.1.86)
Climb the wide, chockstone-filled chimney on the right side of the short
recessed wall.

Claire's Brother   35 feet   Very Severe 4b   (14.4.87)
Starting on its left-hand side, climb the jutting face right of *Difficult Descent*.
(Starting up the centre of the face is HVS 5a.)

Gardeners' Question Time   45 feet   Severe †   (3.12.89)
Low in the grade and with the crux reserved for the final moves. Start 15
feet right of *Claire's Brother*.
Climb up rightwards to the grassy top of a large block at 10 feet. Step
right and climb the slabby wall above, keeping just right of the loose
corner. Belay far back using an extra rope.

Shatterbox   60 feet   Hard Severe 4a †   (3.12.89)
Start right of the previous route at a lower level.
Climb the leftward-slanting flake crack to a ledge at 15 feet. Follow the
chimney to the detached ledge at its top. Finish straight up the wall and
belay far back using an extra rope.

Coccyx   60 feet   Hard Severe 4c †   (14.1.87)
Start near the right end of the wall.
Climb the steep initial wall to a ledge. Move up to reach a vertical crack
and finish to the left. Belay using an extra rope.

Sigmoid Direct   50 feet   Hard Very Severe 4c †   (31.1.88)
A good route. Start in the corner 50 feet left of the descent gully (just
around the arête from *Coccyx*).
Climb to the earthy ledge and finish up the overhanging corner-crack.
Belay a long way back with an extra rope.

Cabbage Patch Kids   50 feet   Very Severe 4c †   (31.1.88)
Start just left of *Loosestone Crack* at a tiny corner.
Climb up past the faultline and up a broken left-facing groove to the top.
Belay a long way back with an extra rope.

Loosestone Crack   60 feet   Severe 4a
Start 20 feet right of *Sigmoid Direct*.
Climb the loose, overhanging chimney. Small boulder belay.

Divine Wind   50 feet   Hard Severe †   (31.1.88)
Start 10 feet west of the descent gully. Poorly protected and therefore not
recommended.

Climb a vague scoop and a crack, move diagonally rightwards onto a cherty prow, and finish straight up. Block belay.

BUTTERY CORNER

Buttery Corner is the slabby buttress with a grassy dome which marks the eastern end of the vegetated undercliff half a mile east of the Coastguard Station. For those not of the bush-wacking inclination an abseil stake above this buttress allows speedy access. **Nesting-season restrictions** apply to the climbs east of Buttery Corner (see Introduction).

Delicatessen   100 feet   Hard Severe   4b   [R]   (15.3.80)
Climb the open groove in the yellow slabby face to the faultline and then the wall above to the left.

** **Gold Mother**   50 feet   E5   6b   [R]   †   (10.91)
Two hundred yards east of Buttery Corner is a long strip roof at one-quarter height. The route tackles the central roof-crack but does not brave the loose wall above. Apparently no hand-jams are required throughout its 10 horizontal feet.
Climb across the curved crack and up the wall to the faultline. Lower off.

Fifteen to One   60 feet   Difficult   [R]   (10.91)
One hundred and fifty yards east again is an obvious detached pillar, some 40 feet high. Behind it is an easy escape route. Climb the chimney to the top of the pillar. A few easy moves over deteriorating rock lead to safety.

Another easy exit (Difficult [R]) is located further to the east, about fifty yards west of a well-defined pinnacle.

Slippery Ledge   OS Ref 975 757

Slippery Ledge is the short cliff immediately to the east of Crab Hole. Sound finishes, reasonable rock, and a secluded atmosphere make this an attractive place to climb. The lower ledges are accessible irrespective of the tide but the area should be avoided in heavy seas.

Nesting-season restrictions apply to the west of Slippery Ledge (see Introduction). Since the first route here, *Ruth*, is climbed with one hand in Slippery Ledge and one in Crab Hole, it too is covered.

Approach.   Start below the village pond in Worth Matravers (readers who are also divers should not take this too literally). Follow the signposted path to Winspit. From here, take the coastal path westwards towards the large, impressive bay of Crab Hole, around which the path deviates. Twenty yards before Crab Hole descend a grassy gully, which leads to a vegetated ledge above the cliff. Abseil from the large boulder 15 yards east of the descent gully.

From the large boulder on top of the cliff, a partly free abseil leads to the start of *Query*, easily recognizable by its question-mark crack. The cliff is bounded on its left by Crab Hole, the skyline arête being climbed by *Ruth*. To the left of the abseil there is a series of roofs, while to the right lies the main section of the cliff with a single roof at two-thirds height. Right of *The Corner*, a couple of small buttresses are followed by a long, low-level roof topped by an easy-angled but loose gully. A short section of higher cliff now follows before the more broken remainder, which leads eventually to Winspit.

Ruth   90 feet   Very Severe [R]   (22.5.82)
A nicely situated though poorly-protected top pitch. Start at the right-hand corner of an overhung bay.
1 30 feet 4b. Climb the corner to the roof and traverse left along horizontal cracks to an alcove.
2 60 feet 4b. Traverse left again to a pile of blocks. Climb the arête, with good views of Crab Hole, to a roof. Move right to easy ground and multiple nut belays.

** **Jackie**   60 feet   Hard Very Severe 5a   (11.5.82)
To the west of the abseil down *Query* is a large roof with another roof above it. The route starts on the arête to the right. Good positions.
Climb the arête and break left onto the slab above the large roof. Traverse left until below the break in the roof and fix good runners. Move up into a groove, step right into a second groove, and continue to the top. Belay on the backwall to the right.

Nautilus   45 feet   Hard Severe 4b   (15.6.71)
Start 15 feet right of *Jackie*, at the left end of a ledge at 9 feet.
Go steeply rightwards up to the ledge. Step left and, by means of an indefinite groove, climb the wall to a ledge below a loose overhang. Move up the wall on the left and exit to the right. Belay on the backwall.

Octopus   45 feet   Hard Very Severe 5b †   (26.4.91)
Starting just left of *Query*, reach left to a crack over the void. Pull up with difficulty to a ledge and continue to another. Step left and climb a black groove to a niche. Swing rightwards from this to gain easier ground.

Query   50 feet   Hard Severe 4b   (15.6.71)
Start at the foot of the abseil beneath a question-mark crack. Strenuous for its grade.
Climb the crack to a large ledge, move left, and follow a corner to the top. Belay on the abseil boulder.

Dorset Non-Rhyming Slang   50 feet   Hard Severe   4b   (7.83)
Start as for *Query*.
Climb the crack to the small roof, move right to a ledge, and up to a large
ledge. Continue straight up to the top, taking care with a jammed block.
Belay on the abseil boulder.

Lunar   60 feet   Severe   (15.6.71)
A wandering line. Start 8 feet right of *Query* at a vague groove in the
lower wall.
Climb the wall by the easiest line to the overhang. Traverse 10 feet left
before moving back right to finish up the groove of *Cuboid*. Belay on the
abseil boulder.

Magic   45 feet   Hard Very Severe   5a   (11.5.82)
This shares much of its climbing with *Lunar* but is worthwhile for its
strenuous crux. Start just right of *Lunar* beneath a wide section of roof.
Climb direct to the cracks in the roof, surmount the roof, and continue to
the top. Belay on the abseil boulder.

Cuboid   60 feet   Very Severe   4c   (15.6.71)
Midway between *Query* and *The Corner* is a small cave partly vacated by
a block. Start on the right-hand side of the cave.
Climb straight up to the narrowest point of the overhangs. Pull over,
traverse left a few feet, and follow the groove to the top. Belay on the
abseil boulder.

Alternate Angle   45 feet   Hard Severe   4b   (22.5.82)
Start 3 feet to the right of the *Cuboid* block.
Climb directly up to the wide crack in the roof, pull over, and move left
before exiting. Belay on the abseil boulder.

Parallel Lines   45 feet   Very Severe   4c   (2.3.80)
Start on a low boulder 10 feet right of *Cuboid*. The top section has some
dubious rock.
Climb over ledges and up the wall to the roof. Cross this where it narrows
at a small V-slot and finish straight up. Belay on the backwall.

Moonshine   45 feet   Very Severe   4b   (30.9.82)
An eliminate but worthwhile. The protection is good though difficult to
arrange, and the climbing delicate. Start 4 feet to the left of *The Corner*.
Climb up and mantel onto a small ledge just left of a tiny prow at 15 feet.
Continue to the top roof, step left, and follow a groove to the top. Belay on
the backwall.

The Corner   45 feet   Hard Severe   4b   (15.6.71)
Climb directly up the large left-facing corner and move onto the right wall
at the top. Belay on the backwall.

Ciao Pupa   45 feet   E3 6a/b †   (18.8.91)
Quite a bold route up the gently overhanging right wall of the corner. Start
at the arête right of *The Corner*.
Pull up onto the wall and climb up its middle, with crux moves past a peg.
Near the top, trend rightwards to finish by the arête. Belay on the
backwall.

Ozymandias   50 feet   E2 5c †   (18.8.91)
The right arête of *The Corner*. Belay on the backwall.

Ten feet east of *The Corner* is a cleft with a boulder bridged across it and a
second one jammed in to seaward. The cave behind the cleft should
appeal to adventurers. When you reach the back of the cave, grab the
treasure, kill the monster, and dynamite your way upwards: **La Rue sans
Issue** (80 feet Hard Very Severe 5b † 18.8.91). The rest of us should
reverse the pitch.

Gymslip   45 feet   Hard Severe 4b †   (26.4.91)
From the bridged boulder, gain the crack on the left-hand side of the roof,
follow it for 10 feet, and go diagonally left to finish up a distinct V-groove.
Multiple belays on the backwall.

Slipshod   45 feet   Severe 4a   (27.10.77)
Start as for *Gymslip*.
Follow the obvious crack in the west-facing wall. Climb the corner above
to the top, taking care when passing a large flake. Exit to the right and
belay on the backwall.

All Square   50 feet   Very Severe 4c   (20.4.80)
Start 15 feet right of *Slipshod* at a short layback crack above a crevice.
Move up to a ledge on the left, continue up, and go awkwardly over a
bulge. Finish by trending left and belay on the backwall.

Spout   70 feet   Hard Severe 4b   (10.11.77)
Start below a corner at the left-hand end of the long low roof.
Pull up onto a ledge and move steeply into the corner. Climb to the top of
the corner and make an awkward move right. Continue right before
climbing leftwards and up over loose blocks to reach the main ledge.
Belay to the left on the backwall.

Cosmic Cabbage   60 feet   Hard Severe 4b †   (2.3.80)
Start at a short crack in a west-facing corner, 40 feet east of the long low
roof. The only route in the area not to end up back on the main ledge.
Climb 15 feet up the crack, left under the overhang, and up to an
ammonite. Step right into the corner and climb it to the top. Brassica
'belay', or use an extra rope to reach the fenceposts.

Winspit
OS Ref 977 761

The sea-cliffs and quarries of Winspit have received a spate of additions in recent years at both ends of the grade spectrum.

Approach. Start below the village pond at Worth Matravers and follow the signposted footpath that runs along Winspit Bottom and passes between the two hills known as West and East Man.

There are three distinct areas here: The Main Quarry has half a dozen routes; Quarryman's Wall provides rather more interest for the extreme leader; and the Eastern Seawalls offer very short tidal climbs, natural rock, and a range of grades. The large white circles constitute an interesting feature of the quarried walls; these are stun marks caused by the blasting.

THE MAIN QUARRY
To the west of the cove at Winspit is a quarried area with several derelict buildings. Two routes start by the rock arch west of these ruins.

Think About It 50 feet E2 (E2) 5c S (1979)
Steep, strenuous climbing with its crux at the top of the groove. Start on the eastern side of the prominent rock arch. Four bolt runners, but the crux is better protected with nuts.
From the large bolthole, 10 feet to the left of the arch, climb a thin zigzag crack to a tiny chert break at 20 feet. Swing right to beneath a shallow, overhanging groove and pull up to a rest position atop a small flake. Climb the black-stained groove to two lower-off bolts.

Things That Make You Go Hmmm 35 feet E3 6a S (22.9.91)
'A sumptuous line of unparalleled mediocrity' climbing the face and hanging corner above the archway. Three bolt runners.
Climb a short arête and a wall to undercuts on the right. Follow the corner on huge buckets to the ledge and two lower-off bolts.

Restless Heart 45 feet E2 6a S (4.12.93)
Start a few feet right of the arch. Four bolt runners.
Cross the right end of the roof, move up with difficulty to a niche, and finish up a crack. Double-bolt lower-off point.

★ Any Old Time 45 feet E2 5c S (11.8.93)
Start 20 feet right of the arch. Four bolt runners.
From the rocky mound, climb a corner-crack, step left, and continue up to a horizontal break. Finish up the right-hand side of the arête to twin lower-off bolts.

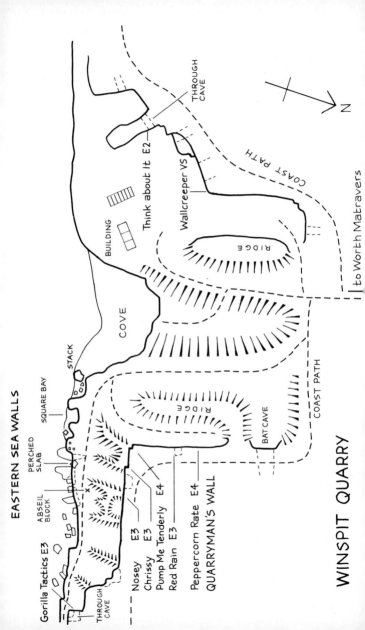

EASTERN SEA WALLS

Gorilla Tactics E3

THROUGH CAVE

ABSEIL BLOCK

PERCHED SLAB

STACK

SQUARE BAY

COVE

BUILDING

Nosey   E3
Chrissy   E3
Pump Me Tenderly E4
Red Rain   E3

Peppercorn Rate E4
QUARRYMAN'S WALL

RIDGE

BAT CAVE

COAST PATH

Think about It E2

THROUGH CAVE

Wallcreeper VS

COAST PATH

RIDGE

to Worth Matravers

N

WINSPIT QUARRY

Post-Coital Snooze   45 feet   Hard Very Severe   5a   S   (18.3.94)
Four bolt runners.
To the right of the arch is a large corner. Climb cracks in the left wall of the corner to two lower-off bolts by a sloping roof.

Further east is a wall between a cave entrance and the right edge of the south-facing wall, before the cliff turns north to form a chasm. Two climbs start here.

Idiot Village   40 feet   E1   5b   S   (11.12.93)
A strenuous, awkward start leads to better holds. Start at the left arête. Four bolt runners.
Climb discontinuous cracks slightly leftwards over the cave to a ledge. Two lower-off bolts.

Wallcreeper   50 feet   Very Severe   4b   †   (24.3.71)
Pull over an awkward bulge at 5 feet and then follow an easy groove.
Make a hard move out right across the flat wall to an obvious finish where the top 5 feet of shattered rock are missing. Belay on the fenceposts.

QUARRYMAN'S WALL
This is the west-facing quarried wall on the east side of the cove. It is a useful refuge from rough seas or strong winds as it is hemmed in by huge piles of spoil from the long-abandoned quarrying. It even has a centrally-located cave in which to weather out showers, not that it ever rains at Swanage!

The Genius of SK   50 feet   E2   5b   S   †   (13.5.94)
The leftmost route on the wall lies immediately left of the large overhung corner. Four bolt runners.
Climb the groove-line to a sit-down finish by the two lower-off bolts.

China in Your Hands   70 feet   E1   5b   †   (10.1.88)
Start below the large, overhung corner at the left-hand end of the wall. Climb onto a ledge above a low roof and follow a diagonal crack rightwards to the large roof. Traverse right past a peg runner and enter the short corner above. Turn the next roof, traverse right on the 'china', and climb a flake to a deep horizontal slot. Double-bolt lower-off point (shared with the next two routes).

Right of the corner is a 30-foot section of cliff which has four strip roofs across it.

★ **Avenging the Halsewell**   60 feet   E5   6b   S   (30.7.88)
Very strenuous, and featuring a *long* stretch. Start in the middle of the strip roofs. Six bolt runners.
Climb up and cross a 3-foot roof at a diagonal crack. Pass another roof to reach a handrail. Make hard moves up over a bulge and cross two more

roofs via a notch to reach a ledge. Continue up a flake to a double-bolt lower-off point.

The Ancient Order of Free-Marblers   60 feet   E4 6a *S*   (13.11.87)
Steep and strenuous. Start on the right-hand side of the strip roofs. Six bolt runners and an *in-situ* thread.
Climb a shallow groove with difficulty and follow a flake over two roofs to a ledge. Step left and continue more easily to a large horizontal break just below the top. Double-bolt lower-off point.

⋆ **Billy Winspit**   60 feet   E5 6b *S*   (29.11.93)
Start 5 feet right of the last route. Six bolt runners.
Climb a wall and the flake crack above to a niche at 40 feet. Warning: blank section ahead! After a good rest, make some reachy moves up from a poor undercut eventually to clasp the two lower-off bolts.

⋆ **Peppercorn Rate**   60 feet   E4 6a *S*   (23.12.87)
A blind crux bulge leads to a compelling thin crack. Low in its grade. Start on the left side of a buttress separating the overhung bay from a more gently-angled bay on the right. Six bolt runners.
Climb the arête to a bulge and continue up to a finger-crack set in a smooth face. Follow this to a hard move and the double-bolt lower-off point beyond.

So Naughty   50 feet   Very Severe 4c *S*   (5.12.93)
Five bolt runners. Good value at this grade.
Climb the right arête for 15 feet, and make a tricky move around it into the corner. Follow the corner (still fairly sustained) to two lower-off bolts.

Insanely Yours   40 feet   E4 6b *S*   (20.3.94)
In the middle of the wall is a cave, which has a low roof to its left. Start below the right-hand side of the low roof. Four bolt runners.
Climb into a groove and trend left across a steep wall. Cross the bulge above to an easing of the angle and the two lower-off bolts.

The next two routes have excellent climbing in their lower sections, but easier climbing on fragile rock for the final 20 feet.

Jargon Eater   60 feet   E2 5b †   (20.12.87)
A steep start gives way to more delicate climbing higher up. Start 5 feet left of the cave at a block-choked crack.
Climb the crack, traverse left, and follow the corner-crack to the roof. Turn it on the right and trend left to the lowest of three successive short wide cracks. Go diagonally back right to exit by the topmost crack. Fencepost belay.

Unseen Ripples of the Pebble   60 feet   E1 5b   (31.12.87)
Start on the left side of the cave. A large assortment of *Friends* is required. High in the grade.

Climb the crack to the roof, step left, and go up the corner-crack to a bulge. Move straight over it and finish as for the last route. Fencepost belay.

Gallows Gore   40 feet   E4 6b † S   (3.1.88)
A boulder-problem above the cave, starting on its right arête. Five bolt runners (the first two shared with *Red Rain*).
Climb up a crack to the horizontal crack. Move left to a knee-lock rest and cross the bulge on widely-spaced holds. Continue to a ledge and two lower-off bolts.

** **Red Rain**   60 feet   E3 (E4) 6a S   (3.1.88/7.1.88)
An excellent, varied pitch with good natural protection which is high in its grade. Start at the right arête of the cave. For some reason the climb has been retrobolted: definitely not necessary.
Climb the cracks to a body-wedge rest under a small roof at half height. Swing right and climb a thin crack to better holds, which lead slightly rightwards to a double-bolt lower-off point.

* **Queen Anne's Men**   65 feet   E3 6a S   (31.12.87)
Start 10 feet right of the cave. Three bolt runners.
Climb via a scoop straight up to a tiny roof. Move left past the stump of a peg to a layback edge. Follow this to a hand-ledge which provides large but glass-smooth holds. Two lower-off bolts above.

Exuberance   50 feet   E4 6b S   (5.8.93)
This three-bolt eliminate climbs directly up the wall and the thin crack above to reach a double-bolt lower-off point. Quite a bold finish.

* **Stonemason**   60 feet   E1 (E1) 5b S   (20.12.87)
Steep and sustained, though easier than it looks. Start 20 feet right of the cave. Three bolt runners.
Climb up, past a hold at 7 feet composed of calcite-cemented rock fragments, to a ledge. Step right and climb discontinuous cracks to another ledge beneath a smooth wall. Two lower-off bolts.

The next four lines are on rather unappealing rock but prove to be enjoyable nonetheless.

Resin Devotion   45 feet   Hard Very Severe 5a S   (13.5.94)
Start at the rib immediately right of the orange corner. Hardest at the bottom. Four bolt runners.
Climb the rib and the slabby groove to two lower-off bolts.

Insect Graveyard   50 feet   E2 5c S   (5.8.93)
This sustained pitch starts 15 feet right of the orange corner. Four bolt runners. It feels run out after the third bolt.

Climb up past a small roof to good sidepulls and continue to the lower-off bolts.

Playtime with Playtex (80 feet E4 6a *S* † 30.7.94) is a mid-height traverse with nine bolt runners. Start as for the next route, move diagonally left to half height, and cross the orange corner to reach *Red Rain*. Climb that route's crux and undercut leftwards before finishing on *Gallows Gore*.

Know What I Mean, Pal? 45 feet E1 5b *S* (5.11.93)
Four bolt runners and a double-bolt lower-off point. The first ascensionist described this line to the left of a chossy corner as 'nondescript but nice'. It is based around a vague corner at one-third height.

Pump Me Tenderly 45 feet E4 6b *S* (9.11.91)
A worthwhile route which starts just before the end of the wall. Five bolt runners. Low in its grade.
Climb up, trend right, and continue up the arête, with balancy moves to gain the lower-off bolts.

At the right-hand end of Quarryman's Wall are two routes in a shallow corner.

Nine Years' Absence 30 feet E1 5c *S* (1.9.93)
A three-bolt line up the right wall of the corner; quite sustained, with a choice of tactics near the top. Two lower-off bolts.

The Vixen 30 feet E4 6b *S* (31.7.93)
Start just to seaward of the last route. Four bolt runners and a twin-bolted lower-off bracket.
With difficulty, climb into a bottomless corner. At the top of the corner, move out rightwards to a powerful finish over a small roof.

The quarried wall now turns through a right-angle and faces the sea. This wall is pierced by a series of quarried caves.

Agonies of a Dying Mind 30 feet E4 6c *S* (4.3.94)
Start behind a big boulder, below a roof at 6 feet. Three bolt runners.
A hard boulder-problem start leads over the roof to a slab. Continue up this and cross the roof to reach two lower-off bolts.

Dick Dastardly 35 feet E4 6b *S* (5.12.93)
Start on the left of a low roof at the left-hand end of the south-facing wall. Three bolt runners. Another hard pitch, which has yet to see a flashed ascent.
Climb up to the horizontal break, step right into the groove in the arête, and gain an undercut with difficulty. More tricky moves lead to a ledge in a corner and two lower-off bolts.

Lips of a Stranger   40 feet   E4 6a *S*   (4.12.93)
Start 30 feet from the western end of the south-facing wall, behind a
boulder on a grassy mound. Bold, with four spaced-out bolt runners.
A hanging starting-sequence leads to a roof. Cross the roof and seek
refuge in a corner, before trending right to the arête and following it to
lower-off bolts.

** Chrissy   50 feet   E3 5c *S*   (31.7.93)
Forty-five feet along the south-facing wall is a roof with an open corner
above. A strenuous start, a tenuous mid section, and especially fine
bridging to finish. Five bolts protect.
After a hanging start, climb up and follow a crack rightwards around a
roof. Climb the technical corner above to twin lower-off bolts.

* Revhead's Hi-Roller   40 feet   E5 6b *S*   (5.6.94)
Start 10 feet right of *Chrissy*. Sustained and with a hard start, especially
for the short. Six bolt runners.
From boulders, pull over the roof. Cross a bulge with difficulty to reach a
short groove. Climb the arête *à cheval* before finishing leftwards to two
lower-off bolts.

Knickerless Crutches   30 feet   E3 6a *S*   (4.12.93)
Start on top of a grassy mound left of a big cave. The finish is harder than
it looks but is less traumatic with a nut runner. Three bolt runners.
Climb a groove (with a smooth, calcite-stained left wall) and its capping
bulge; then follow the crack in the headwall to lower-off bolts.

* The Damnation Game   50 feet   E5 6b *S*   (28.11.93)
One hundred feet along the south-facing wall is a big cave. Start
immediately to its left. Five bolt runners.
Climb over two roofs and up the groove above. Continue up a finger-
crack on the left to two lower-off bolts.

* Lunacy Booth   60 feet   E6 6b/c *S* †   (5.6.94)
Despite starting off a boulder-pile, the hardest route at Winspit is a brutal
proposition. Seven bolt runners.
Reach for the lip of the cave roof, cut loose, and power round on good
holds. Cross the main overhang to a layback flake; climb this and the wall
above to two lower-off bolts.

Nosey   25 feet   E3 6a *S*   (12.11.93)
A one-move wonder, though not so wondrous. Start on the ridge on the
right-hand side of the big cave. Two bolt runners.
Climb the arête direct, with hard moves to the roof followed by a juggy
finish. Two lower-off bolts.

Rampant Love Jugs   40 feet   E2 5c *S*   (12.11.93)
Start at a small cave in the centre of the wall. Four bolt runners.

After a jump-start for two slopers, climb a black bulge to a slabby finish. Twin lower-off bolts.

The south-facing wall is brought to an end by a west-facing wall pierced by a large through-cave. The following three routes *start* on the right side of the cave's western entrance, but the attraction of overhanging rock means that two of them finish above the cave mouth.

★ **Gorilla Tactics**   45 feet   E3 5c S   (5.11.93)
Start on the right-hand wall of the cave. A fine line offering exciting positions. Five bolt runners.
Climb the wall, groove, and roof to a double-bolted lower-off bracket.

★ **Flasheart / Born to Be Free**   40 feet   E1 5b S   (12.89/7.8.93)
Flasheart took a fairly direct line up the buttress immediately right of the cave entrance. The combination of this with an airy finish above the cave gives a spectacular climb. A grade higher if a cunning rest is missed. Four bolt runners.
Climb up the buttress, step right at 15 feet, and follow a short corner. Swing left, move up to the roof, and cross this to reach the lower-off bracket shared with *Gorilla Tactics*.

Rubic's Hex   40 feet   Very Severe 5a †   (12.89)
Start just right of the corner some 15 feet right of the cave.
Climb cracks to a loose ledge and finish up the corner. Fencepost belay.

EASTERN SEAWALLS
The quarrying activity which created the walls described above has left a short clean wall of reasonable rock below the ledge forming the quarryman's track. This ledge continues east after a break to form Winspit East End, reached from above by descending the side of a loose grassy bay. The cliffs below the two parts of the ledge offer some short possibilities. Note that **nesting-season restrictions** apply to the east of the buttress dividing the ledge (see Introduction).

The very short walls below the quarryman's track are reminiscent of the Dancing Ledge Lower Walls, but are in a rather more secluded environment. They require low tide and calm seas. The first feature, close to the boulder-filled cove, is a short stack; behind this an easy descent gives access to the routes as far as *Christine*. East of the stack is a square-cut bay containing the following five routes, which climb the obvious cracks in the back wall. Each is 25 feet long and dates from 27.9.87.
Who Needs Friends? (Very Difficult), **Insectitude** (Severe), **Praying Mantle** (Severe), **Emmy's Roof** (Very Severe), **Dream Topping** (Severe).

Part of the buttress on the right-hand side has fallen, destroying **The Tide's Coming In** and **Three Little Pigs** (both 4.10.87).

To the east of the square-cut bay, past a diamond-shaped boulder and a block perched over a zawn, lies a large sea-level ledge. Behind this ledge is a higher, narrow ledge with a strip roof just above.

The following routes can all be approached by a short abseil, either from belays in the crevasse just back from the cliff edge, or from the rectangular block to the east.

Christine   25 feet   Severe   (11.10.87)
Climb the buttress between the perched block and the sea-level ledge.

One Move Wonder   25 feet   Hard Very Severe 5b †   (1991)
The name aptly describes most of the climbs hereabouts. Start 10 feet from the left-hand end of the strip roof.
Climb to a higher ledge and use a crack to cross the roof. Finish easily.

Can't Touch This   25 feet   Hard Severe 4b   (7.7.90)
Start 8 feet right of *One Move Wonder* and climb the short groove and the easy wall above.

Ceri's Route   25 feet   Hard Severe 5a   (6.7.90)
Start at a thin crack 8 feet east of the large sea-level ledge, just before the strip roof peters out.
Make a difficult move over the roof and climb more easily to the top.

Uncertain Smile   30 feet   Hard Very Severe 5b †   (6.7.90)
Start 15 feet right of *Ceri's Route*, on a narrow ledge.
Move over the roof on small positive holds and climb the steep wall above.

Sunday Joint   30 feet   Hard Severe 4b †   (7.7.90)
Start 6 feet right of *Uncertain Smile*, under a steep flake and an ammonite and climb the deceptively steep wall on good holds.

Cosmic Swing   30 feet   Very Severe 4c †   (9.7.90)
Climb the slab and the crack in the left-facing corner to the large roof. Make a 'cosmic' swing rightwards to the arête and finish up the wall above.

East of Eden   30 feet   E2 5c †   (9.7.90)
High in the grade. From the smaller sea-level ledge, climb easily up to the right-hand side of the jutting block beneath the roof. Climb onto the wall above using small, positive holds, and finish direct.

Cup Final Day   30 feet   E1 5b †   (7.7.90)
Start 8 feet right of *East of Eden*. High in the grade.
Climb up to the roof-crack and gain the final slab on poor jams.

Mark's Route   30 feet   Severe 4a   (7.7.90)
Start at the right-hand end of the ledge.

Climb the corner formed by a jutting block to a small ledge and continue over the bulge above to the final slab.

Nesting-season restrictions apply on a stretch of cliff to the east (see Introduction). No climbs have been reported there, however.

Seacombe

OS Ref 985 766

Seacombe has a relaxed, non-serious environment, the general accessibility of the place and the convenience of the large, grassy terrace above the climbs in the quarry making it an ideal choice for the hard-pressed climber with a family.

Approach. From the village pond at Worth Matravers, follow the sign-posted footpath that leads eastwards down into a valley and over a ridge to Seacombe Bottom. Follow this secluded valley to the sea (1 mile).

Seacombe Bottom meets with the sea at a quarried area where some extensive caves and a chasm cut back into the rock strata on its western side. On this side of the main quarried ledge is a short sea-cliff with a selection of middle-grade climbs. A single, rather esoteric climb is suitably isolated by a large sea-cave to the west. East of the cove lies Cave Zawn with a small cliff-top quarry beyond. This quarry is known as The Gallery; a number of climbs lie on the sea walls beneath.

SEACOMBE WEST
To the west of the quarried area the cliff rears up to its full height above a large sea-cave. After the rubble remains of another sea-cave the cliff-line veers more to the south and the cliffs become more broken, extending in this condition all the way along to Winspit. Little interest has been shown in this part of the coastline and to date only one climb has been recorded here.

Symbolic Stack Dump   100 feet   Hard Very Severe †   (3.8.85)
A poorly-protected route up the buttress between the large sea-cave and the scree formed by the collapse of another sea-cave. This massive fall occurred after the first ascent so the climb may be looser now. Start from the spacious platform at the base of the buttress. *Friend 2* essential.
Approach by abseil from a stake in front of a bush in line with a large flat-topped boulder seaward of the buttress.
1 70 feet 4b. Climb up to a corner formed by a pillar, follow it for a few moves, and swing right into a vague groove. Climb the groove past some dubious blocks and belay on a ledge.
2 30 feet. Ascend a short corner and take the easiest exit over flaky rock. Belay on the abseil rope.

SEACOMBE QUARRY SEA WALLS

The main quarrying activity at Seacombe has left a large, flat grassy platform with a series of steep, loose, and unappetizing walls above. These walls are unlikely to provide the raw material for much worthwhile climbing. More interesting to the climber is the short, sea-washed cliff situated below the quarried ledge. This 40-foot cliff is composed of a series of small bays which harbour a number of steep, though sometimes broken routes on good rock. The cliff is most easily approached by descending the slabby amphitheatre close to some concrete ruins. The descent of the amphitheatre leads to a short, hidden chimney. Although the descent is easy, the amphitheatre is undercut by large roofs, so a rope is advisable for a novice. The platform at the foot of the climbs becomes awash at high tide or in heavy seas.

⋆ **Far from the Madding Crowd**   50 feet   Very Difficult
An enjoyable pitch on solid rock, nicely situated overlooking the big sea-cave. Low in its grade. Start below the western extremity of the quarried ledge, the point at which the cliffs become dramatically larger.
Step out onto the arête and traverse a few moves left before pulling up onto a good ledge. Climb the ramp above to block belays at the top.

An escapable eliminate has been climbed to the right by three 'first ascensionists' at grades averaging Hard Severe.

Jude the Obscure   40 feet   Very Severe 5a   (3.8.85)
Start 20 feet from the western end of the wall, below two leftward-slanting cracks in the upper wall.
Climb up to the cracks and follow them to the top. Block belay.

Yankee Doddle   40 feet   Very Severe 5a   (3.8.85)
Start below a vertical crack just left of an overhang on the upper wall.
Climb up onto a ledge containing a rusty relic of the quarrymen. Gain the crack above and follow it to a rounded finish. Block belay.

To the east (past a poor corner-climb graded Severe) is a steep wall with a jutting block at one-third height which forms a flat ledge. This block is bounded by a niche on its left and a short chimney on its right.

⋆ **Mardon's Hard 'Un**   45 feet   E2 5b/c   (1.8.85)
An excellent climb, strenuous and sustained, and sporting a problematic layback. Start below the left-hand end of the obvious niche at 15 feet. *Friend 3* useful high up.
Climb to the niche. Launch out left up a short layback flake and continue straight up, passing a bulge with difficulty. Block belay.

Heart of the Matter   50 feet   Hard Very Severe 5b   (1.8.85)
A fine pitch, varied and interesting, with some hard moves near the top. Start as for *Mardon's Hard 'Un*.

Move up into the niche and exit right onto the jutting ledge via an unusual hand-traverse and mantelshelf. Pull up rightwards to a small scoop, go leftwards over a bulge, and climb quickly to the top. Block belays.

Ship of Fools   40 feet   Hard Very Severe   5b †   (1.9.85)
An indifferent climb but harder than it looks. Start just right of the short chimney.
Climb up to a ledge and continue up the wall above, to finish up a minute corner. Block belay.

JCB   40 feet   Very Severe   5a †   (5.11.88)
Start at the western end of the amphitheatre bay.
Climb the wide chimney, roof, and easy corner to a block belay.

To the right of the easy way down into the amphitheatre bay is a jutting low roof and then a high roof.

Left-Hand Route   40 feet   E3   6a †   (5.93)
Harder than it looks, but well-protected and aptly named. Start beneath the high roof.
Climb the right corner of the recess to a ledge on the right of a block. Move up with difficulty into the hanging corner and make a ludicrous leftward stretch for a sharp jug. Cut loose and pull up to easier ground.

Harry Seacombe   40 feet   E1   5b †   (1.9.85)
Right of the high roof is a short chimney leading up to a crack in a small roof. Start below this. Now two grades harder after the loss of an overhang (behind one's back) which helped one stay in balance while crossing the roof.
Lean over a rock-pool and enter the chimney as elegantly as possible. Move up and left to a good knee-lock under the roof. Pull over to easier ground and a block belay beyond.

Bold for the Old   40 feet   E1   5b   (1.8.85)
Steep climbing on good incut holds but with no protection until the top wall. Start at a short crack just right of *Harry Seacombe*.
Climb straight up the two walls, passing a break at two-thirds height. Scrambling leads to a block belay a long way back.

Divine Decadence   40 feet   Hard Severe   4b   (15.9.85)
Start on the left-hand side of the second bay east of the easy way down into the amphitheatre bay.
Climb up to a triangular roof, step left, and go up to a leftward-slanting crack and ramp. Follow these and finish up the wall above. Belay on the fenceposts with an extra rope.

Wet, Wet, Wet   45 feet   Very Severe   4b †   (17.1.88)
Start at the back of the overhanging bay. Too cherty to be enjoyable.

Climb to the roof and then out onto the left wall. Bridge the cleft and continue to the top. Belay with an extra rope on the fenceposts.

Got to Go   40 feet   Very Severe 4b   (1.8.85)
Start below the crackline on the right-hand side of the bay.
Climb the crack and difficult roofs to the top.

Most of the easier lines towards the back of the cove were ascended many years ago. They are not described owing to their unsatisfactory rock and the predilection of tourists to sunbathe beneath them. Also, a number of them have been affected by rockfall.

SEACOMBE QUARRY
Jam Up Jelly Tight   25 feet   Hard Severe 4c †   (9.85)
At the right-hand end of the quarry's backwall is a wide crack which proves harder than it looks. Nut belays.

THE GALLERY
This small cliff provides a pleasant secluded venue, with interesting technical climbing on its compact lower wall but with a more blocky top section. The original way down from The Gallery is now dangerously loose and an abseil descent from two large blocks is recommended. The eastern section of the large flat ledge beneath the cliff is sometimes awash at high tide, and the area should be avoided in heavy seas. Belays are either wires on the back-wall or the abseil blocks.

The wall that stretches west from the abseil point and the next wall further to seaward provide all but one of the climbs described below, as well as a worthwhile bouldering traverse. The corner further left is all that remains of the old descent route, and the cliff is bounded at its left end by Cave Zawn. The eastern face of the zawn has been climbed at about Hard Severe. Unfortunately, the face has a very loose finish and is therefore not recommended.

Wolverhampton Wanderer   40 feet   Very Difficult   (10.88)
Start at the left-hand end of the flat wall, beneath a left-facing corner. Beware loose rock.
Climb up to a ledge and follow the corner above for 10 feet. Avoid the loose rock above by breaking out right before continuing to the top.

Percy the Palm   35 feet   Hard Severe 4b   (1987)
Start 10 feet from the western edge of the wall.
Climb up into the sentry-box at half height and follow the left-hand crack to the top.

Suntrap   35 feet   Hard Severe 4b   (3.89)
Climb up to the sentry-box at half height. Move up and out onto the right wall, which is climbed to the top.

The next three climbs all require a forceful approach.

Fiddler on the Roof   35 feet   E1 5c †   (3.5.92)
Start midway between the sentry-box and *Toby's Revenge*. Gear to
protect the crux is very strenuous to place, making the route high in its
grade.
Climb to the roof and step left. Gain the rail on the wall above and swing
rightwards before crossing the roof. Finish straight up.

★ **Toby's Revenge**   35 feet   Very Severe 4c   (10.87)
Start beneath a crack in the strip roof.
Climb the steep lower wall to the roof, storm the overhanging crack, and
finish more easily up a groove.

Adder Crack   40 feet   Hard Severe 4b
Start at the blunt arête formed by two blocks supporting a roof.
Climb up to the slab, step left under the roof, and cross it using a crack.
Finish straight up the wall.

Golden Oldie   35 feet   Severe   (11.87)
Start as for *Adder Crack*. Climb the blunt arête to a large ledge and the
left-hand corner to the top.

Knobcrook Road   40 feet   Very Severe 4c   (5.88)
Start at the left end of the eastern wall.
Climb the corner-crack to the ledge. Step up to the roof and traverse
awkwardly left past the remains of an ancient peg. Go up through the gap
to the top.

Spiderman   35 feet   Very Severe 4c   (10.88)
Start 6 feet right of the corner. An exciting move over the roof.
Climb to the ledge. Continue to the wide roof left of the ammonite and
make a wild pull over to finish.

Jockanesse   40 feet   Severe 4b   (10.87)
Choose a line up the wall to the right of the tiny head-height roof. Walk
rightwards along the ledge and continue up a small corner, which merges
into the easy groove of the next route.

California Here I Come   35 feet   Hard Severe 5a   (11.88)
Start immediately right of a hole at 6 feet.
Hard climbing for the grade leads to a good ledge. Finish up the easy
groove.

Libertine   65 feet   E1 5b †   (3.5.92)
Interesting climbing but poorly protected at the top of the groove. To the
east of the other climbs is a tall cave with a tilted boulder to the east
again. Belay on the boulder, and start a few feet left of a vague groove

which has a more pronounced mid section.
Step onto the black wall and swing right into the groove. Climb up to a ledge and thence to the faultline. Use the corner on the right to gain the crack above the groove and follow it to the top. Multiple belays.

Hedbury Quarry

The climbs at Hedbury Quarry are situated both above and below its quarried ledges. The easier routes lie on the sea walls below the level of the main ledges, where the rock is washed clean and is reasonably sound. In normal conditions access to the sea walls is not a problem, but they should be avoided when the sea is rough. Apart from a few practice aid climbs, the upper quarried walls offer mainly sport climbs; these have lower-off points to avoid the loose material above. Most of these sport climbs are of good quality, despite appearances, and they tend to have more character than the Dancing Ledge bolt routes. The quarry is much quieter than Dancing Ledge too. **Nesting-season restrictions** apply east of the main quarry (see Introduction).

Approach as for Dancing Ledge as far as the stiles. From here, turn right and follow the coastal footpath for a quarter of a mile to a stile. Just beyond the stile a path leads down a ridge into Hedbury Quarry.

At the base of the ridge there is a well-preserved cannon that was last fired over 150 years ago. To its west a cave leads through to a narrower ledge and more quarry workings known as Mike's Corner. Further on at sea-level is the Cul-de-sac Cave, known locally as Pig 'n' Whistle, owing presumably to the noise made by the air escaping from the cleft when pressurized by the sea. The first climbs described in this area tackle the smooth black walls beyond.

THE BLACK WALLS

West of Mike's Corner is an impressive area of smooth black walls above large flat tidal ledges. The quarrymen's name for this area was Scratch-Arse. At the western end of these ledges is a zawn with an easy-angled buttress. Approach all routes except *Knee and a Tall Man* by abseil from a stake 30 feet east of the first stile west of Mike's Corner. Calm seas only. At high tide it is possible to rig up a hanging belay above the sea for *Waiting for the Death Blow*.

Black Wall Avoidance   140 feet   Very Severe   (1977)
Near the westernmost end of the ledges is an earthy corner which forms the edge of a buttress. Loose and not recommended.
1 60 feet 4c. Climb the obvious groove and flake.
2 80 feet 4b. Traverse left for 40 feet and then climb around into an exit

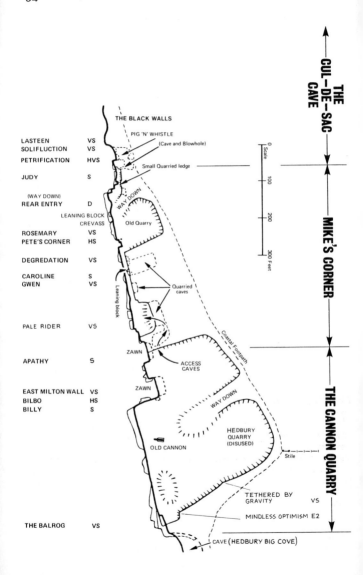

THE BLACK WALLS

PIG 'N' WHISTLE
(Cave and Blowhole)

LASTEEN   VS
SOLIFLUCTION   VS
PETRIFICATION   HVS

Small Quarried ledge

JUDY   S

(WAY DOWN)
REAR ENTRY   D

WAY DOWN

LEANING BLOCK
CREVASS

Old Quarry

ROSEMARY   VS
PETE'S CORNER   HS

DEGREDATION   VS

CAROLINE   S
GWEN   VS

Quarried caves

Leaning block

PALE RIDER   VS

APATHY   S

ZAWN

ACCESS
CAVES

EAST MILTON WALL VS
BILBO   HS
BILLY   S

ZAWN

WAY DOWN

Coastal Footpath

HEDBURY
QUARRY
(DISUSED)

OLD CANNON

Stile

TETHERED BY
GRAVITY   VS

MINDLESS OPTIMISM E2

THE BALROG   VS

CAVE (HEDBURY BIG COVE)

0
Scale
100
200
300 Feet

THE
CUL–DE–SAC
CAVE

MIKE'S CORNER

THE CANNON QUARRY

corner. The belay stake has vanished; make do with several fenceposts.

The next three routes have a serious nature owing to the brittle, shattered rock near the top. The abseil rope is best employed on the steep earthy slopes above.

Knee and a Tall Man   90 feet   E2   5b †   (18.6.94)
From a stake a few feet west of the stile, abseil to a tidal ledge. Start below the right-hand end of a strip roof at 10 feet, near the right-hand end of the ledge. *RP*s useful on the sparsely-protected lower section.
Climb up past the end of the roof, and at 40 feet swing left to a peg. Move up easier ground to two *in-situ* threads and continue up past two pegs to the 'cornice' at the top of the rock. Use the abseil rope to belay and pull out.

★ **Waiting for the Death Blow**   100 feet   E2   5b   (31.7.91)
Enjoyable climbing in an unlikely setting, tempered by a couple of disconcerting moves at the top. Start just right of a small overhang at 10 feet. (Twenty feet right of the last route and separated from it by a break in the ledge.)
Climb straight up the wall past a peg runner to a thin horizontal break. Move left 5 feet, make steep moves to bypass a chert roof on its left, and step back onto a ledge on its lip. Continue straight up deep cracks to a brittle band of rock near the top. Using flat holds 3 feet left of a peg runner, yard up through the steep 'cornice' to a ledge. Use the abseil rope to belay and pull out.

> **Dark Millenium** (100 feet E4 6a † 19.5.91) starts beneath the left-hand end of the half-height roof. It was climbed with four bolt runners before this cliff was designated a bolt-free zone; consequently the bolts may have been removed. This direct line crosses a small roof and uses a diagonal rail to reach a break, before continuing up past a ledge to a swing left and the top. Belay on the abseil rope.

MIKE'S CORNER
The through-cave on the west side of The Cannon Quarry leads to Mike's Corner, a narrower ledge which contains some well-situated bivouac caves. At the western end of Mike's Corner is an easy and fairly obvious descent route, *Rear Entry*, which leads down to large ledges at the fault-line. To the east of *Rear Entry* is a large fallen block, and beyond it is The Crevasse. This can either be climbed across (tricky), or, when the sea is calm, descended by its left wall to reach the sea-level ledges below. Sixty feet further on, *Blood Gully* climbs a large corner which runs the full height of the cliff.

UPPER LEDGE
For those who require some non-serious aid practice and take skin cancer warnings seriously, there are half a dozen 40-foot roof-cracks in the cave

with the leaning block at its entrance. The small cave to the east contains two easy aid climbs: **Benny's Apprentice** (35 feet A1 † 23.7.89) traverses the three walls of the cave; a poor route but it does provide practice for those apprehensive about *Benny* itself. **Spaghetti Western** (25 feet A1 22.5.88) follows the roof-crack closest to the back of the cave.

SEA WALLS
Lasteen   190 feet   Very Severe   (9.4.74)
Follow the faultline westwards from *Rear Entry* until easy scrambling ends at a niche.
1 90 feet 4b. Continue along the faultline to a corner beyond a zawn.
2 100 feet 4c. Traverse 20 feet left along the faultline to gain the edge before the smooth walls. Turn the roof on its left and then go up right to a small ledge (belay possible). Climb left to a ledge and right to the foot of a steep ramp (directly above the belay). Follow this and exit left at the top.

Solifluction   140 feet   Very Severe †   (7.10.79)
Start as for *Lasteen*. Take care to avoid rope drag.
1 60 feet 4a. Traverse the faultline westwards until below an obvious cantilevered block. A short crack leads to a good ledge and belays 10 feet above the traverse.
2 80 feet 4b. Gain a ledge on the right and traverse to the right-hand side of the cantilevered block. Step up onto the block, walk left to a layback crack in a shallow groove, and climb this to a good ledge with a large boulder on it (junction with *Petrification*). Go up a few feet and then left around the arête to a fair exit. Belay on the fenceposts.

Petrification   110 feet Hard Very Severe 5a †   (31.3.72/12.1.80)
Start as for *Lasteen*. Pegs required.
Climb the ramp up to the left on large holds to a small niche on the arête. Climb straight up over a bulge and onto a steep wall below a roof in a corner. (Belay possible by placing pegs.) Traverse out left under the roof, placing a peg runner, to the foot of a steep, loose groove. Go up the groove for a few feet and move diagonally left (second peg placement) to reach a sound ledge. Take the safest line around to the left and continue up rubble to the top.

It is possible to reach the large cave below *Petrification*, the Cul-de-sac Cave, by means of a narrow entrance near *Judy*. This interesting excursion is safe only when the sea is very calm.

★ **Judy**   40 feet   Severe   4a   (10.2.73)
Not a long climb but with exciting positions for its grade. Start 40 feet left of *Rear Entry*.
Climb a short slab, step left across a gap, and traverse left along the slab between the two roofs before climbing to the top.

The wall to the left of the descent route is **Whatnot** (25 feet Severe). The descent route itself, **Rear Entry**, is a 20-foot pitch graded Difficult.

Rosemary   30 feet   Very Severe 4c   (8.4.74)
This starts about 20 feet right of The Crevasse on the continuation ledge. Move up, first right and then left under the roof, to a tiny layback corner-crack. Follow this to the top.

The next three routes start from the sea-level ledge.

Pete's Corner   40 feet   Hard Severe 4a/b   (28.4.72)
No, not *that* Pete! Start at a quarryman's thread on the left arête of *Blood Gully*.
Climb up from the thread and break left slightly to the foot of an obvious corner at 20 feet. Go up the corner and straight over the overhang to the top.

Blood Gully   40 feet   Hard Severe 4b   (Pre-1963)
Start 50 feet right of The Crevasse and climb the prominent corner to the top.

Degradation   60 feet   Very Severe   (28.4.72)
Start right of *Blood Gully* by a small square-cut cave.
1 25 feet 4b. Climb the crack on the right-hand side of the overhang to a ledge.
2 35 feet 4c. Go right a few feet and cross the overhang at a partly-detached (or partly-attached if you're an optimist) block. Continue right for 10 feet to avoid the next overhang and then go up to the top.

The next two routes start from a small, rectangular ledge with an ammonite on it; this is directly below the leaning block in the cave mouth. Approach by abseil from the leaning block or by traversing across from *Blood Gully* (Severe).

Caroline   30 feet   Severe 4a   (12.5.73)
Climb straight up above the ammonite and exit just left of a tiny roof.

Gwen   40 feet   Very Severe 4c   (12.5.73)
From the right-hand end of the ledge, go diagonally right and surmount the overhang at its weakest point. Move left and up to finish.

The routes from *Rawhide* to *Any Which Way but Loose* can be approached by abseil from boulders 20 feet from the eastern end of Mike's Corner. They start from a ledge 20 feet above the sea.

Rawhide   35 feet   Hard Severe 4b   (1988)
Left of the ledge gained by abseil is another ledge; start on its right-hand side.

Climb to a thin finger-ledge, traverse left for 8 feet, and continue to the top on good holds. Block belay.

Pale Rider   35 feet   Very Severe 4c   (30.7.89)
Start on the left-hand side of the ledge gained by abseil.
Climb to the roof and surmount it using a thin crack. Finish straight up and belay on the abseil blocks.

Tightrope   35 feet   Hard Severe 4b   (1988)
Start 6 feet right of *Pale Rider* at the right-hand end of an overhang.
Climb straight up past the overhang and traverse left on its lip for 4 feet. Continue up on good holds and belay on the abseil blocks.

The Good, the Bad and the Ugly   30 feet   Severe 4a   (22.5.88)
Start at the arête. Climb a short V-groove and continue direct on good holds. Block belay.

Any Which Way but Loose   35 feet   Very Severe 4c †   (22.5.88)
Very loose. From the right end of the ledge, climb the crack above the detached block to a roof. Traverse right (difficult) and finish up an arête. Block belay.

Dynamic Uno (Hard Very Severe †† 11.8.74) starts from the sea-level ledge beneath the extreme eastern end of Mike's Corner. Pitch 1 climbs a crack to a ledge on the right arête, but pitch 2 has suffered a rockfall, is now dangerously loose, and has not been reclimbed.

THE CANNON QUARRY
UPPER LEDGE
North of the through-cave to Mike's Corner are some small caves. **The Cat that Ate Marrowbone** (30 feet Very Severe 5a 12.87) is a poor route over the middle of the second cave.

From the descent ridge leading down into Hedbury Quarry, the principal features of the quarried eastern face are easily seen: tiered overhangs on the left-hand side, a blunt, leftward-slanting arête in the middle, and an area of black drainage streaks closer to the sea. All the climbs on this face are to the right of the blunt arête.

Tethered by Gravity   30 feet   Very Severe 4c S   (12.3.94)
Start 5 feet right of the blunt leftward-slanting arête. Four bolt runners.
Cross the first bulge using a large calcite-cemented hold, and the second bulge using holds in a slight corner. Two lower-off bolts.

Goddamn Sexual Tyrannosaurus
                                  35 feet Very Severe 5a S (12.3.94)
Start 15 feet right of the blunt arête. Three bolt runners.
Climb up for 20 feet to the tiny corner which forms the crux. Good holds

are soon within reach and lead to two lower-off bolts.

Ammonitemare   35 feet   E2 6a S   (17.10.93)
Start 30 feet right of the blunt arête. Four bolt runners.
Climb the wall and flake, with hard moves to gain the flake. Two lower-off
bolts.

Of Mice and Men   35 feet   E1 5c S   (18.3.94)
Start 10 feet right of *Ammonitemare*, below a corner at 15 feet. Four bolt
runners.
Cross a small roof to gain the corner. Leaving the corner is more difficult!
Two lower-off bolts above.

Bad Day   35 feet   E4 6a S   (9.6.91)
Start 50 feet right of the blunt arête, at the left-hand side of a very low
roof. Four bolt runners.
Climb to the strip roof and follow a seam with difficulty to reach a jam in a
calcite flake on the right. Move up leftwards and then swing right before
following a shallow corner to two lower-off bolts.

★ **Moves for the Masses**   30 feet   E1 5c S   (13.10.90)
Interesting calcite formations. Start at a very low roof beneath a large half-
height roof. High in the grade. Three bolt runners.
Pull over the roof onto weird calcite holds; follow these upwards and step
left to calcite-cemented flakes. Make a long stretch to better holds and
finish up the shallow corner of *Bad Day* to its lower-off bolts.

★★ **Hangs Like a Dead Man**   30 feet   E3 6a S   (7.3.91)
Powerful climbing on good rock. Start on the right-hand side of the very
low roof. Four bolt runners.
Pull steeply into a scoop beneath a roof, move up, and undercut leftwards
to a big flake. Turn the final roof on its right and continue to two lower-off
bolts.

★★ **Jumping the Gun**   35 feet   E2 (E2) 5b S   (7.3.91)
The best line in the quarry is a diagonal flake 20 feet right of *Moves for
the Masses*. Sustained and strenuous but low in its grade. Five bolt
runners.
Layback leftwards over the initial bulges to a foot-ledge and a rest. Cross
a roof and continue in the same line on good holds to lower-off bolts
shared with the last route.

Into the Realm of Radical Cool   40 feet   E4 6b S †   (18.3.94)
Five bolt runners.
Climb *Jumping the Gun* to its third bolt, leaving the first bolt unclipped to
avoid rope drag higher up. Break out right over the roof and continue to
two lower-off bolts.

Mouth Breather   30 feet   E5 6c † *S*   (9.5.91)
An awkward and painful crux. Start just right of *Jumping the Gun.* Four
bolt runners.
Layback a steep crack to the roof and undercut desperately out left to
enter a short corner. Move past the smaller upper roof and follow a large
flake to a twin bolt lower-off point.

The next three routes are often wet.

Sure Shot   35 feet   E3 5c *S*   (8.10.90)
This climbs a steep line just left of the black-streaked area (10 feet right of
Mouth Breather). Six bolt runners.
Layback diagonally leftwards up flakes to the roof. Follow the corner-crack
and then leftward leading flakes to a block forming a jug beneath a roof.
Step right to the black-streaked break in the roof and move onto a good
ledge. Two lower-off bolts.

Cinderella's Big Score   30 feet   E5 6b   (6.5.91)
Continuously steep climbing with two tricky sections. Start at the bulging
pillar 25 feet right of *Sure Shot.*
Brutal moves over the initial roof (peg runner) lead to a stretch (or a jump!)
out right past a bolt runner for a phallic jug. From here, climb a short
layback crack (*in-situ* thread) and bulges (two bolt runners) to a ledge.
Two lower-off bolts.

It Can't Be Denied   35 feet   E5 6b *S*   (22.10.94)
Start 10 feet right of *Cinderella's Big Score.* Four bolt runners.
Overcome the tricky hanging start to gain a crack within a groove.
Continue up and over the crux bulge. Two lower-off bolts shared with
Cinderella's Big Score.

The next three routes have a common finish and shared lower-off bolts.

Bop Ceroc   35 feet   E3 6a †   (20.4.92)
A variation on *Produced by Fred Quimby,* more technical than that route and
protected by *RPs* on the crux. Left of *The Glue Krux Klan Direct* is a low-level
roof. Start left of the roof.
Climb easily to a ledge at 9 feet and step right to a blank groove. Climb
the groove utilizing the triangular ledge as much as possible to gain a
diagonal crack. Move right and finish up the wall as for *Produced by Fred
Quimby.* Two lower-off bolts.

The Glue Krux Klan Direct   35 feet   E3 6a *S*   (26.9.90)
Start just right of a low-level roof and left of the open corner of *Produced
by Fred Quimby.* Four bolt runners.
Climb steeply to a jug on the rib above the roof. Make technical moves
on calcified nodules to a break. Pull up left and then right before
finishing with difficulty to two lower-off bolts. (The original line (†) went

left from the break and then leftwards up a crack to a *single* lower-off bolt.)

Produced by Fred Quimby   50 feet   E2 6a *S*   (29.6.91)
Start at the open corner nearly 100 feet right of the black-streaked area. High in the grade. Four bolt runners.
Climb large holds and the crack above, and traverse leftwards to a good rest (above the start of *The Glue Krux Klan Direct*). Pull up left and then right before finishing with difficulty. Two lower-off bolts.

Strange Devices   35 feet   E2 5c †   (20.4.92)
Climb up to the bolt of *Produced by Fred Quimby* and follow the crack on the right to a horizontal crack. Move right to the lower-off bolts of *Don's Long Gone*.

Don's Long Gone   30 feet   E3 (E3) 5c/6a *S*   (20.4.92)
Start beneath a prominent crack splitting a roof. Three bolt runners.
Climb a short groove to jugs. Continue over the roof and up the crack to a ledge. Two lower-off bolts.

Mindless Optimism   40 feet   E2 5c *S*   (29.6.91)
The left arête of the corner at the seaward end of the wall. Three bolt runners.
Climb the initial wall to a ledge. Swing left onto the arête and climb this, with committing final moves, to the double-bolted lower-off point.

SEA WALLS
Those routes as far as *Finger Cwack* are located on a section of cliff subject to a high rate of erosion, as evidenced by the loss of three recent additions. They are approached by an abseil close to *Apathy* from blocks 70 feet back.

Apathy   60 feet   Severe   (17.8.74)
In the process of falling apart: not recommended. This climbs the obvious west-facing corner located 60 feet east of the through-cave between *Mike's Corner* and the *Cannon Quarry*. Belay on the abseil blocks.

Gary   55 feet   Severe 4a †   (9.10.89)
Well protected. Start 20 feet right of *Apathy* at a cave with a short chimney and a crack above it.
Climb the sharp arête left of the chimney to its top, swing right to a ledge, and continue up the back wall to the overhang. Traverse 5 feet right and finish with care. Belay on the abseil blocks. (The direct start up the chimney is a grade harder.)

To the right a buttress has slipped away into the sea. As a result **Rubble Trubble** (23.7.89), **Internal Examination** and **Barney Rubble** (both 9.10.89) are no longer with us.

Finger Cwack   55 feet   Very Severe   4b/c   (23.7.89)
The difficulties are short but solid and worthwhile. Start 40 feet right of
Gary at a short corner with a hanging groove above, directly below an
ammonite at 20 feet.
Climb to the overhang and up the crack in the groove above to a ledge.
Step left and climb straight to the top. Belay on the abseil blocks.

Fifty yards west of the old cannon is a prominent west-facing wall with a
raised platform at its base.

East Milton Wall   40 feet   Very Severe   4b   (Pre-1963)
Start just left of the raised platform. Poorly protected.
Climb the wall to the faultline (large *Hex*), cross the overhang at its
weakest point, and continue more easily up cracks to the top.

Bilbo   40 feet   Hard Severe   4b   (22.1.72)
Start from the middle of the raised platform.
Climb the wall to the faultline and then up the obvious 'step'. Continue
fractionally leftwards up the steep wall to the top.

Billy   40 feet   Severe   4a   (30.12.71)
Start to the right of the raised platform.
Climb a small corner to the ledge and follow cracks and grooves slightly
left to the top.

To the east of The Cannon Quarry lies Hedbury Big Cove, a huge and very
impressive sea-cave. *The Balrog* climbs the buttress that separates the main
ledge of the quarry from the cove.

The Balrog   70 feet   Very Severe   (30.12.71/31.8.81)
Descend to the lower ledge that leads into the back of Hedbury Big Cove.
Near the western end of this ledge is a short corner capped by a roof at 8
feet; start here.
1 30 feet 5a. Climb up, avoiding the roof via the crack on the left, to
another large roof at 20 feet. Traverse right and up to a foot-ledge before
moving left (crux) to a corner, which leads to a good stance (the main
ledge can be reached easily from here).
2 40 feet 4b. Climb the wall above to the top of the cliff by a line on the
left. Stake belay.

> The next two routes were climbed with some bolt protection before this
> cliff was designated a bolt-free area; consequently the bolts may have
> been removed. **Sheffield über Alles** (90 feet E6 6b [R] † 8.10.90)
> has one bolt and starts 40 feet right of *The Balrog*, where very steep
> climbing leads to a vague groove. **The Jesus Lizard** (90 feet E6 6b
> [R] † 24.3.91) climbs the bulging wall and groove 10 feet further
> right. Despite its two bolts and six pegs, two sets of *Friends* are
> required. Both routes have some loose rock.

Smokey Hole and Topmast Quarry

OS Ref 994 768

This is the stretch of coastline that runs westwards from Dancing Ledge along to Hedbury Quarry. Several large sea-caves isolate the sections of cliff that have been explored so far. Most of the routes are on the shorter, more solid and clean-cut buttresses situated directly below the two cliff-top quarries. Progress along the base of the cliffs is hampered by the sea-caves, making it difficult to get an overview of the area and necessitating an abseil approach to the foot of each climb. The steep, juggy, and well-positioned nature of the climbing in this area makes it worthy of attention for anyone who enjoys seclusion. **Nesting-season restrictions** apply to both Smokey Hole and Topmast Quarry (see Introduction).

Approach as for Dancing Ledge as far as the stiles. From here, turn right and follow the coastal path westwards about 300 yards past a tiny, unnamed quarry to reach a larger area of opencast workings. This is Topmast Quarry. Just beyond are some planks which offer dry passage over an occasionally swampy area; south of the planks is Smokey Hole, an isolated ledge identified by its twin caves.

SMOKEY HOLE

A pleasant spot with a sideways view of the impressive Hedbury Big Cove and furnished with a very private bivouac cave.

** **Figurehead**   50 feet   E2   5b   [R]   (16.8.85)
An exposed pitch delving into the atmosphere of Hedbury Big Cove. Abseil from the quarryman's thread in the western cave, and belay at the western end of the prominent ledge a short distance below.
Move left along the faultline and then up and left to reach a deep crack. Climb the crack to its top and swing right to the hanging arête. Follow the very steep arête and finish to the right. Belay back on the abseil point.

Epidemic   70 feet   Hard Severe   [R]   (1975)
Abseil from the thread in the western cave to the bottom of a corner-groove.
1 45 feet 4b. Climb the corner-groove to the faultline.
2 25 feet. Above is another groove; climb the wall on its left to the top. Belay using the abseil thread.

Spanish Harlem   70 feet   E1   5b   [R] †   (18.8.85)
A bold finish. Start by abseiling from the eastern cave (the low one) to the base of a large corner. The first to descend will require nuts to keep the rope in contact with the rock.
Climb the corner, with a diversion right half-way up, to overhangs at its

top. Traverse right a few moves, swing out left on a good block, and pull up to a ledge just below the top. Belay on the abseil rope.

The four routes described next are reached by abseil from a stake located 20 yards east of the descent to Smokey Hole. The first person to descend will need to place nuts to keep in contact with the rock. All four routes require calm seas. The first two shared a bolt belay at the start before the agreement which designated Smokey Hole as bolt-free; consequently this bolt may have been removed. *RPs* and the abseil rope *may* suffice.

Slow Dive   90 feet   E6 6b [R] †   (31.7.91)
A bold, stamina climb. Abseil from the stake to a small sea-level ledge. Belay on the abseil rope and *RPs* (see above).
Trend left up a slight groove to a small ledge (runners 5 feet to the left). From the ledge, boldly gain the layback edge above and step left to small holds (vital *Rock* 2). Make difficult moves past a poor peg runner to a good break and cross the 5-foot roof (*in-situ* thread). Continue straight up past two peg runners to a juggy horizontal break at the top (*in-situ* thread). Exit easily on the right to a stake belay.

★ **Diving for Pearls**   80 feet   E5 6b [R] †   (1.12.90)
Bold, high-quality climbing up the centre of the very steep face. High in its grade. Start as for *Slow Dive*.
Climb direct up a slight groove protected by *RPs* and a peg runner to the faultline (*Friend* 3½). Now safer, cross a bulge with difficulty to a peg runner and a hand-ledge. Trend left and then right up the leaning wall to a jug (peg runner to the right) and so gain large flakes (peg runner). Continue to a good exit up slabby rock on the right. Belay on the abseil rope.

★★ **Vapour Trail**   80 feet   E6 6b [R] †   (13.12.90)
Very bold, very overhanging, and on superb rock. Abseil as for *Slow Dive*, swinging right to a hanging belay beneath a peg runner 15 feet above the sea (15 feet left of the *Sea of Tranquillity* zawn).
Climb straight up a blank pillar past the peg runner, and then make hard, serious moves to the faultline (large *in-situ* thread). Now the climb overhangs: pull past a peg runner to a small spike and go strenuously leftwards to a big jug (peg runner); move rightwards with difficulty to a juggy alcove; and surge straight over the final bulges (peg runner and *in-situ* thread) onto the headwall. Pumpy moves lead to a solid top and a stake belay.

★ **Rocket USA**   90 feet   E6 6b [R] †   (31.7.91)
The groove-system overlooking the eerie *Sea of Tranquillity* zawn is extremely steep in its upper half. From the foot of the abseil, traverse easily rightwards for 30 feet to a hanging belay on the left arête of the zawn.
Climb a rightward-facing corner past an overhang to the faultline. Pull

steeply up left (*in-situ* thread) to a rail and go strenuously rightwards to good holds and runners. Crank up the open groove (peg runner on the right) to a deep hole, a *Friend* $2\frac{1}{2}$ placement, and a mid-air rest. Pull straight around the lip to a big jug (two peg runners) and finish slightly left up the headwall. Stake belay.

TOPMAST QUARRY
Back in 1882, bad weather drove the *Alexandranova* onto the rocks here and seventy-seven crewmen perished. Such was the force of the storm that the ship's topmast was found on the cliff-top! The abseil point is at the western end of the quarry.

Sea of Tranquillity   100 feet   Very Severe + A1 [R] †   (18.8.85)
The buttress beneath Topmast Quarry contains a sea-cave. This unique route follows a roof-crack above an eerie pool in the cave. Head-torches would be useful. In order to avoid getting wetter than necessary, it is also helpful to have low tide and calm seas both to enter and to exit from the cave. Abseil 20 feet down and position the rope using a large boulder on the faultline ledge before continuing down around the arête to the west to land on sea-washed boulders. The cave is to the west. Wade into the cave and take a stance at a north-facing wall which just dips into the sea. Use nuts for aid to gain the roof-crack and traverse out right above the pool. Squeeze up into a widening of the crack after 40 feet, and free-climb across a short, south-facing wall, until it is possible to step down onto a slab leading left to a belay 20 feet above the water. Descend and then escape westwards from the cave to the foot of *Epidemic*. Very low tide required. Otherwise swim back to the start of *Zircon*, but beware the currents that flow under the buttress.

★ **Aquamarine**   75 feet   Very Severe [R] †   (17.8.85)
A delightful pitch up the hidden corner that bounds the western edge of the buttress beneath Topmast Quarry. Calm seas are essential. Abseil, locating the rope as for *Sea of Tranquillity*, and continue down a V-chimney to a sea-level ledge on a buttress that just dips into the sea.
1 55 feet 4c. Climb the edge of the south-facing slab until level with the chimney. Traverse right, step across the chimney, and continue diagonally right up its other wall to a bulge. Step around the arête and climb a thin crack to finishing jugs. Belay to the boulder.
2 20 feet. Climb easily up the short steep wall to the right of the belay.

Zircon   65 feet   E1 [R] †   (17.8.85)
Abseil down past the faultline and the obvious groove beneath to a ledge 10 feet above the sea.
1 45 feet 5b. Traverse the lip of the overhang on the left and at the arête climb straight up to finish on a series of huge jugs. Belay on the boulder.
2 20 feet 4b. Step right and climb the corner to the quarry.

Gimme Gimme Shock Treatment
                    80 feet   Hard Very Severe   5a/b [R] † (17.8.85)
A good, steep climb. Abseil as for *Zircon* and start 20 feet to the right at
the eastern end of the ledge.
Move up and right easily for 40 feet to reach the faultline ledge. Gain the
slab on the right, pull over a bulge, and step right onto another slab.
Finish to the right of the overhangs above. Boulder belay.

Dancing Ledge   OS Ref 998 768

Dancing Ledge consists of two large ledges hemmed in by a quarried wall
and separated from each other by a short wall of natural rock. The attrac-
tions for climbers are the accessibility, lack of seriousness, and sheltered
aspect of the area. The ledge is very popular with holiday-makers and
day-trippers in summer. The crowds are swelled by parties of beginners
under instruction on the Lower Wall and, more recently, bolt-boys on their
clip-trips up above. An excellent place for family picnics, swimming, and
getting in that redpoint.

In recent years, Dancing Ledge has become distinctly overused. In an effort
to halt this decline, the quarry's owners, The National Trust, have restricted
its use for climbing and abseiling instruction to five local outdoor activity centres and to groups who apply for permission. This can be obtained from, or
the centres contacted via: Geoff Hann, The National Trust, 1 Marine Terrace,
Studland, Dorset (01929 44259). However, The Trust does allow individual
climbers to use both Lower and Upper Walls.

Approach.   From Langton Matravers, turn off the B3069 into Durnford
Drive (100 yards west of the *King's Arms*) and follow the track to the free
National Trust car-park. Walk south along the track to Spyway Barn and
continue through two fields to the brow of a hill; a well-worn path to the right
leads down to stiles and a further descent to Dancing Ledge just beyond.

UPPER WALLS
Many climbs have been established recently on the quarried walls sur-
rounding the upper ledge. The majority of these climbs are bolted and all
but two have lower-off points so that the loose material at the top is
avoided. The National Trust have stipulated that these lower-off points
should **always** be used, both to avoid stonefall danger and to stop erosion of the cliff edge. Climbing to the top of the cliff and abseiling from it
are not permitted - neither are they desirable, given the shattered and brittle rock near the cliff-top.

All but two of the climbs on the Upper Walls are on the left of the descent
into the quarry. Immediately right of a grill-covered cave is a low-level roof

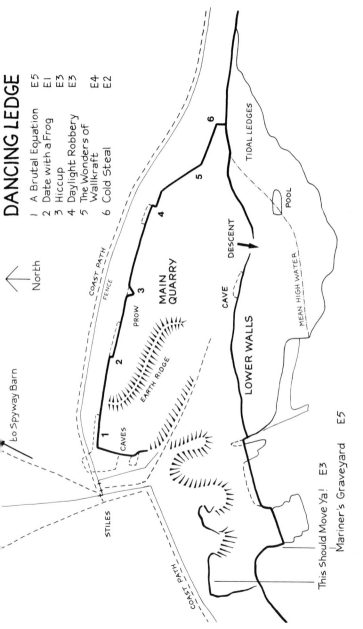

DANCING LEDGE

1	A Brutal Equation	E5
2	Date with a Frog	E1
3	Hiccup	E3
4	Daylight Robbery	E3
5	The Wonders of Wallkraft	E4
6	Cold Steal	E2

← North

to Spyway Barn

STILES

COAST PATH

FENCE

CAVES

EARTH RIDGE

PROW

MAIN QUARRY

CAVE

DESCENT

LOWER WALLS

POOL

MEAN HIGH WATER

TIDAL LEDGES

This Should Move Ya! E3

Mariner's Graveyard E5

crossed by *Idiot Joy Showland*. The wall to the right with a strip of slab at three-quarter height is climbed centrally by *Commander Cody and the Lost Planet Airmen*. A half-height roof is the next feature, with *Today Forever* at its mid point. Further along, *Hiccup* starts beneath a prominent jutting overhang high on the cliff. Beyond, the right-hand side of a low-level roof is the scene of *Daylight Robbery*. Past a smooth orange wall climbed by *Rambling Moses Weetabix* is a section of overhangs; *The Wonders of Wallkraft* aims for an easy-to-spot crack, taking in some of the overhangs on the way. The leftward-leaning corner in the next bay is *Cold Steal*, and *Eye Am the Sky* climbs a short way up the seaward edge of the quarried wall before disappearing around the corner.

Two short routes are located to the west of the descent path. As these finish on a subsidiary (walk-off) ledge and do not pose any stonefall danger, they do not have lower-off points.

Birth, School, Work, Death   20 feet   E2 6a †   (16.9.90)
On the far left-hand side of the quarry, west of the descent path, is a wide double roof. This extended boulder-problem starts on the left-hand side of the roofs above a bad landing.
Climb the roof series into a short scoop. Stake belay.

This Should Move Ya!   25 feet   E3 6a/b   (16.9.90)
This free-climbs an ancient aid route via a wild crux. One peg and two bolt runners. Start below the centre of the double roof.
Climb to the roof, swing leftwards, and jump for a hidden jug. Move left to a projection and exit onto a ledge. Stake belay.

The majority of the harder climbs are situated on the quarried wall to the north and east of the descent path. In the north-western corner of the main quarry is a blocked-up cave. For years an illicit toilet for innumerable members of organized groups, it will now become, it is hoped, a bat-roost once again. Following a geological survey, the rock above the cave has been declared unsafe. Because of this, The National Trust will not permit the two routes above the cave to be climbed. **For Your Arms Only** and **Volx with Friction** have therefore been debolted by climbers.

On its right-hand side, the cave gives way to a low-level roof, the entrance exam for several steep routes.

★ **A Brutal Equation**   35 feet   E5 6a S   (6.6.91)
This one-in-four curling wave of rock is high in its grade. Start at the right-hand end of the second roof. Three bolt runners which look rather suspect, as do the lower-off bolts.
Pull over the strip roof to a large flake formed by the end of the second roof, and move up to a big undercut. Long reaches between jugs lead to tricky moves by the top bolt. Gain a rail and the twin-bolt lower-off point. (Starting from the back of the low-level roof is apparently 6b; it looks harder!)

Shinhead Clash   35 feet   E3   5c/6a   S   (19.6.91)
Start 10 feet right of *A Brutal Equation*, beneath a short corner at the top of the cliff. Four bolt runners, the top one being on *Idiot Joy Showland*.
Pull up strenuously to a standing-position below the second roof. Cross this and swing for a sloping break. Continue up and make a further long reach for a small positive hold. Trend right and finish up the last 10 feet of *Idiot Joy Showland* to its two lower-off bolts.

★ **Idiot Joy Showland**   35 feet   E4   6a   S   (19.5.91)
A sustained pitch with a boulder-problem start situated 15 feet from the right-hand end of the low-level roof. A popular route. Four bolt runners.
Pull over the initial roof with a hard rockover to gain a large bucket. Continue up the leaning wall to two lower-off bolts on the top slab.

★ **Sugar Ray**   35 feet   E5   6a   S   (8.4.92)
Situated 10 feet from the right-hand end of the low roof is a sustained eliminate which pulls no punches. Four bolt runners.
Make a long reach to start and climb straight up; the powerful crux move is centred on a half-height undercut. Finish leftwards to the last route's lower-off bolts.

Names Is for Tombstones (Baby)   40 feet   E4   6b   S   (8.4.91)
Start at the right-hand end of the low-level roof. A strenuous route with a hard crux. Three bolt runners.
From a slight arête, trend leftwards up the steep wall to a twin-bolt lower-off point on the slab above.

Twenty-five yards from the north-western corner of the main quarry, on the south-facing wall, is a large sloping ledge at three-quarters height. Four routes finish on this sloping ledge.

Transparent Birthday Suit   30 feet   E1 (E1)   5b   S   (20.1.91)
Start on the right-hand side of a grassy mound, just left of some thin streaks. Two bolt runners.
Climb straight up and then slightly rightwards, where moving up onto a depression in the sloping ledge above provides the main difficulty. Two lower-off bolts.

Commander Cody and the Lost Planet Airmen
                                    30 feet   E1   5c   S   (28.2.88)
Start where short, thick flakes at the bottom, and just before the ledge, form leftward-facing corners (10 feet right of *Transparent Birthday Suit*).
Retrobolted in spite of the first ascensionist's wish that it should remain bolt free. Originally E2, it is still hard E1 with the bolts. One peg and three bolt runners.
Climb up just left of the flakes; the final moves onto the sloping ledge are the crux. Two lower-off bolts.

The original line in this section, **Ideal World** (E1 5b 7.1.88), started as for *Commander Cody...* before moving right to finish up a detached flake. The flake has since been removed and the original line absorbed by that route and the next.

Squalid Walid and the Druze Blues   30 feet   E1 5c S   (28.2.88)
Start 10 feet right of *Commander Cody...*, beneath a shallow niche high on the wall. Three bolt runners.
Pull up to a bulge, break left and then back right, and finish up the small corner above. Two lower-off bolts.

Ozark Mountain Daredevils   35 feet   E1 5b   (28.2.88)
Start beneath the high niche as for *Squalid Walid and the Druze Blues*.
Pull up to a bulge and then swing right to good holds and a rest. Reach the sloping ledge by going either straight up the wall above or slightly to the right (easier). Scuttle scarily sideways to the lower-off bolts of *Squalid Walid and the Druze Blues*.

⋆ **Date with a Frog**   30 feet   E1 5b S   (13.4.91)
Start just left of the large, half-height roof (40 feet right of *Ozark Mountain Daredevils*).
Climb straight up past two bolt runners to a double-bolted lower-off plate.

Fear of a Black Planet   35 feet   E4 6a/b   (26.9.90)
This bold route starts 20 feet from the left-hand side of the large strip roof at half height. High in the grade, and not recommended owing to the hollow flake.
Climb up past a poor bolt runner, and make reachy moves to gain a peg runner at the roof. Undercut around on hollow holds to flowstone and then a bucket (committing). Lower off a bolt and a thread.

Today Forever   35 feet   E4 6b   (23.3.91)
The black streak 15 feet right of *Fear of a Black Planet* calls for some strange moves.
Climb straight up the streak (bolt and peg runners) to a hand-ledge on the lip of a small roof. Rock over with difficulty into a slight groove (bolt runner) and climb to a *single*-bolt lower-off point.

Chicago Pipe Dream   40 feet   E1 5b S   (5.9.93)
A soft touch which starts above a toilet-shaped hole in the rock, beneath a low triangular roof. Three bolt runners.
Climb a blunt arête, move up right to a ledge, and continue up to two lower-off bolts.

Perpetual State of Confusion   40 feet   E2 6a S   (26.8.93)
Start 15 feet left of the prominent jutting overhang. Three bolt runners.
Make hard moves up the wall and grab the ledge on the left. Once established on it, continue up to two lower-off bolts.

Hiccup　40 feet　E3　5c　　　　　　　　　　　　(11.5.91)
A key feature in the centre of the west-facing wall is a prominent jutting
overhang at three-quarter height. Start beneath this.
Climb the smooth wall past two bolt runners direct to the roof. Move left
around the loose arête to a double-bolted lower-off plate.

Empty Promises　30 feet　E1　5b　S　　　　　　　(22.5.94)
Start under the right-hand side of the three-quarter-height jutting overhang.
Low in its grade with some interesting moves, and more solid than it
appears. Three bolt runners and two lower-off bolts.

★ **All Fall Down**　35 feet　E1　5c　S　　　　　　　(11.11.90)
The middle of the flat wall right of the prominent jutting overhang at three-
quarter height. Straightforward, enjoyable, and sustained.
After some difficult moves past two bolt runners, make a long reach from
good holds past a third to gain the twin lower-off bolts.

Carol's Little Injection　40 feet　E1　5b　S　　　(26.8.93)
Start 10 feet right of *All Fall Down*. Low in the grade. Three bolt runners.
Climb over a slight bulge into a niche before stepping right and back left
to finish. Two lower-off bolts.

★ **Sloping and Hoping**　40 feet　E3　5c　S　　　　(26.8.93)
Start 15 feet right again. Three bolt runners. Sustained.
After a steep, juggy start, a succession of sloping holds leads to twin
lower-off bolts.

Sixty feet right of the prominent jutting overhang at three-quarter height is a
low-level roof with a seat-height ledge beneath it. *Mr Choo Choo* is 10 feet left
of this roof, and *Daylight Robbery* is at its right-hand end.

★ **Mr Choo Choo**　35 feet　E4　6a　S　　　　　　(14.5.91)
Start just right of a ledge at 6 feet. Strenuous and blind.
Steam up past four bolt runners to two lower-off bolts.

Seven Years Solitary　30 feet　E4　6b　S　　　　(13.5.90)
The (non-)line 10 feet right of *Mr Choo Choo*, for which a long reach is a
distinct advantage. Start below a bulge, just left of the low-level roof. Two
bolt runners.
Boulder-problem moves using a layback edge on the bulge allow better
holds to be reached. Continue straight up to a juggy ledge. Two lower-off
bolts.

Disco's Out - Murder's In　35 feet　E4　6a　S　　(17.2.91)
Start at the centre of the low-level roof. Four bolt runners.
Climb over the roof, up the wall, and then rightwards to the lower-off bolts
of *Daylight Robbery*.

★ Daylight Robbery   35 feet   E3 6a *S*   (11.11.90)
The shallow groove at the right-hand end of the low-level roof.
Climb the groove past three bolt runners to a double-bolt lower-off
point.

The next three climbs take direct lines up the smooth orange wall.

★ Double or Quits   35 feet   E5 6b *S*   (7.91)
A fingery number, with three bolt runners to reduce the odds. Start on the left-
hand side of a smooth, orange-coloured sheet of calcite.
Climb over a bulge to a good pocket at the base of the blank wall.
Ascend the wall just right of the bolt-line, using a cornflake for a hold!
Two lower-off bolts. (Climbing the left arête reduces the technicalities to
6a.)

★ Rambling Moses Weetabix and the Secona Park Seven
                              35 feet   E3 6a *S* (27.6.87)
A technical tourist attraction! The first route recorded on the back wall
takes the centre of the orange-coloured face, and is low in its grade.
Climb the centre of the wall past four bolt runners to two lower-off bolts.

Hard Tackle / The Honey Monster
                              35 feet   E3 6a *S* (1992/21.8.93)
The right-hand side of the smooth orange wall. Three bolt runners.
Climb the groove and step left onto the wall. Continue up past a niche
and make some thin moves to reach the lower-off bolts. A grade easier,
but no tick, if you succumb to temptation and grab them!

War of the Wardens   25 feet   Very Severe 4c *S*   (17.5.94)
A better climb than it looks, this starts 10 feet right of the smooth orange
wall. Four bolt runners.
A steep start leads to a ledge and two lower-off bolts above.

Negative Creep   30 feet   E3 5c *S*   (8.4.92)
Low in the grade. A worthwhile route which climbs a series of small roofs
just right of a mound at the base of the cliff. Start just right of the roofs.
Three bolt runners.
Climb diagonally left beneath a large roof to enter a shallow bulging
groove. Jug-pull up the groove and then gain the two lower-off bolts
more delicately. (An easier, left-hand start is also possible.)

Next are two extended boulder-problems which lead to a hanging scoop
and a shared pair of lower-off bolts.

Slap, Bang, on a Hang   25 feet   E3 6a *S*   (22.12.90)
Start as for *Negative Creep*. One bolt runner.
A long reach around the roof at 12 feet leads to the scooped ledge.

Corona Envelope   25 feet   E5 6b *S* †   (22.12.90)
Lightning-fast moves over the right-hand side of the roof *may* lead to the
scooped ledge. Two bolt runners.

Prophets of Rage   40 feet   E5 6b *S*   (7.5.90)
Hard, reachy climbing up the bulging wall 10 feet right of the hanging
scoop of *Corona Envelope*. Five bolt runners.
Undercut leftwards by a diagonal flake to better holds and go strenuously
over the roof into a narrow corner. Continue up to a short crack and trend
right to a good hold. Double-bolt lower-off point.

★ **Haunted by a Million Screams**   35 feet   E4 6a *S*   (17.3.88)
A continuously overhanging line which deserves popularity. Start beneath
a slanting roof at 20 feet. Four bolt runners.
Climb a bulging wall to jugs and thence to a deep slot beneath the
slanting roof. Surmount the roof and continue to the lower-off bolts of the
previous route.

The Ghost of Ian Curtis   40 feet   E6 6c *S* †   (21.7.92)
Start beneath the right-hand end of the slanting roof at 20 feet. Unlikely
climbing through tiered overhangs. Sustained, and protected by four bolt
runners.
Pull over the first roof to jugs and then undercut outwards to a wild knee-
bar 'rest' beneath a blank bulge. Pull on a calcite edge, giving it your all
to reach better holds and a two-bolt lower-off point.

★ **Atrocity Exhibition**   30 feet   E4 6b *S*   (16.9.90)
A steep, solid climb which has some tenuous and blind moves. Start
beneath a rounded roof at three-quarter height. Three bolt runners; a
grade harder if you clip all the old bolts as well!
Make a steep start straight up to a jug at 15 feet. Climb with difficulty up
a left-facing corner and gain a continuation corner. Follow this to two
lower-off bolts beneath the rounded roof.

★★ **The Wonders of Wallkraft**   35 feet   E4 6a *S*   (2.12.90)
A very steep route following the crackline through the roofs just left of a
blunt, bulging prow. Five bolt runners.
Climb 15 feet to a large hold and reach around the roof to a finger-crack.
From another large hold above, use flared jams to cross the top overhangs
to a good pinch-grip and the two lower-off bolts.

A bolted line up the bulging prow has not yet been climbed. It looks very hard
indeed.

Fat Chance Hotel   30 feet   E5 6b/c *S* †   (20.4.88)
Start just right of the blunt, bulging prow (75 feet from the seaward end of
the wall). Four bolt runners and an *in-situ* thread.

Climb the bulge and the blank, hanging groove to better holds. Continue up to two lower-off bolts.

⋆ **Day of the Lords**   20 feet   E3 6b S   (13.5.90)
A short problem over the double roof. Start 10 feet right of *Fat Chance Hotel*. Three bolt runners.
Difficult undercutting leads up to a jug. From here, lean around the second roof to reach calcite clusters and make the crux moves to gain good holds and the lower-off bolts above.

Ken Wilson's Last Stand   30 feet   E4 6b S   (6.5.91)
Start beneath the obvious downward-pointing flake at 18 feet. Three bolt runners.
Climb steeply over the initial bulges to a prominent hold. Make a strenuous reach to an undercut flake right of the prominent flake and continue more easily to the lower-off bolts of *Cold Steal*.

Cold Steal   30 feet   E2 5c S   (22.12.90)
This worthwhile route proves surprisingly difficult and has some strange moves. It takes the leftward-slanting corner with the smooth left wall and features four bolt runners and two lower-off bolts.

John Craven's Willy Warmer   30 feet   Hard Very Severe 4c S   (8.92)
At the bottom of its grade. Three bolt runners.
Climb a groove and cross a bulge to two lower-off bolts.

Taylor Made Tracking Damage   20 feet   E2 6a/b S   (15.12.90)
This hard boulder-problem starts 12 feet right of *Cold Steal* and 35 feet from the seaward end of the wall.
Use a short wide crack to clip a bolt runner and continue with difficulty to the scoop above. Single-bolt lower-off point, or continue to the last route's lower-off bolts.

Option B   35 feet   E3 6a S   (6.9.93)
The line through the roofs just before the right-hand end of the quarried wall. Three bolt runners.
Climb up past the quarrymen's boreholes and over the roof to two lower-off bolts.

Eye Am the Sky   35 feet   E4 6b S   (11.4.92)
Start just before the right arête of the quarried wall. Three bolt runners. This route defines the limit of the bolt zone.
Climb steeply to a fist-sized hole underneath a roof. Swing rightwards onto the seaward face and continue up the blank wall by hard laybacks. Two lower-off bolts.

SEA WALL
The wall between Dancing Ledge and Guillemot Ledge is untouched

by quarrying and for the most part falls into deep water. It has been designated a bolt-free area. However, four bolt-routes have been climbed here, some (but not all) predating the bolting agreement; consequently their bolts may have been removed. **Hieronymus GBH** (70 feet E4 6a 15.12.90) starts from the lowest of the narrow ledges near the left-hand side of this face. It climbs to a break, moves slightly right, and continues up to a lower-off point. **Sea of Holes** (E2 5c S [R] 25.8.94) is 30 feet to the east and is escaped by prusiking. **Song to the Siren** (80 feet E5 6a S [R] 30.10.91) is approached by abseil from a stake 50 yards west of a stile. From a twin-bolt belay, a fairly direct line crosses an overhang and a tufa shield to reach an abseil-rope belay. Thirty feet to the east of *Siren's* stake, an abseil from another stake leads to a belay 20 feet above the sea, the setting-off point for **White Rave** (60 feet E5 6a S [R] 25.8.93), which climbs a steep white sheet and a bulge to a slabby finish and an abseil-rope belay.

LOWER WALLS

The lower ledge is split into three parts, and slopes gently down into the sea. Climbs of most grades up to Very Severe start from these lower ledges, and much harder climbs take up the challenge of the sea-caves between them. Although the easier lines were at one time documented in detail, a full set of descriptions is felt to be superfluous as the wall never exceeds 25 feet in height and its problems are obvious. Only the harder recent additions are described. Elsewhere on the Lower Walls climbers may safely be left to choose their own lines, most of which have undoubtedly been done before.

West of the main lower ledge is a narrow zawn and an even lower ledge. Beyond is another ledge with a sea-cave on either side of it. The following routes are on good rock and tackle some exhilarating airspace above the tiered sea-cave west of the furthest ledge. They are best approached by abseil.

Corridors of Power   35 feet   E4 6b S †   (27.11.93)
Start on an isolated jutting ledge some 10 feet left of *Mariner's Graveyard* pitch 2. Five bolt runners.
A desperate start is followed by a sustained series of steep moves. Bolt belay.

** **Mariner's Graveyard**   90 feet   E5 S †   (19.10.90)
A spare pair of arms is required for this committing adventure, which traverses the lower hanging wall above the sea-cave. A route to yo-ho-ho rather than yo-yo! Twenty yards from the western side of the quarry is a small cave. Abseil from blocks in the cave's mouth to a single-bolt belay on the right side of the sea-cave.
1 50 feet 6a. Seven bolts and four *in-situ* threads. Follow the lowest handrail to an isolated jutting ledge on the left side of the cave. Single-bolt belay.

2 40 feet 6a. Four bolt runners. Pull steeply up to the break above the centre of the ledge. Haul over the roof and continue to a clean-cut exit. Block belay.

★ **The Pump Will Tear Us Apart**   60 feet   E5 6b *S*   (7.10.90)
Superb holds in a sensational position, but a very pumpy route. Feet are an optional extra (but should be carried). Start as for *Mariner's Graveyard*. Seven bolts and four *in-situ* threads.
Pull up, look left, and hand-traverse the rail for 25 feet to the centre of the cave. Climb out and up to a break and a semi rest by a good flake. Continue straight over bulges to the top. Block belays.

★ **Lucretia, My Reflection**   40 feet   E3 6a *S*   (30.9.90)
A gothic pitch on a wild leftward line above the cave. Start as for *Mariner's Graveyard*. Five bolts and three *in-situ* threads.
Pull up to a break and then go strenuously leftwards on a diagonal crack (crux) to gain a hanging slab. Traverse left on deep pockets to the slab's end. Finish leftwards over bulges. Block belays.

Here Comes the Hizbollah   30 feet   E3 6a *S*   (22.2.92)
Start as for *Mariner's Graveyard*. Four bolt runners.
Climb the right-hand side of the corner before launching up around the roof to a series of flat holds (the crux). Continue on good holds to the main ledge.

★★ **Hell's Darker Chambers**   60 feet   E7 6c *S* †   (3.5.92)
West of the main lower ledge is a narrow zawn; start beyond this on the east side of a large sea-cave. This, the hardest route 'down the ledge' ventures into the middle of the cave: mindlessly strenuous but low in the grade. Nine bolt runners.
Pull steeply up to the handrail and traverse left for 30 feet to the centre of the cave. Cross leftwards over the first two roofs via desperate moves on 'slopers'. From the next rail, make a hard swing leftwards and follow a spectacular series of juggy blocks slightly leftwards to the top.

Bust Ya Boiler   50 feet   E6 6b *S* †   (17.10.93)
A steep pitch which starts as for *Hell's Darker Chambers*. Eight bolt runners.
Pull up to the handrail and traverse left for 10 feet, as for *Hell's Darker Chambers*. Climb up through the roofs above, with a reachy crux at the final lip.

Marianas Trenchcoat   35 feet   E4 5c †   (3.3.91)
Another steep line, which swings out above the narrow zawn at the western end of the main ledge.
Jug-haul up the right-hand side of the arch above the zawn to gain a handrail. Swing left for 10 feet and go straight up to a peg runner, before finishing over the roof. Block belay.

In the centre of the lower wall below the main ledge is a cave which periodically sheds part of its roof. Nevertheless, at the time of going to press, there exist three routes over it. Another route is fittingly absent: **Absent Friend** (1.7.90).

Mexican Wave   30 feet   E5 6b †   (22.3.88)
Climb the 20-foot roof-stack on the left side of the cave past two threads (originally *in situ* but now missing.)

Armed and Dangerous (30 feet E5 6b †† 24.7.87), which crosses the centre of the cave roof, has been affected by rockfall and may need cleaning.

A Short Story about Power   30 feet   E4 6b ††   (7.5.90)
A reclean is required as a result of a rockfall near the top.
Pull over the centre of the roof, and swing rightwards (bolt runner) to beneath a short blank wall. Continue strenuously (bolt runner) to the top. Block belay.
A direct start (E5 6c † 27.6.91) crosses the 7-foot ceiling to a prominent pinch-grip on the lip, and then uses 'slopers' to pass a bolt runner and finish as for the original route.

Totally Gone Now   25 feet   E2 5c †   (1988)
In the steepest part of the wall 100 feet east of the cave are two rightward-slanting cracks. Climb the left-hand crack.

Come On Arms   20 feet   E2 6a †   (1988)
Climb the right-hand crack.

Guillemot Ledge   OS Ref 001 768

Guillemot is a popular area for several 'convenience factors', in addition to its good climbing: first, it has car-parking relatively close by; secondly, the jumble of huge blocks at its base provides protection from heavy seas, which means that it is usually still accessible in the winter months; last, the central section of the cliff is located beneath a disused quarry and so has clean-cut finishes.

The cliff has a wide selection of desirable climbs in virtually all the grades. At its western end, where it rises to over 130 feet in height, there exists a steep, white wall that is one of the showpieces of Swanage. This superb face is the realm solely of the extreme climber and is tightly packed with top-quality hard routes.

There is, however, one grade conspicuous by its absence - Very Difficult -

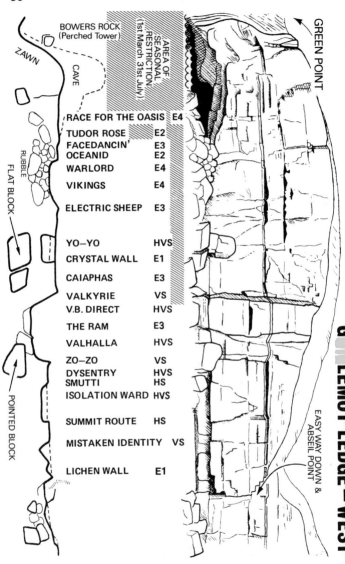

GREEN POINT

BOWERS ROCK
(Perched Tower)

ZAWN

CAVE

AREA OF
SEASONAL
RESTRICTION
(1st March-31st July)

RUBBLE

FLAT BLOCK

POINTED BLOCK

RACE FOR THE OASIS E4

TUDOR ROSE E2
FACEDANCIN' E3
OCEANID E2
WARLORD E4

VIKINGS E4

ELECTRIC SHEEP E3

YO–YO HVS

CRYSTAL WALL E1

CAIAPHAS E3

VALKYRIE VS
V.B. DIRECT HVS

THE RAM E3

VALHALLA HVS

ZO–ZO VS
DYSENTRY HVS
SMUTTI HS
ISOLATION WARD HVS

SUMMIT ROUTE HS

MISTAKEN IDENTITY VS

LICHEN WALL E1

GURNARD'S HEAD – WEST

EASY WAY DOWN &
ABSEIL POINT

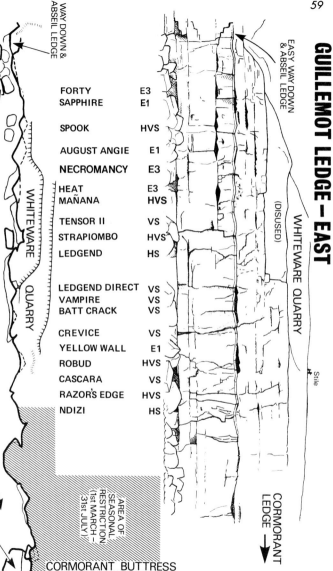

GUILLEMOT LEDGE — EAST

WAY DOWN & ABSEIL LEDGE

EASY WAY DOWN & ABSEIL LEDGE

WHITEWARE QUARRY

(DISUSED)

Stile

FORTY	E3
SAPPHIRE	E1
SPOOK	HVS
AUGUST ANGIE	E1
NECROMANCY	E3
HEAT	E3
MAÑANA	HVS
TENSOR II	VS
STRAPIOMBO	HVS
LEDGEND	HS
LEDGEND DIRECT	VS
VAMPIRE	VS
BATT CRACK	VS
CREVICE	VS
YELLOW WALL	E1
ROBUD	HVS
CASCARA	VS
RAZOR'S EDGE	HVS
NDIZI	HS

WHITEWARE QUARRY

CORMORANT LEDGE

AREA OF SEASONAL RESTRICTION (1st MARCH – 31st JULY)

POINTED

CORMORANT BUTTRESS

the grade of the previous escape route from the area. Since *Exit Chimney* fell down there have been several rescues of parties that had intended to climb it! The easiest route is now *Ledgend* at Hard Severe. Alternatively, seas permitting, and outside the nesting-season, *Cormorant Buttress West* (Severe) provides an interesting exit at neighbouring Cormorant Ledge Another departure - welcome this time - is that of the rickety old fence on the cliff-top. The new fence now provides the belays in Guillemot West.

Quarrying activity above the eastern end of the cliff has left the routes beneath it with safe finishes, but both to the west of the abseil point and to the east of *Robud* the cliff-top is still in its natural state. A number of the routes at Guillemot are affected by a degree of loose rock in their upper part, though the majority should not prove troublesome for the experienced climber. Progress along the bottom of the cliff is usually unaffected by the state of the tide; however, a short section just west of the abseil ledge is sometimes awash. If this should prove impassable then the western end of Guillemot can be gained also by abseiling down the *Valkyrie* buttress, but care is needed with loose rock at the top. **Nesting-season restrictions** apply between Dancing Ledge and *Valkyrie Buttress Direct*, and also to the east of *The Razor's Edge* (see Introduction).

Approach as for Dancing Ledge to the brow of the hill. Head leftwards (east) along this for a short distance and cross a stile in a dry-stone wall. Follow the valley to a wide gully, which leads down to a roomy ledge. From a cemented bar or nut anchors in the corner of the ledge, make a free abseil to the boulders 50 feet below.

GUILLEMOT WEST

West of the abseil point, the boulders give way to a low-level platform (sometimes awash) which extends to a triangular buttress topped by a stack of blocks. *Summit Route* and *Smutti* climb up the sides of this triangle. The cliff now rears up to its full height at the large corner of *Zo-Zo*, which defines the right side of the enormous *Valkyrie* buttress jutting out above a pile of huge blocks. A number of routes attack this buttress: *The Ram* forces a difficult passage to meet with the soaring upper arête; *Valkyrie Buttress Direct* tackles the middle of the seaward face; and *Be-Bop-Deluxe* gives surprising climbing up the golden, west-facing wall. Further on, past the thin flake-line of *Caiaphas*, a massive reclining pillar marks both the start of *Yo-Yo* and the beginning of a very impressive face that stretches across to finish above a large sea-cave. The first distinctive feature in this area is the striking vertical fault of *Electric Sheep*. Further westwards, past the mighty white headwall of *Warlord*, the boulders come to an end at the foot of a steep groove: this is *Oceanid*. Beyond extends the large sea-cave, the upper walls of which sport several more fine routes. *Tudor Rose* weaves an intricate path up the main expanse of the wall and *Dougal the Great* plunges straight into the nightmare of overhanging rock formed by the stepped roofs of the cave.

Dougal the Great   150 feet   E6 [R] †   (4.9.77/12.2.88)
Start beneath the roofs on the right-hand side of the sea-cave at the western end of Guillemot Ledge. The bolts are relics of the climb's original A3 status and are not required for a free ascent.
1 85 feet 6b/c. Climb over two roofs (wedge and peg runner) to a junction with *Race for the Oasis*. (To prevent rope-drag, the initial protection may need stripping at this point.) Traverse 15 feet left (*in-situ* thread) to a nose. Continue past the nose and three old bolt studs to the roof (peg runner). Gain the wall above and continue up past a small overhang (two *in-situ* threads and a peg runner) to a small recessed ledge. Belay here on nuts and a peg.
2 65 feet 5c. From the left end of the ledge, climb the bulging wall (*in-situ* thread) directly to a jutting ledge (*in-situ* thread). With great respect for the condition of the rock, follow the obvious line diagonally leftwards and exit up the leaning chimney.

★ Race for the Oasis   200 feet   E4 [R] †   (27.11.82)
A wandering but nevertheless sustained climb which tackles the roofs of the sea-cave on good rock. Great care is necessary to minimize rope drag on the first pitch. Start below the right-hand end of the cave roof behind a large flat boulder.
1 80 feet 6a. Move up to gain a chimneying position, and then traverse left under the overhang for 25 feet past a peg runner. Climb steeply to a peg runner below another overhang. Swing up right using a doubtful flake to reach a poor rest below a shallow, bottomless groove (small nut and spike runners up left). Make steep and fingery moves up the left rib of the groove and trend rightwards to join *Tudor Rose*. Take a hanging stance at the right-hand end of a narrow roof.
2 30 feet 5b. Traverse left for 10 feet to a good handhold below a very shallow groove. Go up the groove and traverse left again before stepping down to an exposed stance on a small recessed ledge (the oasis). Nut and peg belay shared with *Dougal the Great*.
3 90 feet 5c. Move diagonally right to the faultline (large *Friend* runner) and hand-traverse right along this to a good ledge and a peg runner. From the left end of the ledge move up to a peg runner and a good handhold; now step left slightly and climb boldly up the wall to positive finishing holds. Trend up right, and exit leftwards up an easy groove as for *Nemesis*.

★ Sons of Pioneers   160 feet   E6 [R] †   (28.8.94)
A demanding fabrication of exciting pitches - each having something different to offer! The route forces a line between the upper sections of *Tudor Rose* and *Facedancin'*.
1 60 feet 6a. A bold and very committing pitch requiring good ropework. Climb up to the horizontal chimney under the roof and follow it leftwards for 10 feet (as for *Race for the Oasis*). Drop out of the dark to jugs on the lip and gain a rightward-rising handrail (crucial *Friend 2* in pocket). Follow the rail for 10 feet before crossing the bulge

leftwards to the foot of a slight corner on *Tudor Rose*. Peg and nut belay.
2 30 feet **6b.** Climb to the top of the corner, where a grossly leaning wall appears to bar progress. Move up right to gain a horizontal crack in the bulge (peg runner), and make wild moves over onto the lip. Multiple *Friend 2* and *3* belay.
3 70 feet **6a.** From a position just right of a large ammonite, climb the unprotected wall to better holds and wire runners. Bear right to the distinctive square-cut niche below the white headwall. Continue direct (peg runner on the right) to the long ledge, follow it rightwards, and finish up the corner.

*** **Tudor Rose**   210 feet   E2 [R]   (5.5.74)
An established Swanage classic, low in its grade and mostly on good rock. Difficulties, though intricate and sustained, are nowhere excessive. Start below a long crack just right of the low-level roofs (40 feet right of the large cave).
1 150 feet **5b.** Climb the small bulge and slab to reach the cracks. Pull up steeply into the left-hand crack, climb this for a few feet to where it eases slightly, and traverse left to a good foot-ledge. Continue the traverse to the second of two slight corners (peg runner). Move left with difficulty, and continue up over a jammed block to a small roof. Step left and follow a groove to the faultline (optional poor belay). Climb the steep wall more easily to a good stance and large nut belay in a corner.
2 60 feet **5b.** Climb the slender flake at the right-hand end of the ledge and move up into the shallow groove on the left. Make a long reach to the horizontal crack above, and then traverse right along the break to finish up a short corner as for *Oceanid*. Alternatively, and much harder, step right once the horizontal crack is reached and continue up the very steep wall above.

*** **Facedancin'**   160 feet   E3 [R]   (8.1.83)
A superb route with steep and dynamic climbing on the second pitch. The climb takes a direct, though natural line up the steep wall to the left of *Oceanid*. High in its grade but all the major difficulties are well protected. Start as for *Tudor Rose*.
1 80 feet **5c.** Follow *Tudor Rose* to the foot-ledge 10 feet along that route's traverse. Climb the wall and the short, hanging groove splitting the bulge above. Step right at the top of the groove to reach thread and nut belays at the faultline.
2 80 feet **6a.** Move diagonally right for 15 feet, and then trend back left to a good ledge. Go over a bulge to a peg runner and step right to a series of thin flake-cracks in the steep, white wall. Follow these cracks direct (peg runner) to the ledge traversed by *Tudor Rose*, and finish up the corner on the right.

* **Oceanid**   150 feet   E2 [R]   (5.8.72)
A steep, compelling line. Its quality, however, is marred by the worrying

moves to bypass some dubious blocks at the top of the groove. Start on top of a jumble of fallen blocks, below a slim, square-cut groove in the upper wall (20 feet right of *Tudor Rose*).
1 60 feet 5a. Traverse 10 feet left from the top of the blocks and climb steeply into a niche. Pull out of the niche using a large jug on the right and follow the cracks above until it is possible to step right onto a slab just below the faultline (thread belay).
2 90 feet 5b. Climb up diagonally left to the faultline and up onto the wall above. Move left around a bulge and continue straight up the sustained groove above, before stepping out left to avoid the capping bulge. Finish up the short corner.

⋆⋆ **Fly Crazy but Free** 150 feet E5 [R] (26.9.83)
A desperately fingery and technical pitch up the leaning white wall between *Oceanid* and *Warlord*.
1 60 feet 5a. *Oceanid* pitch 1.
2 90 feet 6b. Move up diagonally left, and then back right above the lip of the overhang to a small ledge and peg runner (as for *Warlord*). Swing left and move up to a niche below the white wall. Climb the twin cracks above, step left, and make a very hard move up to a good horizontal break. Proceed directly up the sustained, leaning headwall past two peg runners.

⋆⋆ **Warlord** 140 feet E4 [R] (21.2.76/28.11.81)
An immaculate classic with a pleasing degree of safety. Steep, *very* strenuous, and with the crux reserved for the final moves.
1 60 feet 5a. *Oceanid* pitch 1.
2 80 feet 5c. Move up diagonally left, and then back right above the lip of the overhang to a small ledge and peg runner. Follow the crack above past various pegs, keeping something in reserve for the short difficult section 15 feet from the top.

⋆⋆ **Vikings** 170 feet E4 [R] (21.8.83)
A very fine route through the roofs and up the superb white wall to the right of the upper section of *Warlord*. Technically absorbing climbing throughout and on good rock. Small wires and *RP*s are essential. Start at the right-hand of two converging cracks.
1 70 feet 5a. Climb about half-way up the right-hand crack and move left into a scoop. Go up a short corner to a slab and traverse left half-way along this to where it is possible to pull through the overlap onto the upper slab (peg runner). Continue leftwards to the thread belay of *Oceanid*.
2 30 feet 5c. Move up right to the roof (large *Friend* placement) and pull over to good holds and a small, sloping ledge. Traverse right on undercuts along the lip, and then go up right to a nut and peg belay below a short corner in the next roof.
3 70 feet 6a. Pull into the short corner and make a spectacular swing over the roof. Move up onto a narrow sloping ledge (peg runner above) before climbing the wall just to its right to a good resting-place by a flake

crack. Pull up left and proceed straight up the wall, passing a good *Friend* 2 placement, to a steep blocky finish on good holds.
Variation
The Horny Hat Finish [R]   (24.8.89)
3a 70 feet 6a. Follow the parent route to the narrow sloping ledge. Climb slightly leftwards and then follow a deep, intermittent crack (parallel to, and a short distance right of, the crack of *Warlord*). Make hard moves where this ends, and finish up a cracked wall.

Electric Sheep 120 feet E3 [R] †   (11.5.74)
An impressive and uncompromising proposition offering difficult climbing in a serious situation on loose rock. Start as for *Vikings*.
1 60 feet 5b. Climb the right-hand crack, surmount the faultline roof (peg runner), and continue to a scoop below a second roof.
2 60 feet 5c. Climb the crack in the roof and continue steeply to the top.

★ **Nemesis** 265 feet E1 [R] †   (14.4.74/1979)
An interesting and exposed traverse of the western wing of Guillemot Ledge. The climbing is serious in parts and sustained. Start at the base of a very large boulder pillar leaning against the cliff.
1 40 feet. Scramble to the top of the pillar.
2 80 feet 5a. Climb the ramp on the left for about 15 feet to the arête, and then traverse left across a wall to a groove. Continue left to a slab and follow this to the thread belay of *Oceanid*.
3 60 feet 5b. Climb up left to the faultline and traverse left along it (the traverse is steep and difficult to start but soon eases). Continue across the slab beyond to a poor belay below an obvious clean-cut corner at the top of the cliff.
4 85 feet 5a. Ascend the steep groove above the stance to an awkward thread runner, traverse right, and continue to a large ledge. Walk left along the ledge (optional stance) and climb the obvious clean-cut corner and cracks above to the top. (The base of the corner is the final stance of *Tudor Rose*, the top pitch of which provides a better finish.)

Yo-Yo 145 feet Hard Very Severe [R]   (24.3.74/1.2.76)
A good line but a poor, loose route. Start as for *Nemesis*.
1 40 feet. Scramble to the top of the pillar.
2 40 feet 4b. Climb the ramp on the left to a small ledge at the faultline (peg belay).
3 65 feet 5a. Step up right and climb a bottomless, slanting groove past a peg runner. Cross a loose, toothed overhang and continue up until it is possible to move right with difficulty to an exposed foothold on the nose. Step left and continue directly to a loose finish.
Variation
3a 90 feet 5a (1 pt aid) [R] †. Move up left over loose rock for about 30 feet to the overhang. Climb a groove in the overhang (10 feet right of the roof-crack of *Electric Sheep*) using a peg for aid, and then traverse up

right past a slab to an overhanging corner. Ascend the corner and move right around a nose to a slab which leads to the top.

Crystal Wall   120 feet   E1   [R]   (10.5.75)
A disturbing route, high in its grade and loose. Start immediately right of the huge reclining pillar. Belay pegs required.
1 60 feet 4a. Climb the crack, step left onto the steep wall, and ascend cracks to the protruding block at the faultline. Place peg belays.
2 60 feet 5a. Traverse right to a corner-crack and climb this (peg runner) to an exposed ledge and a second protection peg. Move up left onto the slab above, continue up into a short corner, and proceed carefully over loose ground to the top.

* **Caiaphas**   130 feet   E3   [R]   (22.9.79)
A high-calibre main pitch, bold and fingery. Start below a short corner 10 feet right of the huge reclining pillar of *Yo-Yo*.
1 80 feet 5c. Climb the corner and continue up, trending right on small holds for 15 feet to reach the foot of a white wall. Traverse 10 feet left to the thin crack. Go up this to a strip roof at the faultline and pull over to reach the bottom left-hand end of the prominent diagonal flake. Follow the echoing flake for 15 feet to a stance and nut belays.
2 50 feet 5a. Continue along the flake and climb the unstable corner to a loose top.

The next two pitches start from a good ledge at 20 feet, some 15 feet left of the big corner. They also end at the same point. The second pitch of *Caiaphas* can be used to finish, but it is rather loose. An alternative, once the belay of *Caiaphas* is reached, is to make a descending traverse to the belay of *Valkyrie*.

* **Deaf Mosaic**   70 feet   E6 6c   [R] †   (28.8.94)
Fingertip climbing on the blank, white face immediately right of the *Caiaphas* flake. The route can be protected well.
Climb direct, fairly easily, to the horizontal break beneath the steep white wall. Gain one- and two-finger holes in the wall, and then climb intricately up the centre (two peg runners) to the main break. From a big undercut, pull over to a jug on the 'shield', and proceed more easily to the belay of *Caiaphas*.

Norseman   70 feet   E5 6a/b   [R] †   (28.8.94)
Steep, technical face-climbing up the thin crack left of the big corner. Climb direct, fairly easily, to the horizontal break beneath the steep white wall. Climb the thin crack with increasing difficulty to a small niche at the main break. Surmount the roof and follow a thin crack in the 'shield' to the belay of *Caiaphas*.

Valkyrie   155 feet   Very Severe   [R]   (11.4.66)
Some nice situations but the climb has a loose and disappointing top

pitch. Start at the foot of the conspicuous corner that bounds the western side of the *Valkyrie* buttress.
1 60 feet 4b. Either climb the corner-crack direct to a stance at the faultline, or, slightly harder, step left at 15 feet and follow the layback crack to the same point.
2 35 feet. Traverse right along the faultline, and belay on the front of the buttress.
3 60 feet 4b. Climb up leftwards for 20 feet to a ledge before traversing left for 15 feet. Climb the left arête and continue left along the obvious line of weakness to a loose exit.

Be-Bop-Deluxe   120 feet   E2 [R]   (6.12.83)
The yellow, west-facing sidewall of the *Valkyrie* buttress gives open face-climbing on rock which is unfortunately rather friable. Start below the crack in the bulge just right of *Valkyrie*.
1 80 feet 5b. Pull up the crack and move rightwards along the horizontal break at the base of the yellow wall. Climb the centre of the wall boldly (peg runner) and bear right to gain a groove leading to the faultline.
2 40 feet 4c. From the stance, step back left onto the wall and follow a shallow corner until it is possible to move right around the arête to the start of a cracked slab. Climb the slab to the top.

Valkyrie Buttress Direct   120 feet   Hard Very Severe   (21.5.67)
Protection is poor on the first pitch. Start below the big roof in the middle of the seaward face of the *Valkyrie* buttress.
1 65 feet 5a. Climb the steep wall and veer left to the edge of the buttress. Move up past the left-hand end of the roof and continue slightly right to a good ledge at the faultline.
2 55 feet 4c. From the centre of the ledge, move up and left to where an awkward mantel gains an overhung ledge. Continue straight up past a peg runner to a fairly sound finish.

The Ram   120 feet   E3   (6.77)
A worthwhile route, fairly strenuous. Start 6 feet right of *Valkyrie Buttress Direct* below a large ledge at 10 feet.
1 80 feet 5c. Climb up bearing right to a corner that passes through an overhang. Move up into the corner and traverse left above the roof for 10 feet (crux), before climbing straight up to ledges.
2 40 feet 5a/b. The sharp arête above is climbed on its left-hand side to the top.

Valhalla   125 feet   Hard Very Severe   (27.2.77)
Start as for *The Ram*. A loose top pitch.
1 70 feet 5a. Climb up to the ledge, and from its left-hand end follow a faint groove and crack to ledges on the left. Move up to the roof and traverse right for 15 feet. Pull up a steep groove and continue more easily to the faultline. Multiple nut belay.

2 55 feet 4c. Climb the corner above to the top.

★ **Zo-Zo** 100 feet Very Severe
Recommended on account of its splendid first pitch, this is an easy tick for its grade and very popular. A number of large nuts are required for protection and the belay. Start at the foot of the prominent corner on the right-hand side of the *Valkyrie* buttress.
1 60 feet 4b. The corner gives sustained climbing to the faultline, where a short leftward traverse gains a good belay ledge.
2 40 feet. Climb the right wall of the groove above, taking care with the large blocks at the top. Stake belay.

Dysentry 100 feet Hard Very Severe 4c   (18.2.79)
The thin crack in the wall right of *Zo-Zo* has a very loose and unpleasant upper section. Start 10 feet right of the corner of *Zo-Zo*.
Climb to the ledge at 6 feet and continue up to the foot of a thin crack. Go up the crack to the faultline (optional belay) and traverse right for 15 feet. Pull over a bulge to a resting-place and continue up over loose ground, trending rightwards to a ledge below an earth cornice. Avoid this on its left and continue up to the top.

About 100 feet to the west of the abseil descent lies a large triangular buttress with a pinnacle of blocks on its top.

Smutti 115 feet Hard Severe   (12.2.67)
Start below the crack that forms the left-hand side of the triangle. A poor route, requiring a steady second on pitch 2.
1 50 feet 4a. Climb up the newly-formed niche or easier rock to its left to gain the crackline. Follow this to the apex of the triangle.
2 65 feet 4b. Climb the difficult corner above until a step to the right can be made. Pull over the bulge to the right on suspect rock and traverse rightwards along a ledge to the grassy gully. Belay on fenceposts. (A direct finish has been climbed but is not recommended.)
Variations
Isolation Ward Hard Very Severe †   (1.9.84)
1a 50 feet 4b/c. Poorly protected. Start midway between *Smutti* and *Summit Route* below a 3-foot roof. Cross the roof on good holds. Climb up leftwards to a ledge, and then go diagonally right up the wall to join *Summit Route* just below the pinnacle belay.
Summit Route Hard Severe   (11.4.66)
1b 50 feet 4a/b. Start below the crack that forms the right-hand side of the triangle. Climb the wall, groove, and crack to the pinnacle.

★ **Mistaken Identity** 70 feet Very Severe 4c   (1976)
A steep, sustained pitch on sound rock. Start 10 feet right of *Summit Route* at the left-hand end of a large low-level roof.
Climb up past the edge of the roof, avoid the guano, and then continue up the wall and cracks above to a ledge. Exit to the right.

True Identity   75 feet   Hard Very Severe 5a †   (9.10.94)
A good route which starts as for its *Mistaken* partner, at the left-hand end of the low-level roof.
Climb up to clear the roof and traverse right past a large thread placement to a ledge. Step right and follow a short crack before crossing the overhang on its right to gain the slab above. Trend right to a shallow scoop in the headwall and finish direct.

Lichen Wall   70 feet   E1 5b   (13.4.74)
Start 20 feet to the west of the entry abseil at the right-hand end of the large low-level roof. A strenuous start and a technical finish.
Climb 10 feet up the wall, pull up to a jug, and traverse left (hard) to gain the arête. Ascend the lichenous wall to a block (stance possible to the left), and then climb the crack above with difficulty to the top.

Michelle   60 feet   Hard Very Severe 5a   (10.5.87)
Starting 5 feet right of the low-level roof of *Lichen Wall*, this has become less independent of that route since a large hand-traverse block 'went AWOL'. Harder for the short at the top.
Climb up and then rightwards over a bulge before traversing leftwards for 10 feet. Climb up slightly rightwards to a roof. Make a long stretch to pull over onto the second lowest rock step of the abseil ledge.

GUILLEMOT EAST

The abseil from the open ledge leads down a short, bulging buttress next to a large rockfall scar, which marks the original extent of the ledge. To the east the unlikely line of *Sapphire* breaches the intimidating overhang that caps an obvious, wide sentry-box situated just below the faultline. A short distance past this, *The Spook* and *August Angie* climb two grooves that lead up to a pair of diamond-shaped roofs. Beyond, a steep, bare wall makes the challenge plain for those who can take *The Heat*. Just past the corner of *Tensor II*, *Ledgend* tackles a prominent ragged crack which is easily spotted from the abseil ledge. Further on, *The Crevice* ascends an overhanging chimney/crack. Next is an interesting, spade-shaped flake in the groove of *Robud*; and to its east *The Razor's Edge* cuts an attractive line up the arête of a slabby buttress. Progress eastwards from this point into Cormorant Ledge has been facilitated by the demise of Cleft Buttress; it is now possible to scramble across from Guillemot to Cormorant either at low tide or if there is a calm sea.

Landslide Victory   50 feet   Very Severe 4b †   (5.4.92)
Still quite loose and dirty from the rockfall. Poorly protected. Start right of the entry abseil, at a diagonal flake crack.
Climb leftwards up the diagonal crack and left along a break to a short crack. Move up delicately and continue left to the main crackline. Continue up this on suspect rock and finish with an airy mantelshelf.

Exit Chimney II the Sequel 100 feet E4 6a † (5.12.87)
The rubber marks on this route date from its days as one side of a
chimney! Start 30 feet right of the entry abseil.
Climb over the roof at a crack. Continue boldly up flakes and a rib to the
roof (*in-situ* thread). Follow twin overhanging cracks with difficulty to the
faultline and continue directly up the wall above on big holds. Belay with
an extra rope to the fenceposts.

Forty 110 feet E3 6a † (30.4.77/10.83)
An unfriendly route with a poor finish. Low in its grade. Start part way
between the rockfall scar and *Sapphire*.
Avoiding the first pitch of *Sapphire*, climb up to the overhang and pull
directly over past a peg runner (crux). Follow the groove above, mostly on
its right-hand side, to gain the faultline and an optional stance. Finish
straight up on loose rock. Belay with an extra rope to the fenceposts.

⋆ Sapphire 110 feet E1 (3.4.72)
A trade route of the area with solid rock throughout and a safe but
imposing crux. Start 60 feet right of the abseil ledge, at a wall below a
prominent, open sentry-box just below the faultline.
1 45 feet 4b. Climb the poorly-protected wall to the wide sentry-box.
2 65 feet 5b. Move up to the faultline and swing left onto a slight
arête. Surmount the roof, passing two peg runners to reach the next set
of overhangs (crux). Traverse right underneath these and follow a crack
around a bulge to the top. Belay with nuts on the backwall of the
quarry.

Immediately east of *Sapphire* are two connected diamond-shaped roofs with
twin grooves beneath them. The left-hand groove is *The Spook* and the right
one is *August Angie*.

⋆ The Spook 110 feet Hard Very Severe (31.3.74)
A very popular route, impressive and with a bold finish.
1 60 feet 5a. Climb the groove to the roof and traverse right beneath it
to gain a steeper groove, which leads to the faultline. Belay to the right.
2 50 feet 5a. Climb the wall above to a small roof. (The peg has almost
completed its metamorphosis into rust, but there is an unlikely large nut
placement up left behind a spike.) Pull up onto the steep wall above the
roof via a suspect hold and continue to the top. Belay with nuts on the
backwall.

⋆ Toiler on the Sea 110 feet E5 † (6.6.87)
Start at the arête between *The Spook* and *August Angie*.
1 60 feet 6b. Climb boldly up the front face of the arête to the roof (peg
and *in-situ* threads). Pull over into a niche (peg runner), bridge out (peg
runner over the roof), and follow the shallow groove-line on the right to the
faultline.
2 50 feet 5b. Climb diagonally left for about 25 feet past a peg runner

to gain a protruding ledge. Step left onto the nose and continue up to the top.

August Angie   125 feet   E1   (28.10.73)
A good route with sustained difficulties. Pitch 1 is poorly protected and requires care to avoid rope drag. Start beneath the right-hand of the two prominent grooves.
1 85 feet 5b. Climb the groove past a peg runner and continue with difficulty to the roof and a second peg runner. Traverse right under the roof to a ledge below a corner (optional stance). Climb the corner to the faultline and traverse awkwardly left to a good ledge.
2 40 feet 4c/5a. Climb the wall just right of the belay to the roof. Move right around the arête to a break in the overhangs and climb up through this to the top (strenuous). Belay with nuts on the backwall.

★ **Necromancy**   110 feet   E3 5c   (11.8.90)
Protection is sparse, but what there is is good. Start 15 feet right of the groove of *August Angie*.
Climb a short wall and go strenuously through a break in the roof. Swing rightwards on a line of incuts to a peg runner at a good flake. Continue boldly straight up to the large ledge. Now go up and rightwards to a superb jug and a clean-cut exit onto a ledge. Finish easily. Block belay.

★ **The Heat**   115 feet   E3   (7.4.74)
Some excellent climbing but with a bold and sparsely-protected first pitch up a steep wall; a serious route. Start 30 feet right of *August Angie* from a ledge beneath the left-hand end of a large roof at 40 feet.
1 50 feet 5c. Climb the short wall to a ledge (peg runner). Move left (another peg runner) and ascend the wall above with difficulty on small holds to a belay ledge.
2 65 feet 5a/b. Follow the corner, and then move right and up to the faultline. Move left around a nose (peg runner) and traverse left to below a V-shaped overhang. Climb up over this, and belay using a block on the right.
Variation
★ **The Big Heat**   70 feet   E3 5c †   (6.6.87)
An extension to *The Heat* up the wall above. Climb the crux wall of *The Heat* and then, eschewing the welcoming ledge on the left, press on up the wall above (two peg runners). Block belay on the ledge. Scramble out.

Mañana   110 feet   Hard Very Severe   (5.5.63)
Worth doing despite a badly-protected and delicate start. Start at the right-hand end of the initial ledge of *The Heat*, below a large roof.
1 50 feet 4c. Climb easily right to a ledge at 10 feet below a microscopic, roof-capped corner. Step delicately right onto a slight rib and move up past a bent peg runner to a shallow groove; this leads to a good stance on the right of the big roof.
2 60 feet 5a. Climb the short wall on the left passing a peg runner to the

faultline (difficult). Alternatively, but no easier, move 5 feet left before going up to the faultline. Continue to the top more easily. Block belay.

Funeral Pyre   100 feet   E3 †   (6.5.87)
Start beneath a wide and very shallow scoop before the next corner. A bold first pitch.
1 50 feet 5c. Climb slightly rightwards and then back leftwards to foot-ledges. Continue up the steep, unprotected scoop to the stance of *Tensor II*. Large block belay.
2 50 feet 5a. Using the massive peg on *Tensor II* as a side-runner, walk 8 feet left and balance up the slabby arête to the faultline. Finish, as for *Tensor II*, by surmounting the overhang just to the right and following the groove to a block belay at the top.

★★ **Tensor II**   115 feet   Very Severe   (8.12.73)
A Swanage classic with absorbing and contrasted pitches. It is at the top of its grade, and especially hard for locals who are unused to the style of climbing required for the crux. Probably the most popular route at Guillemot. Start at the corner.
1 70 feet 4c. Climb the corner-crack until level with the first roof on the left. Follow a series of undercuts leftwards beneath the roof, and climb a slight bulge to a good stance and a large flake belay.
2 45 feet 5a. Clip the chunky peg runner and then make some thin and delicate moves up the slab to the faultline. Surmount the overhang above and follow the groove to the top. Block belay.

★ **Strapiombo**   100 feet   Hard Very Severe 5a   (27.3.67)
The corner-crack of *Tensor II* and the chimney above provide an enjoyable outing at an amenable standard.
Climb the corner-crack to a peg runner above a spike and continue up on poorish rock to the roof. Turn it on the right and climb the chimney to the faultline. Follow a broken crack on good holds to a ledge and continue up on sound rock to the top. Stake belay.

Helen's Return   100 feet   E2 5b   (5.87)
Start below the west-facing wall immediately right of the corner-crack of *Tensor II*.
Climb the centre of the wall, move right to avoid the overhang on *Strapiombo*, and follow the arête above the initial crack of *Ledgend* to the faultline. Continue more easily up the steepening wall and exit over small overhangs into the quarry above. Stake belay.

About 200 feet east of the abseil point, and visible from it, lies a conspicuous flake crack in a steep wall. This is *Ledgend*.

Ledgend   120 feet   Hard Severe   (11.4.66)
A popular route, and likely to become more so since the demise of *Exit*

Chimney. However, it is high in its grade and requires some care near the top.

1 75 feet 4b. Climb a crack rightwards to a ledge below the flake crack and follow this on good holds to its top. Move right (optional belay) and climb the corner-crack to the faultline. Traverse right and belay in the middle of the ledge.

2 45 feet 4a. Continue right to the end of the ledge and step out rightwards over the void. Climb up for about 15 feet and follow a traverse-line leftwards to reach the end of the lower quarried ledge. Stake belay.

Graffiti Bombers of New York City 100 feet E2 5c † (20.12.86)
Start on the ledge just right of *Ledgend*.
After a boulder-problem start to gain an *in-situ* thread, climb the arête past another *in-situ* thread to the faultline; from here, climb a shallow, poorly-protected groove to the top. Stake belay.

★ **Ledgend Direct** 95 feet Very Severe (12.2.67)
An invigorating climb up the well-protected, steep corner that meets with the upper section of *Ledgend*. Start 30 feet right of *Ledgend*.

1 55 feet 4c. Climb a short wall followed by the corner, which steepens towards the top, to gain a small faultline ledge on the left (junction with *Ledgend*). Multiple nut belay.

2 40 feet 4a. Step out rightwards over the void. From here, climb up for about 15 feet and then follow a traverse-line leftwards to reach the end of the lower quarried ledge. Stake belay.

Vampire 90 feet Very Severe 4c (27.6.82)
An eliminate up the arête starting as for *Ledgend Direct*. The crack in the arête can be reached direct at 5b; better in line but unbalanced in difficulty.
As for *Batt Crack*, climb a short wall to a ledge and go diagonally right to the base of a corner. Continue diagonally left to climb the crack in the arête to the faultline. Surmount the overhang using an ammonite and continue straight to the top passing to the left of a large flake. Belay using nuts on the backwall of the quarry.

★ **Batt Crack** 120 feet Very Severe (25.3.67)
Start as for *Ledgend Direct*.

1 60 feet 4b/c. Climb a short wall to a ledge and go diagonally right to the base of a corner. Follow this to the overhang, traverse right, and belay on a good ledge.

2 60 feet 4a. Climb the groove and flakes behind the belay and then move right and up to a ledge. Move up to another ledge and pass the small roof above at its left-hand end. Nut belays on the backwall of the quarry.

Twenty feet to the right of *Ledgend Direct* is an overhanging chimney/crack which gives a poor route.

The Crevice   120 feet   Very Severe   (28.3.67)
1 60 feet 4c. Climb the steep wall to the chimney/crack and ascend this to a stance shared with *Batt Crack*.
2 60 feet 4a. Climb the groove above for a few feet and swing out onto the right wall, which is climbed by moving slightly right and up to a peg runner beneath slabby blocks. Continue leftwards to the top. Nut belays on the backwall.

★ **Friends from the Deep**   130 feet   E3 †   (6.5.87)
Start 5 feet right of the overhanging chimney/crack of *The Crevice*.
1 80 feet 5c. Climb up to a slot and a thread runner. Traverse 5 feet right, cross a bulge, and continue up to a rest on *Yellow Wall*. Traverse left to a flake and climb with difficulty up a thin crack (thread runner) to the faultline. Belay to the left in the corner of *The Crevice*.
2 50 feet 4c. Move 5 feet right before climbing rightwards to exit through a V-shaped overhang. Nut belays.

Twenty feet right of the overhanging chimney/crack of *The Crevice* is a large groove containing a prominent spade-shaped flake. This is *Robud*.

★ **Yellow Wall**   140 feet   E1   (3.4.72)
A splendid route, sustained and full of interest. Start just to the left of *Robud*.
1 70 feet 5b. Climb up the wall and move slightly left to reach a downward-pointing spike. Traverse left and pull over a bulge past a peg runner into a shallow groove. Continue up and take a cramped stance atop a wedged boulder.
2 70 feet 5a. Climb up and steeply right beneath overhanging blocks; now pass the overhang to gain a small ledge. Move up and across the traverse of *Robud*, and traverse rightwards around the arête into a corner with a prominent projecting flake. Climb the corner and exit slightly left. Nut belays on the backwall.

★ **Robud**   140 feet   Hard Very Severe   (26.3.67)
A commendable climb. Start at the foot of the groove.
1 70 feet 5a. Climb the groove to the spade and move right to the edge of the overhang. Follow the small groove above (peg runner) to a tiny stance and multiple nut belay.
2 70 feet 4c. Climb diagonally left, passing a prominent overhang to finish near *The Crevice*. Nut belays on the backwall.

Cascara   150 feet   Very Severe   (30.6.68)
Quite a good first pitch. Pegs should be carried for the first belay. Start as for *Robud*.
1 100 feet 4b. Climb the groove of *Robud* for a few feet to a ledge and traverse right to a shallow groove. Climb this groove to the faultline and move awkwardly right to a stance on the nose. Peg belay not *in-situ*.
2 50 feet 4b. Move rightwards to a short wall; climb this and the slab

above to a rotten overhang and a thread runner. Move left and continue directly to the top. Belay well back on the stile.

The Razor's Edge   145 feet   Hard Very Severe   (14.9.69)
This climbs the steep groove in the arête of the slabby buttress right of *Robud*. Start 20 feet left of this groove below a short, undercut slab (directly beneath the shallow groove of *Cascara*).
1 80 feet 4c. Gain the slab, and traverse right for 20 feet to the main groove. (Alternatively, the groove can be reached direct but this is harder.) Follow the groove, move rightwards around an overhang, and continue up to a stance and thread belay.
2 65 feet 4b. Step over a small overhang into a groove and climb it to a peg runner at its top. Finish by trending left up a slab and a corner. Belay well back on the stile.

★ **Younger Days**   110 feet   E3 6a [R] †   (6.6.87)
This climbs the arête proper. Start 10 feet to its right.
Climb easily for 25 feet until the arête steepens and then layback its right-hand side (*in-situ* thread) to the faultline. Continue more easily up the wall above. Stake belay.

The Eastern Girdle
                              425 feet   Hard Very Severe (1 pt aid) [R] (29.6.74)
A traverse of Guillemot East, starting from *Ndizi* and ending on the abseil ledge. The original start and finish have been destroyed by rockfall and the **final pitch has not since been climbed**. If it is not feasible, finish up *Sapphire*, thereby making the grade E1.
1 50 feet 4a. Climb the slab and then move right to belay in the corner below the faultline.
2 40 feet 5a. Climb the corner and hand-traverse left along the faultline (very steep) to the thread belay of *The Razor's Edge*.
3 75 feet 5a. Move left along the faultline and swing around an overhang into *Robud*. Climb down to and across the bottom of the spade-shaped flake to a good spike runner. Cross the left wall into *The Crevice*.
4 125 feet 4a. Follow the faultline leftwards, mostly easy, to a good block belay on *Mañana*.
5 60 feet 4a. Traverse into *The Heat*, descend the corner, and move into *August Angie*. From a peg, abseil down and swing across to a small stance in the corner-crack.
6 75 feet 4a ††. Traverse left for 20 feet and climb the wall on small holds until a flake can be lassoed for protection. Move down and swing into the corner using a good flake. Climb the corner to a ledge and move left under the roof past a peg to reach the abseil ledge.

Ndizi   160 feet   Hard Severe [R]   (21.3.67)
A disappointing climb which covers some loose ground. Start at the base of slabs on the left-hand side of a small bay (to the left of a huge rockfall scar).

1 90 feet 4a. Climb the slabs and move right to a corner below the faultline. Step down to the right, and climb a wall to a stance and belay at the faultline.

2 70 feet 4a. Continue up and traverse right across a friable wall to a groove. Follow this over suspect blocks to a grassy finish. Belay to the fenceposts a long way back.

Cormorant Ledge
OS Ref 004 768

Cormorant Ledge and its western neighbour Guillemot Ledge form a continuous stretch of cliff endowed with a broad spectrum of climbs of all standards in a quiet, secluded environment. Some of the routes on the central part of the cliff are unfortunately plagued by poor finishes and, although few are overtly dangerous, care should always be taken. Several of these routes have a stake runner to help protect their top sections. To increase security, an ice-hammer or even a nut-key can be used as a last resort to fashion holds in the earth slope.

Note. Stakes tend not to stay in place for long in this area, so belays are usually on fenceposts. Some are better than others and, in any case, it is advisable to use more than one.

The collapse of Cleft Buttress has removed the physical barrier between Cormorant and Guillemot. Nowadays, they are differentiated more by their respective ease of access: a high tide at Cormorant, unlike Guillemot, prevents progress along the base of the cliff. With familiarity, access is still possible to many of the routes on the eastern and western wings, although caution should be exercised before abseiling in if the sea is rough. **Nesting-season restrictions** apply west of *Sea Cow* and east of *Oran* (see Introduction).

Approach as for Dancing Ledge to the brow of a hill. Head leftwards (east) along this for a short distance and cross a dry-stone wall. Cut diagonally across the valley to meet the Coastal Path and reach another stile, which is set in the stone wall above Guillemot Ledge. Continue eastwards for approximately 250 yards until a grassy ramp in the cliff edge allows a careful descent into Reform Quarry. If approached from the east, Reform Quarry is located about seventy yards west of the point at which the path is diverted inland to avoid a landslip area.

1. Twenty yards east of the descent into Reform Quarry large flakes form a short arête on the back wall and there is a stake to the right. From here, a free-hanging abseil leads down a west-facing wall to a large boulder at the start of *Wall Street*.

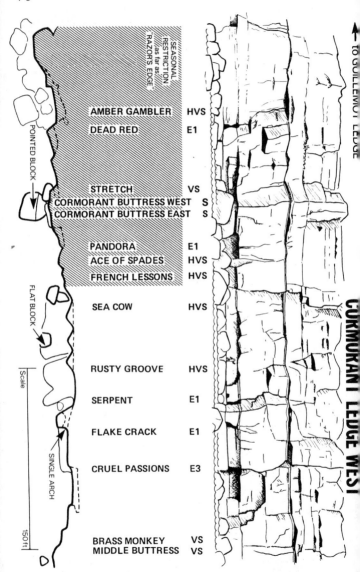

TO GUILLEMOT LEDGE

CORMORANT LEDGE WEST

POINTED BLOCK

FLAT BLOCK

SINGLE ARCH

Scale

150 ft

SEASONAL RESTRICTION as far as "RAZOR'S EDGE"

AMBER GAMBLER	HVS
DEAD RED	E1
STRETCH	VS
CORMORANT BUTTRESS WEST	S
CORMORANT BUTTRESS EAST	S
PANDORA	E1
ACE OF SPADES	HVS
FRENCH LESSONS	HVS
SEA COW	HVS
RUSTY GROOVE	HVS
SERPENT	E1
FLAKE CRACK	E1
CRUEL PASSIONS	E3
BRASS MONKEY	VS
MIDDLE BUTTRESS	VS

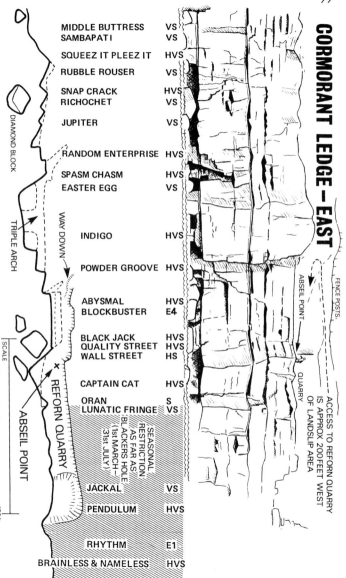

CORMORANT LEDGE – EAST

MIDDLE BUTTRESS	VS
SAMBAPATI	VS
SQUEEZ IT PLEEZ IT	HVS
RUBBLE ROUSER	VS
SNAP CRACK	HVS
RICHOCHET	VS
JUPITER	VS
RANDOM ENTERPRISE	HVS
SPASM CHASM	HVS
EASTER EGG	VS
INDIGO	HVS
POWDER GROOVE	HVS
ABYSMAL	HVS
BLOCKBUSTER	E4
BLACK JACK	HVS
QUALITY STREET	HVS
WALL STREET	HS
CAPTAIN CAT	HVS
ORAN	S
LUNATIC FRINGE	VS
JACKAL	VS
PENDULUM	HVS
RHYTHM	E1
BRAINLESS & NAMELESS	HVS

DIAMOND BLOCK

TRIPLE ARCH

WAY DOWN

REFORN QUARRY

ABSEIL POINT

SCALE

150 ft

ABSEIL POINT

FENCE POSTS.

ABSEIL POINT

QUARRY

ACCESS TO REFORN QUARRY IS APPROX 200FEET WEST OF LANDSLIP AREA

SEASONAL RESTRICTION AS FAR AS BLACKERS HOLE 1st MARCH - 31st JULY)

2. [R] Abseil from a stake below the 36th fencepost east of the stile above the Whiteware Quarries. At the foot of the abseil, beneath Cormorant Buttress, is a large boulder, which is usually unaffected by the sea.

3. Since the collapse of Cleft Buttress, which bounded the western end of Cormorant, the cliff can be reached via the short entry abseil for Guillemot Ledges. Calm seas or low tide required.

CORMORANT MAIN AREA

The abseil from Reforn Quarry descends a juggy wall split by the distinctive crack of *Wall Street*. To the west across an overhung bay filled with large boulders is the Triple Arch, an interesting formation requiring a low crouch to get through to the base of an impressive cleft - *Spasm Chasm*. A flat platform (awash at high tide) passes below a series of low roofs to where a slight buttress with a groove is climbed by *Middle Buttress*. The platform ends at a trough below *Cruel Passions*. Beyond, through the Single Arch, *Serpent* climbs a compelling, overhanging corner-crack. More low roofs lead to the big corner of *Sea Cow*, with an impressive headwall on its left flanked by the prow of Cormorant Buttress. Further west the cracks and roofs of *Dead Red* and *Ambler Gambler* are followed by an unstable area resulting from the collapse of Cleft Buttress. (This fall caused the demise of *The Cleft, Cleft Buttress, The Connexion, Neptune's Wall,* and *Zimbalist*.) Guillemot Ledge lies beyond.

** **Ambler Gambler**   130 feet   Hard Very Severe [R]   (13.6.71)
An excellent route, well endowed with protection and on good rock. Forty feet west of the abseil down Cormorant Buttress is a sentry-box cave. This is to the east of the rockfall area which divides Guillemot from Cormorant Ledges. Start on a ledge below flaky cracks on the left-hand side of the sentry-box.
1 80 feet 5a. Climb up to the cracks and follow them to the faultline. Traverse right with difficulty to a good ledge and thread belays.
2 50 feet 5a. Move up to a ledge above the belay and climb the steep wall above to a roof. Surmount the roof to reach some large blocks and continue up to a stake belay.

** **Dead Red**   120 feet   E1 [R]   (13.4.74)
A taxing climb, steep and strenuous. The initial wall is poorly protected, and the close proximity of the rockfall scar may imply some instability on pitch 2. Start just right of the sentry-box.
1 70 feet 5b. Climb to a ledge and then up to the roof. Traverse left under this to reach cracks, which lead up to a ledge and thread belays shared with *Ambler Gambler*.
2 50 feet 4b. Climb the deepest of the short grooves above the belay. Go up a steep wall above to some large blocks, step left, and pull over the top. Stake belay.

The abseil descent often used to enter the western end of Cormorant Ledge runs down the projecting prow of Cormorant Buttress (see approach notes for more details, but remember that this entry point is seasonally restricted). This abseil leads to the top of a large boulder, which provides the start for *Stretch*, *Cormorant Buttress West*, and *Cormorant Buttress East*.

Stretch   140 feet   Very Severe [R]   (12.10.69)
A worthwhile route, with the final crack providing an interesting crux.
1 80 feet 4b. Follow the groove of *Cormorant Buttress West* for 10 feet to a thread runner. Traverse up left around the arête to a shallow, slabby groove, and climb this on the right until it is possible to move back left to a good ledge and thread belay.
2 60 feet 4c. Climb easily to the prominent crack up to the left and gain it from the left. Climb the crack and continue to a stake belay.

** **Cormorant Buttress West**   110 feet   Severe [R]   (11.10.69)
The premier route of its standard at Swanage, giving quality climbing high in its grade and situated on a serious section of cliff. Start on top of the large block at the foot of the prominent buttress. Some large *Hexes* required for pitch 2.
1 50 feet 4a. A tricky boulder-problem start leads up left into an easy-angled open groove, which is climbed on monster-sized holds to a large ledge on the left at the faultline. Belay here on good threads.
2 60 feet. Pull up onto the wall, traverse right for 10 feet, and move up to a ledge. Climb the flake crack above to gain the top of the buttress and the abseil stake beyond.

Cormorant Buttress East   120 feet   Severe [R]   (11.10.69)
As well as destroying *Cormorant Buttress Central*, rockfall has left this once enjoyable route with a loose finish. Slightly harder than its companion climb. Start on top of the large block at the foot of the prominent buttress.
1 60 feet 4a. Make some tricky moves to enter the groove on the right, and climb up and diagonally right onto the slab below the faultline overhangs. Pull through these at a break near their centre and continue straight up to belay at the base of a deep corner.
2 60 feet. Climb the corner to its top. Traverse left using dubious handholds, and then step down and across to a mud slab. Climb up loose blocks to the top and belay on the abseil stake.

* **Pandora**   140 feet   E1 [R]   (22.4.73/11.8.84)
A varied climb on good rock, with a difficult roof to start and a fine top pitch. Start 40 feet east of Cormorant Buttress below a prominent crack in the wide, low-level overhang.
1 40 feet 5c. Climb the crack and pull strenuously around the lip onto the wall above. Continue easily for 20 feet to a stance and belay.
2 40 feet 4a. Easy ground leads up and left around a small roof to belay as for *Cormorant Buttress East*.
3 60 feet 5a. Traverse right for 10 feet and climb up to the second of two distinct triangular roofs. Traverse right along a good crack to

footholds and pull up into a small niche. Step back left and climb steeply on good holds to a final jug and the top. Stake belay.

★★ **Ace of Spades**   105 feet   Hard Very Severe [R]   (7.9.79/8.80)
Between the prow of Cormorant Buttress and the large corner of *Sea Cow* is a steep, white wall that leans at the top. This excellent route takes a direct line up the centre of the wall on good rock throughout, saving its best moments until last. Start at a short corner 10 feet right of *Pandora*.
1 50 feet 4c. From a ledge, pull into the short, steep corner and escape out right. Step back left into the crack above, which widens into a groove, and follow it to a comfortable ledge and block belays.
2 55 feet 5b. Move up and bypass the nose of rock to gain a groove. Follow this to the top roof and step right with difficulty to a peg runner. Pull up steeply leftwards past a good wire-placement, and either mantelshelf neatly onto the ledge above or grovel over like everybody else. Stake belay.

French Lessons   130 feet   Hard Very Severe [R] †   (11.8.84)
Start below a prominent corner (25 feet right of *Ace of Spades*). Long slings are required to avoid rope drag on pitch 2. The route has the same finish as *Ace of Spades*.
1 50 feet 4b. Go up the wall to the corner and follow this until a traverse left at the faultline leads to a commodious ledge.
2 80 feet 5b. Climb the groove above to a protruding block and step left above it onto a slabby wall. Ascend cracks diagonally left to reach a horizontal break and follow this left below a small overhang to join *Ace of Spades*. Climb to the roof above and step right with difficulty to a peg runner. Pull up steeply leftwards and make an awkward mantelshelf to finish. Stake belay.

Sea Cow   120 feet   Hard Very Severe   (19.10.69/8.79)
Having a loose finish, the large, right-facing corner-system proves less enjoyable than appearances might suggest. Start 10 feet right of the corner and immediately left of some low roofs.
1 40 feet 5a. Climb directly up the wall and assorted flakes to belay on the right below a shallow groove which breaks through the overhanging ground above.
2 80 feet 5a. Climb up to the groove and follow it to a projecting block. Move left to a ledge and continue to traverse left for 15 feet to reach a steep corner. Go up this to a stake runner and continue up leftwards to a stake belay.

Sunset Finish   110 feet   Hard Very Severe   (24.10.87)
Start beneath a roof-crack above a narrow inlet some 40 feet right of *Sea Cow*.
1 50 feet 5a. Pull over the roof, step left, and continue easily up to follow a crack on the right through a bulge to the faultline.

2 60 feet 5b. Climb diagonally leftwards to two pointed blocks (thread) and then up to a finger-crack, which leads to the flaky overhang above. Step left and then back right on the lip; then climb a crack over a roof to the top. Stake belay.

Rusty Groove 110 feet Hard Very Severe (17.8.72/13.1.80)
Some good and surprisingly technical climbing in places but with a loosish top. Start 5 feet right of *Sunset Finish* and 20 feet left of the Single Arch, at a break in the low roofs.
1 50 feet 5a. Climb the broken groove and then the corner with difficulty to a large ledge at the faultline.
2 60 feet 5a. Traverse left for 15 feet and go up to a chimney/corner formed by a large jutting block. Climb this, moving out right at the top to gain a good ledge. Continue up slightly rightwards over blocks to finish. Stake belay.

Serpent 110 feet E1 (18.10.69/12.4.74)
Pitch 1 gives superb climbing up the twisting corner immediately west of the Single Arch. However, the top pitch is loose, precarious, and badly protected. This is best avoided by making a long rightward traverse above the faultline into *Flake Crack*, which reduces the standard to HVS. Start below the attractive corner, which leans steeply at about 30 feet.
1 50 feet 5a. Climb the corner and pull over with difficulty onto a ledge. Belay just down from the faultline.
2 60 feet 5a. Climb up into a groove above. Move left for 5 feet, up, and back right into the groove. Go up this for a few feet, traverse left across a slab onto blocks, and continue up left into a corner which leads to the top. Stake belay.

Flake Crack 120 feet E1 (22.8.71/24.4.82)
Strenuous on the crux, passing the small roof above the faultline. Start immediately east of the Single Arch at the foot of a flaky crack.
1 70 feet 5c. Climb up the crack for 15 feet before moving diagonally right across the wall and up a short corner to the roof. Swing left along the break below the roof to two pegs and pull over with difficulty to a good stance beyond.
2 50 feet 4a. Climb the corner above, and follow a series of ledges out right to steep grass and a long earth slope leading to a stake belay.

⋆ **Stern Mistress** 180 feet E1 † (13.8.84)
A sneaky route with a very exposed and committing second pitch.
1 60 feet 4b. Follow *Flake Crack* until it is possible to traverse easily right along a series of flakes. Belay on large nuts below the big roof.
2 40 feet 5b. Take care to minimize rope drag on this pitch. Step right from the stance and descend an easy slab to reach a projecting foothold on the edge of the roof below. Traverse rightwards with mounting excitement along the very lip of the roof and pull into an overhanging groove. Climb this (strenuous) and belay at a comfortable stance above.

3 45 feet 4c. Climb up to a roof and surmount it gently. Move up and traverse out left beneath a second roof to gain the grassy ledge above.
4 35 feet. Finish directly up the easy slab above and scramble up a long earth slope with care to a stake belay. A preplaced rope to pull out on is justifiable.

★ **Cruel Passions**   170 feet   E3   (27.4.80/24.4.82)
Some varied but fairly serious climbing, which breaks through a daunting series of defences. Low in its grade. Midway between the Single Arch and *Middle Buttress* is a distinctive line running the full height of the cliff. Start to the right of this, below the eastern end of a low-level roof.
1 80 feet 5b/c. Climb a short steep wall to a good ledge. Step left into a small bottomless corner and traverse left along the lip of the roof using an obvious undercut hold. Continue diagonally leftwards for 20 feet to a rest beneath a very large bulge. Pull around leftwards past a poor peg and climb steeply up to reach a line of deep flakes on the left. Belay here using large nuts.
2 55 feet 5b. Go up a short slab above the belay to runners in the roof. Step back down and climb the side wall with care to reach massive jugs on the lip of the roof. The orange groove above leads steeply to good runners and a ledge around to the right. Step right and climb past a deep crack to where a 10-foot traverse right gains a belay shared with *Stern Mistress* in a small corner.
3 35 feet. *Stern Mistress* pitch 4.
Variation
Adults Only †   (19.8.84)
1a 40 feet 6a. The obvious direct start over the roof (bigger than it looks) to join *Cruel Passions* below its crux bulge.

★ **Brass Monkey**   110 feet   Very Severe   (31.3.72)
Good situations and a reasonable finish.
1 60 feet 4b. Follow *Middle Buttress* for a few feet until a traverse left, just above the overhang, gains a corner. Climb the corner to the faultline.
2 50 feet 4c. Climb the wall above to a bulge and pull over on good holds (strenuous). Continue up to an overhanging crack and follow this with difficult moves to pull out at the top. Carry on up over blocks and grass to a stake belay.

Middle Buttress   140 feet   Very Severe   (18.10.69)
A popular route, climbing a shallow groove in the slight buttress located midway between Single Arch and Triple Arch. Start below the groove on a good ledge above the boulders.
1 110 feet 4c. Climb the groove for 25 feet, traverse rightwards around the arête, and go up a slab to reach the left end of the faultline roof. Pull onto the face, step right, and continue to a block protruding from the wall. Gain the block from the left and follow the layback crack above to a good ledge.
2 30 feet. Scramble up the earth slope to a stake belay.

Sambapati   150 feet   Very Severe   (28.7.74)
A worthwhile route with a relaxed start and a good finish. Start as for
Middle Buttress.
1 50 feet 4a/b. Climb up and rightwards to reach a shallow groove,
which is followed until a slab on the right can be crossed to reach a
stance below a roof.
2 70 feet 4c. Climb the groove on the right for 15 feet and traverse left
along a narrow ledge until below a smooth wall. Climb the wall and a
crack to reach a good ledge shared with *Middle Buttress*.
3 30 feet. Scramble up the earth slope to a stake belay.

★ **Squeez It Pleez It**   110 feet   Hard Very Severe †   (26.4.80)
A rewarding, well-protected first pitch. Start beneath a short, steep crack
20 feet right of *Middle Buttress*.
1 50 feet 5a. Follow the crack to a resting-place after 20 feet at the foot
of a slight diagonal ramp. Follow the ramp rightwards on superb holds as
far as another crack, which splits the bulges above. Climb this crack with
difficulty to a short slab and a good faultline ledge.
2 60 feet 4b. Go up a short corner above and move diagonally right to
reach the foot of a corner shared with *Rubble Rouser*. Follow the corner,
escaping leftwards at the top to a stake belay.

Rubble Rouser   125 feet   Very Severe   (11.4.74)
To the east of *Middle Buttress* is a tiny bay. Start at the foot of the steep
corner at the back of this depression, some 25 feet right of *Squeez It Pleez
It*.
1 60 feet 4c. Follow the corner for a few feet, surmount an awkward
bulge, and go up more easily to where the rock steepens. Move
rightwards onto the wall, continue to the faultline, and belay above the
arête on the right.
2 65 feet 4b. Climb easily up left for 25 feet to a corner, which is
followed to blocks and a steep earthy finish.

Snap Crack   140 feet   Hard Very Severe †   (26.8.79)
A fine first pitch climbing the striking crackline in the wall right of *Rubble
Rouser*. Pitch 2 makes a long traverse to the right in search of an
independent exit. Start at the arête right of *Rubble Rouser*.
1 65 feet 5a. Pull up onto a very slight rib and continue to a small
overhang below the crackline. Good holds lead over the overhang and
some bold moves gain the crack. Go up this until high holds enable the
arête to be reached, and follow it to the faultline.
2 75 feet 4c. Step onto the wall above the belay, and traverse right for
25 feet along the lip of the roofs until it is possible to pull through a break
into a slight corner. Move left into a bay to bypass the roof, and climb a
wide crack past a ledge to a ledge on the right. Go up over large blocks
and finish past a stake runner. Stake belay.

Excalibur   145 feet   Very Severe   (20.4.75/22.8.79)
Immediately left of the low-level roofs that run eastwards to the Triple Arch
is a line of flakes that lead up to the right of a protruding arête. Start in the
corner below these flakes.
1   75 feet   4b/c.   Climb up for 10 feet and then leftwards to a rib. Follow
the diagonal crack into the groove of *Rubble Rouser*. Continue up this until it
is possible to traverse into the centre of the right wall. Go up the wall to the
faultline and move right to a stance shared with *Snap Crack* above the
arête.
2   50 feet   4b.   Climb easily up left for 25 feet to a corner, as for *Rubble
Rouser*. Go up it for a few feet and make an interesting hand-traverse right
along a good horizontal crack to gain a slab. Cross the slab to a good
ledge and belay on the right.
3   20 feet.   Follow steep rock and earth rightwards to reach a stake
runner; continue to a stake belay above.

Ricochet   110 feet   Very Severe   (18.4.71)
Start as for *Excalibur*.
1   60 feet   4c.   Climb cracks to gain a faint horizontal fault at 30 feet.
Step right with difficulty and ascend a big flake to easier-angled ground.
Move up and right to belay on the faultline as for *Jupiter*.
2   50 feet   4b.   *Jupiter* Pitch 2.

Jupiter   110 feet   Very Severe   (11.10.70)
Start from a low ledge at a point some 40 feet west of the Triple Arch.
1   60 feet   4c/5a.   Climb to the roof at its weakest point and make a
difficult move over into the small groove above. Climb the face to the right
of this groove to a small ledge. Move back left and climb the open corner
to the faultline. Belay to the left.
2   50 feet   4b.   Climb up above the belay, moving left and then right to a
small groove. Follow this to a slab leading left to some large blocks.
Continue carefully, passing a stake runner, to belay further up at a second
stake.
Variation
1a   60 feet   Hard Very Severe   5b   †   (13.8.84).   Pull directly over the
roof 6 feet left of *Jupiter* and follow a direct line up to the corner above.
Belay at the faultline on the left.

Random Enterprise   120 feet   Hard Very Severe   †   (12.1.80)
An interesting first pitch. Start on the western edge of the archway of
Spasm Chasm, below a crack leading to a bulge.
1   60 feet   5a/b.   Climb a short corner to a roof and move right to gain
the crack that leads steeply to a bulge. Swing around the left side of this
bulge (crux) and pull over on to a slab, which is followed to a short,
shallow groove. Belay here just below the faultline.
2   60 feet   4c.   Gain the faultline and follow the overhangs above
diagonally left until some awkward moves gain a square-cut groove. Go
up this for 10 feet to join *Jupiter* at a curving, wide crack and move easily

left to some large blocks. Continue to the top passing a stake runner *en route*. Stake belay.

Spasm Chasm   165 feet   Hard Very Severe ††   (29.3.75)
The prominent chasm gave great climbing apart from a horrendous finish over unstable blocks and earth, for which a preplaced rope was recommended. However, the top section has fallen, leaving a very steep and loose corner which has not been reclimbed. Start at the back of the archway which forms the west side of the Triple Arch. Pegs required.
1 60 feet 5a/b. Climb up the back of the cave and chimney out under the roof until a difficult move can be made onto the right wall. Belay on the right, in a niche below a roof overlooking the chasm.
2 55 feet 4c. Move right around the roof, continue diagonally left, and place pegs to belay at the faultline.
3 50 feet. The original description was: 'Go up the wall on the left to the roof and traverse left into a corner. The corner is followed until the preplaced rope can be used to pull over the rubble above.'

Bachelor Boy   160 feet   Hard Very Severe ††   (3.4.72)
Not recommended; it shared with *Spasm Chasm* the need for a preplaced rope in order to negotiate a dangerously loose finish. The finish is even more dangerous since the rockfall, and the route has not been reclimbed. Start, if you must, from boulders to the right of the cave entrance, below the west-facing wall of the Triple Arch buttress.
1 70 feet 4b. Climb the wall for 40 feet, until it is possible to move left (some loose rock) and up a groove to the faultline.
2 90 feet. The original description was: 'Climb diagonally left under the overhang and move around into the finishing corner of *Spasm Chasm*. Pull over the rubble above using the preplaced rope.' This pitch may be avoided by a 30-foot traverse rightwards along the faultline to the belay on Easter Egg, known as **Fledgling's Flight** (4c/5a † 10.7.83).

★ **Easter Egg**   120 feet   Very Severe   (11.4.71)
A fairly steep and absorbing first pitch, which is less demanding than it looks; low in its grade. Start as for *Bachelor Boy*.
1 80 feet 4b/c. Climb the centre of the wall on good holds to a flake at 30 feet, traverse right, and follow a groove on the arête to reach the faultline. Traverse right to a ledge on the seaward face of the buttress and climb a wall above to a good stance and thread belay below a corner.
2 40 feet 4b. Climb the corner to a large block. Move carefully around this to the left and continue straight up to the top. Stake belay.

★ **Calm, Calm**   155 feet   E2 †   (14.7.91)
Start round to the right of *Easter Egg* (about 15 feet left of *Rage, Rage*) below a block. Pitch 1 is well protected, solid and sustained, swimming in jugs between the roofs, and technical at the second roof. High in the grade.

1 75 feet 6a. Climb up to the overhang at the block, pull through, and follow the ragged crack rightwards to a roof. Cross this with difficulty and carry on to the thread belay of *Easter Egg*.
2 80 feet 4a/b. Climb the obvious weakness left of *Easter Egg*. Stake belay.

Rage, Rage   170 feet   E3 †   (14.7.91/27.10.91)
The first 25 feet provide bold, strenuous, and exhilarating climbing on which the protection is hard won. Start in the middle arch of the Triple Arch, from a thread belay on a ledge 10 feet up. This climb (and *Indigo*) can be approached at high tide by abseiling to the thread belay of *Easter Egg*; from here a climbing rope can be used doubled to abseil diagonally right (facing in) to the start of the route.
1 70 feet 6a. Climb up to a chicken-head where the angle drops back to vertical. If no ornithologists are about, bite it off, and continue straight up to a corner. Follow this to a thread belay at the faultline.
2 100 feet 4c. Not recommended; better to traverse left and finish up *Easter Egg*. Otherwise, follow the corner-crack directly above the belay on worrying rock to an appalling finish. Stake belay.

Indigo   150 feet   Hard Very Severe   (7.8.77)
This follows a crackline up the south-eastern edge of the Triple Arch buttress. Start as for *Rage, Rage*.
1 70 feet 5a. A precarious traverse right leads to protection and a steep crack. Follow this to the faultline. Move 10 feet left to belay on a good thread in a small corner.
2 80 feet 4b. Move back above the first pitch. Climb up using the right wall to reach an overhang. Step left and go through the break to follow a groove to the top. Stake belay.

Powder Groove   130 feet   Hard Very Severe   (30.4.72)
This route climbs corners bounding the eastern side of the Triple Arch buttress to an unpleasant exit. Start from the boulders 20 feet east of the Triple Arch.
1 60 feet 5a. Traverse left into a corner capped by a roof at 20 feet. Turn the roof on the left (committing) and continue up the wall and corner until about 10 feet below the faultline. Move right to a small corner and up to a sheltered stance just below the faultline. Block and nut belays.
2 70 feet 4b. Follow the loose corner above to the top, and then continue up 30 feet of steep earth to the descent path. Belay to a stake far down the path to the right. Alternatively, to avoid the earth slope, from 5 feet below the top of the rock go 15 feet right and then up to a solid exit. Stake belay.
Variation
1a 60 feet 5b † (8.9.90). Traverse left into the roof-capped corner as for *Powder Groove*. Move up to the roof and turn it on the right. Follow the crack to the belay of the parent route.

Abysmal   120 feet   Hard Very Severe   (13.1.78)
Start in the middle of the overhung bay immediately east of the Reforn
Quarry abseil point.
1 90 feet 5a. Climb a short corner until above the roof at 10 feet and
traverse left into the corner. Go up this to a roof and traverse left
underneath it across an east-facing wall to gain the main arête. Climb a
bottomless groove for a few feet and swing around onto the seaward
face, which is climbed to the faultline. Move diagonally right through an
obvious break to easy-angled rock. Thread and nut belays a few feet
further up.
2 30 feet 4b. Climb the crack behind the stance to a stake belay in the
foliage up to the right.

Blockbuster   160 feet   E4 †   (6.10.84/13.10.84)
Very strenuous. Start as for *Abysmal.*
1 80 feet 6a. Climb a short corner until above the roof at 10 feet and
traverse left into the corner which leads up to a big roof (as for *Abysmal*
so far). Traverse right to the first weakness in the roof, pull through, and
continue rightwards to a hanging stance below a corner.
2 40 feet 4b. Go up the faultline, step left, and pull
rightwards through the overhang. Traverse 20 feet left to a thread belay
just left of the final pitch of *Abysmal.*
3 40 feet 4c. Climb the groove just left of the belay to the top. Stake
belay in the foliage up to the right, as for *Abysmal.*

★ **Tape and Ape**   130 feet   E5 †   (27.10.91)
Tape is recommended for this 10-foot roof-crack, which has an obligatory
toe-hang at the lip! A nut was preplaced near the lip on the only ascent to
date. Start as for *Abysmal.*
1 50 feet 6b. Climb straight up to the roof. Tenuous jams and wild
moves across the roof-crack lead to a hanging stance just above the lip.
2 40 feet 5c. Move up a few feet and then left to gain a vague crack
with a spike in it. Climb up the crack to the faultline, leftwards to a break,
and up to easy-angled rock. Follow this diagonally leftwards to the thread
belay of *Blockbuster.*
3 40 feet 5a. Climb the crack above the stance and continue to the top.
Stake belay high up amidst the vegetation.

★ **Black Jack**   180 feet   Hard Very Severe   (10.3.74)
An entertaining expedition that weaves its way through some impressive
roofs. Start beneath the corner bounding the right-hand side of the
overhung bay.
1 100 feet 5a. Climb the corner to the faultline, passing a roof half-way.
Traverse left along the faultline for 25 feet to a break in the roof and pull
over onto the wall above. Multiple-nut belay 15 feet to the left.
2 80 feet 4c. Climb the steep wall to the right of the belay until it is
possible to traverse right above the big roofs. Continue up a slight groove
to finish as for *Quality Street* onto a good ledge. Multiple-nut belay.

★★★ Quality Street   100 feet   Hard Very Severe   4c   (10.2.74)

A tremendous pitch, steep and satisfying, and always on good rock. At the bottom of its grade. Start immediately right of a niche at the foot of the west-facing wall, just left of *Wall Street*.
Climb directly up to a flake at 30 feet and move up rightwards to a niche at the faultline (optional belay). Pull up left onto the steep wall above and climb quickly to reach a roof. Move left around this into a corner and follow the crack above to a good ledge. Multiple-nut belay.

★ Wall Street   100 feet   Hard Severe   (29.3.70)

A disjointed route well fortified with large holds. Start at the foot of a juggy wall on the right-hand side of the overhung bay. The route follows the prominent crack in the centre of this wall before going rightwards along the faultline to the arête.
1 60 feet 4a. Climb the wall on superb holds, trending rightwards to meet the crack. Go up to a bulge, step right, and continue past a ledge to the faultline. Traverse right to the arête and belay just above on a good stance.
2 40 feet 4b. The slight groove directly above the belay is climbed steeply to the top and a multiple-nut belay. A secure finish.

Wall Street Crash   105 feet   Hard Very Severe   (9.6.84)

A worthwhile route, which is low in its grade and solid throughout. Start directly below the obvious crack in the juggy wall.
1 60 feet 5a. Pull up around the left-hand end of the large roof to good holds in the crack above. Traverse rightwards above the lip of the roof and follow flakes in the wall above to the faultline. Step left and pull up a short wall to reach the belay of *Wall Street* on the right.
2 45 feet 4c. Traverse left for 10 feet and pull over a bulge to a small overhang. Surmount this and then step left to finish awkwardly up a thin crack. Multiple-nut belay.
Direct Start
1a 50 feet 5b/c (31.7.82). From the top of the boulder beneath the large roof, make a fierce pull over the lip to gain the flakes of the parent route.

Captain Cat   100 feet   Hard Very Severe   (15.7.79)

Start as for *Oran*.
1 60 feet 4c. Follow *Oran* to the foot of its corner and climb up left easily to the foot of a thin crack in the centre of a yellow wall. Climb the crack and pull over the overhang above to a thread and nut belay up to the right.
2 40 feet 5a. Climb the wall behind the stance for 10 feet and move up left into a shallow groove. Follow this to a gap at the left-hand end of a long, narrow roof. Pull through the gap into the quarry above.

★ Oran   100 feet   Severe   (27.3.70)

An enjoyable route, bold at the start of the second pitch, giving the easiest exit from the eastern end of the cliff. Start below a hidden corner 30 feet

right of *Wall Street*, just past a large, low-level roof. Low tide required.
1 60 feet. Climb up to a ledge at 15 feet and follow the corner to the faultline. Traverse right to belay on a good ledge around the arête.
2 40 feet 4a. Continue up the obvious line above on flat holds and trend slightly right to belay on the quarried ledge.

Lunatic Fringe   135 feet   Very Severe [R] †   (7.9.79)
The rock deteriorates above the faultline. Start as for *Oran*.
1 80 feet 4c. Follow *Oran* to the foot of its corner and move diagonally right until it is possible to move up and around the arête onto a slab. Cross this to steep cracks and follow a chimney to another steep crack on the right. Go up a bottomless corner above to the faultline and climb a wall to belay on the right below a roof.
2 55 feet 4b. Traverse about 35 feet to the right on loose rock to a short corner. Go up this to a good ledge and finish up a second short corner on the right onto the quarried ledge.

REFORN QUARRY EAST
The ledge at the eastern end of Reforn Quarry is stepped down about 6 feet to form a lower level. Below this, *Jackal* takes a direct line up the cliff to finish beside a tower of perched blocks at the western end of the sunken ledge. *Pendulum* climbs the most easterly corner that finishes in the quarry. Access to both of these routes is by abseil down the line of *Jackal* from nut anchors in the backwall of the quarry. Two further routes, *Rhythm* and *Brainless and Nameless* are approached by abseil down the buttress to the east of the sunken ledge to reach a sea-level ledge just visible from above.

Jackal   90 feet   Very Severe [R] †   (30.9.79)
Abseil from the western end of the sunken ledge to a nut belay but no stance 15 feet above the sea. Pegs required.
1 50 feet 4c. From the belay, climb up left via a shallow groove, until it is possible to move right, and follow a layback crack to the faultline. Poor but protected stance to the right; place pegs and *Friends* to belay.
2 40 feet 4b. Step up left onto a ledge at the faultline and move a few feet left around an arête. Continue upwards and then traverse right under a large, dubious block to a groove which leads to the quarried ledge.

* Pendulum   100 feet   Hard Very Severe [R] †   (22.9.79)
A fine, steep first pitch. Start by abseiling down *Jackal*, but continue on further to gain a ledge leading right to a good platform beneath a huge roof. Alternatively, it is possible to abseil as for *Rhythm* and hand-traverse left to the start of the route. Pegs required.
1 60 feet 4c. Climb the corner, steeply at first, until good holds at the faultline lead right to a good ledge; place pegs and nuts to belay.
2 40 feet 5a. Traverse back left to the top of the corner. Climb up awkwardly, and continue up to the right around a small roof to reach the quarried ledge.

Variation
2a 40 feet 5a [R] † (30.9.79). Traverse back left to the top of the corner and move up left onto the slab. Follow the roof above to the left until a series of steep mantelshelf moves gains the quarried ledge.

Rhythm   130 feet   E1 [R] †   (3.8.80)
An unprotected first pitch and a worrying 'belay' at the top. Abseil from nuts in the backwall down the buttress to the east of the sunken ledge. This leads to a sea-level ledge. Pegs required.
1 30 feet 5b. Go straight up to a roof at 25 feet and swing up left on to a small flat ledge; place pegs and nuts to belay.
2 100 feet 5b. Traverse right along the lip of the overhang to a loose-looking block. Climb up to an earthy ledge and follow a shattered wall on the right to overhangs. Step left and exit up a grassy gully to dreadful nut belays. Scramble leftwards into Reform Quarry.

Brainless and Nameless 120 feet   Hard Very Severe [R] † (16.8.80)
Abseil as for *Rhythm* to the sea-level ledge and traverse right until the ledge ends below a prominent hanging flake which leans rightwards. Start here. Another 'John Wayne'-style belay at the top.
1 50 feet 5a. Climb the flake crack until it peters out. Move up and right to gain a small bay below another hanging flake. Go up past the flake to the faultline and traverse a few feet left. Belay up to the left in a small niche.
2 70 feet 4a. Climb up leftwards and follow a chimney behind a tottering tower to the top. The ground above the route is a crevassed landslip area; belay on whichever boulders are currently at the surface. (The fenceposts are far away and very shaky!)

Blackers Hole   OS Ref 007 768

For a long time Blackers Hole was regarded as an unpromising area. The initial impression of mediocre rock and a predominance of poor finishes turned free-climbing attention elsewhere. Overlooked and neglected apart from several good routes in the lower grades, the main attraction remained the sensational *Laughing Arthur*, providing A3 climbing across an awesome sea-cave.

The area's true potential was highlighted when *Polaris* ventured into the intimidating terrain to the left of the massive cave and sparked off a renewal of interest in the cliff. Major additions were made in the cave area, and free ascents of *Procrastinating Giant* and, finally, *Laughing Arthur* have cleaned up most of the remaining aid points. For the connoisseur of major sea-cliff undertakings, *Polaris*, *Laughing Arthur*, and *Infinite Gravity* must rank among the best in the South-West.

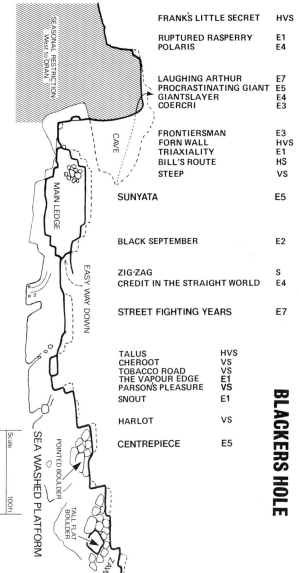

FRANK'S LITTLE SECRET HVS

RUPTURED RASPERRY E1
POLARIS E4

LAUGHING ARTHUR E7
PROCRASTINATING GIANT E5
GIANTSLAYER E4
COERCRI E3

FRONTIERSMAN E3
FORN WALL HVS
TRIAXIALITY E1
BILL'S ROUTE HS
STEEP VS

SUNYATA E5

BLACK SEPTEMBER E2

ZIG-ZAG S
CREDIT IN THE STRAIGHT WORLD E4

STREET FIGHTING YEARS E7

TALUS HVS
CHEROOT VS
TOBACCO ROAD VS
THE VAPOUR EDGE E1
PARSON'S PLEASURE VS
SNOUT E1

HARLOT VS

CENTREPIECE E5

SEASONAL RESTRICTION
West to ORAN

CAVE

MAIN LEDGE

EASY WAY DOWN

SEA WASHED PLATFORM

POINTED BOULDER

TALL FLAT BOULDER

ZAWN

Scale

100ft

BLACKERS HOLE

Nesting-season restrictions apply to the climbs left of *Frontiersman*, including those in the sea-cave (see Introduction).

Approach.
1. From the car-park at Durlston Country Park (parking fee charged), follow the tarmac road that leads down across a wooded valley towards the lighthouse. Soon after crossing the bridge, cut across to the cliff-top path. Walk three-quarters of a mile to two tall, white pylons (above Fisherman's Ledge). Continue westwards past two stone walls to a slight path on the seaward side of the fence. This path leads down gently westwards to an easy ramp and rock steps descending to the Main Ledge. Continue down to the sea-level ledge for Blackers Hole East.

2. For Blackers Hole Far West, follow the coast path westwards from Blackers Hole. Just after the path is diverted inland around a landslip area is a long, steep, grassy gully. Abseil from a stake down the gully to a second stake. This abseil is optional, but a certain E8 leader is lucky to be alive after losing his footing here. From the second stake, abseil to the right (facing in) to land on a boulder. Leave the abseil rope in place. Lowish tide and calm seas required.

3. For *Frank's Little Secret* and *Polaris*, walk 180 yards west from Blackers Hole to a deep gully with a mud-slide at its top. Thirty yards east of this is a grassy hollow near the cliff edge with two hard-to-spot stakes on its eastern side. An abseil leads to a large ledge at the base of the routes, which is exposed only at low tide. Leave the abseil rope in place.

BLACKERS HOLE FAR WEST
Some 150 yards west of the huge cave is a cliff flanked by jutting overhangs. The cliff stretches eastwards from the abseil point and is accessible only from low to mid tide in calm seas. All the climbs except two end at *in-situ* lower-off points (in order to avoid the loose rock above), so the only exits from the area are *Aboriginal Script*, *Dreamtime*, or the abseil rope. The latter should be secured to the higher boulders so that retreat is not cut off. Since the lower-off bolts date from the first ascent, they should be **checked** on abseil before they are relied upon.

It has now been agreed that this area should be bolt-free apart from the lower-off points for climbs from *I Am Stone* to *True Nature's Son*. **Aboriginal Script** (70 feet E5 6b [R] † 11.90) was climbed before the agreement with a bolt runner; consequently the bolt may have been removed. The route climbed the seaward face of the buttress immediately left of the abseil, taking in a large roof on the way.

★ **Dreamtime** 70 feet E2 5b [R] †   (25.4.87)
The line of the abseil; the right-hand side of the roof-capped buttress. No time for dreaming as the base of the route is often wave-swept. Climb the arching flake past a small ledge to the faultline. Step left and continue up

the flake past an *in-situ* thread. Belay on the abseil stake.

Immediately right of the roof-capped buttress is an unclimbed chimney-line and then a flat wall protected from the sea by boulders.

I Am Stone   80 feet   E2 5c [R] †   (27.10.89)
Start on top of a high flat boulder 25 feet right of the unclimbed chimney-line.
Climb up a short flake, then steeply leftwards to a thin break, and up left onto a ledge. Go rightwards up a slab to the faultline and rightwards over a bulge to easier ground by a flake. Traverse right easily for 20 feet to a double-bolt lower-off point.

★ **Melancholia**   75 feet   E2 5b [R] †   (27.10.89)
A combination of good moves, rock, and protection make the blank groove just right of *I Am Stone* a worthwhile climb.
Climb a thin crack to jugs beneath the groove. Enter it steeply and trend right up a succession of good small holds (peg runner) to the faultline (*in-situ* thread). Pull over the bulge, step right, and continue to the double-bolt lower-off point.

Another Youth Explodes   75 feet   E3 6a/b [R] †   (27.10.89)
A steep climb starting beneath the corner before the sea-level platform.
Climb the leaning groove to jutting ledges at 25 feet and a good nut on the left. Follow the rightward-trending ramp to reach the faultline beneath the large ceiling. Clip a peg runner on the lip, and then from a footlock reach around for a jug. Pull onto the slab (*in-situ* thread on the right) and continue direct to a double-bolt lower-off point shared with the last two routes.

★ **Whispers Deep**   75 feet   E2 5c [R] †   (24.10.89)
An enjoyable and well-protected climb taking the central line of the crag, an *Elysium*-style crack. Start 50 feet right of the roof-capped buttress from a sea-level platform.
Climb steeply up the thin crack on good holds to a small roof (*in-situ* thread) and thence to the faultline. Climb a short, steep wall, pull over the right-hand side of a large overhang, and gain a break (*in-situ* thread). From good holds, layback to 'jugland' at the next break. Bolt and *in-situ* thread lower-off point.

True Nature's Son   75 feet   E4 6a [R] †   (25.10.89)
A technical pitch with a succession of bouldery problems. Start 20 feet right of *Whispers Deep*, on top of the first boulder past the sea-level platform.
Climb directly up an unprotected and technical wall to reach wire placements in a thin break at 20 feet. Pull over a slight roof and up a hard, blind crack (peg runner) to slabby ground. Step left and climb the roof-crack and the wider crack above to two *in-situ* threads. Swing

strenuously left, and press on leftwards up bulging rock to gain the lower-off point of *Whispers Deep*.

Loneshark (40 feet E4 6a [R] † 25.10.89) gave strenuous climbing from near the right-hand side of the boulder-beach. Its crack, roof, and ledge are all still there, but the two threads which constituted the lower-off point are gone.

Follow Approach 3 to reach the remaining routes in Blackers Hole Far West.

Supergrass (100 feet E4 6b [R] † 8.9.90) was climbed before the designation of the cliff as bolt-free; consequently the bolt may not be in place. Dead low tide required. Starting 20 feet left of the abseil, pitch 1 took a bold and intricate line up to the belay of *Frank's Little Secret* before following pitch 2 of that route.

★ **Frank's Little Secret**   100 feet   Hard Very Severe   [R]   (7.8.77)
A pleasant and enjoyable route on solid rock throughout. Start at the foot of the abseil. If the tide is in, a hanging stance may be taken 10 feet above the ledge.
1 70 feet 4c. Climb the left-hand crack to a small overhang. Traverse right and move up to the large overhang. Step back left and climb the crack above until a move right gains a good nut belay below a flake-line.
2 30 feet 4c. Climb the flake-line to the top and belay on twin stakes.

★★★ **Polaris**   215 feet   E4   [R]   (13.8.78)
A committing route of great character and quality. Although the main difficulties have good protection, failure on the top pitch would cause major problems. The variation third pitches can be approached by abseil from the main route's belay stake. Nuts should be placed to keep in contact with the rock. Start as for *Frank's Little Secret*.
1 90 feet 5a. Climb the left-hand crackline to a small overhang. Traverse right and move up to the large overhang above. Follow the faultline rightwards to the arête or, slightly better, traverse across lower down to reach the arête and climb it to regain the faultline. Continue across to a nut belay beneath a large, open groove.
2 45 feet 6a. Step down and move across to the main arête. Climb the very steep, thin crack until it is possible to swing out right onto a wild hand-traverse across the extremely overhanging wall. This traverse is short but ends in the crux: a pull up and right (*Rock 4*) onto the lip of the big roof. Take a belay on a tiny slab using nuts and a peg.
3 80 feet 5c. Starting 6 feet right of the corner, climb the overhanging wall to a hidden peg by a small corner. Move across left and follow a slanting crack into the base of the large groove for a much needed rest before the difficulties above. Climb the sustained groove, passing a slight bulge near the top to gain a slab. Climb this to a stake belay.

Variations
Ruptured Raspberry   E1 [R]   (1979)
2a 95 feet 5a. A particularly evil pitch, loose and manky. Climb the
open groove above the first stance, moving right at the top to reach a
stake belay well back.

★ **Nuke**   E4 [R] †   (1.3.80/10.87)
3a 90 feet 6a. A wild pitch. From the second stance, on the lip of the
large roof, climb diagonally left along the obvious flake until a 'wicked'
move gains a perched block on the arête. Continue more easily up loosish
rock to a stake belay.

★ **Bolt the Blue Sea?**   90 feet   E5 [R] †   (15.10.94)
A strenuous encounter with the sinuous crackline in the acutely
overhanging left wall of the *Polaris* corner.
3b 90 feet 6b. Climb the back of the corner and pull over a bulge to a
niche on *Polaris*. Swing left onto the wall immediately (peg runner), and
follow the crack to good flake holds (peg runner); these flakes lead
diagonally leftwards to exit onto the sharp left-hand arête. Either belay on
wires here or scramble out to a stake belay.

Weapons of Sound   90 feet   E5 [R] †   (2.10.94)
Very protectable, after the start, and at the bottom of the grade.
3c 90 feet 6a. From the right-hand end of the stance, move up and then
right to gain a line of pockets (*in-situ* thread). Move up to a hand-ledge
and climb a short groove. Break right across the overhanging right wall of
the corner on finger-pockets to a break. Continue up the wall to easier
ground and a stake belay.

★★ **Enter the Void**   90 feet   E6 6b [R] †   (2.10.94)
A brilliant pitch, largely on good pocket holds, in very atmospheric
environs. Low in its grade.
3d 90 feet 6b. From the right-hand end of the stance, move up and then
right to gain a line of pockets (*in-situ* thread). Move up to a hand-ledge
and traverse right to another pocket-line. Follow deep pockets (peg
runner) to a good vertical slot. Climb straight up the blunt, leaning arête,
with hard moves to gain the ledge above. Step right and climb a slab to
rubbly ledges and a stake belay.

BLACKERS HOLE WEST

From the western end of the Main Ledge, *Forn Wall* ventures out onto the seaward face while, to its left, *Frontiersman* tackles the centre of the steep, white
wall. Around on the west-facing wall, the cliff gains in height before meeting
with a vast sea-cave. *Coercri* climbs the centre of this face while the daunting
arête bounding the side of the cave provides the venue for *Giantslayer*. The
sea-level ledges stop here, so it is necessary to traverse the retaining wall to
gain the shingle beach at the back of the cave. Starting from this beach, *Procrastinating Giant* heads up into the overhanging rock above the entry traverse, and *Laughing Arthur* climbs the enormous main roof. Westwards
from the cave entrance an unmistakable overhanging groove undercut by
a large roof can be seen: this is *Polaris*.

The following five overhanging monsters start from the back of the huge cave. Gain access to the cave along *Blackers Hole Traverse*. In the cave a tyrolean can be arranged for gear, seconds, the climbing press, etc. The approach to the cave and the steepness of the rock make all the climbs here serious propositions, sport climbs included.

★★★ **The Schwarzechild Radius**   200 feet   E6 + A1 *S* [R] †   (23.2.93)
A superb soaring line up an extremely intimidating section of cliff. Crawl westwards from the pebble beach at the back of the cave to a small promontory. Calm sea necessary.
1 80 feet 6b. Thirteen bolt runners. Jump to start and attack an extremely leaning wall (the crux) to reach a juggy shakeout at 30 feet. Follow a very steep narrow corner to a projecting hand-ledge at the faultline. Climb up a bulging rib and trend left near its top to a hanging belay. This overhangs the start by 35 feet!
2 60 feet A1. Eight bolt runners and two *in-situ* threads. Swing diagonally leftwards on a series of large flakes to meet the 20-foot roof-crack. Tighten your stomach and launch out to the lip. Twin-bolt belay on the slab above. (The pitch has been 'worked' at 6b but has yet to be redpointed.)
3 60 feet 5b. Three bolt runners. Climb across to the right and then up the bulging buttress, with a huge reach *en-route*, to a clean-cut finish. Stake belay.

★★★ **Laughing Arthur**   360 feet   E7 [R] †   (6-8.8.70/28.8.89)
'Simply the greatest roof-climb in Britain' with 110 feet of overhang! Good protection, some *in-situ*. However, patches of doubtful rock remain and the route is high in its grade. Start (15 feet left of the original route's groove) at the back of the cave. The original route, which tackled the roof-crack in one pitch, was A3.
1 90 feet 6b. Climb the bulges (*in-situ* thread) to a large flake and resting-place (*in-situ* thread above). Traverse right (peg runner) into the groove at a recess. Power rightwards to good holds (*in-situ* thread and two peg runners) and follow the groove on large holds (peg runner) until a 10-foot leftward traverse gains a resting-place. Continue slightly leftwards on guano to small ledges at the main roof. *In-situ* belay.
2 60 feet 6b. The Big One! Step up to the roof-crack, 'summon the power, shut out the fear and go'. The hanging sidewall offers assistance occasionally with a difficult section passing the dip half-way along ('head bar' rest possible). At the lip, pull out right onto a small oasis of verticality, and a take a hanging stance on twin bolts in a position of horrendous exposure.
3 30 feet 6b. Follow the roof-crack, using hanging blockwork, past a flared section until you can layback into the vertical. Pull out left onto a slab, and belay on two *in-situ* threads and a bolt. Very, very exposed!
4 80 feet 5a. Traverse easily left to the smooth slab, a rare commodity at Swanage, and move leftwards to climb the centre of the clean grey area to the ledge-system. Belay on large nuts and *Friends*.

5 100 feet. Traverse left along the ledge for 75 feet, until it is possible to climb over a rock step onto steep ground and the top. Stake belay.
Variation
Coma II   E5 *S* [R] †   (25.11.89)
A mind-blowing 'escape' pitch from *Laughing Arthur*, which ploughs through the tiered overhangs above the belay at the end of pitch 2 and shares its upper section with *Infinite Gravity*. It can be approached by abseil.

3a 60 feet 6b. Pull up on a projecting boss to clip a peg runner. Now climb a rightward-slanting, overhanging arête (bolt runner) and gain a huge jug (bolt runner). Move slightly left past a rail (bolt runner) to the top break. Hand-traverse out on small holds (peg runner) to bypass the roof and gain hidden buckets and a resting-ledge right on the lip (frighteningly exposed!) Belay here on two bolts. Pull out on a rope preplaced on two stakes hidden in a hollow 30 feet below the top.

▸ **Infinite Gravity**   140 feet   E8 6b *S* [R] †   (8.92)
This monumental 'jugathon' up the huge impending arête right of *Laughing Arthur* is a 'total mindbomb'; it overhangs forty-five degrees all the way and comes complete with twenty-two bolt runners.
Cut loose and climb the leaning wall, with hard moves to enter a severely overhung V-groove. Layback to a shakeout at the top of the groove before crossing a bulge to reach a block. Follow a vague crack past several roofs to another block on the lip of the largest roof. Undercut desperately leftwards to a poor shakeout at a change in angle where the rock turns white. Push on leftwards, following a good crack for 15 feet, and gain a handrail by strenuous stretches. Swing left for 10 feet to a huge hold on *Coma II*. Follow rails diagonally leftwards over the overhangs to emerge into the light at a small ledge equipped with a double-bolt belay. Pull out on a rope preplaced on a double stake belay.

▸ **Naked and Savage**   90 feet   E7 6b [R] †   (23.8.90)
Outrageously overhanging climbing taking the soaring groove above the start of *Procrastinating Giant*. An all-weather pitch. Start on the eastern side of the beach at the back of the sea-cave.
Climb the thin crack in the leaning wall below the obvious corner (two peg runners). Go up this corner (peg runner) until a wobbly jug on the left wall enables a resting-niche and a cluster of peg runners to be reached (this is where *Procrastinating Giant* traverses right). Pull into and follow the leaning continuation groove. The final undercling provides the crux, protected by a peg runner and poor *in-situ* thread runner, and leads to a vertical crack. Follow this to a huge jug and double-bolt lower-off point. After lowering, it is apparently possible to pendulum out from the cave to the access ledge, thus avoiding *Blackers Hole Traverse*.

Procrastinating Giant   180 feet   E5 [R] †   (11.8.74/10.10.83)
A substantial undertaking. This impressive free route mostly follows the original aided line; however, the traverse section of pitch 1 on thin blades

is avoided by utilizing a long overlap 10 feet higher. Start as for *Naked and Savage*. A preplaced rope is advisable at the top.
1 80 feet 6a. Climb the thin crack in the leaning wall below the obvious corner (two peg runners). Go up this corner (peg runner) until a wobbly jug on the left wall enables a resting-niche and a cluster of peg runners to be reached. Traverse delicately right below the overlap and take a hanging stance where it ends.
2 30 feet 5b. Climb the corner to a couple of peg runners on the right wall. Swing around the arête on the right and belay on a peg and an *in-situ* thread.
3 70 feet 6a. Pull straight over the bulge above and make a long reach for a good pocket and an *in-situ* thread. Move up left (peg runner) and surmount the final overhang on large holds to easier but looser ground. Move right and pull up the steep grass slope on the fixed rope.

** **Monsters of Rock**   140 feet   E6 [R] †   (3.9.89)
Named *Monster Rock* in the *Rockfax* guide. A direct line through *Procrastinating Giant*. Start in the sea-cave, at its eastern edge. A preplaced rope is advisable for the exit.
1 70 feet 6b. Traverse right along the faultline to the centre of the blank wall (old peg runner). Move up to good pockets where fingery pulls (peg runner) lead to a hidden jug. Make some more hard moves (peg runner) up left to a large incut and an old peg runner. Swing right with difficulty to a flake (*in-situ* thread) and move up to the strip roof (old rusted peg runners). Undercut right a few feet and take a hanging belay as for *Procrastinating Giant*.
2 70 feet 6a. Climb easily the corner above, past some old peg runners, as for *Procrastinating Giant*. Continue nearly up to the top roof, avoiding a doubtful rock fang. Pull out on a jug and strenuously gain another. Swing precariously right onto the exposed arête (peg runner) and good holds on the other side. Surmount the bulge (peg runner and *in-situ* thread) and trend right on bulbous holds. Pull out on a rope preplaced on twin stakes.

Blackers Hole Traverse   50 feet Hard Very Severe 5a [R]   (6.8.70)
Start at the eastern outer edge of the sea-cave.
Swing down and around the arête. Follow the faultline past some old lumps of metal and a poor peg before descending to the boulders and the shingle beach at the back of the cave.

The west-facing wall which flanks the huge sea-cave has five routes on it, although two of these may not exist for long.

The single pitch of *Giantslayer* consists of three straight sections. The first and third are in line, with the second section to their left. Two sport climbs were added more recently; the bolting on their direct lines retrobolts *Giantslayer* and violate the Dorset bolt agreement; they will be removed. **Marble Halls** (85 feet E5 6b *S* [R] † 29.8.93) is an unbalanced line up the arête, while **Cold Empty Cross** (85 feet E4 6a *S* [R] † 29.8.93) starts and finishes as for *Giantslayer*.

⚑ Giantslayer 140 feet E4 6a [R] †   (24.9.83)
Giantslayer climbs up the hostile ground on the west-facing wall, finishing up *Procrastinating Giant*. A demanding lead without the above-mentioned bolts, which may well be removed. A fixed rope to finish is advisable but not imperative. Start at the base of a leftward-leaning ramp. Climb up a rib, swing left below a small roof, and move diagonally left to the prominent arête. Follow a sustained crackline up the curiously textured wall to reach a resting-place below an *in-situ* thread and peg runner. Finish as for *Procrastinating Giant* pitch 3: Pull over the bulge above the thread on superb holds, and make a long reach for a good pocket and an *in-situ* thread. Move up left (peg runner) and surmount the final overhang on large holds. On the easier but looser section above, move right and pull up the steep grass slope on the fixed rope.

⚑ Coercri 120 feet E3 [R]   (1980/28.8.83)
A fine route giving difficult and well-protected climbing up the west-facing wall. Start at the base of a leftward-leaning ramp, as for *Giantslayer*.
1 80 feet 5c. Follow the ramp to a peg runner at its top. Make a difficult move to start a thin crack on the right, which is climbed to a good ledge.
2 40 feet 5c. Follow another ramp up leftwards to a peg runner and pull directly over the bulge on good fingerholds to easier ground. Climb up rightwards and then continue directly up to the top on reasonable rock. Stake belay.

Scarface (Hard Very Severe + A1 [R] 27.10.75) has been largely super-seded by the first pitch of *Cosa Nostra* and the second of *Coercri*. However, its aid section, over the roof directly above the belay of *Coercri*, has not yet been free-climbed. A preplaced rope is required for the loose exit.

Cosa Nostra 100 feet E2 5c [R] S   (21.4.88)
Exposed climbing up the left arête of the seaward-facing wall. Start on the seaward side of the arête. Climb a bulging crack before trending left onto the arête and the start of a diagonal ramp (peg runner). Step right immediately and follow the arête to a niche. Move rightwards over a bulge and up a crack to easier ground. Trend left to a ledge near the top and belay on a preplaced rope. Pull out on the rope.

Frontiersman 100 feet E3 5b   (4.6.83)
Good strenuous climbing, although scary on the traverse at the top. Start on the sloping, sea-level platform in the centre of the seaward-facing wall. Just right of a groove-line is a slabby wall; climb this to a roof at half height. Move around the right-hand side of the roof and go back left to the base of the white wall. Move up slightly leftwards and then straight up to a flake, from where a 15-foot traverse right gains the good ledge at the top of *Forn Wall*. Pull up the earth slope on a rope preplaced on a stake.

Forn Wall 50 feet Hard Very Severe 5a
A worthwhile route. Start at the westernmost edge of the Main Ledge.

Climb the arête and move diagonally left to a crack in the seaward face.
Climb to the left of the niche and continue up the wall to the top. Pull up
the earth slope on a rope preplaced on a stake.

MAIN LEDGE

The Main Ledge is a very large platform located well above the waves; it
stays dry in all but the worst sea conditions. On the wall bounding the
west side of the Main Ledge, *Bill's Route* pulls over the obvious roof at 15
feet before following a series of ledges leading up to a long earth slope.
This route and its neighbours would provide pleasant climbing were it not
for this earth slope. 'Dangerous in the dry, suicidal in the wet' sums it up,
so a fixed rope comes into its own here. The backwall of the Main Ledge consists of a series of stepped roofs capped by an even more unpleasant top,
which makes lower-off points obligatory. The artificial routes which once
tackled these overhangs have been superseded by an array of demanding
free-climbs. It provides an ideal venue for 'the disciples of power', especially
when other areas are out of condition owing to rough seas or poor weather.
However, much of the fixed protection on the backwall is in need of replacement; the grades assume this is done.

**The following four climbs all require a preplaced rope to safe-
guard the exit over the earth slope at the top.** Use the stake on
the grassy promontory above the western side of the Main Ledge.

Triaxiality   50 feet   E1 5b   (9.2.80)
Start at the foot of the arête bounding the western side of the Main Ledge.
From the Ledge, climb to a roof and pull over it to gain a steep crack.
Follow this to a ledge at the top. Pull up the earth slope on the preplaced
rope.

Flyover   50 feet   Hard Very Severe 4c   (1.66)
Start below a break in the roof at 15 feet.
Pull over the roof to a good ledge and climb the cracks in the overhanging
wall past a peg runner to a ledge. Pull up the earth slope on the preplaced
rope.

Bill's Route   55 feet   Hard Severe 4b
Start as for *Flyover*.
Climb up to the roof and swing boldly over it onto the ledge above (as for
Flyover). Follow a series of small ledges up to the right, move back left at
the top to pull over, and gain the earth slopes above. Pull up to the top on
the preplaced rope.

Steep   50 feet   Very Severe 4c   (1968)
Fairly serious in its upper part even with a preplaced rope for the earth
slope. Start below the left-hand of two corners to the right of *Bill's Route*.
Climb the corner and step across left to a ledge at 30 feet. Continue up to
the earth and pull out on the preplaced rope.

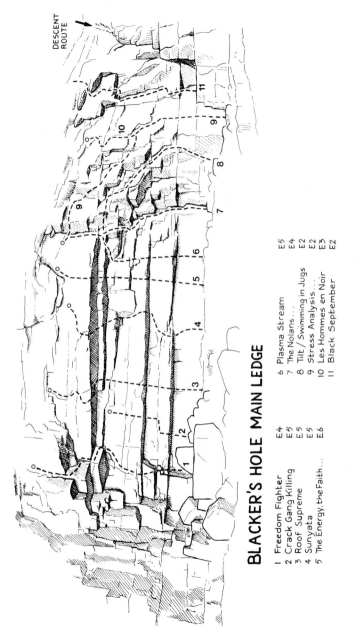

BLACKER'S HOLE MAIN LEDGE

1 Freedom Fighter	E4	6 Plasma Stream	E5
2 Crack Gang Killing	E5	7 The Nolans….	E4
3 Roof Supreme	E5	8 Tilt / Swimming in Jugs	E2
4 Sunyata	E5	9 Stress Analysis….	E2
5 The Energy, the Faith….	E6	10 Les Hommes en Noir	E3
		11 Black September	E2

DESCENT ROUTE

Variation
Overhang Start (55 feet E1 5b). Climb the crack in the roof
immediately left of the corner and then step right to join the parent route.

⋆ **Freedom Fighter**   40 feet   E4   6a/b   (3.2.88)
Start on the left-hand side of the overhung bay at a short corner. Highly
entertaining.
Climb very steep flakes and traverse left under two large roofs (peg
runner) to a wide corner-crack. *In-situ* nut and peg lower-off point.

⋆ **Crack Gang Killing**   30 feet   E5   6c †   (18.11.88)
Start 15 feet right of the short corner. Those of normal stature should start
from a boulder or with a pole-vault.
Climb the series of roofs past a ring-peg runner, a bolt runner, and another
peg runner to a twin-bolt lower-off point beneath the top roof.
Direct Start (6c/7a † 4.89). A desperate problem; only for the tall. Cross
the 5-foot ceiling from the back to the first peg runner. No boulders
allowed!

⋆ **Roof Supreme**   40 feet   E5   6c †   (11.6.88)
A 'bulky outing' with long reaches, starting 5 feet left of a niche in the
lower wall. The top peg has broken off; the grade assumes its
replacement.
Using a pile of boulders to reach the lip, climb up and cross a roof to a
flake (peg runner). Move up to 'resting'-jams (suspect *in-situ* thread). Pull
over the top ceiling with difficulty to the left of a peg runner. Swing right to
a jug (peg runner) and climb up to a bolt and double-peg lower-off point.

In the centre of the backwall are two carvings. One of these is Om, the roar of
infinity, yet also the stillness of pure being.

⋆⋆ **Sunyata**   35 feet   E5   6b   (6.2.88)
A superb test-piece for the cellar generation. Start just left of the Buddhist
carvings near the centre of the backwall. The *in-situ* nut is heavily corroded.
Pull up and traverse right for 10 feet (two peg runners). Cross the roof (*in-situ* nut) to a rest in a niche. Trend left over the top two roofs (peg runner)
to good holds. Peg and bolt lower-off point to the right.

⋆⋆ **The Energy, the Faith, the Devotion**
                              35 feet   E6   6c/7a †   (12.3.88)
Only for the tall. Start 10 feet right of the Buddhist carvings.
Cross the desperate and reachy roof (bolt runner). Continue over two
smaller roofs (peg runner and *in-situ* thread) and pass the top roof using a
pocketed crack (*in-situ* thread and bolt runner). Double-peg lower-off point.

⋆ **Plasma Stream**   35 feet   E5   6c/7a †   (1988/13.4.89)
Utterly heinous! Impossible for the short? Start 10 feet from the end of the
main lower roof.

Surmount the hard, blank roof, pass the second roof (*in-situ* thread on a flake), and go up to the third. Swing right and gain the corner above. *In-situ* nut and thread lower-off point.

★ **Guano on My Face**   80 feet   E4 6a †   (27.12.88)
'If it's not worth a star we'll give it a spaceship!' A traverse of the back wall starting as for *The Nolans Meet Impulse Manslaughter*.
Climb up, traverse left along the hanging flakes, and descend the groove left of *Freedom Fighter* to the ground.

The Nolans Meet Impulse Manslaughter
                                      35 feet   E4 6b † (21.1.88)
A real battle. Start on the right-hand side of the overhangs.
Climb flakes in the overhanging corner and cross a 5-foot roof to reach a vague corner. Follow this (peg runner) to an *in-situ* thread and nut lower-off point (shared with *Plasma Stream*).

★ **Tilt / Swimming in Jugs**   40 feet   E2   5b   (8.10.67/6.2.88)
Well protected but strenuous and therefore high in the grade. Start at the base of the diagonal crack in the sidewall just right of the recessed backwall.
Climb leftwards up the crack and flakes before swinging left into a corner. Use the previous route's lower-off point.

Stress Analysis of a Strapless Evening Gown
                                      45 feet   E2 5b † (20.2.88)
Start at the base of the descent steps.
Climb to a ledge at 8 feet, gain a flake, and traverse left past a fang to a resting-place. Continue diagonally left past a square-cut block and a suspect shield into a corner. Climb to the roof and traverse left on sharp, shelly rock to a corner. Lower-off point as for *Plasma Stream*.

Les Hommes en Noir (30 feet E3 6a † 3.2.88) is a poor route, starting as for *Stress Analysis of a Strapless Evening Gown*. A stake and fixed rope need to be placed. Climb to a ledge at 8 feet, gain a flake, and continue up the hairline crack to better holds. Pull up leftwards to an easing beneath the bulges and lower off the preplaced rope.

Black September   60 feet   E2 5c   (17.9.83)
A varied route. Start just above the foot of the descent steps, to the left of a clean corner.
Using a wide crack, climb the bulge and step right into the corner. Follow this to the first roof, step right, and pull over (crux) onto the wall above. Turn the second roof on the left and swing back on top of it. Surmount the final bulge with difficulty using dubious holds to gain the ledge above. Belay here on multiple nuts. Traverse off with care to the descent route on the right.

BLACKERS HOLE EAST

Scrambling down from the eastern end of the main ledge leads to the foot of a slabby area where *Zig-Zag* weaves its way up to a flake near the top. To the right is a large cave with a triple-stepped roof breached in three short pitches by *Street Fighting Years*. Further on, above a higher platform, is a steep wall climbed by *Tobacco Road*, with the *Vapour Edge* tackling its right arête. Further eastwards the cliff is set back in a succession of corners accessible only at low tide. The first corner gives *Parson's Pleasure*, while *Harlot* climbs the east-facing wall of the second corner. The second corner itself is as yet unclimbed in its entirety and is flanked on the right by the smooth, imposing *Centrepiece* wall. A rockfall has destroyed two routes at the right end of this wall. Climbs further east all involve wading or an abseil approach, as well as fixed ropes to overcome the steep, bare earth slope.

** **Zig-Zag**   95 feet   Severe

A well-established classic of the area. Start just east of the Main Ledge in a small corner at the foot of a diagonal crack.
1 50 feet 4a. Climb up easily rightwards along the crack and surmount the bulge above at its weakest point. Above, an undercut crack leads back left to a belay on an overhung ledge.
2 45 feet 4a. Traverse right along another ledge, move delicately across the slab, and climb up via a big flake to the top. Belay on a stake to the right.

The area of rock crossed by *Zig-Zag* also has two direct lines. The easier of the two, **Parallel Lines** (80 feet Hard Very Severe 5a † 11.8.92), starts 8 feet right of the small corner and passes through a shallow groove just right of the *Zig-Zag* belay ledge. **Straight Lines** (80 feet Hard Very Severe 5b) starts below the top of the initial crack of *Zig-Zag*, and is centred around a shallow grey groove at half height. Both climbs belay on a stake to the right, backed up by *Friends* in the backwall.

Luxury Liner   185 feet   E2   (10.6.81)

An absorbing outing with some good climbing on the traverse between the cave roofs. Start 10 feet right of *Zig-Zag*.
1 50 feet 5b. Cruise up over a small bulge to the start of the second crack on *Zig-Zag*. Traverse horizontally right and with difficulty enter a short, steep corner, which is situated by the lip of the big roof. Pull up out of the corner and belay here on *Friends* and nuts.
2 75 feet 5b/c. Hand-traverse rightwards along the break for 25 feet to meet a rounded bulge. Avoid this by descending to reach good holds on the lip of the main cave roof. Continue traversing until a hard move right gains a scoop and a good rest at its top. Traverse easily right for 10 feet to a hanging belay on good nuts beneath an open groove.
3 60 feet 4c. Hand-traverse rightwards and then shuffle along a ledge for 20 feet. Descend the blunt flake of *Talus* and continue down to the ground. (This is pleasanter than finishing up *Talus*.)

★ **Credit in the Straight World**   80 feet   E4 6a   (20.8.83)
Bold and technical climbing up the wall overlooking *Zig-Zag*. Start 20 feet
right of *Zig-Zag* at a rockfall scar.
Climb the left-hand side of the alcove formed by the rockfall and the bulge
above to a short, steep wall. Move right to reach an undercut and pull
over onto the slab above. Follow the easy flake/crack for 10 feet, step
right, and climb the steep wall to a finger-jug at the base of a small groove
on the right. Move up and then left to the top. Belay on a stake shared
with *Zig-Zag*.

Absence Makes the Heart...   110 feet   E3 6a   (23.2.86)
Start at a rib on the left-hand side of a wide cave.
Climb the rib, bulges, and a short groove to a ledge. Move up rightwards
across a shallow groove and climb the headwall (peg runner) slightly right
to the top. Belay on a preplaced rope, which is then used to pull past a
short broken section at the top.

★ **Street Fighting Years**   120 feet   E7 †   (22.8.89)
Wild, wild roof-climbing through the centre of the large triple-roofed cave.
'A last great problem for roof machines only!' An *in-situ* nut at the lip of
the first roof and a peg on the lip of the second are now missing but this is
thought not to alter the grade.
1 40 feet 6c. Climb to the 15-foot roof and follow the right-hand of two
diagonal cracks on isolated jams, travelling feet first to the lip. Pull around
to a double *in-situ* thread belay.
2 30 feet 6b. Move up to the next ceiling and cross it past a huge jug
(old peg runner) with hard moves at the lip into a small corner. Swing up
right to a big hold before stretching up to the horizontal break. Take a
hanging belay by an old bolt-stud using *Friends* and large nuts.
3 50 feet 6a. Pull over the top overhang at a thin crack to reach jugs.
Ascend an easy groove in the headwall and go leftwards to finish as for
Absence Makes the Heart... Belay on a preplaced rope as for that route.

It Sank the Ship, Now Eat the Lettuce 90 feet E1 5b † (22.7.87)
A traverse of the lowest hanging wall of the cave. The two threads placed
for *Street Fighting Years* are not allowed as there is plenty of good natural
protection nearby! Start at the right-hand edge of the cave.
Climb over ledges onto the wall and traverse left keeping up by the roof.
When the far corner is 5 feet away, descend a crack to the lip. Continue
to the corner and use strenuous undercuts to reach the ledge on the left.
Step left and descend to the deck.

A Dose of the Malhams (60 feet E6 6b † 7.8.90) was climbed
before this section of cliff was designated bolt-free. It used three bolt
runners; consequently these bolts may have been removed. The climb
took the overhanging arête, blank roof, and wall to the flake-line of
Talus and an abseil escape.

Talus 160 feet Hard Very Severe (27.6.71)
This route has a highly unstable top pitch, which is best avoided
completely. Just beyond the large cave to the east of the Main Ledge is a
wide ledge at 8 feet situated beneath a steep headwall. Start here. Pitch 1
takes the left-hand of two prominent flakes in the lower wall.
1 60 feet 4c. Climb up leftwards to a 3-foot roof split by a flake crack.
Surmount the roof and follow the crack above to a ledge and peg belays.
2 100 feet 4c. Traverse left along the ledge and continuation crack to
beneath loose blocks. Climb these blocks and the loose crack above until
about 10 feet from the top. Exit left on horrendous rock.

Cheroot 90 feet Very Severe 4c (9.9.67/c.1974)
A good line but with unbalanced difficulties and a loose finish. Start as for
Talus.
Move up and climb the right-hand of the two flakes to a smooth slab.
Continue up left of a small roof to a distinct diagonal crack. Follow the line
of the crack out leftwards and finish to the left over loose rock. Belay with
an extra rope on the fenceposts.

Rufty's Roll Up 85 feet E1 5b † (11.8.92)
Start from the right-hand end of the ledge.
Climb straight up the wall, past an obvious white jug, to a vertical crack in
the headwall (10 feet left of the main crack of *Tobacco Road*). Finish
straight up. Stake belay on the right.

★ **Tobacco Road** 80 feet Very Severe 4c
Steep, well-protected climbing on good rock. Start from the right-hand end
of the wide ledge at 8 feet.
Climb up easily rightwards to two vertical cracks and follow these to a
ledge below the headwall. Move left up a ramp onto the smooth wall.
Traverse horizontally right past a wobbly jug and climb directly up cracks
to a groove, which is followed up rightwards to the top. Stake belay.

★ **The Vapour Edge** 90 feet E1 5b (27.3.83)
Elegant, well-positioned climbing up the arête to the right of *Tobacco
Road*. Start below the left arête of the big overhung corner situated about
200 feet east of the Main Ledge.
Climb easily up the arête to a ledge at 40 feet. Trend up rightwards to the
foot of a very thin, vertical crack (just left of the arête) and climb this
direct. Continue up the wall above to good finishing holds. Belay with an
extra rope on the fenceposts.

★ **Parson's Pleasure** 80 feet Very Severe (4.10.75)
Enjoyable climbing leads to a steep and troublesome finish. Start as for
The Vapour Edge.
1 40 feet 4a. Climb up the arête for a few feet and out right to a smooth
corner in the east-facing wall. Climb the corner to a large sloping ledge
and good thread belays below a roof.

2 40 feet 4c. Follow the chimney on the right of the roof to a good ledge. Climb the final corner and a bulge on its left (strenuous) to a wide ledge. Go left along the ledge and up earth and grass to a stake belay.

Bloodlust 80 feet E5 6a/b † (8.89)
An eliminate giving 20 feet of independent roof-climbing along the crack formed by a huge, sagging block. Start as for *Snout*.
Scramble up into the recess, step out right, and pull up into a restricted overhanging corner. Climb leftwards across the crack to a constricted semi rest. Continue along the roof-crack until it is possible to jam around the lip. Finish up *Parson's Pleasure* pitch 2.

★ **Snout** 80 feet E1 (11.10.75/1.6.80)
An intimidating and mentally confusing first pitch. Start at a large recess 20 feet east of *Parson's Pleasure*.
1 40 feet 5a/b. Scramble up into the recess and step out right to pull up into a restricted overhanging corner. Lean out backwards to reach the bottomless wall behind, chimney-traverse right, and go up the groove above. Exit left at the top to a stance on the wall.
2 40 feet 5a. Climb up above the first pitch on good holds to an obvious thread formed by a flake; move up over this to a fair finish. Stake belay.

★ **Havana** 80 feet E4 6a/b † (15.10.94)
Plentiful protection and a thrilling finale are the main characteristics of the direct line, which aims for the obvious thin crack in the undercut headwall right of *Snout*.
From the right-hand side of the recess, climb direct on good holds and pull over a small roof awkwardly. Continue in the same line to the bulge beneath the headwall. Reach good holds on the lip (*in-situ* thread) and then follow the thin crack with some difficulty to easier ground and the large ledge above.

Buttend 90 feet Hard Very Severe (3.4.76)
Start as for *Snout* in the large recess.
1 40 feet 5a. From the right-hand edge of the recess, traverse right to a protruding ledge. Surmount the roof above the ledge (peg runner) and continue up the wall to a belay at a horizontal break on the left of the arête.
2 50 feet 4c. Move around the arête, step up onto a block, and continue up the slabs above to a corner on the left. Move out to a ledge on the arête and climb up awkwardly onto a higher ledge. From the right, finish over the rubble bank above. Stake belay.

Once It's Gotcha 80 feet E5 6b † (15.10.94)
The ability to harness reserves of power whilst under duress is needed for this exacting venture. The climb is based upon the arête at the right-hand side of the face.
Climb straight up the arête for 20 feet to a niche at the foot of a crack

running up its right-hand side. Swing left beneath a roof to a jug (vital *Friend 2½*), and then improvise up the left-hand side of the arête, with committing moves to reach horizontal breaks. Bear slightly leftward to a flake beneath the corner of *Buttend*, which is followed to the top.

Harlot   85 feet   Very Severe †   (25.4.76)
A meretricious climb of little merit, on account of some large suspect blocks. Start at a crack in the east-facing wall of the second large corner east of the Main Ledge.
1 35 feet 4c. Pull into a niche with difficulty and continue up a smooth-sided chimney to reach a stance and belay.
2 50 feet 4b. Move left with difficulty to the arête and go up this, before stepping right to gain a large ledge up above. Continue over the top to a stake belay.

The next smooth wall is taken centrally by *Centrepiece*. The belay stake for the three routes on the wall is located at the very edge of the third hollow east of the descent to Blackers Hole. All three routes require a preplaced rope to finish.

The Equalizer (70 feet E5 6b † 31.5.87) climbed the left-hand side of the *Centrepiece* wall. It used a bolt runner before it was agreed that bolts on this section of cliff should be restricted to certain belays; consequently the bolt may have been removed.

** **Centrepiece**   70 feet   E5 6c   (5.9.86)
A last great problem of yesteryear. Climb the centre of the wall (*in-situ* thread) and then ascend the crux crack. Continue past a peg runner to a ledge and belay on a rope preplaced on a stake.

** **Not Forgotten, No Fade Away**   70 feet   E5 6b †   (5.9.86)
Climb directly through the bulges and up the smooth wall right of Centrepiece. Belay to a rope preplaced on a stake.

To the right of *Not Forgotten, No Fade Away* two routes have perished in a rockfall: **Personality Clash** (4.6.83) and **Black Shag** (12.10.75).

Made in Britain (70 feet E4 6b †† 4.7.87) is approached by abseil from a stake just west of the second wall west of the Fisherman's Ledge pylons. The route has not been climbed since the initial pillar fell down. Above the remains of the pillar and the calcite sheet (*in-situ* thread and peg), a groove is followed to a stake and thread belay. Prusik up the abseil rope.

Friends of the Earth   135 feet   Hard Severe 4a †   (29.7.75)
Pleasant and varied climbing, which can be reached only at low tide and in a calm sea. The finish is up a *long* crumbly earth slope, so it is necessary to preplace a fixed rope from a stake located in a small hollow

below the second wall west of the pylons. The route finishes directly below this stake. Starting from the eastern extremity of the sea-level ledge, wade to the first cave, traverse around this, and wade across the second cave to reach the seaward ledge on a pillar supporting the roof. Climb up from the right-hand end of the ledge for 30 feet to a large ledge. Continue up the right-hand groove to a big flake, step left onto a slab, and then move up right to a slab at 70 feet. Prusik up the fixed rope to overcome the desperately loose earth slope above.

The Cattle Troughs Area   OS Ref 015 768

A discontinuous sea-level ledge extends throughout this area, beginning at the cave of Conner Cove and coming to an end just before the western limit of Boulder Ruckle. The breaks in this ledge form the boundaries for seven separate sections, each of which has its own entry point. From west to east these sections are: Fisherman's Ledge, The Promenade, Unknown Ledge, Flake Ledge, The Jumble, Cattle Troughs, and finally Amphitheatre Ledge.

In this area there is a series of amphitheatre-shaped depressions in the cliff. Starting from the east, the normal direction of approach, the first of these rock amphitheatres (The Half Moon) is above Amphitheatre Ledge. The second and third (The Pulpit and The Lecture Theatre respectively) lie within Cattle Troughs. The fourth is The Jumble and the fifth Flake Ledge. The final two depressions are situated above The Promenade. It is important to note that the amphitheatres at Cattle Troughs, The Jumble, and Flake Ledge can be viewed only from the cliff edge, whereas the others are obvious from the walk along the main cliff-top path. A short distance past The Promenade two large white pylons mark the location of Fisherman's Ledge.

Approach. From the car-park at Durlston Country Park (parking fee charged), follow the tarmac road that leads down across a wooded valley towards the lighthouse. Soon after crossing the bridge, cut across to the cliff-top path. Follow it westwards to a stone wall where Durlston Country Park gives way to The National Trust's *Belle Vue* estate. Continue on for 150 yards to a depression in the cliff-top with a semi-circular cliff beneath; this is Amphitheatre Ledge. From here the following options are open to you.

Fisherman's Ledge From the top of Amphitheatre Ledge, continue along the path to two tall, white pylons. The main ledge at Fisherman's is just to the west of these. From here, there are four choices.
1. Make an airy free-hanging abseil from one of the belay stakes to the main ledge below.
2. Revese *Helix*. This finishes at the top of the west-facing wall of Connor

Cove and may be difficult to locate on a first visit, as well as being intimidating to descend.
3. For the routes in Connor Cove, abseil in as described below.
4. Diving into the sea from above *The Conger* in order to solo, dripping wet, up *Freeborn Man* has been done, but is not unreservedly recommended.

The Promenade From the top of Amphitheatre Ledge, continue along the path until a tiny quarry, Chilmark Quarry, can be seen. This is situated above the eastern end of The Promenade. Between the quarry and the two tall, white pylons are two rock amphitheatres. Abseil down the **westernmost** of these amphitheatres, which is located about 75 yards east of the pylons. The abseil descends the line of *Danglefoot*, a relatively simple climb to solo down when it is familiar. The abseil point is normally the drilled thread located on the ledge above the amphitheatre. However, the grass slope above has slipped, depositing a large pile of earth on the ledge. Until this clears, use a stake just to the west, on the side of the amphitheatre.

Unknown Ledge Traverse in from the eastern end of The Promenade (easier) or the western end of Flake Ledge (quicker).

Flake Ledge From the ledge at the top of Cattle Troughs, walk westward to an amphitheatre. Continue to the *next* amphitheatre, scramble down a few feet, and walk east along a narrow ledge to a short chimney. Descend the chimney and scramble down to ledges at the bottom.

The Jumble From the ledge at the top of Cattle Troughs, follow the long ledge westwards to an amphitheatre. Climb down slabs until forced eastwards to a short corner, which leads to some slabs and the bottom.

Cattle Troughs From the top of Amphitheatre Ledge, a narrow path contours along the cliff edge past several belay stakes and ends at a large ledge where rucksacks are best left. Climb down easy rock on the western side of a large depression in the cliff (The Lecture Theatre).

Amphitheatre Ledge
1. Abseil from two iron stakes down the eastern side of The Amphitheatre to the ledges below. A traverse eastwards (Very Difficult) leads as far as *The Roaring Forties*.
2. East of The Amphitheatre is a deep hollow. For climbs from *In a Big Sky* to *Arapiles Syndrome*, abseil from a stake below a thorn bush east of the hollow. The abseil rope should be left in place to assist the unpleasant exits.

FISHERMAN'S LEDGE
Compact and sometimes pocketed rock in Conner Cove, overhangs aplenty in the main area, and some ludicrous propositions in the eastern cave all ensure that Fisherman's Ledge ranks as a major Swanage attraction. Although lacking the height of the main cliffs, the majority of the climbs here are on excellent rock and have sound, clean-cut finishes. The sub-

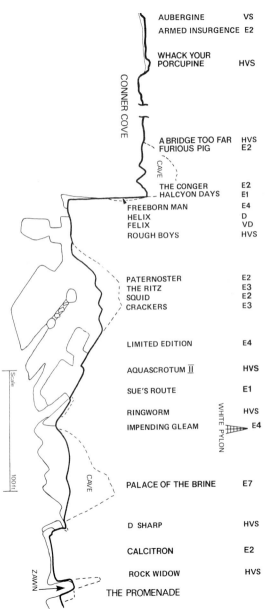

AUBERGINE — VS
ARMED INSURGENCE — E2

WHACK YOUR PORCUPINE — HVS

CONNER COVE

A BRIDGE TOO FAR — HVS
FURIOUS PIG — E2

CAVE

THE CONGER — E2
HALCYON DAYS — E1
FREEBORN MAN — E4
HELIX — D
FELIX — VD
ROUGH BOYS — HVS

PATERNOSTER — E2
THE RITZ — E3
SQUID — E2
CRACKERS — E3

LIMITED EDITION — E4

AQUASCROTUM II — HVS

SUE'S ROUTE — E1

RINGWORM — HVS
IMPENDING GLEAM — E4

WHITE PYLON

PALACE OF THE BRINE — E7

CAVE

D SHARP — HVS

CALCITRON — E2

ROCK WIDOW — HVS

ZAWN

THE PROMENADE

FISHERMAN'S LEDGE

Scale

100 ft

sport of cliff-jumping has enjoyed a renaissance here, sometimes involuntarily combined with deep-water soloing. A nice place, too, for sunbathing, swimming, or even a spot of fishing. However, when the sea is rough, virtually all the routes at Fisherman's become inaccessible and the ledges are awash.

A mile west of the lighthouse are two tall, white pylons. The main ledge at Fisherman's resides just to the west of these, while Fisherman's West, local name Conner Cove, is the stretch of short cliff forming a shallow bay just beyond.

FISHERMAN'S WEST/CONNER COVE

Around the arête to the left of *Helix*, an overhanging wall faces west and meets with an interesting sea-cave split by a bottomless chimney. The centre of the overhanging wall gives the forceful *Freeborn Man*, whereas the traverse out along the lip of the cave roof to gain the bottomless chimney provides a more amenable but equally impressive outing, *The Conger*. The obvious corner on the left-hand side of the cave proves to be *A Bridge Too Far* and, further west, *Aubergine* climbs an east-facing corner-crack. The short, smooth wall of very compact rock continues westwards to a large, rectangular recess, the home of *Ruffy Tuffy*. Further on, before a large sea-cave, are two delights for the deep-water soloist, *Fathoms* and *...And Captain Blood's Cavern*. A prominent straight crack splitting a smooth, east-facing wall can be seen from all along this section of cliff; this crack is *The Law* and, the arête to the left is *Decayed*. The coastline beyond is capped by a long, steep earth slope and eventually merges with Blackers Hole East.

Access to the first four climbs is by abseil from a stake directly below a bramble bush, 50 yards east of the second wall west of the pylons. This abseil leads down a long earth slope to an excavated ledge atop the arête of *Decayed*. For the first two climbs, continue down the western side of the arête and for the other two, carry on down the east-facing wall.

★ **The Garden of Earthly Delights**   230 feet E3 †   (5.8.90)
A wild traverse across the lip of the sea-cave left of *Decayed* using the prominent handrail. Before abseiling in, place a fixed rope, as for *Friends of the Earth*, on a stake in a small hollow below the second wall west of the pylons. Calm seas required. Belay 25 feet left of the arête of *Decayed*.
1 90 feet 5c. Walk 20 feet left and climb a slab to the horizontal crack beneath the roof. Follow the crack leftwards over the cave until a higher crack can be used to reach a bottomless groove in the east-facing wall. Hanging belay.
2 40 feet 5b. Descend to the very bottom of the groove and follow the crack again to reach a ledge on *Friends of the Earth*. Thread Belay.
3 100 feet 4a. (As for *Friends of the Earth*.) Climb a groove to a big flake, step left onto a slab, and then move up right onto another slab. Prusik up the long, steep earth slope using the fixed rope.

Behind the start of *The Garden of Earthly Delights* two routes, **Boys Keep Swinging** and **Everybody's Downfall** (both 27.2.88), have fallen down. It was the name that did it!

Decayed 65 feet E2 5b †   (1.1.80)
Bold. Start from the right-hand side of the ledge about 10 feet above the sea.
Climb up the wall and step right onto a small ledge. Move right onto the arête and follow it to the top of an obvious flake. Swing right onto a ramp of poor rock and continue along this to a corner. Hand-traverse left, and belay on the finishing ledge using the abseil rope.

★ **The Law** 80 feet E3 5c   (16.5.80)
A strenuous pitch up a steep off-fingers crack in a remarkably smooth, east-facing wall. Start from a sea-level ledge just to the right of the crack.
Move up and hand-traverse left to gain the bottom of the crack. Climb the crack with difficulty and exit left at the top. Use the abseil rope to belay on the ledge above the arête.

★ **Inspector Clouseau** 80 feet E4 6a †   (24.2.88)
A winter seepage line. Start 10 feet right of The Law.
Climb the smooth, white wall via twin cracks. Finish leftwards at the capping bulge to join *The Law*. Belay on the abseil rope.

The cliff to the east, known to the *cognoscenti* as Funky Wall, is heavily eroded at the top and therefore of lesser height. At the western end of this section is the abseil stake for the next six routes. The abseil leads to a ledge.

★★ **...And Captain Blood's Cavern** 80 feet E3 6a   (8.8.90)
The arching overlap above the eastern corner of the next sea-cave is a well-situated classic, high in its grade, which attracts the crank-or-splash brigade. From the bottom of the abseil, traverse left for 30 feet to a flake crack.
Drop down and traverse left for 15 feet to the end of the handrail. Make a hard move up to an undercut crack and follow this to a bulge. Move left to an arête and up to an overhang. Cross this and finish up a corner. Stake belay.
Variation
★★ **Davey Jones' Lock-off** 80 feet E4 6a †   (8.94)
Follow the parent route before moving left on the lip of the cave to a foot-ledge. Climb up to undercuts and thence to the top.

★★ **Fathoms** 80 feet E3 5c   (8.9.86)
Strictly a summer route; well worth doing when dry. Start as for *...And Captain Blood's Cavern*.
Climb up and then leftwards into a groove, which is followed to a superb jam at its end. Pull over and exit rightwards on friable rock. Poor belays.

Donald, Where's Your Trousers? 45 feet E1 5b   (8.9.86)
Start as for *...And Captain Blood's Cavern*.
Climb diagonally right between undercuts and follow a short layback
flake leftwards to an easier finish. Poor belays.

Amazonia 40 feet E1 5b †   (4.6.93)
From the bottom of the abseil, move left to a small ledge. Start here.
Climb onto the shelf on the left and move steadily leftwards and upwards.
Take the bulge on its left and finish on jugs.

The Rise and Dear Demise of the Funky Nomadic Tribes
                    40 feet   Hard Very Severe 5b (27.8.79)
From the left-hand end of the ledge, climb the small crack and flakes direct
to the top.

★ **The Friendly Ranger from Clontarf Castle** 40 feet E2 5c (27.8.79)
Low in its grade.
From the right-hand end of the ledge, climb the wall and cracks straight to
the top.

For the next five routes, either abseil from a stake 30 feet west of *Aubergine*,
or abseil down that route and traverse west to a large, rectangular recess.

The Friendly Landlord of Durlston Castle
                    40 feet   Hard Very Severe 5a † (6.9.86)
Start at a rib 40 feet right of *The Friendly Ranger from Clontarf Castle*, and
10 feet left of the rectangular recess. Climb the right-hand side of the rib,
moving leftwards near the top.

On the Third Day 40 feet E3 5c   (8.9.86)
From the left end of the recess, climb a flaky groove to a roof. Move right
and ascend a flake-line to a rounded finish.

★ **Moving Away from Rufty Tufty** 40 feet E4 5c †   (1988)
Poorly protected but above deep(ish?) water. Start as for *Rufty Tufty*. Mantel
onto a ledge at 8 feet and climb diagonally left up the vague ramp to better
holds. Move leftwards to a vague crack, which leads to a hard finish just to
the right.

★★ **Rufty Tufty** 40 feet   Hard Very Severe 4c   (7.9.86)
Start at the right-hand side of the recessed ledge. Mantel onto the ledge at
8 feet and climb the pocketed crack before stepping right to finish. Stake
belay.

★ **Rufty Tufty Vivisects His Mummy** 40 feet E3 5c   (8.9.86)
Superb but poorly-protected climbing on deep finger-pockets. Start as for
Rufty Tufty. Mantel onto the ledge at 8 feet and climb straight up the brown
scoop to a stake belay.

⋆ Hallucinating Freely　40 feet　E5 6b †　　　　(29.8.89)
A serious lead but with great moves. The rectangular recess has a smaller continuation recess to its right. Start on the right-hand side of this second recess. The *Rock 2* was preplaced on the first ascent. Climb a series of lay-back fins (vital *Rock 6*) and surmount a bulge to an incut (vital *Rock 2*). Continue precariously up the headwall (the crux) to an easier, scooped finish. Stake belay.

⋆⋆ End of the Innocence　45 feet　E4 6b †　　　　(29.8.89)
A fine, well-protected pitch based around the high roof left of *Aubergine*. Start on the right-hand side of the smaller recess, as for *Hallucinating Freely*. Step right and climb rightwards up a short wall to a corner. Make a tricky move to gain good holds before undercutting right under the roof. More hard moves now lead to large finishing holds and a stake belay.

⋆⋆ Tempting Truancy　40 feet　E4 5c †　　　　(9.9.86)
Sustained climbing up the wall 10 feet left of *Aubergine*, with a poorly-protected lower half.

About 200 feet west of *The Conger* is an obvious depression in the cliff. Below this point is a small ledge just above the sea with a flake crack rising up from it; this is *Aubergine*. Abseil to the ledge from large nuts, backed up by a small stake 20 feet to the east.

Aubergine　40 feet　Very Severe 5a　　　　(1.3.70)
An unusual climb at this grade for Swanage. With increasing difficulty but perfect protection, climb the crack to the top.

Armed Insurgence　40 feet　E2 5c †　　　　(15.4.84)
Start 15 feet right of *Aubergine*. A runner was preplaced on the final moves for the first ascent.
Climb the wall using small pockets to a short, horizontal crack. Move up and slightly right over bulging rock to a 'dinner-plate' and finish up the steep headwall above. Stake belay.

A ramp-line right of *Armed Insurgence* was climbed and well named **Totally Insignificant and of Unparalleled Mediocrity** (8.9.86), though this is totally insignificant now that it has fallen down.

Whack Your Porcupine　40 feet　Hard Very Severe 5a　　(8.9.86)
Start at a groove to the right of a cluster of small roofs.
Climb the groove and finish leftwards. Nut and *Friend* belays.

That Disillusioned Feeling When You See Your Jumper Disappear Beneath the Waves　40 feet　Very Severe 4b　(6.9.86)
The easy-angled groove 20 feet right of the small roofs leads to a nut belay.

Ruurd Ruum 50 feet E3 5c †   (8.9.86)
Start 30 feet right of the small roofs. High in the grade. Low tide required.
Climb a slightly rightward-trending crack and finish up a groove on the
right.

Leap of Faith 50 feet E3 5c   (6.93)
Start at the large corner around the buttress from *Ruurd Ruum*.
Pull up onto the small ledge on the left and continue up the arête on
pockets. Move leftwards around the bulge and continue to the top.

Tsunami 50 feet E4 6b †   (6.93)
Climb the large corner for 10 feet (as for the next route) before
moving onto the left wall. Climb the wall and pull over the roof on
delicate jugs (the crux). A short corner leads to the top. Stake belay
immediately.

A Bridge Too Far 70 feet Hard Very Severe 5a   (9.79)
Start at the large corner.
Climb the corner to the roof and step down rightwards to a foothold on
the arête. Bridge 'too far' across the chimney and continue rightwards to
finish as for *The Conger*. Multiple-*Friend* belays.

Zawn Yawn 40 feet Very Severe 4c   (8.9.86)
Start as for *A Bridge Too Far*.
Traverse right at low level, climb the chimney, and continue rightwards to
finish as for *The Conger*. Multiple-*Friend* belays.

The wall to the right is climbed by **Crime Wave** (45 feet E1 5b † 6.93).

★ **Furious Pig** 40 feet E2 5c   (3.89)
A unique and rather atmospheric route. Abseil down the undercut pillar
immediately left of *The Conger* to a hanging belay five feet above the sea,
at the bottom of a completely undercut arête.
Above are two slight grooves. Climb the left-hand groove to a large block
on the left. Layback a flake on the right to the finish of *The Conger*.
Multiple-*Friend* belays.

★ **The Great Shark Hunt** 40 feet E4 6a   (3.89)
Start as for *Furious Pig*.
Swing rightwards across the overhanging wall and pull up into the right-
hand groove. Follow it steeply to the finish of *The Conger*. Multiple-*Friend*
belays.

★★★ **The Conger** 100 feet E2 5c   (7.9.69/9.79)
An outlandish and weirdly atmospheric climb across the lip of the sea-
cave to the west of the main ledge. A route that should definitely not be
missed. A perfect deep-water solo. During winter the slabs are usually wet
and the climb is out of condition as a result. From the main ledge, traverse

along the sea-level fault beneath the west-facing wall and belay in a niche just before the sea-cave.
Continue the sea-level traverse for 15 feet to a smaller niche and climb a short, greasy chimney to gain the hanging slabs. Cross these slabs until stopped by a smooth wall. Make a hard move (crux) to pull around into the bottomless chimney. Move up to large holds at the top of the chimney and bridge across to more good holds. Pull across, go around the arête, and continue up left over compact but brittle rock. Multiple *Friend* belay.
Variations

★ **Snap Crackle and Plop** 90 feet E3 5c   (11.9.90)
A direct finish to *The Conger*. 'Deserves a star for sheer thrill power.'
Follow *The Conger* to the bottomless chimney; continue straight up the overhanging wall on brittle flakes and deep pockets until a large spike can be used to finish.

★ **Jellied** 90 feet E3 5c.   (3.8.90)
An exciting right-hand finish to *The Conger* which has some friable rock.
Follow *The Conger* to the bottomless chimney and pull up to jugs. Traverse rightwards over the huge roof to emerge on the jutting prow. Exit easily.

★★★ **Swordfish Trombones** 60 feet E5 6b   (27.9.87/1989)
Bizarre climbing in wild positions.
Climb the initial chimney of *The Conger* and step left to the slab. Go up left onto a small trapezoidal slab. Swing right and pull up to a niche, and cross the large roof to good holds on the lip. Pull around with difficulty and finish easily up a leftward-leading slab. Belays low on the right, supplemented by stakes up to the right.

★ **The Musharagi Tree** 70 feet E2 5c   (1.8.88)
Start in the niche as for *The Conger*.
Climb the bulging arête and flake left of the niche on pockets and finish up the final corner of *Halcyon Days*. Alternatively, for a more amenable (E1) outing, start by trending right from the slab of *The Conger*.

★ **Halcyon Days** 75 feet E1 5b   (9.79)
A worthwhile route which is high in the grade, having an intimidating but well-protected crux. Unfortunately, the initial groove is often wet. Start as for *The Conger*.
Climb the overhanging groove to an awkward resting-place, and continue up the corner-crack above. Stake belay well back to the right.

   Herman Borg's Basic Pulley Slippage (70 feet E5 6c 1993)
   takes the left arête of the west-facing wall and the leaning scoop above, but employs a bolt in this bolt-free zone. The bolt has since been removed.

★★★ **Freeborn Man** 70 feet E4 6a   (8.79)
A brilliant pitch, sparsely protected but on some of the best rock at

Swanage. The deep, watery landing provides some security if one is faced with an all-out disaster. Start on the sea-level fault on the right-hand side of the west-facing wall.

Traverse left and pull up from the sea-level fault. Step left and climb easily to the left-hand end of a horizontal flake. Follow a line of superb finger pockets diagonally right and move up with difficulty to a large pocket on the lip of the small overhang. Swing left to another pocket and make further hard moves to pull over onto the slab above. Finish easily and belay well back at a stake.

Troubled Waters   70 feet   Hard Very Severe   5a   (15.7.85)
A virtually unprotected eliminate up the concave wall a few feet right of *Freeborn Man*. Escapable at half height but high in the grade. Start as for *Freeborn Man*.

Traverse left along the sea-level fault and pull onto the slab. Climb rightwards until below the pocketed bulge near the right-hand edge of the wall. Launch up to gain a short layback crack and pull around onto the *Helix* slab, which is followed to the top. Stake belay well back.

Helix Arête   50 feet   Hard Very Severe   5a
Climb the arête that bisects the line of *Helix*.

FISHERMAN'S EAST
A descent of the slab and steep, juggy wall of *Helix* (Difficult) leads to the western end of the main ledge. Just to the east lies a tiered maze of projecting roofs that jut out to create a formidable barrier across the back of the bay. On the left-hand side of this, *Paternoster* climbs out of a small niche while, to the right, *Squid* tackles the distinctive roof-crack below the widest part of the overhangs. Further right the roofs peter out next to a stark, white wall: the testing *Limited Edition*, now running to a second edition after a rock-fall hereabouts, still takes a direct line up this wall. Further to the right, past the latest incarnation of the *Aquascrotum* corner, *Vigilante* permits a mean passage up a smooth wall.

To continue eastwards necessitates clambering up onto two huge boulders, walking round the corner below the bulging arête of *Ringworm*, and descending to the foot of an overhanging crack: *The Impending Gleam* powers its way through the bulges above. The large cave beyond forms the vaults of the highly impressive *The Mind Cathedral*. This cave can be crossed at very low tide to reach the flat *Calcitron* wall, the eastern side of which is terminated by a smooth sided zawn and the end of the scrambling. A 6a traverse can be made above the zawn to reach The Promenade.

** **Helix**   50 feet   Difficult
A delightful excursion with a surprising degree of exposure. Start at the extreme western end of the main ledge, just before the cliff turns a right-angled corner.

The initial black wall is littered with glorious holds. Climb the wall, aiming

for a good ledge on the arête. Traverse to a corner on the left and follow a superbly situated slab past a rusty quarryman's stake to easier ground above. Stake belay far back.
Variation (50 feet Very Difficult). Climb the prominent crack in the west-facing wall to reach the ledge. Finish up the left edge of the slab.

Felix   50 feet   Very Difficult
Start just right of a wide crack.
Climb up the black wall on big holds and follow the slabby corner above to the top. Stake belay over to the right.

Rough Boys   60 feet   Hard Very Severe   5a/b   (4.8.84)
Some good, well-protected climbing but escapable at two-thirds height.
Start 10 feet right of the wide crack.
Climb the black wall on huge holds to a ledge. Take the corner above to a ledge on the left and finish steeply up a crack. Stake belay.

★ **Bon Firé**   60 feet   E2 5c †   (4.89)
Start, as for *Rough Boys*, 10 feet right of the wide crack.
Climb the black wall on huge holds to a ledge. Traverse right to a crack and go up to the left-hand end of the large roof above the hanging slab.
Move onto the headwall and traverse 15 feet right to a big hold. Continue direct on flakes and finish leftwards.

★ **The Wey of All Men**   90 feet   E3 †   (25.3.89)
Well protected but high in the grade. Start, as for *Rough Boys*, 10 feet right of the wide crack.
1   40 feet   4c. Climb up to clear the overhang and traverse right just above its lip to a slab. Continue rightwards to belay near the end of the slab.
2   50 feet   6a. Climb the roof-crack with difficulty to good holds.
Continue direct via a thin crack to the top. Stake belay.

★★ **Mayhem on the Terraces**   380 feet   E3 †   (6.7.87-25.10.87)
A girdle of Fisherman's East, at just below half height, from *Rough Boys* to the finishing groove of *The Impending Gleam*. (The first three pitches can be combined with the second pitch of *Squid* to give a highly recommended E2.) Pitch 6 has suffered a rockfall and has **not been reclimbed**.
1   40 feet   4c. Climb up until just past the first ledge on *Rough Boys* before moving right and down onto a slab. Cross it rightwards until stopped by a short wall. Stance on foot-ledges.
2   30 feet   5b. Traverse the overhung and undercut wall to a small ledge, the belay of *The Ritz*.
3   30 feet   5b. Traverse with hands at ledge-level around an undercut prow to the belay of *Squid*.
4   30 feet   5c. Step right and go down under a roof, reversing part of *Crackers*, and then go rightwards to a stance in the corner. Belay on large *Friends* above. (Back-rope advisable for second.)

5 70 feet 6a. Traverse right past an old peg runner to a resting-place on the left-hand side of a huge block. Continue with spaced out protection to a peg runner on *Limited Edition*. Step down and around the corner to belay.
6 30 feet 5a ††. The large overhang has 'calved', leaving a similar feature 10 feet higher. The original description may well require no change: 'undercling the roof above to gain the corner of *Aquascrotum*.'
7 40 feet 5c. Move down; follow the break rightwards for 30 feet across a smooth wall and belay on *Sue's Route*.
8 70 feet 5b. Take care with rope-drag on this pitch. Descend below the roof half-way across the bay and turn the arête as for *Ringworm*. Traverse around another arête and then more easily to reach an overhanging arête with a jutting ledge. Swing around on this to the steep groove of *The Impending Gleam*. Aerial belay.
9 40 feet 5a. Climb the groove to a sound finish. Stake belay.

★ **Quo Vadis Direct**   90 feet   E2 5c †   (1.3.79/1981)
An interesting pitch up the buttress left of *Paternoster*. Start just left of *Paternoster*. These two routes are invariably greasy low down; they prove much easier when dry.
1 30 feet 5c. Go up and pull through the first roof at a niche. Traverse left between the roofs to below a short groove (peg runner high up). Move up onto the slab above to belay.
2 60 feet 5a/b. Hand-traverse right a few moves before breaking through the overhang. Move up left onto an arête and climb to the start of an open groove. Follow this groove, surmount the final overhang, and continue to the top. Stake belay.

★ **Paternoster**   100 feet   E2   (30.5.76)
A notorious HVS in the early days, it has a surprisingly awkward first pitch. Start just right of two vertical cracks.
1 70 feet 5b. Climb up to a small niche beneath a roof before swinging left and moving up into a chimney. Move up around a corner on the right to a cramped resting-spot and continue up the square-cut groove. Traverse left beneath the roof for 10 feet and climb another (wider) square-cut groove. Exit left at the top onto a small stance.
2 30 feet 5a. Climb the groove above to finish on loose rock. Stake belay to the right.

★ **Bad Young Brother**   100 feet   E4 6b †   (28.5.88)
Start as for *Paternoster*.
Gain the small niche and move leftwards over the crucial roof (two *in-situ* threads) to gain the groove on *Paternoster*. Climb strenuously over the bulges above (peg runner) to good holds and then up twin cracks just to the left. Continue straight to the top via the large flake and crack above (*in-situ* thread). Stake belay.

★★★ **The Ritz**   100 feet   E3   (11.78)
An improbable line, giving a well-protected classic. Start as for *Paternoster*.

1 50 feet 5a/b. Gain the small niche, step right, and pull into a chimney. Swing right along the roof and climb a groove to the next roof; layback this to an improbable perched stance. Large nut belays.
2 50 feet 6a. Cross the roof using a crack on the right and join *Squid*: step left onto the arête, climb a corner, and continue to a stake belay.

★ **Squid**   115 feet   E2   (6.8.67/1975)
A fun route with the difficulties confined to a short struggle around the lip of the main roof. Extend the protection at this point to avoid rope-drag on the top section. On the right-hand side of the overhung bay is a west-facing wall; start here at a diagonal crack.
1 50 feet 4c. Follow the crack up leftwards to a sloping ledge beneath a small roof. Ascend the small chimney to the left and step right to a good ledge.
2 65 feet 5c. Climb out across the roof on jams and pull up into a short chimney below another large roof. Traverse left past a small corner to the arête (optional belay). Climb the corner above to a stake belay at the top.

Crackers   100 feet   E3 †   (9.79)
Lack of protection on the second pitch makes this a serious route. Start as for *Squid*.
1 40 feet 5b. Climb the blind groove above the start of *Squid*. Exit left at the top before moving up and left to belay as for *Squid*.
2 60 feet 5c. Move left and up around a small prow and continue rightwards to below a groove. Make a weird move over the roof to enter this short groove and finish straight up. Stake belay over to the left.

★ **Mental as Anything**   100 feet   E4 6b †   (22.12.87)
The huge double roof right of *Crackers* requires long reaches and wild heel-hooking. Highly exposed.
Climb past a big ledge and go leftwards up a shallow groove to a blocky overhang (two *in-situ* threads). Pull over the next roof to good holds in a scoop, undercut 5 feet rightwards, and cross the top roof to more good holds. Finish up the corner's cracked right wall. Stake belay.

Rock around the Block   100 feet   E2 †   (29.11.87)
Start at the left-hand end of the rock pool, at a groove. Mostly large *Friends* and nuts required.
1 70 feet 5c. Climb easily to a ledge and then up to the roofs. Traverse right past a poor peg runner to a chimney and go up a short wall with difficulty to a block roof. Traverse right to the end of the block and pull up on top of it.
2 30 feet 5a. Step left into a bottomless, overhanging corner. Pull out of it, step left, and continue to the top. Stake belay.

Rock around the Block Direct   90 feet   E3 6a   (15.2.88)
From the start of *Rock around the Block*, climb rightwards and up the

chimney to rejoin the original route. Take the block roof direct via the crack on its left side and continue to the top. Stake belay.

My Wildest Dreams   90 feet   E4   6a †   (3.4.88)
Varied and exciting. Start midway between *Rock around the Block* and *Sting in the Tail*. The climb has been affected slightly by rockfall near the top and a flake has loosened somewhat.
Step over the rock-pool and climb the blank wall to a square roof at the base of a huge block (*in-situ* thread). Go up the smooth groove on the right and over a roof to a hollow flake (*in-situ* thread). Continue through a large overhang (*in-situ* thread) to a rest on the right and finish up the blunt arête. Stake belay.

Sting in the Tail   90 feet   E4   5c   (11.7.86)
Start on the right-hand side of the rock-pool. Very marginal protection. Climb to a roof, up the flake crack on its left-hand side, and up the wall on the right. Gain the ledge from the right (vital *Friend $1\frac{1}{2}$*). Continue up over a roof to the base of a corner. Move right at two-thirds height to flakes and finish left up the corner (poor peg runner). Stake belays.

** **Limited Edition**   80 feet   E4   5c/6a   (17.5.80)
A superb pitch giving difficult climbing up the centre of the prominent white face. The initial and middle sections of the route have been altered by rockfall. Start by a tiny rock-pool.
Climb easily up a shallow sentry-box via a flake to a small roof. Rock over rightwards onto a jug with difficulty and climb up rightwards to a resting-place beneath a shallow right-facing corner (old peg runner on the left). Ascend the corner to its capping roof, pull out left onto the headwall, and continue up to a slight groove (peg runner). Continue to the top and belay on a stake.

Aquascrotum II   60 feet   Hard Very Severe   5a †   (12.2.67)
At the eastern end of the main sea-level platform, two huge boulders form a higher ledge. This route climbed the obvious seaward-facing corner above the boulders, before moving steeply left to avoid a bulge at the top. A sizeable fall at half height has altered this corner yet again. (*Aquascrotum III*?) Beware loose rock.

* **Vigilante**   60 feet   E5   6b   (3.4.88)
A sustained and bold route which requires many small wires and small *Friends*. The grade presupposes that the first of the two peg runners, which has snapped off, is replaced. In addition, both ascents to date have employed an *in-situ* nut at 20 feet.
From the large boulders, climb directly up the centre of the blank wall, finishing slightly left near the top. Stake belay.

Sue's Route   60 feet   E1   5b   (1968)
A good route, awkward to protect and with a few technical surprises.

Start 20 feet right of the corner of *Aquascrotum II* from a high ledge.
Move up to a ledge at 6 feet and ascend the thin crack above to another
ledge. Continue up the crack with increasing difficulty until some good
flakes can be reached, and then continue to the top. Poor stake belay over
to the left.

★ **Girl from the Snow Country**   60 feet   E1   5c   (3.4.88)
Start as for *Sue's Route*.
Climb a diagonal flake rightwards onto a slab on *Ringworm*. Pull over the
roof and follow a pocketed calcite vein to the top. Stake belay.

Ringworm   80 feet   Hard Very Severe   5b †   (10.7.77)
Start on the high ledge below an undercut leftward-slanting slab.
Pull over the overhang and climb up the slab to a second overhang. Move
right and turn the arête with difficulty. Traverse 10 feet further right to
another arête and a resting-place. Continue steeply up on good holds in
honeycomb rock to the top. Stake belay.

★ **All Quiet on the Southern Front**   70 feet   E3   5c   (20.6.87)
Start from the end of the high ledge. Poorly protected.
Climb over a bulge, past a spike, and up the face to a jammed block.
Trend slightly right to a clean exit. Stake belay.

The following climbs as far as *The Beautiful and the Damned* all require low
water and a calm sea. They start in a large cave.

★ **The Impending Gleam**   80 feet   E4   5c   (1983)
Strenuous, sustained, and well-protected climbing on good rock
throughout. Unfortunately the initial section is often wet. Start beneath the
prominent crack on the western edge of the big cave.
Climb the overhanging right arête to gain a niche below the roof. Pull out
over this and continue up the steep groove above to a sound finish. Stake
belay.

★ **Temple Redneck**   100 feet   E6 †   (21.2.93)
This impressive route up the arête on the left side of the cave has good
rock and a sensational crux. Take wires to supplement the six bolt runners
and *in-situ* thread.
1 80 feet 6c. Climb a steep, shallow groove in the arête and then pull
up right to a rail. Head diagonally leftwards close to the arête on hidden
incuts to meet the large roof (*in-situ* thread). Swing left to a no-hands rest.
Continue across the overhang and diagonally leftwards up a sustained
leaning wall to the belay alcove of *The Mind Cathedral*. Belay on wires
and an *in-situ* thread.
2 20 feet 5a. *The Mind Cathedral* pitch 2.

★★★ The Mind Cathedral   110 feet   E6 †   (21.5.88)

An awesome line through the roof of a huge cave, though it is not known to have been climbed since a key flake was pulled off. Start at the wide chimney on the left side of the cave.

1 90 feet 6b. Climb the chimney (*in-situ* thread) and move out right onto the hanging right wall. Launch up the forty-five degree overhanging groove to the apex of the cave and climb out using flakes to a handrail (*in-situ* thread). Follow this (*in-situ* thread) to a niche on the lip. Intergalactic belay on wires and an *in-situ* thread.

2 20 feet 5a. Climb straight up the headwall. Stake belay.

The left wall of the back of the cave is the start of a hard bolted project.

★★★ Palace of the Brine   100 feet   E7 6c S †   (21.9.91)

'The best single pitch I've ever done!' said the first ascensionist. A magnificent hard line which arcs out through the roof of the cave. Twelve bolt runners and a peg runner show the way. Start on a ledge in the right-hand corner of the cave, beneath a blank wall.

Climb the wall, trending right to a sloping crack, and then diagonally rightwards to near the top of a flake-line; follow this to a semi-rest at the roof. Lean out and crucifix to jugs at the start of the main groove in the roof. Jams, a weird bridge, undercuts, and free swings all lead towards the lip. Pass under a dip on better holds and then lock for glory on good flakes. Ascend a short wall to a clean-cut exit, the belay stakes, and convalescence.

★★ Drunken Butterfly   80 feet   E6 6b/c S †   (25.3.93)

The wildly overhanging groove in the roof left of *Paparazzi News*. Start at a nut belay in an alcove at 25 feet on the right wall of the cave. One peg and seven bolt runners.

Move up left and then directly up the face to the base of the groove. Climb diagonally leftwards up the severely overhanging sidewall to a no-hands rest in an aven. Undercut powerfully leftwards to the lip and a huge jug. A short groove leads to a stake belay.

★ Paparazzi News   90 feet   E6 6b †   (17.2.88)

This climbs the shallow groove topped by big roofs 10 feet left of *Cave Rave*. Follow an easy flake to a ledge and climb the blank groove to undercuts. Power 10 feet right, almost to the arête, and go directly through the roofs into a shallow groove. Move up to jugs and swing left to a large exit corner. Stake belay.

★★ Cave Rave   80 feet   E5 6a   (14.11.87)

Spacebound but relatively safe. Start 15 feet left of the deep chimney on the right-hand side of the cave, from a small ledge at 20 feet.

Climb the groove with increasing difficulty and go through the roofs. Clip an *in-situ* thread at the top roof and swing left for 5 feet to an exit corner (peg runner). Stake belay.

The Beautiful and the Damned   75 feet   E5 6a   (12.6.88)
Start as for *Cave Rave*. A serious start and finish.
Step right to a shallow groove and climb boldly up to jugs and a peg
runner. Pull over the roof and go up a short hard groove to an *in-situ*
thread on *Cave Rave*. Move rightwards at the top roof to good holds (*in-situ* thread) and pull over to a cleaned finish. Stake belay.

The next seven routes all start from a ledge which is most easily gained by
abseil. The abseil stake is located immediately west of the rocky outcrops
beneath the cliff-top pylons. (Alternatively, at low tide, traverse east from
The Mind Cathedral cave.)

D Sharp   80 feet   Hard Very Severe 5b †   (10.2.80)
On the eastern arête of *The Mind Cathedral* cave is a deep chimney with a
groove to the right. Start from the ledge, beneath the groove.
Follow the groove for 40 feet to a niche below the overhangs. Around the
arête to the right is a series of cracks. Climb these, which have had four
unnecessary *in-situ* threads since the advent of *Test Department*, and
continue up flaky rock to the top. Stake belay.

★ **Test Department**   80 feet   E1 5b   (10.7.86)
Between *The Mind Cathedral* cave and the narrow zawn at the end of
Fisherman's Ledge is a flat wall. This route, up the left side of the wall, is
quite sustained and technical for its grade.
Move up rightwards onto the front face and climb it (three *in-situ* thread
runners) to join *D Sharp*. Continue up deep cracks harbouring four more
in-situ threads and finish up a flaky wall. Stake belay.

★ **Damage Case**   80 feet   E3 5c   (11.7.86)
Start at the straight crack right of *Test Department*.
Follow the crack with difficulty to a widening at 30 feet. Keep following it
past six *in-situ* thread runners to a flaky wall and a stake belay.

★ **Calcitron**   80 feet   E2 5b   (11.7.86)
The crack in the middle of the flat wall. The rock has an uninspiring
appearance but it gives sustained and enjoyable climbing with good
protection.
Climb the leftward-trending crack (*in-situ* thread) and then an overhang
into a small groove (*in-situ* thread). Follow a finger-ramp rightwards and
finish straight up a juggy crack (*in-situ* thread) to a final slab. Stake belay.

Rock Widow   90 feet   Hard Very Severe 5a   (24.4.76)
At the extreme eastern end of Fisherman's Ledge is a niche overlooking an
overhung zawn. Start here.
Ten feet to the left of the stance is a shallow groove. Climb this for a few
feet and traverse left until below a corner just before the arête. Climb up
steeply into the corner and ascend it to the top. Belay on nuts and threads
well back towards the fence.

Concubine   90 feet   E1   (25.4.76)
Start as for *Rock Widow*.
1 50 feet 5a. Ten feet to the left of the stance is a shallow groove. Climb
this groove strenuously and surmount a bulge. Move into the chimney and
follow it to a belay in the cave above.
2 40 feet 4c. Traverse out left around the west arête to a slab and
groove, which are climbed to the top. Belay on nuts and threads well over
the top.

Clever Dick   35 feet   E1 5c †   (28.8.89)
Start at the extreme eastern end of Fisherman's Ledge, next to an
overhung zawn.
Climb down to clear the roof and undercut strenuously into the cave.
Traverse more easily rightwards to the first stance of *Benny*, and finish up
that route.

THE PROMENADE
An interesting section of cliff, above a wide platform that is awash in rough
seas. This platform, The Promenade, runs along the bottom of the entire area
and can be easily identified when viewed from the top of Cattle Troughs 100
yards or so to the east. Despite, or perhaps because of the impressive barrier
of roofs that adorn The Promenade, a large number of new Extremes have
been climbed here. However, the area has a good selection of routes of
all standards which deserve greater popularity.

To the west of Cattle Troughs, past the depressions in the cliff that give the
descent routes into The Jumble and Flake Ledge, is a tiny quarry, Chilmark
Quarry. This is situated above the eastern end of The Promenade. The western limit of The Promenade is marked by two large, white pylons on the cliff-
top.

For the approach, see the introduction to The Cattle Troughs Area (page
110).

PROMENADE WEST
On the traverse west from *Danglefoot* several awkward moves are required
to cross a narrow zawn to an obvious chimney, *Revelation Chimney*. A short
distance further on, *Winking Wall* attacks a weakness in the overhangs. The
next eye-catcher is the uncompromising roof-crack of *Godfodder* before The
Promenade comes to a final abrupt halt at a smooth-sided zawn. A continuously surprising expedition, *Benny*, disappears into the depths of this zawn
before eventually reappearing out of a big hole in the face above. In order to
stay dry while continuing westwards from The Promenade into Fisherman's
Ledge it is necessary to cross the wall above the zawn of *Benny*: this is *The
Eastern Traverse*.

The Eastern Traverse   25 feet   5c   (1987)
This short trip starts at the western end of the ledge at a deep zawn which

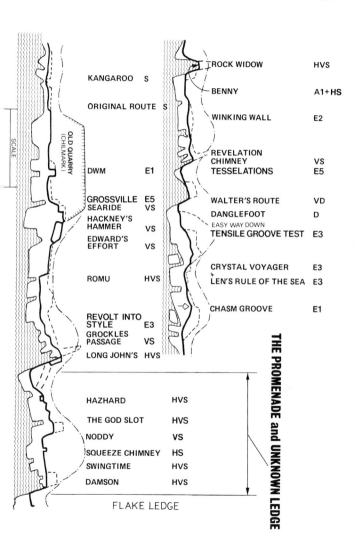

KANGAROO S

ORIGINAL ROUTE S

OLD QUARRY (CHILMARK)

SCALE

DWM E1

GROSSVILLE E5
SEARIDE VS

HACKNEY'S HAMMER VS

EDWARD'S EFFORT VS

ROMU HVS

REVOLT INTO STYLE E3

GROCKLES PASSAGE VS

LONG JOHN'S HVS

ROCK WIDOW HVS

BENNY A1+HS

WINKING WALL E2

REVELATION CHIMNEY VS
TESSELATIONS E5

WALTER'S ROUTE VD

DANGLEFOOT D

EASY WAY DOWN
TENSILE GROOVE TEST E3

CRYSTAL VOYAGER E3

LEN'S RULE OF THE SEA E3

CHASM GROOVE E1

THE PROMENADE and UNKNOWN LEDGE

HAZHARD HVS

THE GOD SLOT HVS

NODDY VS

SQUEEZE CHIMNEY HS

SWINGTIME HVS

DAMSON HVS

FLAKE LEDGE

forms a sea-cave. Protected by a chunky peg runner. The return trip (from east to west) is 6a.

Crimes against the Soul   70 feet   E5 6a †   (8.4.89)
A steep problem which is quite bold. Start as for *The Eastern Traverse*.
Pull onto the wall above the sea-cave as for *The Eastern Traverse* (peg runner). Climb diagonally right along a slanting wall to the main overhang and a vital, blind *Hex 7* placement on the lip. Cross the overhang to reach jugs and move leftwards with difficulty (bolt runner) into a V-groove. Climb the groove on good holds past a large *in-situ* thread to easy ledges. Nut belay. Scramble off to the right.

*** **Benny**   180 feet   A1 + Hard Severe   (24.4.76)
Weird and wonderful. A surreal, unique, and committing expedition into the depths of a hidden zawn. Best savoured on a hot summer's day. Calm seas are required, however, together with a degree of caution, as this climb has been the scene of a fatality, a rescue, and several duckings. The aided entry traverse is on *in-situ* slings supplemented by some nuts; pegs need not be carried. Start at the far western end of The Promenade on the edge of a smooth sided zawn.
1 40 feet A1. Step down onto the side wall of the zawn and traverse along this to a rock bridge below a huge chimney at the back.
2 60 feet. Climb up the chimney on large holds, move out at the top, and belay in the cave mouth.
3 80 feet. Step out of the cave and traverse right with difficulty to the east arête. Follow a ledge leading right to easy ground and move up to a drilled-thread belay or the stile beyond.

Hot to Trot   70 feet   E5 6c S †   (19.6.94)
Start about 10 feet right of the zawn. Seven bolts, a peg, and two *in-situ* threads.
Cross the boulder-problem roof and climb the bulging, white wall and the rib above to two lower-off bolts. Starting via the bottomless sentry-box on the left is 'only' 6b, but involves hideous body-wedges and head-bars!

** **The Gangster Lean**   80 feet   E3 5c S   (22.7.86)
Starting 20 feet to the right of *Benny*, this climbs the undercut, bulging wall. Seven bolts and two *in-situ* threads.
Break through the roof at a narrowing and go diagonally left. Climb through bulging rock to a good crack below the right-hand side of a prominent roof. Bypass the roof to the right and go up a leftward-leading ramp, to finish up the blunt arête. Two lower-off bolts.

* **Seppukku**   80 feet   E3 5c   (3.89)
This good pitch climbs straight up from the start of *The Gangster Lean*.
Layback through a narrowing in the initial roof and pull over another to a big jug. Surmount the next roof on jugs to reach undercuts in the final overhang (*in-situ* thread). Move left to the base of a thin crack in a vague

rib; climb this (crux) protected by small wires to large holds and a good slot. Continue more easily on incuts to the top where small wires protect a careful rightwards exit. Belay to a preplaced rope tied to the stile.

★ **Chicago Peace** 80 feet E3 6a † (31.1.87)
A technically sustained route starting from the large niche 15 feet right of *Seppukku*.
Step leftwards out of the niche and pull through the bulge. Trend rightwards with difficulty over bulges to a peg runner. Climb the left-facing groove to the top. Poor belays up the slope.

★ **J J Burnell, King of the Bass** 80 feet E2 5b † (7.4.89)
An enjoyable, well-cleaned pitch starting from the large niche.
Climb easily rightwards up a slab to a narrowing in the roof. Layback over on large holds to a horizontal break (runners on the left). Step up right onto a small ledge and continue direct on more big holds to a clean-cut exit. Stake belay.

Just Another Victim 35 feet E6 6b *S* † (10.6.94)
The hanging roof-crack 15 feet left of *Godfodder* is easy - for its grade! Five bolt runners.
Pull over the roof to enter a short groove. Lean out to a rail before embarking upon the main roof-crack. Cunning footwork and a hidden jug should see you to the lip, whereupon easy climbing leads to two lower-off bolts.

★ **Godfodder** 90 feet E6 † (27.5.91)
The 15-foot roof-crack in the overhung bay is a superb, well-protected proposition.
1 50 feet 6c. Climb the pillar in the centre of the bay past an *in-situ* thread to the roof-crack. Make an intricate series of moves to jugs over the lip. Belay on a foot-ledge on the lip using a deep crack up to the right.
2 40 feet 4b. Trend rightwards up an easy but sparsely-protected wall to a clean-cut finish. Stake belay.

The bolts to the right protect an uncompleted project.

A Boschboy, a Trad, and a Funky Dredd
70 feet E3 6b † (14.4.91)
A boulder-problem crux safeguarded by *in-situ* gear is followed by an easy but run-out section.
Start as for *Winking Wall* up a diagonal crack. Now launch straight over the roof (bolt runner) on a hidden one-finger hold to reach a good hold in the form of a spike (bolt runner). Continue up the wall, trending leftwards to a clean-cut exit as for *Godfodder*. Stake belay.

Winking Wall 80 feet E2 6a † (10.4.77/6.6.84)
An unbalanced route, with a disconcerting and insecure crux. Start

midway between the overhung bay and *Revelation Chimney* at a leftward-slanting crack.
Follow the crack and then pull steeply up to a horizontal fault. Traverse right to the break in the overhangs and climb this past a poor peg runner to gain the shallow groove above. Ascend the groove to a suspect flake, step right, and continue on good holds to the top. Stake belay above.

Magnesian Days (80 feet E2 6a † 26.4.86) follows *Winking Wall* until just past its peg; it then traverses 10 feet right to a slabby prow and climbs straight up to an exit crack. Stake belay.

Empowerless   30 feet   E4 6b S   (29.8.94)
Start 5 feet right of *Winking Wall*. Four bolts and a peg protect this short, sharp problem up the wall and over the roof. Two lower-off bolts on the slab.

★ **Revelation Chimney**   80 feet   Very Severe 4c   (28.3.76)
This tackles the unmistakable smooth sided chimney above the narrow zawn 60 feet west of *Danglefoot*.
Climb a short slab on the left side of the zawn to small ledges. Ascend the chimney above, move out to the lip, and climb a crack and flakes to the top. Stake belay above a rock step. (The original start up the steep south-facing wall is harder.)

The west-facing wall by *Revelation Chimney* has two routes.

★ **Waves Become Wings**   70 feet   E5 6b S †   (19.6.94)
A clear, crisp day is needed for success on this very sustained line on smooth, compact rock. High in the grade. Eight bolt runners.
Step across the gap and climb the fingery wall to a good jug just above a small roof. Continue over bulges with difficulty to a shallow rightward-leaning groove on *Birth Pains of New Nations*. Finish as for that route by following the groove and the easier wall above to two lower-off bolts.

★ **Birth Pains of New Nations**   80 feet   E6 6b   (8.10.86)
A superb yet serious pitch. The lowest bolt is badly cracked - as you would be if you were lashed by sea-spray throughout the winter - but there are small wire placements on this initial section. Start in the centre of the face right of *Revelation Chimney*.
Climb up to the bolt runner and then rightwards to a good slot. Move over the bulge to jugs and a peg runner. Continue leftwards over a bulge (blind, committing, and strenuous) and up a vague groove. Continue up an easier wall to two lower-off bolts at the top. Four bolt runners on this section, which is shared with *Waves Become Wings*.

★★ **Tessellations**   80 feet   E5 6b   (10.7.86)
Desperate but with much *in-situ* gear, 'a mosaic piece of intricate

technicality'. Start below the seaward face of the arête right of *Revelation Chimney.*
Climb a rib to a break and swing left (*in-situ* thread) onto the arête. Pull through bulges (three peg runners and bolt runner) to vertical ground. Step right to a flake and continue up the arête (four *in-situ* threads) to the top. Stake belay.

★ **Total Seizure**   45 feet   E6 6c *S* †   (28.11.87/11.6.94)
The original climb, *Seizure*, started as for *Tessalations*. This direct version starts up a groove to the right. Eight bolt runners.
Climb the groove and cross the 8-foot roof. Trend left up the severely bulging wall past a jammed block. Finish in a scoop over the lip, where there are two lower-off bolts.

★ **Solid State Logic**   40 feet   E7 6c *S* †   (12.5.91)
This power climb tackles 20 feet of overhang and has all bolt protection apart from an initial wire. 'So incapacitating it's difficult to breathe between moves.' Start on the left-hand side of an overhung bay.
Climb slightly leftwards up the back of the bay before going out past an unhelpful hanging wall to a better hold. Continue over the final bulges and pull rightwards into a slabby groove. Escape off easily to the right.
Multiple-nut belay backed up by a stake far to the left.

Aerial Pursuit   100 feet   Hard Very Severe   (6.5.84)
Worryingly loose at the top. Start as for *Walter's Route.*
1 20 feet. Climb the crack in the bulge to the amphitheatre.
2 80 feet 5a. Traverse easily below the overhang. Move left with increasing difficulty to gain an obvious but exposed foothold on a small arête. Continue towards a projecting block, surmount it, and climb up until it is possible to cross diagonally right to the base of a shallow groove. Climb the groove to the top. Multiple-nut belay backed up by a stake far to the left.

Walter's Route   40 feet   Very Difficult
Start 20 feet left of *Danglefoot* at the end of the ledge.
Climb up to a ledge, overcome the crack in the bulge, and so gain the amphitheatre. Follow a flake to a drilled-thread belay on the floor of the large ledge.
A variation start up the crack around to the left is usually just as its name suggests: **Greasy Walter** (Hard Very Severe 5b).

PROMENADE EAST
To the east of the *Danglefoot* descent is an overhung bay. *Tensile Groove Test* attempts to sidestep the roofs on the left side of this bay, while *Crystal Voyager* takes off up cracks in the bay's right wall and swings out along a highly exposed handrail. Above the next gap in the platform an impressive crack in an arête tells of *Len's Rule of the Sea* while, beyond, *Chasm Groove* starts out from a small corner below an enormous roof. Further eastwards around a

corner is the black, bulging buttress of *Original Route*, above a narrow, often wave-washed section of the ledge. Next is a slight bay climbed by *DWM* and to the east a large bay offers the interesting *Sea Ride* up its centre. Further on, two severely overhanging sections are split by the west-facing wall of *Sargasso*. Beyond is a cave, the home of *The Futurist*. There then follow a selection of roof lines, with *Howling Stone* crying loudest for attention. The Promenade ends at a deep black cave where *Grockles' Passage* takes an unlikely line for its grade. A short scramble across a zawn and through an arch (if it is still there!) offers easy access to Unknown Ledge.

Danglefoot   40 feet   Difficult
Just to the east of two deep breaks in the sea-level ledge, a short steep wall gives access to the bottom of an easy-angled amphitheatre. This is the line of the descent route.
Move up, traverse 5 feet right, and surmount the bulge, which is easier than it looks, to gain the amphitheatre. Scramble up to a drilled-thread belay on the ledge above.

The Flail Trail   40 feet   Hard Very Severe 5a S   (29.5.85)
The curving prow 15 feet right of *Danglefoot* is a fine little pitch, but did it really need three bolt runners?
Climb the wall just left of the arête to a break at 15 feet and follow the prow diagonally right to reach a handrail. Swing right a few feet and pull over onto the slab using huge solution pockets. Twin-bolt belay.

★ Violent Breed   40 feet   E5 6c †   (19.4.88)
Dynamic, and harder than its neighbour. Start 10 feet right of the left-hand arête of the overhung bay. A wire was preplaced on the first ascent.
Climb up a bottomless chimney. Swing left and climb over the bulges (bolt runner and *in-situ* thread) to jugs at the top.

★ Down in the Sewer   40 feet   E5 6b   (23.5.87)
Start as for *Violent Breed*.
Climb up a bottomless chimney and cross the roof using a jug on the lip. Continue up an overhanging groove with difficulty to the handrail on *Tensile Groove Test*. Swing left, pull up on the jammed flake (*in-situ* thread), and exit on huge pockets.

★★★ Tensile Groove Test   50 feet   E3 6a   (11.10.86)
Start as for *Violent Breed*. Great fun but very strenuous.
Climb to the roof, step right, and go up a corner to the main roof. Hand-traverse back left (crux). Layback up to a hollow flake (*in-situ* thread) and finish over the final roof on pockets.

★★ Crystal Voyager   90 feet   E3 5c   (14.11.76/20.4.80)
A superb pitch, exposed and intimidating. Start on the right-hand side of the overhung bay at cracks leading up to the right-hand end of the lowest of the roofs.

Climb the awkward cracks to a small niche. Traverse right for 5 feet and continue along the prominent 'handrail' formed by a large hanging block. Move straight up the wall to the corner above, surmount the overhang, and climb the groove to the top. Stake belay.

★ Len's Rule of the Sea   70 feet   E3 6a   (2.8.83)

This tackles the overhanging groove in the undercut arête some 25 feet right of *Crystal Voyager*, above a break in the ledge. The initial section is bold and technical; thereafter, the holds improve with progress up the route. Unfortunately, the main difficulties are invariably wet; they have been graded accordingly.

Climb the black corner and traverse right for 5 feet to a good handhold in a tiny bottomless groove. Traverse right again above the lip of the overhang and follow the steep crack to a resting-place in a recess. Pull over the overhang using a large chockstone and continue up the crack to the top.

Volts Discharge   50 feet   E4 6b †   (2.11.86)

The *in-situ* thread runner is now *ex situ*; replace it for the grade to stand. Start a few feet left of *Mr Gymnasia*.

Climb the two roofs a few feet left of *Mr Gymnasia* to reach good holds. Trend left over another roof to an easy exit. Nut Belay.

Mr Gymnasia   50 feet   E4 6a †   (16.6.85)

Twenty feet east of *Len's Rule of the Sea* is a slight trench in the rock platform with a jammed boulder to seaward. The fault which formed the trench continues as a very thin crack in the bulging wall; start here. A strenuous pitch but on perfect rock.

Climb rightwards with difficulty through the initial bulge. Continue straight up past an obscured *Friend* placement (still difficult) to reach good holds at half height. Climb on more easily to finish just left of the runnel. Continue up the amphitheatre to a stake belay on the left.

Load It for Me   50 feet   E4 6b/c †   (4.10.86)

A dynamic route with a hard start and a bold upper section which has ground-fall potential from 30 feet. Although the first peg runner was preclipped on the first ascent, this apparently does not affect the grade. Start 6 feet right of *Mr Gymnasia*.

Climb the crux roof (peg runner) to better holds (peg runner). Continue slightly rightwards and up the runnel to the top. Stake belay on the left.

The Garage Mechanic   40 feet   E6 6c S †   (10.5.93)

Start just left of a small pool. Five bolt runners. A powerful roof-problem with a pleasant top wall.

Undercut out to a good edge, from which cunning static moves lead over the lip to better holds. Continue more easily up the bulging wall to two lower-off bolts.

★ **Coming in a R-U-S-H**   50 feet   E4 6c †   (21.2.87)
Start beneath the groove of *Chasm Groove*. A very hard start coupled with an exposed upper section.
Jump up to clip an *in-situ* thread runner at the lip, and then boulder out the initial roof. Follow *Chasm Groove* to the second overhang before traversing rightwards above the large roof to a poor peg runner in a shallow groove. Move up to a break and go rightwards to finish more easily. Stake belay.

Chasm Groove   60 feet   E1 5b   (19.4.69)
On the left-hand side of a colossal roof is a diamond-shaped rock-pool. Start beneath this roof, in a small corner to the right of the pool. Move up the corner and traverse left along the lip of the overhang until above the rock-pool. Place a peg for protection and climb the groove above, exiting left up a short slab. Peg belay.
Direct Start (6a/b † 1987). A boulder-problem up the hanging arête to the left of the normal start.

Although it remains unclimbed, the huge roof does serve a purpose apart from fuelling double-figure E-grade dreams: it provides protection from the rain for boulder-problems on the short backwall. This afternoon suntrap has four problems and a traverse. Spotter essential!

Ride the Lightning (80 feet E3 6c † 3.93) starts 20 feet right of the initial corner of *Chasm Groove*; sustained climbing at low levels leads rightwards to the arête. **Juggernaut** (15 feet E3 6c † 3.93) climbs the large overhang (no, not the huge one!) past two jugs. Jump off from the second jug after a committing crux. Five feet to the right is **Jack-knife** (20 feet E3 6b/c † 3.93), another committing problem. Climb leftwards past a pod and a sidepull to a flake before swinging left to a jug on *Juggernaut*. Jump off. Fifteen feet left of the seaward arête is a shallow, rightward-leaning groove. **Techno Sketching** (15 feet E2 6b † 3.93) climbs this to a handrail and another jump down. **Puddle Jumper** (15 feet E1 6a † 3.93) reaches the same high point via the right wall of the groove.

Boongary   60 feet   Very Severe 4c   (13.2.78)
Poorly protected but worth doing. Start on the seaward side of the arête between the huge roof and a narrow section of the ledge. Climb up and trend left to where a long reach gains good holds. Continue up an easy slab to a large ledge. Multiple nut belays. (The quarryman's thread is unfortunately in a loose block.)

German New Order   30 feet   E4 6c   (18.9.86)
A short test-piece in the style of Rubicon Wall. Start 15 feet right of *Boongary*. The grade given predates the loss of the first bolt-hanger. Climb a short, leaning wall past two bolt runners to better holds at the break. Cross the roof and belay on the slab.

Blitzkrieg 30 feet E4 6c † (14.12.86)
An extremely technical problem which succumbs to a dynamic approach. Start 25 feet right of *Boongary*, beneath a solitary bolt runner. Climb the short bulging wall, the crux roof, and the slab above.

Big Brother Is Watching 25 feet E4 6b † (14.3.87)
Start 40 feet right of *Boongary*, below the left-hand end of the large strip roof. A desperate exit. Climb up to a niche below the roof and swing left along a wide break. Pull over leftwards to sloping holds and step left before moving over to easy ground. Block belay.

Kangaroo 40 feet Severe 4a
A nice little climb up the bulging black buttress situated 60 feet east of *Boongary*, where the sea-level platform is at its narrowest. Follow the overhanging crack in the buttress (strenuous to start). Belay on a ledge in the west-facing corner above. Scramble off up slabs.

Distant Early Warning 40 feet E1 5c (6.9.86)
Climb the roof right of *Kangaroo* to a prominent 'mushroom' jug. Continue more easily straight to the top.

Original Route 50 feet Severe
Start at the east-facing corner to the right of *Kangaroo*. Quite high in the grade. Climb the wall just to the right of the buttress and swing left up onto the seaward face. Work left to avoid the overhangs and continue up to belay on a ledge in a west-facing corner. Scramble up slabs to finish.

★ **Cool and the Gang** 40 feet E1 5b (26.4.86)
Start as for *Original Route*. Climb straight up to a roof-crack, and cross it to gain a hidden hold on the arête. Finish more easily.

Up on the Catwalk 50 feet Hard Very Severe 5a (27.9.86)
Start 5 feet right of *Original Route*. Climb a slabby wall to the large roof. Traverse rightwards between the overhangs for 20 feet and exit up a short groove.

Genetix 40 feet E4 6a † (12.4.87)
Start 15 feet right of *Original Route*. Climb through two roofs past two *in-situ* threads to a semi rest. Cross the final roof and finish up a blank groove. Nut belay.

★ **To Fever Pitch** 40 feet E4 6b (6.9.86)
Superb, strenuous, and sustained. Climb a short groove left of *Stakk Attakk* and go over a double roof on the left to a jug. Swing right and up over the final bulges.

Stakk Attakk 40 feet E2 5c (29.5.85)
Start at the eastern end of the narrow section of ledge, at a short hanging

rib. Well protected at the crux, but not so higher up. Climb the short rib and step right to below the central weakness in the second roof. Pull over this to better holds, and continue up the left side of a large undercut block to finish easily into the quarry. *Friend* belay just to the right.

DWM   40 feet   E1 5c   (1963/15.5.77)
East of the narrow section of ledge lies a small bay composed of light-coloured rock. Climb the left-hand corner of the bay and gain a ledge on the left with difficulty. Climb back right and up to the top. Block and nut belays immediately.

⋆ **Zeitgeist**   40 feet   E5 6b   (12.7.86)
Start on the right side of the bay. Steeper than it looks but low in the grade. Climb up the groove past a projecting peg and finish boldly up above a severely weathered *in-situ* thread runner. Block belay.

A Quantum Jump for Apekind   40 feet   E4 6a †   (26.11.87)
The roofed arête right of Zeitgeist. The peg runner has disappeared since the first ascent. A grade harder if it is not replaced. Climb leftwards over the first two roofs with *RP* protection to good holds and a space vacated by a peg runner. Pass the third roof to reach ledges and a block belay.

Ocean of Violence   50 feet   E3 6a †   (16.6.85)
A sustained and gymnastic climb up the conspicuous crackline bisecting the roofs between the bays of *DWM* to the west and of *Sea Ride* to the east. Follow the crackline with difficulty over two progressively larger roofs. Easier climbing now leads to a solid exit. Belay on the back wall of the quarry using nuts and *Friends*.

⋆⋆ **Grossville**   60 feet   E5 6a   (18.10.86)
The huge prow on the left-hand side of the large bay containing *Sea Ride* features some outrageous moves. Pull up rightwards to a large jug and make difficult moves up (peg runner) to another jug. Continue (peg runner) to the roof and pull over. Swing left and up and climb a jammed fin. Finish more easily to a block belay on the right.

⋆ **Wingwalker Extraordinaire**   50 feet   E4 6a †   (14.11.87)
Start at the back of the large bay, on its left-hand side. Climb up to a jammed block at 20 feet (as for *Joyride*). Traverse left and go over a roof-crack, and then up steeply to regain *Joyride* at its *in-situ* thread. Swing leftwards to finish up the flying prow. Block belay.

Joyride   60 feet   E2 †   (1985)
An unusual eliminate that proves especially difficult for tall climbers.
1 40 feet 5b. Climb up to a jammed block at 20 feet. Move diagonally right through a large bulge and belay on a small prow beneath the capping roof. (Junction with *Sea Ride*).

2 20 feet 6a. Traverse out left between roofs (exposed and constricted) to an *in-situ* thread, and pull around the roof to reach a block belay in the quarry.

★ **Sea Ride**   40 feet   Very Severe   4c/5a   (31.5.69)
Entertaining, with a well-protected crux. Start to the right of two short clefts in the back wall of the large bay (below, and approachable by abseil from, the eastern end of Chilmark Quarry). Climb a slabby wall and follow a corner to the roof-crack. Overcome the roof by strange moves and gain the quarried ledge. Block belay.

Hackney's Hammer   60 feet   Very Severe   4c   (Pre-1963)
An interesting pitch with a tricky exit. Start 10 feet right of *Sea Ride*. Climb the huge block and the groove up to its left. From the final square-cut groove, exit delicately left. Block belay on the quarried ledge.

Sexaphone   40 feet   E6   6b †   (13.10.87)
A horrific and graunchy route. Start from the huge block on the right-hand side of the bay. Cross the flared 10-foot roof-crack with great difficulty and an *in-situ* thread runner to better holds. Continue up the very shallow, blank groove past a peg runner to the top. Stake belay.

★ **Space Threshold**   45 feet   E2   5b †   (23.3.86)
Start 10 feet right of *Sexaphone*, from the top of the huge block. Climb a scoop to the roof, swing right through a roof-crack, and go right again below the second roof. Pull around the large flake and continue straight up to the top. Stake belay.

★ **Edward's Effort**   80 feet   Very Severe   4c   (16.6.74)
Good climbing but with some worrying moments when one discovers the final overhang is a detached block. Start 50 feet right of *Sea Ride*, just right of the chimney formed by the huge block and the main cliff. Climb the wall for 20 feet to a small sentry-box. Move out right from the its top and go up to an overhang. Surmount this, and a second overhang to the right, before taking the third overhang direct. Continue to the top. Stake belay.

All Apologies   65 feet   E3   6b *S* †   (29.6.94)
The bulging arête to the right is climbed with one *in-situ* thread and five bolt runners. Climb straight up through the bulge on a series of hidden holds to easier ground. Continue up the edge of the wall past a slanting ramp. Follow a blind crack in the arête to a large flake over the top. Two lower-off bolts.

★★ **Strangled in Black**   80 feet   E4   6a   (18.10.86)
Start 15 feet right of *Edward's Effort*. Four *in-situ* threads and one peg runner. From a slab, pull rightwards over the bulge to a jug, before

moving over to easy ground. Continue via a faint groove-line up through bulges to a stake belay.

Titter Ye Not, Mrs!   70 feet   E3 5c †   (4.90)
An eliminate with good though hidden gear which starts between *Strangled in Black* and *Romu*.
Climb directly through bulges, with a strenuous pull-out leftwards to gain an alcove. Continue up past a good flake crack before moving right past an old peg runner into the corner of *Romu*. Layback straight over the top roof to a solid finish. Nut or *Friend* belay.

Romu   90 feet   Hard Very Severe   (31.5.69)
This climbs the impending groove to the left of a severely overhanging section of the cliff. Start 30 feet right of the chimney by *Edward's Effort*.
1 35 feet 4c. Pull up onto the small nose just right of the groove and surmount the bulge above (poor peg runner). Climb the overhanging groove and belay on pegs on a slab.
2 25 feet 4c. Make a difficult step down to the left and traverse left for 25 feet to another peg belay.
3 30 feet 4c. This pitch is the top of *Edward's Effort*. Climb up the groove behind the slab, over an overhang, and up onto a large, detached block. Follow a short overhanging corner and scramble up to a belay.

Sargasso   50 feet · Hard Very Severe   4c †   (11.7.86)
Climb as for *Romu* up past the poor peg runner, go diagonally right to a ledge on the arête, and finish up slabs to the right.

★ Fat Necrosis   40 feet   E4 6b   (6.9.86)
Hard to start and dry only in summer. Climb the roof-crack and chimney 10 feet right of *Romu*.

The bulging rock 10 feet right of *Fat Necrosis* was bolted and climbed after this section of The Promenade was designated bolt-free (**Liquid Steel** 30 feet E6 6c *S* † 13.7.94). The bolts may have been removed.

★ The Futurist   60 feet   E5 †   (4.11.86)
The roof-crack rising from the cave is dry only in summer. Start at the rib on the right-hand side of the cave.
1 30 feet 6b. Climb the rib to the roof and swing left with difficulty to gain the crack (neatly avoiding the first 10 feet of roof-crack - only 15 feet to go!). Follow the crack past four *in-situ* threads to a huge thread on the lip. Pull over to easy ground and belay immediately.
2 30 feet. Climb the easy corner to a stake on the right.

Berserka   30 feet   E4 6b   (12.7.86)
Start 10 feet right of *The Futurist*.

Climb the scoop to the roof and step right. Climb out rightwards through the lip with difficulty. Nut belay immediately. Scramble out.

The following roof lines are often wet:

Revolt into Style   35 feet   E3 6a   (9.7.85)
The first roof line starts where the ledge becomes narrower again. A hard start and some strenuous moves to overcome the final roof make this route high in its grade.
Pull through the initial roof (more difficult than it looks) to a poor rest in a niche below the second roof. Move out to an *in-situ* thread runner at the lip, pull over, and continue to jugs and a belay. Scramble out.

Ape Crap   35 feet   E2 5c   (9.7.85)
A strenuous and well-protected problem that tackles the roof line where the ledge is at its narrowest.
Climb the bulging crack to the roof and surmount this with long reaches. Continue to jugs at the top. Belay and then scramble out.

Distortion Plan   35 feet   E4 6a †   (14.4.87)
Overcome the bulging crack right of *Ape Crap* and cross the 8-foot roof (*in-situ* thread) to good holds and easy ground above. Take a nut belay before scrambling out.

⋆⋆ **Howling Stone**   50 feet   E3 6a   (7.7.85)
A wild, exciting climb up the very overhanging arête just left of *Grockles' Passage*. High in the grade and harder for the short.
Follow the steep crack in the arête to a niche at 20 feet. Step right around an overhang and move up to a semi rest beneath a 5-foot roof. Pass this roof with difficulty and continue 'out there' up the arête on spaced jugs. A solid finish leads to a stake belay.

⋆ **Grockles' Passage**   80 feet   Very Severe   (27.7.75)
An intimidating route that is easier than it looks from the bottom. Start 10 feet before the deep, black cave at the eastern end of the sea-level platform.
1 50 feet 4c. Climb just left of the steep arête for 15 feet, and follow the chimney/groove to a small ledge. Move out left under a suspect block and up to belay on a ledge on the arête.
2 30 feet. Exit up the right-hand side of the gully to a stake belay.

Long John's   70 feet   Hard Very Severe 5a   (1968)
Start on the eastern side of the cave at the end of The Promenade.
Climb up leftwards over blocky overhangs to reach the right-hand side of a smooth, white wall. Move up and then left across the top of this square wall to the arête. Continue to the top. Belay on fenceposts using an extra rope.

To the east is an arch. A short traverse (Very Difficult) and a step through this portal leads to Unknown Ledge.

UNKNOWN LEDGE

Although not difficult to reach nowadays, Unknown Ledge is a secluded spot that receives little attention, despite having several interesting climbs that are worth investigating. Sandwiched between The Promenade and Flake Ledge it has a wide platform at the bottom. However, the cliff should be avoided if the sea is rough.

For the approach, see the introduction to The Cattle Troughs Area (page 110).

At the western end of the ledge is an arch, all that remains of the buttress on which **Thunder Wall** (22.7.71) was situated. In the centre of the cliff the prominent fault above a cave gives the excellent *The God Slot*. Further on, past some wet overhangs, *Damson* is the plum line of the enclosing wall.

Hazhard 100 feet Hard Very Severe 5a †   (1.11.75/17.4.82)
Start at an 8-foot high pedestal at the western end of the ledge.
Climb the pedestal and move awkwardly right below a small overhang into a shallow groove. Follow this groove to a large overhang (peg runner). Step left, climb the chockstone-filled corner, and exit right onto a prow. Traverse right for 10 feet and continue easily rightwards across the slab to cracks which lead past a small bulge to a long ledge. Multiple nut belays. Walk out rightwards along the ledge.

Blast Suburbia 100 feet E1 †   (8.10.86)
Start as for *Hazhard*.
1 70 feet 5b. Climb up, and at 20 feet break diagonally right to a niche. Pull over the roof-crack above to a sloping ledge.
2 30 feet 4a. Climb the groove for 15 feet, step right, and traverse an easy slab for 20 feet. Continue up to a good ledge and nut belays. Walk off rightwards.

★ **Jesus and Mary Chain** 90 feet E3 6a †   (28.9.86)
Excellent open climbing starting 10 feet right of *Hazhard*.
From a porthole, climb a thin crack to gain the wall and an undercut block up to the right. Continue diagonally rightwards and follow the groove on the right of the large overhangs to a wall and a good ledge. Nut belays. Walk off rightwards.

★★ **The God Slot** 90 feet Hard Very Severe 5a   (5.12.76)
An intimidating but compulsive pitch, well protected and on sound rock. This climbs the impending groove above a cave. Start on the right wall of the cave, 10 feet left of the arête.
Climb up until level with the roofs. Move up with difficulty until below the large, top roof and go left to an optional stance in the chimney. Continue past a thread runner out onto the arête and move up into the groove. Step left and belay on the ledge using several nuts. Exit to the right.

Noddy   70 feet   Very Severe 4c   (5.3.67/17.11.77)
To the right of *The God Slot* is a weakness which gives a poor, unbalanced route.
Climb the arête right of *The God Slot* to the overhangs at 20 feet. Make a strenuous move to enter the corner, continue diagonally right, and finish up through a square-cut notch. Nut belays on the ledge. Walk off rightwards.

Squeeze Chimney   40 feet   Hard Severe 4b   (5.3.67)
Climb a slab and place protection at the base of the wide chimney above. Bridge up the chimney and pull out leftwards before traversing right and slightly up for 20 feet to a good stance and belay.

Doppler Shift   35 feet   Hard Very Severe 5a †   (9.7.85)
A bold pitch but with short-lived difficulties, this climbs the right-hand of two short grooves. Start beneath the arête just right of *Squeeze Chimney*. Climb up to the strip roof and continue past a solitary *Friend* placement into the right-hand groove. Long pulls lead to easy ground and a belay. Scramble out via the amphitheatre on the right.

Swingtime   50 feet   Hard Very Severe 4c   (2.5.82)
An interesting climb which starts as for *Doppler Shift*.
Climb the arête to the strip roof and traverse right under it for 25 feet to a break at its right-hand end. Move up into a scoop on steep rock to where an overhang bars the way. Swing left on good handholds for a few moves to a ledge and mantelshelf onto it with difficulty. Continue to assorted belays in the amphitheatre.

Swingtime Direct   40 feet   E2 6a †   (27.9.86)
Only marginally straighter than the original! Start at a crack 10 feet right of *Swingtime*.
Climb the difficult bulge to gain the traverse. From the end of this, finish up the groove right of the parent route's upper scoop.

★ **Damson**   80 feet   Hard Very Severe 5a   (21.11.76)
Start at the eastern end of Unknown Ledge where a steep traverse leads across a bare wall to Flake Ledge.
From half-way along the traverse, climb up the obvious diagonal crack to a roof. Move left and up to a chimney; climb it and finish up the wall on the right. Stake belay.

To continue eastwards into Flake Ledge it is necessary to traverse the steep side-wall of the zawn. This is very intimidating but proves to be well furnished with footholds and jugs all the way: **Unknown Ledge Traverse** (Severe).

FLAKE LEDGE
Often neglected and overlooked, Flake Ledge is a worthwhile little place with some attractive lines. The cliff, situated east of Unknown Ledge, has reason-

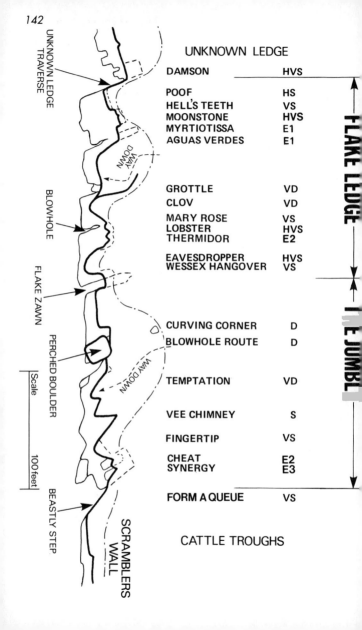

UNKNOWN LEDGE TRAVERSE

UNKNOWN LEDGE

DAMSON	HVS
POOF	HS
HELL'S TEETH	VS
MOONSTONE	HVS
MYRTIOTISSA	E1
AGUAS VERDES	E1
GROTTLE	VD
CLOV	VD
MARY ROSE	VS
LOBSTER	HVS
THERMIDOR	E2
EAVESDROPPER	HVS
WESSEX HANGOVER	VS
CURVING CORNER	D
BLOWHOLE ROUTE	D
TEMPTATION	VD
VEE CHIMNEY	S
FINGERTIP	VS
CHEAT	E2
SYNERGY	E3
FORM A QUEUE	VS

FLAKE LEDGE

THE JUMBLE

BLOWHOLE

FLAKE ZAWN

PERCHED BOULDER

Scale

100 feet

BEASTLY STEP

WAY DOWN

WAY DOWN

SCRAMBLERS WALL

CATTLE TROUGHS

able rock on most routes and access is simple. The ledges at the bottom become awash in rough seas, however, and the routes on the eastern side are prone to dampness.

For the approach, see the introduction to The Cattle Troughs Area (page 110).

The descent route divides Flake Ledge into two parts. To the west of the easy way down lies an impressive blocky buttress situated above a raised, rectangular ledge. Splitting the middle of this buttress is the unmistakable crackline of *Moonstone*.

To the east is a slight bay with a blow hole beneath the cracked arête of *Lobster* and the diagonal groove of *Chalkfree*, while further to the east *Wessex Hangover* ventures into steep ground above Flake Zawn.

The Coral Prison   80 feet   Very Severe 4c   (7.7.85)
Giving pleasant climbing on good rock, this takes the west-facing wall above the traverse-line connecting Flake Ledge with Unknown Ledge. Start from a large block below the arête.
Climb the arête for 10 feet and traverse diagonally leftwards into the centre of the face (crux). Continue straight to the top on good holds. Stake belay above the path.

Poof   70 feet   Hard Severe 4a   (9.63)
Worth doing. Start as for *The Coral Prison*.
Move up the arête and around the left side of the band of roofs. Continue up over several small roofs keeping to the zawn side of the buttress at all times; then move slightly left towards the top. Stake belay above the path.

★ **Hell's Teeth**   70 feet   Very Severe 4c   (9.63)
A fine pitch giving steep and exposed climbing up the face of the buttress. Start at a short corner 10 feet right of *Poof*.
Climb easily up to a tiny corner in the roof above. Pull over leftwards and continue to a good block runner. Move up a few feet, step across right into the bottom of an overhanging groove, and follow it to the top. Stake belay above the path.

★ **Moonstone**   70 feet   Hard Very Severe 5a   (13.11.76)
Steep but well-protected climbing up the conspicuous crackline that runs directly up the centre of the buttress. Stake belay above the path.

Myriotissa   70 feet   E1 5b   (15.6.74/2.4.78)
Some bold and committing climbing to gain the chimney above the large block.
Climb to the top of the large block. Move left and climb up to the left-hand end of the roof before traversing right to the chimney. Follow the chimney to the top and a stake belay to the left above the path. (The chimney can

be gained directly but this is harder and requires a peg to be placed for protection.)

Aguas Verdes   50 feet   E1 5b   (21.11.76)
Start 15 feet right of the large block, below a bottomless corner (west of the easy way down). Low in the grade.
Climb the groove to the roof. Pull up rightwards to reach a diagonal crack and continue up to nut and flake belays in the amphitheatre.

Three climbs take the west-facing wall overlooking the easy way down.

Glove   30 feet   Very Difficult
From the base of the descent chimney, climb the short crackline. Stake belay.

Grottle   35 feet   Very Difficult   (10.63)
A popular and enjoyable little route that is usually unaffected by the state of the sea. Start 10 feet east of the descent chimney above the level of the main ledge.
Climb straight up via a crack to finish in a shallow bay. Stake belay.

Clov   45 feet   Very Difficult   (11.63)
Sparsely protected but on good, positive holds. Start on the bottom ledge 20 feet to the east of the descent chimney.
Climb up a few feet, move right, and then continue straight up, aiming for a groove on the left of a pillar near the top. Finish to the left, almost joining *Grottle*. Stake belay.

Mary Rose   70 feet   Very Severe 4b   (10.10.82)
A slight route. Start 35 feet to the east of the descent chimney.
Climb to a layback crack near the arête at 20 feet. Ascend the crack, trend rightwards, and finish direct. Stake belays on either side of the path.

★ **Lobster**   70 feet   Hard Very Severe 5a/b   (4.8.74)
This tackles the wide crack in the overhanging arête directly above a blowhole. Well protected.
Follow the crack strenuously to a ledge. Continue more easily to stake belays as for *Mary Rose*.

★ **Thermidor**   80 feet   E2 5b   (6.7.79)
Strenuous and technically interesting climbing. Start beneath a groove just right of *Lobster*.
Climb the groove for 25 feet to a bulge. Swing up to a resting-spot on the left and climb cracks to a roof about 15 feet from the top. Move out and climb the left arête to the top. Belay as for *Mary Rose*.

Chalkfree   80 feet   E1 5b †   (27.9.86)
The long diagonal groove.
Climb *Thermidor* for 20 feet, move right, and climb up the overhanging

groove. Surmount a small roof and continue straight up the wall past another roof. Stake belays as for *Mary Rose*.

Eavesdropper   80 feet   Hard Very Severe 5a/b   (3.6.70)
Spectacular positions but often damp. Take care to avoid rope-drag. Twenty feet right of *Lobster* is an easy slab with a good stance on top. Start here.
Climb the groove to the roof and traverse left, past an undercut block, and go around the overhanging nose into a steep corner (junction with *Chalkfree*). Go up the corner and step right onto a ledge. From the right-hand end of the ledge, climb straight up on reasonable rock to the top. Stake belays on either side of the path.

Make Like a Bird   60 feet   Hard Very Severe 5a †   (11.7.90)
Start from the stance on *Eavesdropper*. Care is required with poised blocks on the upper section.
Climb rightwards to a large flake forming a roof, and move rightwards up and around it. Continue over two more roofs, with an awkward pull leading to shattered rock, which proves to be just adequate. Continue up to a stake belay.

Wessex Hangover   60 feet   Very Severe 4b   (1971)
At the eastern end of Flake Ledge is a 20-foot crack to the left of Flake Zawn, which leads to an exposed finish above the zawn. Start beneath this crack.
Climb the crack to the jutting overhang. Move right under this and climb up a short hard groove. Move right again under another overhang and then climb the cleft to block and nut belays above.

The crossing of Flake Zawn, known as **Blindman's Buff**, requires a committing fall across onto the far wall followed by a strenuous pull onto the nose.

THE JUMBLE
At the western limit of The Jumble, *Wessex Way* climbs a slab to join *Wessex Hangover* for an airy finish above Flake Zawn. Next some short mild climbs such as *Curving Corner* are located behind a huge boulder, with slabs above and to the east, where the easy way down lies. *Vee-Chimney* is a popular route around the corner to the east, whilst there are fewer takers for the demanding boulder-problems of *Synergy* and *Cheat*, which take twin cracks in a large roof.

For the approach, see the introduction to The Cattle Troughs Area (page 110).

Wessex Way   60 feet   Hard Severe 4b   (6.9.86)
Start at the westernmost edge of The Jumble. Climb the slab next to Flake Zawn and continue straight up over the bottomless cleft as for *Wessex*

Hangover. Block and nut belays. Scramble off.

Below the easy descent slabs is a huge perched boulder. A number of small problems have been climbed behind this. On the western side of the recess behind the boulder is **Curving Corner** (Difficult), with **Mutation** (Very Difficult) a few feet to the right. **Blow Hole Route** (Difficult) tackles the chimney in the wall behind the boulder. Finally **Temptation** (Very Difficult) climbs the seaward-facing wall just to the right again.

Vee-Chimney 25 feet Severe
This climbs the black chimney situated in a corner immediately east of the easy way down. Low in its grade.

The short, steep right wall of the corner gives two protectionless but worthwhile climbs, and the start of a third.

Fingerrip 30 feet Hard Very Severe 5c
Start below the slight groove in the wall close to *Vee-Chimney.*
An insecure start up the groove followed by a step left leads to much easier climbing and a stake belay.

Fingertip 35 feet Very Severe 5a
Start below the right-hand side of the wall.
Climb directly up the wall to the right-hand side of the large scoop above. Continue on better holds to a stake belay.

Crazy Fingers 60 feet E1 6a †   (19.5.87)
Climb the right arête of the wall and hand-traverse the lip of the roof rightwards for 15 feet to the prow before *Cheat.* Pull over and finish easily.

Around the corner, just before *The Beastly Step*, is a large roof split by twin cracks.

Cheat 50 feet E2 6a   (25.7.71/30.6.84)
The left-hand crack. A safe but taxing roof-problem.
Pull straight up to the roof and surmount it to gain a good ledge above. Continue easily up the crack to a stake belay.

Synergy 60 feet E3 5c †   (1969/1977)
The right-hand crack.
Surmount the roof to the right of the crack and climb the groove above. Step right and continue to a small overhang and peg runner. Continue directly to the top. Stake belay.

From the large boulders at the east end of The Jumble a series of steep moves leads across to Cattle Troughs: **The Beastly Step** (Very Difficult).

CATTLE TROUGHS

Easy access and reasonably sound rock makes Cattle Troughs a useful area within which to gain an initial impression of Swanage. A number of routes here will be found suitable for novice climbers. Although a relatively safe environment under normal conditions, the cliff is nonetheless subject to the vagaries of the sea and, as on any sea-cliff, a belay should always be taken at the foot of a climb. If conditions are rough then Cattle Troughs should be avoided; the area is **dangerous** in heavy seas.

For the approach, see the introduction to The Cattle Troughs Area (page 110).

CATTLE TROUGHS WEST
Immediately west of the descent route is a short corner, *Chockney*, a pleasant initiation into the lower grade routes at Cattle Troughs. To the left of the corner, a buttress and a flat wall give several further routes that will be found amenable to the novice. The ledge continues westwards past more easy-angled rock known as Scrambler's Wall. Beyond, past a steep sea-level traverse, lies The Jumble.

Form a Queue   60 feet   Very Severe   4c   (17.8.86)
Start on a narrow ledge just left of the main ledge.
Step up left onto the small buttress at the left-hand end of the ledge and move up to leftward-slanting undercuts. Follow these to the half-height ledge and climb an obvious layback crack to the top.

The Beastly Traverse   100 feet   Very Difficult
The high-level traverse from Cattle Troughs into The Jumble is an enjoyable little expedition with nice positions yet few difficulties. Start at the western extremity of the main ledge just before the start of *The Beastly Step*. Chicken-head belay at foot-level.
Climb easily up leftwards for 20 feet and step down onto a good ledge above the lip of a roof. Continue across at this level to gain the ledge and then an optional stance on *Cheat*. Climb the left-hand crack above for 10 feet, move around the arête on the left, and follow the final section of *Fingertip* to a stake belay.

To the east an easy-angled section of cliff, Scrambler's Wall, provides a multitude of simple climbs, none of which warrants detailed description.

East of Scrambler's Wall is a flat face followed by a slight buttress. Several lines are possible here, the best two being: **Inspiration** (25 feet Severe), which climbs the middle of the flat face to a stake belay; and **Consolation** (25 feet Severe), the right-hand side of the buttress's seaward face via a short groove (stake belay).

⋆ **Chockney**   25 feet   Very Difficult
The obvious wide corner just to the left of the descent route has probably

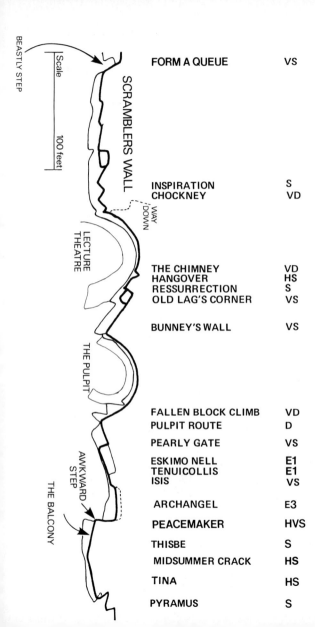

BEASTLY STEP

Scale

100 feet

SCRAMBLERS WALL

FORM A QUEUE   VS

INSPIRATION   S
CHOCKNEY   VD

WAY DOWN

LECTURE THEATRE

THE CHIMNEY   VD
HANGOVER   HS
RESSURRECTION   S
OLD LAG'S CORNER   VS

BUNNEY'S WALL   VS

THE PULPIT

FALLEN BLOCK CLIMB   VD
PULPIT ROUTE   D

PEARLY GATE   VS

ESKIMO NELL   E1
TENUICOLLIS   E1
ISIS   VS

AWKWARD STEP

THE BALCONY

ARCHANGEL   E3

PEACEMAKER   HVS

THISBE   S

MIDSUMMER CRACK   HS

TINA   HS

PYRAMUS   S

received more ascents than any other route at Cattle Troughs. Although a favourite choice for introducing climbing to novices, the initial moves are surprisingly troublesome, especially for the short. Stake belay.

CATTLE TROUGHS EAST
A continuous ledge about 10 feet above the sea runs along the base of the cliff and provides an easy approach to all the routes in this area. At the eastern end of the large depression known as The Lecture Theatre, a pedestal block sits at the foot of *Old Lag's Corner* and bounds the left side of a short, steep wall, *Bunney's Wall*. Eastwards around the corner a second depression, The Pulpit, has a choice of easy exits while *Pulpit Route* climbs a diagonal line of slabs on its right-hand edge. A steep wall now stretches eastwards to meet with a line of overhangs that form an arch near the top of the cliff. *Eskimo Nell* investigates a shallow groove in the middle of this wall and *Archangel* takes an uncompromising line up through the apex of the arch. Continuing east, either a steep hand-traverse or a descent to sea-level ledges leads to The Balcony, a narrow ledge which leads past *Midsummer Crack* to stop just short of the chimney climbed by *Pyramus*.

Note: although most routes in Cattle Troughs East are fairly short, a full rope-length will be required to reach the belay stakes on the narrow path above.

The Chimney   35 feet   Very Difficult
In The Lecture Theatre, to the right of its slabby section, is a conspicuous chimney. Start here.
The chimney requires some technique and is finished out to the right. Belay on the good ledge or continue up to a stake belay on the path above. The groove directly above the top of the chimney provides a more stimulating finish at Severe 4a (and fairly high in that grade).

★ **Hangover**   35 feet   Hard Severe   4b
A splendid climb, well worth doing. Start 6 feet right of *The Chimney*. Climb directly up the wall, past a bulge half-way, to gain a large ledge. Belay on this or continue up to a stake on the path.

★ **Resurrection**   35 feet   Severe   4a
A lovely pitch with good holds all the way. Start a few feet to the right of *Hangover* in the centre of an ill-defined buttress.
Climb straight up to a recess and finish slightly to the right. Either belay on the good ledge or continue easily to a stake belay on the path.

Perfection   35 feet   Severe
A worthwhile route, starting as for *Resurrection*.
Follow the edge diagonally rightwards before taking a shallow groove to the top.

Old Lag's Corner   40 feet   Very Severe   4c   (13.8.84)
Start at the foot of the corner with a prominent pedestal block at its base.

Some very polished footholds.
Climb the corner direct to the top overhangs, traverse right a few feet, and pull up on projecting blocks to gain the large ledge above. Belay here or continue up a short wall to a stake belay on the path.

★ **Bunney's Wall**   30 feet   Very Severe   5a
At the eastern end of The Lecture Theatre, just before the cliff turns a corner into The Pulpit, lies a short, vertical wall. A number of testing problems have been worked out here of which this is the best. Start just right of centre.
A difficult and unprotected start gains easier ground following the slanting crack to the top. Nut and block belays.

Around the arête, the west side and the back of The Pulpit amphitheatre provide two useful descent routes for this part of the cliff.

Fallen Block Climb   40 feet   Very Difficult
A pleasant little climb, though lacking in character. The 'fallen block' has long since gone.
Follow a more or less direct line up the wall on the eastern side of The Pulpit. Belay at a stake a long way back.

★ **Pulpit Route**   45 feet   Difficult
A gentle beginners' route that gives a relaxed introduction to the area. Some delicate moves at the top of the slab make this fairly high in its grade. Start below the conspicuous diagonal slab at the eastern edge of The Pulpit amphitheatre.
Pull up steeply and climb the slab, before traversing left around the arête onto easier ground near the top. Stake belay a long way back on the path. (The alternative of continuing straight up the very narrow slab is slightly harder.)

Pearly Gate   45 feet   Very Severe   4c
Start at the crack on the right-hand side of the initial slab of *Pulpit Route*. Follow the easy crack, step right, and climb the flakes above to a roof. Move left and up the break to a stake belay at the top. Alternatively, from the roof make a long step right to climb around the edge of the roof and to the top (harder). Stake belay.

★ **Eskimo Nell**   60 feet   E1   5b   (24.9.67/16.2.69)
A commendable route and surprisingly technical. Start a few feet to the right of *Pearly Gate* below an obvious, shallow groove just left of a half-height overhang.
Climb onto a huge block and then straight up to a ledge at the bottom of the groove. Climb the groove to the top. Stake belay. (Avoiding the upper groove by a parallel line gained by a wide step out right reduces the standard to serious VS.)

Tenuicollis   60 feet   E1 5a   (25.5.75)
To the right of *Eskimo Nell* is an overhang at half height. This poorly-
protected route starts below the right-hand side of the overhang.
Climb up to a short groove and swing left onto the seaward-facing wall.
Move left again and continue up over ledges (some sloping) to reach a
very small corner about 15 feet to the right of the finish of *Eskimo Nell*.
Climb the corner with difficulty and continue to a stake belay.

★ **Isis**   60 feet   Very Severe 4c   (1963)
Good situations on firm rock makes this a deservedly popular pitch. Start
at the foot of the groove that bounds the left edge of the high arched
recess.
Climb the groove until a wide step can be made below a rusty peg onto
the lip of an overhang. Step left again and climb the overhang-choked
groove up to the right until forced left after about 15 feet. Continue up two
short walls to a stake belay by the path.

Tekneeque   60 feet   E1 5b †   (24.7.91)
Start just right of *Isis*. Poorly protected and high in its grade.
Climb boldly straight up the steep wall to the downward-pointing tongue
of rock on the left side of the high roof. Use this to move left before
finishing straight up. Stake belay on the path.

Archangel and *Hobbit* have seen several accidents.

Archangel   60 feet   E3 6a   (5.5.74)
An unfriendly route as 'the crux hits you just when you think you've done
it!' Changes to the rock above the roof have made this route harder. Start
in the centre of the high arched recess.
Climb up to the roof. Pull through the apex of the arch to a strenuous and
scary finish. Stake belay on the path.

Peacemaker   60 feet   Hard Very Severe 5a   (8.2.89)
Start at the wide corner-crack on the right-hand side of the high arched
recess. Varied climbing.
Climb up the corner to a foot-ledge near the top and step right onto the
slab using a large side hold. Make fingery moves slightly right to gain a
solid finish. Stake belay.

Hobbit (60 feet Very Severe 4b) climbed up and around the right-hand
side of the arch before continuing up the centre of the slab and finishing
as for *Thisbe*. A serious, poorly-protected route which has now been
superseded by more direct lines.

Only Thisbig   50 feet   Hard Very Severe 5b †   (23.6.90)
Serious and unforgiving in its upper reaches, the hard variation finish to
Hobbit now has a tight but independent start.
Climb the narrow facet just right of the chimney and finish up the middle

of the slab. Twin stake belay on the path above.

To the east, a step down leads to sea-level ledges; the higher ledge beyond is known as The Balcony.

Thisbe   50 feet   Severe   4b/c
A balancy start close to the ground leads to easy but poorly-protected climbing on good rock. Start 10 feet right of *Peacemaker* on the lower ledge.
Step delicately up (no hands required!) and gain the faultline (you will need them now!). Continue slightly rightwards to finish up the open corner on the right-hand side of the slab. Scramble up the long slope to a twin stake belay on the path.

Frisbee   50 feet   Very Severe   4c †   (19.5.91)
Start 25 feet right of *Peacemaker* on the sea-level ledge. The crux is well protected, something which cannot be said for the easier climbing above. Climb to the faultline, follow a leftward-slanting crack, and continue up the blunt arête. Stake belay on the path.

Midsummer Crack   40 feet   Hard Severe   4c
Start 8 feet from the left end of The Balcony at a thin crack which, although short, is a tricky problem.
Climb the crack with difficulty to better holds up on the left. Continue up leftwards for 10 feet and finish direct. Scramble up the long slope to a twin stake belay on the path.

Tina   50 feet   Hard Severe   4a   (5.87)
This route has been affected by rockfall. An awkward start.
Climb the crack at the right end of The Balcony to a small ledge, move left, and pull up leftwards onto easier ground. Scramble up the long slope.

Pyramus   50 feet   Severe
The chimney at the eastern extremity of Cattle Troughs is loose and unpleasant towards the top; not recommended. Start at the end of the ledge.
Step down and around the arête, and climb the chimney above finishing to the right. Scramble up to the path and a twin stake belay.

Little Red Watering Can   100 feet   Hard Severe   4a   (1968)
A loose and poorly-protected climb starting from Cattle Troughs and finishing via a hanging amphitheatre. Bears absolutely no similarity to a well-known and similarly-named Cornish classic! Start as for *Pyramus*.
Step down and move across the chimney of *Pyramus* to the next arête to the east. Pull up onto this, move right into a corner, and continue up to an overhung ledge. Traverse right along the ledge and climb up the back of the shallow amphitheatre on loose rock to the top. Stake belay just below the path.

AMPHITHEATRE LEDGE

Two fields west of the lighthouse is a stone wall which marks the western limit of Durlston Country Park. From the stile in this wall, the cliff-top path continues above Boulder Ruckle Far West for 150 yards to where a deep rock amphitheatre drops down to sloping ledges at sea-level: Amphitheatre Ledge. The easier routes here have brittle rock and loose finishes. However, there are a number of worthwhile steep climbs on the leaning wall east of The Amphitheatre proper.

For the approach, see the introduction to The Cattle Troughs Area (page 110).

Varina   80 feet   Severe 4a   (1968)
A sparsely-protected line up the east arête of the amphitheatre. Serious for its grade. Mainly small wires required.
Follow the arête with little difficulty and step right near the top to finish steeply up a small corner on brittle rock. Belay on the abseil stakes. (A harder alternative is to climb the wall between the arête and *Solitude* before moving left to join the parent route below the top.)

Solitude   90 feet   Very Severe 4b   (16.12.66)
Start 30 feet east of The Amphitheatre at the end of the ledge.
Climb a slight groove for 10 feet and step right to a bigger groove. Climb this and then continue up rightwards to reach the abseil stakes.

★ **Atomic Road Hero**   100 feet   E5 6b   (14.12.86)
The leaning face 10 feet right of *Solitude*.
Climb straight up past three *in-situ* thread runners and move slightly right (peg runner) to a large undercut. Move diagonally left over the top of the wall (low *in-situ* thread) to a slabby corner and join *Solitude* to finish (*in-situ* thread).

★ **Theory of Everything**   90 feet   E5 6b †   (23.3.90)
This eliminate has sensational moves by good gear and starts 10 feet right of *Atomic Road Hero*.
Climb the wall on good holds to the leaning upper face and step left to beneath the spidery central crack. Layback quickly up to jugs, make some hard moves just left of a peg runner, and continue to the top of the wall to reach buckets. Finish slightly leftwards on solid blocks to a clean-cut exit. Belay on a rope preplaced on the abseil stakes.

★★ **Zoolookologie**   100 feet   E5 6a   (8.8.86)
A strenuous pitch.
Follow *Theory of Everything* up the easy lower wall to mid height. Climb cracks past an *in-situ* thread and go over a solid bulge to a ledge. Finish up the groove above. Belay on a rope preplaced on the abseil stakes.

Shelob (90 feet Hard Very Severe 4c 1973) is not recommended, being dirty, loose, and very unpleasant. From the left-hand end of the ledge 30 feet right of *Solitude*, climb up for 20 feet, left for 15 feet, and up avoiding the overhangs on the left. Continue diagonally right over large blocks to an earthy ledge. Place a protection peg and climb the loose, earthy wall to the top.

In a Big Sky 80 feet   E2 5c †   (8.6.86)
Some care is required on the upper reaches of this leaning wall. Start from a large, sloping ledge 35 feet right of *Solitude*.
From a flake, climb straight up via thin cracks past five *in-situ*; threads. Near the top, move right with difficulty to easier ground and a ledge. Belay on, and then pull out on, the abseil rope (see Approach 2).

Land of the Leaning 90 feet   E2 †   (7.6.86)
Start on the large, sloping ledge, as for *In a Big Sky*.
1 20 feet. Climb the flake (*in-situ* thread) and go rightwards easily for 10 feet to a small ledge above a zawn. Nut and *in-situ* thread belay.
2 70 feet 5b. Climb cracks slightly rightwards up the wall. Step left and back right at their end, and continue up easier ground past an *in-situ* thread runner. Belay on, and then pull out on, the abseil rope (see Approach 2).

** **World in Action** 90 feet   E5 6a   (11.4.87)
The unrelenting wall above a small faultline ledge some 20 feet left of an obvious rightward-slanting crack.
Climb a bulging arête (peg and *in-situ* thread) to easier ground (*in-situ* thread) before going left to the upper wall. Follow a thin, disjointed crack past two *in-situ* threads to a jug. Continue directly via a shallow groove to a cleaned exit. Belay on, and then pull out on, the abseil rope (see Approach 2).

Arapiles Syndrome 110 feet   E3 5b †   (5.4.86)
Start beneath the obvious, rightward slanting crack (which is climbed by *Pogor*).
Swing leftwards to an obvious crack and climb it to an overlap at two-thirds height. From here, go diagonally right by means of two short traverses, and exit onto a long ledge. Belay on, and then pull out on, the abseil rope (see Approach 2).

Boulder Ruckle   OS Ref 019 768 to 028 768

Boulder Ruckle is the premier cliff at Swanage, a formidable expanse of rock that stretches without a break for over half a mile from Subluminal to Amphitheatre Ledge. The length and uniformity of the Ruckle can prove dis-orienting as it has only one really obvious feature, the prow of the *Marmolata* buttress. This is the impressive buttress that juts out towards the eastern end of the cliff, which can be clearly seen all the way from Subliminal. The cliff consists of an endless repetition of grooves, cracks, roofs, and recesses, the similarity of which makes identifying individual climbs difficult, even though the routes themselves often follow strong natural lines. With such a wide range of fine climbing to be enjoyed, in a variety of grades, the area will no doubt continue as the focus of Swanage climbing for those visitors who get past Subliminal or Dancing Ledge.

Although Boulder Ruckle never exceeds 130 feet in height, it remains a serious place to climb. Access is generally by free-hanging abseil and there are few easy exits, an aspect compounded when faced with a rough sea and the harrowing and precarious nature of some of the finishes. Boulder Ruckle is not an environment for the inexperienced or the accident-prone and it is recommended that climbers should be competent at a standard of at least VS as well as being capable of prusiking out should the need arise. A 150-foot rope will be needed to abseil to the boulders at the base of the cliff and should be left in place in case of an emergency as well as to indicate your presence in the area. Some sort of prusiking device should always be carried. Progress along the bottom of the Ruckle is affected in several places by high tide, and in rough seas many sections are impassable. Caution is advised before abseiling in when conditions are poor unless one is familiar with the area.

The main abseil entry points into Boulder Ruckle have been used to divide up the area into five sections. The introduction for each section is described **in the normal direction of approach from the main abseil points**. Detailed information concerning any tidal considerations is provided along with the location of the easiest escape routes for that section. Details of the main abseil points are given in the Boulder Ruckle approach diagram. Care should be taken when the tide is high or the sea is rough as the nearest abseil point to the route required may not necessarily provide the best approach to it. Although it is possible to abseil into the Ruckle almost anywhere, the entry points described here all lead to boulders above the sea and are free from an excess of loose rock on their tops. To give assistance in finding the routes, the most distinctive climbs have been marked on the diagrams with their distance in metres east and west of the *Marmolata* buttress. **Nesting-season restrictions** apply between *Finale Groove* and *Marmolata*, and between *Gimcrack* and *Via Christina* (at Subliminal). See Introduction for full details.

Approach. From the car-park at Durlston Country Park (parking fee charged), follow the road that leads down across a wooded valley towards the lighthouse. Soon after crossing the bridge, cut across to the cliff-top path. Boulder Ruckle is the section of cliff that stretches westwards from here to a point just beyond the stile marking the boundary of the Country Park.

BOULDER RUCKLE FAR WEST
At the western extremity of Boulder Ruckle is a magnificent wall of awesome

steepness, seamed by cracklines. This, *The Lean Machine* wall, is bounded on its right by *Apex Corner*. To the east around the corner is the distinctive yellow ramp of *High Noon*, and further on a high, flat-topped pedestal leans against the foot of a slab marking the start of *Primrose Hill*. The prominent open corner capped by massive roofs is the habitat of *The Orange-Throated Gronk*. East again is an important venue for the muscle-bound, the *Ocean Boulevard* wall. This grossly overhanging wall is well protected from the sea and remains open to climbing when many other parts of the Ruckle prove inaccessible. The striking, overhanging crack in the left arête is attacked by *Barracuda*, and a series of parallel cracks to the right show the way for *Ocean Boulevard*. *The Last Hurrah of the Golden Horde* follows a line of weakness in the wall directly above the start of the considerably easier left-to-right rake of *The Ramp*, the main reference point hereabouts.

Access to this area is normally by a partially free-hanging abseil from the top of *The Ramp*. However, progress along the boulders from *The Orange-Throated Gronk* towards *The Lean Machine* is possible only when the tide is low and the sea fairly calm. The routes on *The Lean Machine* wall can be approached at high tide by an intimidating and committing abseil down the wall, which has the advantage that the abseil rope is available for the final loose section of the climbs and the disadvantage that it shows how steep the wall actually is! In calm seas only, an escape westwards from *Apex Corner* is possible by following the traverse of *Paradise Street* to Cattle Troughs. With a low tide and very calm seas this same stretch can be passed by a sea-level traverse.

Paradise Street   Hard Severe 4b   (15.5.65)
A traverse in seven pitches from the western limit of Boulder Ruckle past Amphitheatre Ledge to the ledges of Cattle Troughs. The climb starts from the westernmost boulder in the Ruckle and follows the prominent fault along the base of the cliff, with a technical start and a strenuous hand-traverse further on. Route-finding is obvious and no detailed description is needed. In reverse (and with the descent to the boulders at the end by abseil) then the standard is only Severe. *Paradise Street* should **not** be relied upon as an easy exit from the Ruckle as the first section is often out of reach on account of the waves.

The following routes as far as *Apex Corner* are topped by a friable wall. While it is possible to climb this wall, it is an unpleasant experience easily avoided by using a rope preplaced on the alloy belay stake.

Pogor   170 feet   E1   (30.6.85)
The main pitch climbs the obvious, rightward-slanting crack/flake immediately left of *Gaston*. The name, Czechoslovakian for 'beware', refers to the final rubble wall, which can be overcome by means of a preplaced rope.
1 50 feet 4b. *Gaston* pitch 1.
2 120 feet 5b. Climb the wall to the right of the crack, and then the

crack itself to gain a large ledge. Walk right and belay on the preplaced rope before pulling out on it.

Gaston   160 feet   Very Severe   (16.6.68)
This tackles the loose corner line left of the end of the boulders. An unpleasant route, not worth doing. Start on the most westerly boulder in Boulder Ruckle. A rope preplaced on the belay stake is advisable to safeguard the finish.
1 50 feet 4b. Traverse left near sea-level for about 15 feet and climb a wide chimney for 10 feet. Walk left along the wide ledge, and belay below a short V-corner capped by an overhang.
2 110 feet 4b. Climb the right wall of the corner on good holds and continue up right into another corner. Follow this past a ledge to a wider ledge 20 feet higher. Belay on the preplaced rope, which can then be used to pull up over the looser material above.

The Roaring Forties   110 feet   E2 †   (14.6.87)
Start as for *Gaston*. Easier than it looks.
1 30 feet 4b. Traverse left at sea-level to a wide chimney. Climb this to the faultline.
2 80 feet 5b. Surmount the overhang and go diagonally right to the arête. Ascend its left side (peg runner) to the top ledge. Belay on, and then pull out on, a rope preplaced on a stake.

⋆ Sirius   120 feet   E2 5b   (10.5.80)
An excellent pitch - steep, sustained, and very tiring, though with good protection. Start as for *Gaston*, on the left-hand side of *The Lean Machine* wall at the foot of the obvious crackline. A rope preplaced on a stake is advised to assist the finish.
Pull up onto the wall and climb the groove to the faultline. Swing over the bulge above and climb the cracks for 70 feet to a niche below an overhang. Surmount the overhang and belay to a preplaced rope on the ledge. Pull up the rope to the top.

⋆ Wild at Heart   120 feet   E4 6a †   (19.9.92)
There is a fairly continuous thin crack close to *Sirius*. Though escape into *Sirius* is possible, the line feels quite natural.
Climb the groove to the faultline as for *Sirius*. Swing rightwards over the bulge and climb up 8 feet before transferring to the crack on the left. Plough on, aided and abetted by large incut holds, until technical moves up a very thin crack enable a step right to a short corner beneath a roof. Pull leftwards over the roof and belay on the ledge above using a preplaced rope.

⋆ Punks in Power   130 feet   E5 6a/b   (15.9.85)
Exhausting climbing with a powerful crux at the top; the route follows a line of cracks between *Wild at Heart* and *The Lean Machine*. Protection is good, but spaced out higher up. A devastating pitch. Start in the

centre of the wall as for *The Lean Machine*.
Climb *The Lean Machine* to a large jug 5 feet above the faultline. Traverse left along a handrail into a diagonal crack rising from *Sirius*. Follow the crack rightwards and move left with difficulty to gain a hollow, black flake. Continue boldly up the obvious line and follow isolated holds up the calcite wall above. From the large blocks, move rightwards over the lip and climb a thin slab, trending right to reach the top ledge. Belay on a preplaced rope.

★★★ The Lean Machine   130 feet   E5 6a   (11.6.83)

A stupendous route weaving its way up the centre of a wildly leaning wall and finding good holds where they count most. It is well protected, strength permitting, and presents a testing exercise in energy conservation. Start from a boulder against the middle of the wall.
Climb a thin crack to the faultline and go left for a few feet to a deeper crackline veering up rightwards. Follow this on large holds until a long reach gains a superb jug in black rock at a vague horizontal break. Move right and pull up to more good holds. Reach left to a jug, which is used to enter a shallow niche. Make blind moves up right (crux) to finger-slots in a thin crackline and follow this to a good flake. Move up into an easier-angled groove with sparse holds at the top of the wall, and continue up the slabs above. Belay on a rope preplaced on a stake.

Buzz Cocked   130 feet   E5 6a/b †   (22.3.90)

A well-protected eliminate, which makes the most of the space on the upper wall between *Punks in Power* and *Green Machine*.
Follow *Surge Control* to its vague horizontal break. Hand-traverse left 10 feet to the point where *Punks in Power* breaks out left. Continue up a diagonal crack to arrive at the shallow niche on *The Lean Machine*, where a long undercut move allows holds up left to be reached. Precariously layback the rib above to 'jugland' and the finish of *Punks in Power*. Belay on a preplaced rope.

Green Machine (130 feet E5 6a 5.3.87) has only a small amount of

independent climbing. Follow *Surge Control* to a junction with *The Lean Machine*, which is climbed to its shallow niche. Go directly up the crack and the left-hand groove above. Cross the slab and belay on the preplaced rope.

★★ Surge Control   130 feet   E5 6a/b   (18.7.85)

Start just left of the corner at a thin crack.
Climb a short wall to the faultline and follow a hard, thin crack to a jug in a prominent slot at 25 feet. Continue up to join *The Lean Machine* at an area of black rock, and make long reaches (as for *The Lean Machine*) to gain better holds at a vague horizontal. Climb diagonally right to a small recess, pull up out of this with difficulty, and step left to a good flake. Finish as for *The Lean Machine* up the groove and slab above. Belay on a preplaced rope.

The Roaring Boys 130 feet E6 6b (1.8.87)
An eliminate searching for difficulty - and finding it! Start as for *Surge Control*.
Climb a short wall to the faultline and follow a hard, thin crack to a jug in a prominent slot at 25 feet. Swing right along a break and climb the wall in line with a blind crack to the small recess on *Surge Control*. Move diagonally right and up a layback fin to jugs (*in-situ* thread). Continue straight up onto a slab and belay on a rope preplaced on a stake.

A half-height leftward traverse of *The Lean Machine* wall has been climbed, starting from the belay of *Apex Corner*. **The Men They Couldn't Hang** (E4 5c † 1989). Finish up *Sirius*.

Apex Corner 100 feet E1 (12.7.63)
The large corner bounding the right-hand side of *The Lean Machine* wall. Awkward to start and steeper than it appears, with sandy and dubious rock once the corner is quitted. Low in its grade, however.
1 40 feet 5a. Climb the left wall to the corner-crack and follow it to a good stance.
2 60 feet 4c. Continue up the corner to a small ledge below overhangs. Climb diagonally left across the sandy slab and pull out on a rope preplaced on a stake.

The next pair of climbs ascend the slabby right wall of *Apex Corner*. This is the longest slab in the Ruckle, almost reaching to the cliff-top. The two routes cross near the faultline and their cruces are on either side of a small prow near the top.

Charge of the Wild Horsemen 120 feet E1 5b (29.8.88)
Start at a small subsidiary corner 10 feet seaward of *Apex Corner*.
Follow the corner to a flake, where easier slabby climbing up a thin crack leads diagonally right to the faultline. Move straight up the groove above and continue up on the right side of the prow. Pull over the bulge on dusty jugs to reach the final slab. Exit rightwards to a stake belay.

Charge of the Light Brigade 120 feet E1 5b † (19.5.91)
Start 20 feet seaward of *Apex Corner* at a very shallow groove just before the arête. Slightly harder than the previous route, with forceful climbing required on the prow.
Climb the groove to a block and step left onto the main slab. Continue directly to small ledges on the left-hand side of the prow close to the top. Swing rightwards onto the prow and use hidden layaways up right to reach easier ground above. Exit rightwards up slabby rock. Stake belay.

The Lusty, Decadent Delights of Imperial Pompeii
130 feet E4 (18.4.89)
A very steep crux and rotten, friable rock on pitch 2. Start 15 feet right of the right arête of *Apex Corner*.

1 60 feet 5a. Pull strenuously onto a projecting ledge. Climb a short wall and follow a groove, which leads to a sloping ledge near the faultline.
2 70 feet 6a. Climb flakes up to the right (to place protection), and then launch leftwards across the wall, past a good flake, to jugs. Continue up the bulging arête to two *in-situ* threads by a niche, and then to a square ledge. Climb a slight groove to a juggy finish and a stake belay.

Alien Hum   130 feet   E3   (8.9.86)

Twenty feet east of the right arête of *Apex Corner* is a groove-system.
1 60 feet 5a. Climb a deep groove to a sloping ledge below the faultline.
2 70 feet 5c. Five *in-situ* thread runners. Climb a steep diagonal crack (friable rock) and traverse left to a wide bay. Climb this on its left-hand side to the overhangs, and from the last *in-situ* thread finish diagonally leftwards. Stake belay.

★ Gnarly Scar Tissue   120 feet   E5 6b †   (5.9.89)

A direct assault on the big wall 30 feet east of *Apex Corner*. An excellent solid route with good protection.
Climb a shallow groove to good holds, step right, and go up a continuation groove to a slab and flake at the faultline (optional belay). Power up a thin crack in the severely overhanging wall (crux) to reach jugs beneath a roof with an *in-situ* thread above its lip. Undercut strenuously rightwards and pull around to another roof for a shakeout. Continue up (peg runner) to a good crack bounding projecting blocks, and pull over a bulge into a juggy alcove. Stretch over the capping bulge to an excavated ledge, from which solid blocks lead to the top. Stake belay up to the right.

High Noon   120 feet   E2   (11.5.80)

Start where a groove leads to a sloping ledge at the faultline. Above is a prominent, rightward-leading, yellow 'ramp' (in reality a wall).
1 30 feet 4c. Climb the groove to a bulge, step right, and pull over onto the sloping ledge.
2 90 feet 5b. Climb the yellow wall on the right to a resting-place. Continue to a small, loose overhang and pass this on the right to reach easier-angled rock. Climb over loose rock to a stake belay.

★ I Got the Spirit   100 feet   E6 6b †   (22.3.90)

A route of *The Lean Machine* qualities, only steeper! Start at a short steep corner. Good protection.
Bridge the steep corner to jugs (*in-situ* thread) and then fire up the finger-crack in the leaning wall to the faultline. Continue with difficulty past a peg runner to a good block and a semi rest just above. Cross a roof via a diagonal crack to a scoop beneath another roof. Pull directly over (peg runner), and pass a large hold to reach a slab beneath a rubble wall. Belay on a preplaced rope and then prusik out.

Primrose Hill   140 feet   E1   (13.7.79)
Although not technically hard, the route is loose and has a serious finish.
Start at the base of the distinctive, high, flat-topped pedestal that leans
against the cliff 150 feet east of *Apex Corner*.
1 50 feet 4b. Scramble up to the top of the pedestal and follow a crack
to reach a broad slab below the faultline.
2 90 feet 5a. Go up to the faultline and climb the right-hand of two
short, bottomless corners. Move diagonally right along the obvious line of
hanging flakes and overhangs until they peter out at a shallow groove.
Climb this groove to a loose finish. Stake belay.

Yellow-Bellied Fink   130 feet   E4 †   (7.11.87)
A big, demanding route. Start off a boulder just to the right of a short tidal
section.
1 70 feet 5c. Climb a thin crack to a cherty slab, and follow a groove
and then a crack until this fades above the faultline. Continue with
difficulty to better holds, and step left into a shallow scoop under the roof
to take a poor stance. (It may be best to continue, to avoid the poor stance
and help protect the second.)
2 60 feet 6a. Climb a big flake to a sloping ledge and then a difficult
bulging wall (peg runner) to good holds. Move rightwards onto a good
ledge and continue to a stake belay.

The Orange-Throated Gronk   200 feet   E2   (30.4.77)
A serious expedition, which heads up to the centre of the topmost of the
big roofs 100 feet west of *The Ramp*. The route then escapes left along a
strenuous undercling. Beware of rope-drag on the main pitch. Start at the
foot of a wide chimney.
1 50 feet 4c. Climb the chimney to an overhang and traverse right for
15 feet. Follow a short crack and bear left to a stance on a sloping ledge.
Belay on nuts and a peg.
2 150 feet 5b. Move right and follow a flake-line to a bulge. Surmount
this and continue up a short shallow groove to a roof. Traverse rightwards
to a highly suspect thread. Climb directly up (crux) to meet the roof and
follow a long traverse back left, until a final strenuous pull gains a perfect
stance but no belay! Fight the rope-drag to climb the corner above and
exit to the left at the top. Stake belay.

Le Jaune Mecanique   140 feet   E3   (21.6.86)
Start beneath the arête 20 feet right of *The Orange-Throated Gronk*, at a
step in the rock platform. (The extreme left-hand end of the *Ocean
Boulevard* wall.)
1 70 feet 5c. Climb past an *in-situ* thread onto the left wall of the arête
and continue up, clipping another, to a shallow groove. Step right and go
up just left of the arête (*in-situ* thread) to a peg and *in-situ* thread belay on
the faultline.
2 70 feet 5b. Move up to a peg runner at the overhang and go around
right to a small ledge on *Barracuda*. Finish as for that route. Stake belay.

BOULDER RUCKLE ACCESS

AMPHITHEATRE
LEDGE
(THE HALF MOON)

150 feet west of the stile, two fields west of the lighthouse, is a slight rise in the cliff path. Abseil from a large alloy T stake to a platform at the base of THE LEAN MACHINE.

BOULDER
RUCKLE
FAR WEST

45 feet east of the first stile, two fields west of the lighthouse, is a stake at the head of an earthy runnel. Abseil from this down THE RAMP.

THE RAMP

BOTTOMLESS BUTTRESS

BOULDER
RUCKLE
WEST

THUNDERBALL BAY

← Abseil Stakes

▨ Seasonal Restrictions
1st March to 31st July

┼→ North

200 yards west of Marmolata Buttress is a yellow post below the third stone wall west of the lighthouse. Just down from this are two yellow stakes; an abseil from these leads to boulders at the foot of ULYSSES.

PILLAR BAY

BOULDER
RUCKLE
CENTRAL

450 yards west of the lighthouse is a jutting prow which can be easily seen from the cliff top. This is the Marmolata Buttress. Abseil from a stake on its top to the boulders below.

MARMOLATA
BUTTRESS

BOULDER
RUCKLE
EAST

Abseil from a large, tubular stake found approx. 190 yards west of the lighthouse. This descends the line of OLD FAITHFUL to a fin-backed boulder above the level of high tide.

BOULDER
RUCKLE
FAR EAST

Starting by the foot of GREASY CHIMNEY, at the western end of Subluminal, traverse horizontally west for 80 feet, to the corner of WAR, then descend more easily to boulders. (This is the NUTCRACKER TRAVERSE in reverse.)

SUBLUMINAL

to the Lighthouse

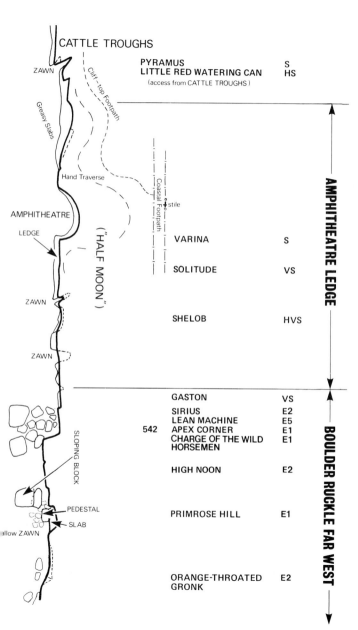

CATTLE TROUGHS

ZAWN

Cliff-top Footpath

PYRAMUS   S
LITTLE RED WATERING CAN   HS
(access from CATTLE TROUGHS)

Greasy Slabs

Hand Traverse

Coastal Footpath

stile

AMPHITHEATRE

LEDGE

("HALF MOON")

VARINA   S

SOLITUDE   VS

ZAWN

SHELOB   HVS

ZAWN

AMPHITHEATRE LEDGE

GASTON   VS

SIRIUS   E2
LEAN MACHINE   E5
542   APEX CORNER   E1
CHARGE OF THE WILD   E1
HORSEMEN

HIGH NOON   E2

SLOPING BLOCK

PRIMROSE HILL   E1

PEDESTAL

SLAB

shallow ZAWN

ORANGE-THROATED   E2
GRONK

BOULDER RUCKLE FAR WEST

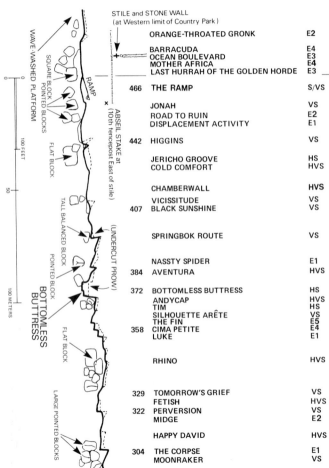

STILE and STONE WALL
(at Western limit of Country Park)

	ORANGE-THROATED GRONK	E2
	BARRACUDA	E4
	OCEAN BOULEVARD	E3
	MOTHER AFRICA	E4
	LAST HURRAH OF THE GOLDEN HORDE	E3
466	THE RAMP	S/VS
	JONAH	VS
	ROAD TO RUIN	E2
	DISPLACEMENT ACTIVITY	E1
442	HIGGINS	VS
	JERICHO GROOVE	HS
	COLD COMFORT	HVS
	CHAMBERWALL	HVS
	VICISSITUDE	VS
407	BLACK SUNSHINE	VS
	SPRINGBOK ROUTE	VS
	NASSTY SPIDER	E1
384	AVENTURA	HVS
372	BOTTOMLESS BUTTRESS	HS
	ANDYCAP	HVS
	TIM	HS
	SILHOUETTE ARÊTE	VS
	THE FIN	E5
358	CIMA PETITE	E4
	LUKE	E1
	RHINO	HVS
329	TOMORROW'S GRIEF	VS
	FETISH	HVS
322	PERVERSION	VS
	MIDGE	E2
	HAPPY DAVID	HVS
304	THE CORPSE	E1
	MOONRAKER	VS

WAVE-WASHED PLATFORM

SQUARE BLOCK
POINTED BLOCKS

RAMP

FLAT BLOCK

ABSEIL STAKE at
(10th fencepost East of stile)

TALL BALANCED BLOCK

POINTED BLOCK

(UNDERCUT PROW)

BOTTOMLESS
BUTTRESS

FLAT BLOCK

LARGE POINTED BLOCKS

0

100 FEET

50

100 METERS

300	MOONRAKER	VS
290	SNOWDROP	E1
	RAINDROP	HVS
	THUNDERBALL	HVS
282	JO	HVS
	THOR	HVS
	RELAX AND SWING	E5
	SARDINE SPECIAL	E5 + A1
	THIRD WORLD	E4
254	DOG WATCH	E3
	CORAL SLABS	E3
	MONGOOSE	E3
239	RAINBOW	VS
	VIPER	HVS
	ASP	VS
215	ENOS	VS
207	CLOUD NINE	E1
	HARD DAY'S NIGHT	HVS
	THE CAT SKINNER	HVS
	ULYSSES	E1
	THE GRIM REAPER	E1
172	SCYTHE	E3
	GOLD FEVER	E4
150	LITTLE MATTERHORN	VS
	ILIUM	E1
	LITTLE YELLOW JUG	HVS
	LARUS	HS
	BILLY PIGG	E1
120	RATTLER	E1
	FISH SUPPER	E2
	SINBAD	E1
	MICKEY MOUSE	E3
106	BUCCANEER	E2

THUNDERBALL BAY

PILLAR BAY

CAVE

FLAT BLOCK

POINTED BOULDER

tiny concealed CAVE

PEDESTAL BLOCK (above large pile of blocks)

THE PILLAR

ROCK COLUMN

BIG YELLOW CORNER

SCALE

100 FEET

3rd Stone wall West of Lighthouse

2 YELLOW STAKES

BOULDER RUCKLE — WEST

BOULDER RUCKLE — CENTRAL

166

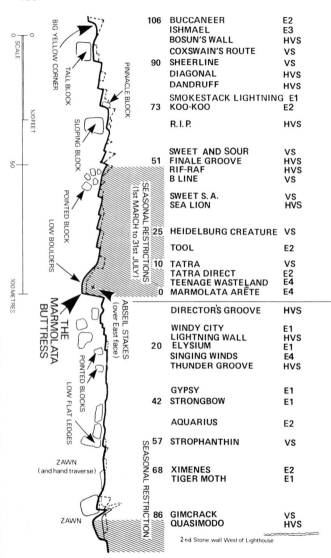

BOULDER RUCKLE — CENTRAL

106	BUCCANEER	E2
	ISHMAEL	E3
	BOSUN'S WALL	HVS
	COXSWAIN'S ROUTE	VS
90	SHEERLINE	VS
	DIAGONAL	HVS
	DANDRUFF	HVS
	SMOKESTACK LIGHTNING	E1
73	KOO-KOO	E2
	R.I.P.	HVS
	SWEET AND SOUR	VS
51	FINALE GROOVE	HVS
	RIF-RAF	HVS
	B LINE	VS
	SWEET S.A.	VS
	SEA LION	HVS
25	HEIDELBURG CREATURE	VS
	TOOL	E2
10	TATRA	VS
	TATRA DIRECT	E2
	TEENAGE WASTELAND	E4
0	MARMOLATA ARÊTE	E4

BIG YELLOW CORNER
TALL BLOCK
PINNACLE BLOCK
SLOPING BLOCK
POINTED BLOCK
LOW BOULDERS

SCALE
0
100 FEET
50
100 METRES

SEASONAL RESTRICTIONS
(1st MARCH to 31st JULY)

THE MARMOLATA BUTTRESS

ABSEIL STAKES (over East face)

POINTED BLOCKS
LOW FLAT LEDGES
ZAWN (and hand traverse)
ZAWN

SEASONAL RESTRICTION

BOULDER RUCKLE — EAST

	DIRECTOR'S GROOVE	HVS
	WINDY CITY	E1
	LIGHTNING WALL	HVS
20	ELYSIUM	E1
	SINGING WINDS	E4
	THUNDER GROOVE	HVS
	GYPSY	E1
42	STRONGBOW	E1
	AQUARIUS	E2
57	STROPHANTHIN	VS
68	XIMENES	E2
	TIGER MOTH	E1
86	GIMCRACK	VS
	QUASIMODO	HVS

2nd Stone wall West of Lighthouse

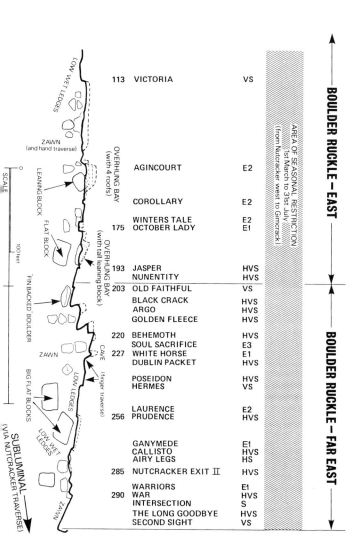

BOULDER RUCKLE — EAST

BOULDER RUCKLE — FAR EAST

SUBLUMINAL
(VIA NUTCRACKER TRAVERSE)

AREA OF SEASONAL RESTRICTION
1st March to 31st July
(from Nutcracker west to Gimcrack)

SCALE

0

100 feet

LOW WET LEDGES

ZAWN
(and hand traverse)

OVERHUNG BAY
(with 4 roofs)

LEANING BLOCK

FLAT BLOCK

OVERHUNG BAY
(with tall leaning block)

FIN BACKED BOULDER

ZAWN

CAVE

(finger traverse)

BIG FLAT BLOCKS

LOW LEDGES

LOW WET LEDGES

ZAWN

113	VICTORIA	VS
	AGINCOURT	E2
	COROLLARY	E2
	WINTERS TALE	E2
175	OCTOBER LADY	E1
193	JASPER	HVS
	NUNENTITY	HVS
203	OLD FAITHFUL	VS
	BLACK CRACK	HVS
	ARGO	HVS
	GOLDEN FLEECE	HVS
220	BEHEMOTH	HVS
	SOUL SACRIFICE	E3
227	WHITE HORSE	E1
	DUBLIN PACKET	HVS
	POSEIDON	HVS
	HERMES	VS
	LAURENCE	E2
256	PRUDENCE	HVS
	GANYMEDE	E1
	CALLISTO	HVS
	AIRY LEGS	HS
285	NUTCRACKER EXIT II	HVS
	WARRIORS	E1
290	WAR	HVS
	INTERSECTION	S
	THE LONG GOODBYE	HVS
	SECOND SIGHT	VS

∗∗ Barracuda   140 feet   E4 5c   (1.4.79/1.4.83)
Start by the step in the rock platform at the western end of the *Ocean Boulevard* wall. This unrelenting climb tackles the prominent overhanging crack just right of the big arête and requires a forceful approach.
Climb a tiny corner, a bulge, and the crack above, which steepens dramatically as it approaches the faultline. Pull over the bulge above to gain a small ledge. Make some tricky moves up and right; then continue straight up until it is possible to finish out to the left. Large stake belay.

Tuna Lick   140 feet   E4 6a †   (4.10.87)
An eliminate between *Barracuda* and *Ocean Boulevard* giving the most strenuous outing on the wall.
Climb the small corner of *Barracuda* and then go up the blank wall to a horizontal break. Follow a sustained flake crack to the faultline and continue strenuously over the bulge to a rest on *Barracuda*. Follow *Barracuda* to finish.

∗∗∗ Ocean Boulevard   130 feet   E3 5b   (3.79/21.11.81)
An immaculate and continually absorbing classic. Though easier and better protected than its neighbours, it is nonetheless a demanding piece of climbing. Start 15 feet from the left-hand end of the wall on the right side of a flat rock platform.
Follow the flake-line, taking the left-hand line where it divides, to a poor rest at the faultline. Climb the crack in the bulge above and step left to a small ledge. Follow the crack to a resting-place on the left, and continue via a flake to a fairly sound finish directly above. Large stake belay.

∗∗∗ Mother Africa   140 feet   E4 5c   (5.6.83)
A tremendous route and very sustained. This follows in its entirety the rightward-slanting crackline in the upper wall. Start 15 feet right of *Ocean Boulevard* below a flat ledge surrounded by white calcite.
Climb on good holds to the ledge and move up the thin crack with difficulty to the faultline. Traverse left a few feet to a vertical slot and surmount the bulge (peg runner), pulling up leftwards into the rightward-slanting crackline. Follow this crack, past a semi rest on a monster-sized jug, and finish up the shallow continuation groove (several peg runners). Large stake belay.
Variation
∗ The Great Hunter House Milk Robbery (130 feet E4 6a 23.10.83/16.10.85) pulls straight over the bulge at the faultline. It then continues up cracks to a peg runner, where a step left gains the parent route.

∗∗∗ Wall of the Worlds   130 feet   E4 6a   (12.6.83)
A stunning route taking a line of thin cracks and a long, shallow groove in the overhanging wall to the left of *The Last Hurrah of the Golden Horde*. Technically difficult as well as strenuous. A good selection of small and medium wires is required. Start midway between *Mother Africa* and *The*

Last Hurrah of the Golden Horde below some thin cracks in the bulging lower wall.
Climb to a tiny ledge at 20 feet (a few feet down and right of the calcite ledge on *Mother Africa*). Follow thin cracks up rightwards to a large spike runner at the faultline and pull directly over the bulge above. Move up past a flake to a small flat ledge and climb the shallow groove to a superb hidden jug. Continue to a peg runner and move right to easier ground. Climb up past an *in-situ* thread to the top. Large stake belay.

The Last Hurrah of the Golden Horde 130 feet E3 5c
(19.2.72/1976)

A serious, nerve-racking route, with weak holds and reasonable but spaced-out protection; Jerry Cornelius would have been proud of it! Start at the base of *The Ramp*, beneath a grossly bulging wall split by cracks. Climb up to a large ledge at 20 feet, traverse left, and go up the crack to the faultline. Pull over the bulge above to reach the base of a pillar. Climb this pillar carefully to a niche and continue up a crack on loose rock. Finish straight up and belay on a large stake to the left.

BOULDER RUCKLE WEST
The partially free-hanging abseil from the top of *The Ramp* deposits one beneath the chimney of *Jonah*. *The Ramp* starts a short distance to the west, beneath the leaning mass of the *Ocean Boulevard* wall; it provides a relatively fast means of escape since the rightward-leaning ramp itself has few difficulties and the suspect wall at the top can be easily overcome by using the abseil rope. However, the safest exit from the Ruckle is *Due Care and Attention* some 30 feet right of the abseil. Immediately right of *Due Care and Attention*, rough seas necessitate a short traverse across a wall to reach the groove of *Higgins*; this is recognizable by its large jammed boulder. Two hundred feet further on, and unmistakable from anywhere hereabouts, is the undercut prow of *Bottomless Buttress*. This is closely followed by the uncompromising roof-cracks of *The Fin* and its twisted twin, *Cima Petite*. One hundred and fifty feet of scrambling leads to a pointed block in front of a yellow-stained wall, the start of *Moonraker*. Next, the *Thunderball* bay may offer some close encounters with the waves; its long, low-level roof has low boulders beneath. This roof is breached by several routes, the most readily discernible being the deep corner of *Jo* situated above a cave at the bay's western end. Just around a vague corner is an east-facing wall where *Mongoose* climbs a large hanging flake. As one continues a short way east past a pointed boulder at the start of *Viper*, a huge alcove above the faultline shows where an overhang has fallen off *Cloud Nine*. Past the easily recognizable pedestal block marking the beginning of *The Cat Skinner* is a pointed boulder and the large east-facing corner of *Scythe*. The recommended abseil for the climbs hereabouts gives a dramatic and exposed descent to the start of *Ulysses*, just to the west of *Scythe*.

Boulder Ruckle West is well endowed with protective boulders at its base and in normal conditions no problems will be encountered when traversing along the bottom. In heavy seas however the two sections mentioned above, close to *Higgins* and in the *Thunderball* bay, may prove to be impassable.

The Ramp   110 feet   Severe   (c.1957)
An escape route but fairly serious for its grade; the holds on the final section are dubious and are often covered with earth dislodged by abseiling. The grade assumes the abseil rope is used to prusik up the final rock section and the earthy runnel above. Start below the conspicuous ramp-line on the right-hand side of the impressive, overhanging *Ocean Boulevard* wall.
1   90 feet.   4a.   Step off a tilted boulder and use a short rightward-facing edge to move up to the ramp; follow this easily to a good ledge and pedestal block just below the top.
2   20 feet.   Using the abseil rope, ascend the wall above and exit to the left of some doubtful-looking blocks. Continue up the earthy runnel to a stake belay. (Climbed free, this pitch is 4c, making the overall grade an unpleasant VS.)

The Boulder Ruckle Girdle Traverse
               3500 feet approx.   E1 (1 pts aid) [R]   (26.4.69/1978)
A mammoth expedition along the unmistakable horizontal faultline that runs almost the full length of Boulder Ruckle. Unfortunately, the route has been affected by two major rockfalls, at the western end of Pillar Bay and to the west of the quadruple overhangs in Boulder Ruckle East. The sections from *Ulysses* to *Little Matterhorn* and from *Victoria* to *Agincourt* have not, as yet, been reclimbed. Provisional descriptions for these pitches have been included to aid the adventurous. It is important to remember that the base of the cliff from *Strophanthin* to Subluminal cliff is not passable at sea-level except at low water, and not even then if the sea is rough, so take care when attempting this part of the girdle. Start as for *The Ramp*. No technical grades are available; who's going to check them for the *next* guidebook?!
1   120 feet.   Climb up the ramp and follow the horizontal fault to the groove of *Higgins*. Step down and belay on the large jammed boulder.
2   110 feet.   Pull around the prow and traverse across beneath the large roof. Continue along the faultline to a corner with a smooth wall on its right.
3   60 feet.   Cross the wall and another similar wall on small holds.
4   30 feet.   Step across the corner and follow it to a stance on the arête of *Bottomless Buttress*.
5   80 feet.   Traverse the wide bay along the faultline and belay on the opposite side of a pedestal in the sentry-box of *Silhouette Arête*.
6   60 feet.   Step up to the faultline and traverse across to the arête. Continue on around to another arête and belay in a corner just beyond as for *Luke*.
★ **7**   80 feet.   Follow the faultline for about 25 feet to below a short corner (peg runner). Step down a few feet and traverse to a layback crack. Regain the faultline and continue to where the lower face sets back in to

form a roof (peg runner high up). Step right to a ledge on the lip of the overhang and follow this for about 30 feet to a short chimney. Belay on the faultline above.

8 20 feet. Follow the faultline to a good ledge.

9 80 feet. Continue to another large ledge and belay at its right-hand end.

10 120 feet. Continue along the faultline over some difficult ground to belay on an arête under a roof.

11 40 feet. Continue to a corner below the top pitch of *Thor*. Belay on the large but doubtful-looking part of the ledge above the *Thunderball* bay.

12 130 feet. Continue to where the ledge becomes broken.

13 40 feet. Continue to the corner of *Rainbow*, easily recognized by the prominent wedged block in the corner below the stance.

★ **14** 20 feet. Cross the face delicately just above the faultline to a peg runner in a diagonal crack. Undercuts lead on until it is possible to step down onto a ledge. Belay in the niche of *Viper*.

15 20 feet. Move around the corner and belay on a ledge 6 feet below.

16 70 feet. Reverse the corner for about 10 feet and follow the traverse-line to the next vertical break. Regain the faultline.

17 50 feet. Continue along and around an arête to the spacious belay ledge of *Enos*. Step down and traverse right (with the faultline at head-level) to a sloping belay in a corner about 20 feet left of a large pedestal block.

18 40 feet. Follow the faultline, placing a peg for protection half-way, and belay on a good ledge as for *Ulysses*.

19 80 feet ††. **Not reclimbed** since the fall which destroyed *Blinking Crack*. A line needs to be found going rightwards to the arête and across the raw corner of *Scythe* to the corner of *Blow the House Down*.

20 50 feet. From the corner, move down a few feet and traverse rightwards above a horizontal crack to a large detached column (reversing *Blow the House Down*). Climb the column and belay on its top, as for *Little Matterhorn*.

21 80 feet. Traverse rightwards along the faultline to a ledge on the arête.

22 80 feet. Move around the arête and across a corner. Traverse the wall with difficulty to where the ledge reappears and continue to a stance 15 feet to the right of the exit corner of *Billy Pigg*.

★ **23** 100 feet. Cross a V-chimney and follow the ledge to the arête. Climb awkwardly across the corner (peg runner) and continue with difficulty along the faultline to reach a stance on a large ledge above the prow of *Sheerline*.

24 40 feet. Continue to the large detached block on *Dandruff*.

★ **25** 80 feet. Traverse around the arête, below the detached block, to a crack. Step down to a pointed ledge and move across into the corner of *Koo-Koo*. Small foot-ledges lead across the face to where the ledge reappears. Belay just beyond the overhanging groove of *RIP*.

★ **26** 120 feet. Follow the ledge to a corner with a large roof immediately above. Climb down a crack in the face and then step down and across into the corner. Move back up to the faultline and over to the corner of

Finale Groove. Cross this with difficulty to reach a good ledge. Belay by the detached block of *Sweet S A.*

27 80 feet. Climb across the corner and continue easily over to another corner where the ledge ends. Belay on the arête as for *The Heidelberg Creature,* recognizable by the flakes jammed in the corner below.

★ **28** 40 feet. Move down to a ledge and cross the face to gain a cramped ledge up to the right on the faultline. Take a hanging stance 10 feet above in the corner of *The Tool.* The second belays on the cramped ledge.

★ **29** 90 feet. From the foot of the corner, follow a ledge to a flake crack, climb this, and move right to a roof. Step around to a groove and a peg runner and move down a few feet to a ledge. Follow it delicately right to a ledge at shoulder-height and pull up to join the groove of *Tatra Direct.* Climb down the overhanging chimney and belay in the niche of *Tatra.*

30 35 feet. Traverse right for 15 feet to a large sloping ledge, pull up to the faultline above, and continue rightwards to a belay as for *Tatra* on a ledge on the nose of the *Marmolata* buttress.

31 20 feet. Cross the east facing wall of the *Marmolata* buttress via the obvious traverse line (peg runner) to a stance in the big corner of *Marmolata* itself.

32 70 feet. Move right and follow *Director's Groove* diagonally right along a ragged crack to join *Ashes and Diamonds* just above the bulge. Reverse the bulge (difficult) and belay at the faultline.

33 80 feet. Reverse *Ashes and Diamonds* for about 15 feet until it is possible to traverse right. Continue over broken ground to the groove of *Lightning Wall* and climb this to a stance and belay.

★ **34** 50 feet. Step around into the corner beneath the roof, move across on jams, and make a long reach to place a peg for protection. Swing down onto a small ledge on *Elysium* and traverse right with difficulty across the wall (peg runner) until the faultline forms a ledge again (peg runner). Traverse the ledge to a multiple-nut belay on *Thunder Groove.*

35 50 feet. Follow the faultline to the short V-chimney of *Gypsy,* cross this to a sloping ledge (peg runner), and continue to where the faultline becomes dished out and forms another sloping ledge (peg runner). Belay beyond this.

36 50 feet. Follow the faultline to a belay on *Strophanthin.*

37 100 feet. Follow the faultline to a belay on *Gimcrack.*

38 40 feet. Move across into a corner opposite the belay ledge, reverse the corner, and belay at a good stance.

39 30 feet. Climb the scoop behind the belay using a layback crack, move right at the top, and belay at the faultline.

40 80 feet. Continue along the faultline to the end of the ledge above a shallow zawn.

41 80 feet ††. **Not reclimbed.** The previous description was: 'Move into the corner beneath the roof and step down on to a large wedged flake. Descend the right-hand side of the flake to a ledge just left of a sloping slab, cross the slab to an overhanging corner and climb this to a ledge under the roof. Follow the ledge until it is possible to place a peg for protection in the roof and to step down onto the face. Continue to the very large ledge atop The Arch.' However, the ledge has gone, following the demise of The Arch.

42 60 feet ††. Also **not reclimbed** since The Arch fell. 'Follow the faultline around the corner and make an awkward few moves to pass beneath a projection of rock. Continue along the faultline to a small stance just before a shallow bay capped by large overhangs.'

★ **43** 55 feet (1 pt aid). Climb around into the corner under the roof (peg runner) and reverse this corner for about 15 feet. Traverse right to a good ledge at the back of the bay. The second man climbs across to the peg and, using this, tyrolean traverses across to the belay ledge.

44 60 feet (1 pt aid). From the middle of the belay ledge, step down, traverse right a few feet, and move up to a small ledge. Move right again and climb a smooth, shallow groove just before the arête with a peg for aid. Follow the faultline and belay at a good ledge on a narrow prow.

45 100 feet. Follow the faultline along easy ledges.

46 100 feet. Continue easily again until a difficult section is reached. Belay on the arête as for *The Golden Fleece*. (At the beginning of the next pitch is a slender finger of rock projecting from the faultline.)

★ **47** 80 feet. Cross the short wall towards the corner. When opposite the finger of rock, lean across and pull up onto it, and then continue a few feet to a short corner. Move around past a peg runner into a corner under the roof, traverse right, and continue more easily to a ledge in the corner of *White Horse*.

48 50 feet. Move down and follow the faultline over some difficult ground to a belay point where the ledge reappears.

49 50 feet. Continue across the corner and carry on until a smooth wall is reached. Belay as for *Prudence*.

★ **50** 60 feet. Move into a corner and cross the smooth wall with difficulty, placing a peg for protection in a small hole (in the face above) about two-thirds of the way along. Continue to a corner and follow the faultline to a good ledge and belay.

51 60 feet. Follow the faultline with fluctuating difficulty to a good belay ledge at the foot of the corner of *War*.

52 80 feet. Traverse the faultline as for *The Nutcracker Traverse* to reach the western end of Subliminal. Congratulations!

The First Och-Aye of the Tartan Army   110 feet   E3   (23.7.83)

An excursion onto the overhanging wall above *The Ramp*. Start to the right of the start of *The Ramp* beneath a crack.

1 60 feet 4c/5a. Climb the crack, passing a large detached block with care, to gain a sloping ledge. Continue up more easily to a ledge on *The Ramp*.

2 50 feet 5b. Move up and traverse out left on good holds to a peg runner in a horizontal crack. Climb the wall slightly left to reach an undercut flake, and move up leftwards to follow a series of jugs and a shallow groove to the top. Stake belay.

★★ **Indian Pacific**   130 feet   E4   5c   (15.3.86)
A magnificent girdle of the *Ocean Boulevard* wall, starting 75 feet up *The Ramp* at a block belay.
Move up and traverse left on good holds to a peg runner in a horizontal crack. Climb along a vague break (peg runner low down) to a niche on *The Last Hurrah of the Golden Horde*. Step down and across into *Wall of the Worlds*. Step up, and then climb on pockets past *The Great Hunter House Milk Robbery* (peg runner). Move up and left again to good holds on *Mother Africa* (peg runner). Continue left and finish as for *Ocean Boulevard*. Stake belay.

Screaming Blue Messiah   60 feet   E3   6a   (18.5.86)
This climb up the wall right of *The First Och-Aye of the Tartan Army* top pitch has an *in-situ* thread and a peg runner. Start at a block belay 75 feet up *The Ramp*.
Step left and climb steepening thin cracks with difficulty to the top break. Finish up a short groove and an unpleasant earth slope to gain a stake belay.

Old Ghosts (Scare Me Most)   100 feet   E3   †   (10.4.93)
The line of the abseil gives a serious start and a strenuous mid section, but these are broken by a rest on *Jonah*.
1 80 feet 6a. Climb the slab of *Jonah* before making hard moves over the bulge above to gain an outstanding (in both senses of the word) jug. Some more good holds lead to a rest on the right. Move back left and follow cracks to a ledge. Climb a short wall and belay at the top of the ramp.
2 20 feet 4a. *Jonah* pitch 2.

Jonah   100 feet   Very Severe   (1974)
A mediocre route up the crack-system which defines the right-hand side of the buttress below the top of the prominent ramp. Start at the foot of the abseil from the top of *The Ramp*, 40 feet right of that climb's starting-point.
1 80 feet 4b. Climb a slab and a crack to a short corner leading to the faultline. Continue carefully up the chimney to a good ledge and pedestal block (belay shared with The Ramp).
2 20 feet 4a. Traverse right and move up to a roof. Bear left and continue up a wall to the earthy bank above. Stake belay.

Road to Ruin   110 feet   E2   (5.11.83)
This takes the steep headwall up and to the right of the corner-line of *Jonah*. The climbing on the second pitch is strenuous. Start at the foot of a rib 25 feet right of *Jonah*.
1 60 feet 4a. Climb the rib to a short wall, and continue up a groove on the left to a stance at the faultline.
2 50 feet 5b. Climb the wall to the right of the belay for 10 feet and step left onto a flake. A difficult move gains good holds on the right and a crackline, which leads to the top on friable rock. Twin belay stakes.

Due Care and Attention   110 feet   Hard Severe   (6.65)
Poorly protected for its initial 30 feet, and some rubble at the top requires
care, but overall the safest easy exit from the Ruckle. Start on a narrow
ledge beneath a wide, shallow groove.
1 80 feet 4a. Climb the easy groove and exit from it onto a slab (crux).
Climb the stepped crack on the right, which leads up to the final open
groove of *Jericho Groove*. Large nut belay.
2 30 feet 4a. Climb the crack in the groove to the top. Stake belay.

Displacement Activity   110 feet   E1 †   (21.10.84)
Although the top pitch is steep, the climbing proves delicate rather than
strenuous. Start as for *Higgins*.
1 70 feet 4c. Climb to the overhang at 15 feet and swing left on to the
blunt arête. Move up and leftwards to the bottom of a shallow groove.
Follow this and cross easier ground to belay at the foot of a crack (the
final crack of the last route).
2 40 feet 5b. Pull up onto the wall on the left and move left to a large
incut foothold. Climb the vague depression above past a peg runner,
taking care with the final handholds. Twin belay stakes.

Higgins   110 feet   Very Severe   (29.6.68)
A challenging first pitch, and some doubtful blocks in the final groove that
are difficult to avoid. Start 50 feet east of the entry abseil at a prominent
groove sporting a sizeable wedged block in its mid section. (This corner
bounds the left end of a very large roof at the faultline.)
1 50 feet 4c. Climb up and pull around the initial overhang into the
corner. Climb this to a comfortable stance atop the jammed boulder. (Or,
less vulnerable to stonefall, continue up and left to the optional stance on
Jericho Groove.)
2 60 feet 4b. Climb the groove to the top, passing an overhang with
care. Stake belay.

★ **Jericho Groove**   130 feet   Hard Severe   (Pre-1963)
An interesting and popular introduction to the Ruckle with a splendid first
pitch. Some loose rock at the top requires care but should not present any
difficulty. Start at the foot of a crack 25 feet right of *Higgins*.
1 70 feet 4a. Climb the crack in the wall and continue up leftwards to a
corner below the big roof. Move up the corner with a hard move to
overcome a bulge, and then traverse left above a prow to gain the corner
of *Higgins*. Belay on top of the jammed boulder.
2 60 feet 4a. Climb the groove above to a small bulge at 15 feet, step
left, and follow ledges up to the left to an open groove (optional stance).
Climb the crack in the groove to the top. Stake belay.

Herem Roof   120 feet   E4 †   (12.10.87)
Spectacular climbing across a seemingly blank roof, which requires the
human-plank manoeuvre: levitating horizontally from foot-jams!
1 70 feet 6a. Climb the first section of *Jericho Groove* and continue to

the overlap in the centre of the 8-foot roof. Cross this to a jug on the lip (*in-situ* thread). Belay on the slab above.
2 50 feet 5a. Climb the bulging wall, stepping right to bypass the final overhang. Slabby ground leads to a stake belay.

Cold Comfort   130 feet   Hard Very Severe   (1.1.80)
Start 50 feet east of *Higgins* at a tiny V-niche.
1 80 feet 4c. Move up into the little niche, climb up leftwards, and follow the obvious, slanting ramp to the large roof above. Hand-traverse right and climb a short V-chimney at the end of the roof. Belay using many poor nuts and *Friends* on the slab up to the left.
2 50 feet 4b/c. A worrying pitch. Climb up and over a small overhang before following a deep flake-line diagonally right. At its end, move right and finish steeply up a slight corner. Belay on bushes and a stake far to the right.

Chamberwall II   140 feet   Hard Very Severe   (6.4.69)
This poor route has an unstable top pitch and is not recommended. Start 10 feet right of *Cold Comfort*.
1 70 feet. Climb a short crack, move up past a large hole, and ascend a corner to the faultline. Go up a small V-groove, placing a peg for protection, and take a stance on the left. Peg belays.
2 70 feet. Move up diagonally right for 20 feet, before going up and back left, following the line of least resistance. Exit left up a slight groove.

Chamberwall   130 feet   Hard Very Severe   (6.4.69)
Similar to the previous route and likewise not recommended. Start at a rightward-slanting slab.
1 60 feet. Climb the slab and move right at the top into a groove. Continue to a good stance at the faultline. Peg belays.
2 70 feet. Follow the easiest line rightwards and up to the top.

Vicissitude   160 feet   Very Severe   (23.10.70)
An interesting line but with a serious exit. Start at a V-groove with an overhang at its base just right of the slanting slab.
1 60 feet 4a. Climb the groove, step left, and continue up the slab to a stance.
2 100 feet 4c. Move up rightwards to the top of a slab, and step down to the right onto another slab. Continue across this until above a small corner. Surmount the overhang above and ascend the groove on the right to the top. Exit with care. Stake belay.

★ **Black Sunshine**   150 feet   Very Severe   (24.10.71)
Two really nice pitches, solid and varied throughout. Start below a shallow scoop, immediately left of the big boulder marking the start of *Springbok Route*.
1 80 feet 4c. Climb up the scoop to a thin, undercut flake and climb this to a good foothold on the left. Move up and traverse 20 feet right to a

corner and a slab. Climb the slab to a stance on the left at the faultline.
2 70 feet 4b. Climb directly up to the overhang above, traverse right for 10 feet, and surmount the overhang on good holds. Continue to a stake belay over the top.

Springbok Route   130 feet   Very Severe   (28.8.66)
Very loose at the top and not recommended. Behind a large, tall boulder is a rightward-facing corner at the left end of a large roof at 20 feet; start here.
1 60 feet 4c. Climb the corner past two overhangs to a stance at the faultline.
2 70 feet 4b. Traverse right for 15 feet to a short groove. Climb up and diagonally right for about 25 feet to a small ledge, before following a groove on doubtful rock to the top. Stake belays.

> **Celibacy Screws You Up** (120 feet E4 6b 4b †† 1989) used a bolt runner before Boulder Ruckle was declared a bolt-free zone; consequently the bolt may have been removed. To complicate matters, a block at the lip of the roof has now fallen. The route has yet to be reascended and the grade merely reflects its previous state. Starting 30 feet right of *Springbok Route*, the climb crossed the large roof and belayed in a crack on the left. It then continued up past the faultline before moving into the groove of *Springbok Route* to finish.

* **Nassty Spider**   125 feet   E1   (26.7.75/10.6.84)
Exciting moves to cross the roof. Start at the right-hand end of a large roof at 20 feet (20 feet left of *Bottomless Buttress*).
1 60 feet 5c. Climb the wall and crack to good runners beneath the roof. Move up and reach out to clip an *in-situ* sling attached to a peg on the lip of the roof; now pull leftwards to large chert holds above the roof. Traverse left on jugs and follow a crack to a secure stance just below the faultline.
2 65 feet 5a. Climb up diagonally right following two stepped roofs. Move right again and pull over a bulge with care to join *Aventura*. Follow the corner above to a sound finish and a stake belay. (The original finish is spoilt by loose rock: this went back left around the rib to a little ledge, up right past an overhang (peg runner), and left to the top.)

Routes in this area are easily located with reference to the large, stepped roofs at 20 feet, which provide the exposure for *Bottomless Buttress*.

* **Aventura**   110 feet   Hard Very Severe   (29.8.64)
The large block forming the roof on pitch 2 provides the superb crux of a memorable climb. This block appears to have tilted slightly, however, and as a consequence the route can no longer be unreservedly recommended. A three-star route for all but one unlucky person? Start at a cave below the corner just west of *Bottomless Buttress*.
1 50 feet 4b/c. Climb up out of the cave and follow the corner above,

until it can be quitted for an ammonite thread belay up and to the right on
the faultline.
2 60 feet 4c. Move up and left to a wide crack in the roof. Pull as gently
as possible over the sagging roof (even more intimidating than it used to
be) and climb the cracks above to a ledge. Follow a corner to a sound
finish and a stake belay.

★ Judgement Day   110 feet   E2 †   (10.4.92)
Enjoyable climbing with a roof that proves easier than it looks. Start
midway between *Aventura* and *Death Is a Gift*.
1 50 feet 4c. After a steep start, climb up the blunt cracked arête to the
left-hand end of the triangular roof. Move up to flakes on the right and
continue to the faultline. Ammonite thread belay.
2 60 feet 5c. Step right and climb to a square-cut niche in the lower
roof, beneath a zigzag crack in the main roof. Cross this 6-foot roof,
traverse left, and finish up a wall. Stake belay.

Death Is a Gift   130 feet   Hard Very Severe   (2.78/11.83)
Start below a roof-capped corner on the left-hand side of the bottomless
buttress. Safer than its name suggests, but with little independent climbing
on pitch 2.
1 60 feet 5a. Climb the corner and traverse rightwards to turn the roof.
Carry on easily to the faultline and an ammonite thread belay.
2 70 feet 4c. Move up for 15 feet and traverse to the right-hand end of
the roofs. Contrived climbing up the short wall, just left of the orange scar
taken by *Bottomless Buttress*, leads to a stake belay on the left.

★ Bottomless Buttress   120 feet   Hard Severe   (16.6.64)
Some 300 feet east of the abseil from the top of *The Ramp* is a jutting nose
of rock that is undercut by large stepped roofs at 20 feet, a useful
landmark. Start immediately right of the buttress at the foot of a corner.
1 60 feet 4a. Climb the corner for 15 feet, and then go leftwards across
the wall onto the front of the buttress. (Optional belay to reduce rope-
drag.) Follow two narrow cracks to the faultline ledge. Belay on large
nuts.
2 60 feet 4a. Move up for 15 feet and traverse right to the edge. Climb
the raw corner above and exit left with care at the top. Stake belay.

Between *Bottomless Buttress* and the roofs of *The Fin* and *Cima Petite* lies an
orange-coloured bay, the scene of a large rockfall in 1976. The three routes
that now lie amidst the rubble have been replaced by four:

The Dead Can't Judge   110 feet   Hard Very Severe 4c †   (9.6.90)
Some suspect rock above the faultline. Start as for *Bottomless Buttress*.
Climb up the crack to the faultline and then past three roofs. Finish straight
up as for *Bottomless Buttress* to a stake belay on the left.

Andycap   130 feet   Hard Very Severe   (2.7.77)
Some poor rock near the top and not very well protected either. Start 15
feet right of *Bottomless Buttress* by a tiny cave.
1 65 feet 4b. Climb the crack above the cave and the flakes above to
the faultline. Belay on a ledge 15 feet to the right, as for *Tim*, very sensibly
out of line with the top pitch!
2 65 feet 4c. Traverse back left to a pillar and climb this until a flake can
be used to gain a crack on the right. Follow the crack to where it becomes
blocked and place a peg runner. Using the right wall, gain the
continuation of the crack and climb it to the top, placing a second peg
runner. Care is needed on the upper part. Stake Belay.

Tim   120 feet   Hard Severe   (30.4.77)
A pleasant first pitch; thereafter dirty and uninteresting. Start at the foot of
the ragged crack 30 feet right of *Bottomless Buttress*.
1 50 feet. Climb the crack and belay at the faultline.
2 40 feet. Traverse left for 20 feet and make an awkward step up onto a
ledge in a corner. Belay on a large ledge above.
3 30 feet 4a. Finish up *Bottomless Buttress*: climb the corner on the left
and exit left with care at the top. Stake belay on the left.

★ **Silhouette Arête**   120 feet   Very Severe   (14.5.78)
Extremely exposed climbing up the hanging arête more than compensates
for a mediocre first pitch. Start just right of *Tim*, below a flake purported to
resemble south-eastern England.
1 60 feet 4a. From the Isle of Wight, grasp The Wash and continue on
good holds to a small ledge. Traverse right and follow a short corner to a
sentry-box.
2 60 feet 4c. Traverse right along the faultline for 15 feet and pull up
onto the wall above. Move right and climb the arête to an overhang
harbouring a peg runner. Surmount the overhang and continue to a large
flake. An easy groove leads to the final ledge of *Cima Petite* and a stake
belay beyond.

★ **The Fin**   130 feet   E5   (24.7.83)
A sensational route which, after a serious start, gives excellent jamming
across a horizontal ceiling. Right of *Silhouette Arête* is a short corner; start
at the overhanging groove right of this (60 feet east of *Bottomless Buttress*).
1 70 feet 6a. Climb the groove to a bulge and surmount this leftwards
using fingerholds in the chert (poor peg runner). Move up to a good
resting-place below the roof. Cross the roof on positive jams to a welcome
chockstone above the lip, and follow the corner above to the faultline.
2 60 feet 4c. Traverse left onto the prow and climb the arête on superb
holds, as for *Silhouette Arête*, to a peg runner at an overhang. Climb the
rib and easy groove to a stake belay at the top.

★ **Cima Petite**   130 feet   E4   (6.11.77/29.11.81)
An impeccably-sculptured exercise in roof technique which unfortunately

has a rather disturbing upper section. Start 10 feet right of *The Fin*, below a large roof split by an inviting diagonal crack.

1 60 feet 6a. Climb the steep crack, move left, and ascend a steep wall past a poor peg runner to another peg runner at the roof. Exposed and dramatic moves across the roof are followed by easy climbing up a crack to the faultline. Belay to the left.

2 70 feet 5a/b. Move back right and up a corner for a few feet until a traverse right gains an arête. Climb this arête (*Friend 3* useful) and surmount the roof above. Move left into a corner and out again, to finish up the main arête. Stake belay.

Luke   130 feet   E1   (26.7.75)
Suspect holds on the top pitch make this a worrying lead. Start as for *Cima Petite*.

1 75 feet 4c. Climb the crack in the corner for 20 feet, traverse right to a deep crack, and follow it to the faultline. Belay slightly to the left.

2 55 feet 5b. Step back right and climb the corner to a roof. The crux: move rightwards around the roof and straight up to the top. Stake belay.

Rhino   130 feet   Hard Very Severe   (15.3.75)
Thirty feet right of *Luke* is a corner leading to a slim flake which reaches up to the faultline.

1 50 feet 4c. Climb the corner to a resting-place and follow the flake/groove to the faultline. Belay slightly to the right.

2 80 feet 4c/5a. Climb up steeply for 10 feet and traverse right for 20 feet to a corner. Move up this for a few feet and traverse right with difficulty into the prominent upper corner of *Tomorrow's Grief*. Climb the corner and exit right at the top. Stake belay.

★ The Earth's at Flashpoint   130 feet   E3   5b †   (24.3.90)
A solid, varied line which crosses *Rhino*. Start 15 feet right of *Rhino* from a large boulder.
Climb a short corner to ledges beneath a continuation corner. Swing left underneath a roof to stand on a block, and climb the front of the pillar (peg runner) to the faultline (optional belay, as for *Rhino*). Climb up to the huge ammonite in the roof, move leftwards over the roof, and then step back right. Finish straight up on positive holds (peg runner) to the exit of *Luke*. Stake Belay.

Nuclear Sunset   120 feet   E3 †   (23.5.87)
An unbalanced climb with the difficulties confined to the roof. Start at a 20-foot corner 20 feet left of *Tomorrow's Grief*.

1 70 feet 6a. Climb the corner and the crack above to the centre of a 5-foot roof. Cross this, passing an *in-situ* thread, and move up to a small belay ledge in a corner.

2 50 feet 4c/5a. Traverse right and finish up the corner of *Tomorrow's Grief*. Stake belay.

★ Tomorrow's Grief   105 feet   Very Severe   4b/c   (21.10.73)
A worthwhile and popular route, but some care is required on the upper section. Start 80 feet east of *Luke*, below a juggy crack leading up to an obvious exit corner.
Follow the crack on superb holds past a roof to the faultline. Step up off the faultline ledge, and bridge across to a small corner on the left. Climb up and then right to a good ledge below the top corner. Climb the corner to a rightward exit at the top. Stake belay.

Fetish   120 feet   Hard Very Severe   (30.3.75)
Start below an open groove on the front of the buttress immediately right of *Tomorrow's Grief*.
1 60 feet 4c/5a. Climb a short crack and traverse 10 feet right to pull through a break in the overlap. Ascend the groove to the faultline.
2 60 feet 4b. Climb up diagonally left across the wall to a short groove that leads to the top. Stake belay.

Perversion   120 feet   Very Severe   (17.7.66)
An unfriendly route which is serious for its grade. The second pitch is badly protected and dangerously loose. Not recommended. Start 15 feet right of *Fetish*, at a corner that reaches up to the faultline.
1 60 feet 4b. Pull strenuously through the overhang and climb the corner to the faultline. Belay at a good ledge on the left.
2 60 feet 4b. Climb straight up above the belay, step right, and follow the groove to the top. A steep and unpleasant pitch. Stake belay.

Midge   120 feet   E2   (2.7.77)
A fine, strenuous start, but the top pitch is a scary experience where loose rock is combined with ground-fall potential; not recommended. Start immediately right of *Perversion* below a diagonal line of cracks.
1 60 feet 5b. Surmount the overhang with difficulty and follow the flakes diagonally right before heading straight up to the faultline.
2 60 feet 5a. Climb the crack to the overhangs, and traverse right around a rib for 15 feet until beneath a prominent jutting overhang. This seems better than any other alternative, so pull over with difficulty and move right before continuing up to the top. Stake belay amidst the bushes.

★ Happy David   120 feet   Hard Very Severe   (19.6.77)
An interesting route on reasonable rock, with a bold and committing crux. Start below a smooth, triangular roof at 20 feet, some 40 feet right of *Perversion*.
1 70 feet 5a. Surmount the overhang and move up to the roof. Pull around this on the left, move up a short crack, and go right to the arête. Climb the overhanging corner to a ledge and continue to the faultline. Belay on a good ledge as for *The Corpse*.
2 50 feet 5a/b. Move up above the ledge and trend rightwards, until good holds lead to a peg runner below the main roof. Pull over the roof on the left (crux) and continue up slabby rock to the top. Stake belay.

The Corpse 130 feet E1 †   (12.7.75)
The second pitch has suffered a rockfall and is now loose and serious; not
recommended. Start below the steep corner just west of the pointed block
of *Moonraker*.
1 65 feet 5a. Climb the right wall to the bulge and surmount this
strenuously to gain the easy corner above. Belay on a good ledge to the
left at the faultline.
2 65 feet 5a. Move left along the ledge for 15 feet and climb the wall
above to an overhang. Go up right to a good runner and then back left
above the overhang. Continue up the depression above and finish on the
right. Stake belay amongst the bushes.
Variation
Stiff Start †   (29.11.81)
1a 55 feet 5a/b. Midway between the prominent corners of *Perversion*
and *The Corpse* is a short undercut corner leading to a blank bulge. Climb
this and step left around the arête. Move easily up and right to a belay at
the left-hand end of the faultline ledge.

William McGonagall 50 feet E4 6a †   (1989)
This route starts midway between *The Corpse* and *Moonraker* and is a trip
to the faultline ledge only.
Climb cracks to a section of roof a few feet lower than the rest. Continue
steeply up and follow a flake crack to the faultline. Block Belay.

Moonraker 120 feet Very Severe   (14.9.64)
High in its grade, with some hard climbing to start and a disappointing
top pitch. Start where a pointed boulder leans against a yellow-stained
wall, some 60 feet east of *Fetish* and 50 feet west of the *Thunderball* bay.
1 50 feet 5a. Climb a shallow, yellow-stained groove to better holds and
follow a corner past a prominent ledge to the faultline.
2 70 feet 4b. Climb the slight depression above for 10 feet; then go
awkwardly up rightwards past a peg runner to gain the edge of a small
nose (some loose rock). Easier climbing leads up right to another corner
and a delicate exit over loose blocks. Stake belay.

★ **Sun Streets** 120 feet E2 †   (31.8.86)
A fine, airy route.
1 60 feet 5b. Climb the short groove right of *Moonraker* to its capping
roof. Pull out left and go up 10 feet before traversing back right on the lip
to a hanging arête, which leads to the faultline.
2 60 feet 5c. Pull over the roof and climb a strenuous crack just right of
the arête to the roof on *Snowdrop*. Step left onto the arête and continue
directly up a compact rib to a stake belay.

★ **Snowdrop** 120 feet E1   (31.3.75)
Exciting and intimidating on its second pitch. Start at the clean-cut corner
25 feet right of *Moonraker*, just before the western end of the *Thunderball*
bay.

1 60 feet 4c. Climb the corner to a hanging stance at the faultline.
2 60 feet 5b. Climb up to the overhangs and escape out left onto the
arête. Follow this until it is possible to move back onto the lip of the final
roof. Continue to the top and belay on a stake.

Raindrop 120 feet Hard Very Severe (12.6.77)
A loose top pitch, and high in its grade. Start from boulders immediately
east of *Snowdrop*, below a crack in an overhang at 15 feet.
1 50 feet 5a/b. Climb to the crack in the overhang and pull onto the
wall. Continue to a leftward-slanting crack and follow it to the faultline.
Hanging belay in the corner to the left as for *Snowdrop*.
2 70 feet 5a. Move back above the crack and surmount an overhang
(peg runner above). Now go diagonally right to the arête. The arête is
steep and the rock dubious; climb it past a peg runner, and belay at a
stake.

★ **St Elmo's Fire** 120 feet E3 (13.7.86)
Exposed climbing with a bold start. Start 10 feet right of *Raindrop* on a
boulder.
1 60 feet 5c. Struggle around the roof and continue just left of the arête
to a break. Step right and climb the arête to the faultline.
2 60 feet 5c. Climb a crack just right of the arête and then the arête
itself to a roof. Continue over this (hidden protection crack on the right) to
easier climbing and a stake belay.

★★ **Thunderball** 110 feet Hard Very Severe (11.7.63/7.6.75)
An engaging route of great character. The climb is high in the grade
with an unprotected start (unless you have a *Friend* $2\frac{1}{2}$) and a top pitch
which breaks through some daunting overhangs. Start 25 feet right of the
corner of Snowdrop, at the left-hand side of the wide, overhung
Thunderball bay.
1 60 feet 5a. Pull through the overhang on good holds and cross the
bulge above to a resting-place. Climb diagonally right to the arête,
delicately around into a small corner, and up this easily to the faultline.
2 50 feet 5a. From the end of the ledge, climb the left wall to a small
roof. Turn this on the left and traverse back right below the large roof. Pull
through the break above with difficulty and climb a corner to the final
roof. Exit up to the left and scramble up to a stake belay.
Variation
Lunatic 120 feet E3 5c † (12.11.86)
A direct version of *Thunderball*.
Climb the overhang and bulge of *Thunderball* and carry on straight up the
groove to the faultline. From the end of the ledge, climb the left wall to a
small roof. Turn this on the left and pull straight over the large roof above,
before stepping left to finish. Stake belay.

★★ **Jo** 105 feet Hard Very Severe (16.6.68/31.3.75)
An enjoyable climb passing through impressive ground for its grade. Start

at the western end of the *Thunderball* bay, where a deep cavern is concealed by roofs.

1 55 feet 4c. Climb the right wall of the cave easily to a ledge on the arête beneath the roof. Bridge up, pull into the corner above, and follow this to a comfortable stance at the faultline. Various nuts and a small thread.

2 50 feet 5a. Move up onto the wall above the belay and continue up right to a steep bulge. Pull over to a good nut runner and make a strenuous move to gain the foot of a smooth groove. Climb the well-protected groove to the top and exit right onto a small ledge. A reasonably sound finish leads to a stake belay.

★ **Thor**   140 feet   Hard Very Severe   (7.6.75/11.7.63)
A good route with a tortuous and interesting start. Beware rope-drag on the first pitch. Start 15 feet right of *Jo* beneath a large roof.

1 75 feet 4c/5a. Climb to a niche below the roof. Hand-traverse left around the bulge, pull up onto the lip of the roof, and move up rightwards across a wall to gain a groove. Follow this for 10 feet before traversing back left to a corner-crack, which leads to a belay at the faultline.

2 65 feet 5a. Traverse rightwards along the faultline and climb the wall above diagonally right to a groove. Climb the groove until forced out left, move up, and go back right above the bulge. Continue to a stake belay at the top. (Better but harder if the groove is climbed direct.)

★★ **Relax and Swing**   160 feet   E5   (23.7.83)
An amazing climb, its major attraction being the extensive gymnastics required to cross the seemingly ludicrous 20-foot roof. Demanding throughout. Start (as for *Thor*) 15 feet right of *Jo* beneath a large roof.

1 40 feet 6a. Climb to the roof, where a complicated series of manoeuvres leads out rightwards along the crack. Pull around the lip with considerable relief and take a hanging belay in the square-cut corner.

2 50 feet 5b. Avoid the large roof above by a traverse left to the arête. Climb up to a corner-crack and follow it easily to the faultline (as for *Thor*).

3 70 feet 5c. Climb the shallow groove above for 15 feet. Traverse diagonally right beneath a smooth wall to a thin crack at its right edge. Follow the crack, and step left at the top to finish. Stake belay.
Variation

3a 60 feet 5c † (23.7.83). This, although the original and more direct pitch, is loose at the top. Pull straight onto the upper wall and move rightwards to a smooth area split by a very thin blind crack (just left of the crack mentioned above). Follow the crack (*RPs*) by using small fingerholds on the right before stepping back left above it to a steep finish. Stake belay.

Sardine Special   120 feet   E5 (1 pt aid) †   (19.9.76/7.6.87)
A desperately strenuous first pitch that was originally A2. Start beneath the short, hanging corner right of *Relax and Swing*. Since the first free ascent the boulder used to gain the lip of the roof has shifted. The

alternative method of gaining the lip, using a 25-foot finger-crack in the roof, has yet to be climbed, and *may* just push up the grade!

1 50 feet 6b. From a human pyramid imitating the absent boulder, pull directly over the roof to enter the corner above. Move up and traverse right just below a roof to a crack. Cross the next roof on widely-spaced jugs to gain the left-hand groove.

2 70 feet 5a. Climb the chimney/groove to the faultline, step right, and continue to a roof. Traverse right and move up into a short groove, which is followed to the top.

Third World 120 feet E4 (1 pt aid) † (25.6.83)

Perplexing and very strenuous on its crux roof. It is especially awkward to arrange the required protection. Start 50 feet right of *Jo* underneath a boss of rock.

1 60 feet 6a. Climb to the ledge immediately right of the boss. Move out left (awkward) and place a *Friend* for protection above the lip with difficulty. Cut loose and make a wild swing from a good hold above (some assistance from the rope was used to stop swinging off the hold on the first ascent). Place a nut to supplement the *Friend* and traverse left along the lip until an awkward pull gains better holds and a resting-place under a small roof. Step right and climb a short crack for a few feet until a traverse right leads to easy ground. Follow the easy crack to the faultline.

2 60 feet 5a. Traverse 15 feet rightwards along the faultline to a crack at the foot of a long groove. Climb the groove to the top. Twin-stake belay.

Jug Index 110 feet E4 † (29.11.87)

A vicious problem.

1 50 feet 6b. Gain the ledge and cross the 6-foot roof, past an *in-situ;* thread and a jug on the lip, to a square-cut corner above. Continue easily to the faultline.

2 60 feet 5a. *Third World* pitch 2.

Dogwatch 130 feet E3 † (1.4.72/1980/9.6.90)

The initial roof-crack is no more since the collapse of the right-hand roof. What remains is enjoyable but unbalanced, as the strenuous crux is followed by much easier climbing. Start at the eastern end of the *Thunderball* bay's long low roof.

1 70 feet 5c. Climb up past the right-hand end of a ledge to the roof. Undercut leftwards for 8 feet and then out to the lip. Follow the crack above through a bulge, and belay in the corner just beneath the faultline.

2 60 feet 4c. From a ledge on the left, pull up leftwards on suspect rock, and follow the groove to the top on better rock. Stake belay.

Coral Slabs 120 feet E3 † (14.7.79/1980/28.4.95)

A difficult start, much harder since the rockfall which affected its neighbour, but this soon relents to give more straightforward climbing. Start at the eastern edge of the *Thunderball* bay, just right of *Dogwatch*.

1 60 feet 5c. Climb the initial wall to a bulge, step out rightwards, and pull up into a bottomless corner (peg runner). Cross the left wall with difficulty and move up to the ledge above. Continue left and up to a chockstone belay in the corner just below the faultline as for *Dogwatch*.

2 60 feet 5a. Pull over the roof on the left and continue up a corner for a few feet. Climb diagonally right to where the roof peters out and go up a short corner. Move left a fraction and finish up a slight groove in a steep wall.

Mongoose   120 feet   E3   (29.6.69/10.75)

The initial section of this climb has become much looser. A great pity as the strenuous and awkward climbing above to move under the hanging flake is a memorable experience. Start around from the *Thunderball* bay below a wedged block at 15 feet.

1 60 feet 5b. Climb up onto the block. Continue with difficulty up a small groove on the left to better holds below the roof. Jams and widely-spaced footholds lead out left under the roof to a steep groove. Climb this, past a resting-place and a thread runner, and belay at the faultline.

2 60 feet 4c. Climb up the corner above to a ledge. Follow a crack to just below a small roof and traverse right across the slab to finish up an obvious corner. A pleasant and sound exit. Stake belay.

★ Future Primitive   120 feet   E4   (5.11.83)

A superb jamming problem across a 6-foot roof which is similar to *Cima Petite*, though slightly harder. Start 5 feet right of *Mongoose* at a groove leading up unpleasant-looking, overhanging rock.

1 70 feet 6b. Enter the groove from the right and follow it to a roof. Traverse 10 feet right to some undercuts and pull up right to an unstable ledge below the big roof. Swing left and follow the roof-crack, until a difficult pull around the lip gains an easy groove leading to the faultline.

2 50 feet 5a. Climb a groove on the right to a flat ledge. Step back left and follow a crack-and-groove-system just right of the arête to the top.

Vicky the Viking   130 feet   E2 †   (10.9.90)

Start as for *Rainbow*.

1 60 feet 5c. Follow *Rainbow* for 15 feet, move leftwards, and then go up to a roof. Surmount the roof with difficulty and climb the crack above to the faultline.

2 70 feet 5a. From above the first pitch of *Rainbow*, climb up to a roof. Traverse right under this for 20 feet and climb directly up for a further 20 feet. Move around an arête and finish up a chossy groove.

Rainbow   150 feet   Very Severe   (26.3.67)

Loose at the top but otherwise quite pleasant. To the east of the *Thunderball* bay, past a prominent roof at 45 feet, is a square-cut corner sporting a prominent wedged block. Start below this corner.

1 90 feet 4b. Pull onto a rib and climb past a doubtful bulge to a crack. Follow the corner to the faultline and traverse easily left to belay at the foot of a groove.
2 60 feet 4b. Climb the groove, trending right to a ledge. Move right into a steep corner, which is climbed to a finish slightly left at the top. Scramble up grass to a stake belay.

⋆ **Get outta Your Armchair and into This**
                                   110 feet   E5 6a † (16.10.94)
The narrow face right of the corner of *Rainbow*; sustained and with two bold sections, one of which can be mitigated by a large *Friend* runner. Start 10 feet from the corner.
From the right-hand side of a shallow recess, step right onto a blunt undercut rib. Climb the rib to a bulge, and make a tricky move over this to better holds and gear. Continue straight up the blankening wall and make a thin move to reach the faultline (*Friend* $3\frac{1}{2}$ or *4*). Cross the roof and follow a diagonal crack, before climbing over the right-hand side of another roof. Go up flakes to join the rounded arête on the right and a solid exit groove. The final slope is a little steeper than usual, so a preplaced rope could be forgiven.

Viper   145 feet   Hard Very Severe   (29.8.64)
Very loose and unprotected in its upper part, this is a steep, traumatic experience advisable only for the manic depressive. Start 40 feet right of *Rainbow*, to the left of a distinctive pointed boulder.
1 85 feet 4c. Climb the short, rounded arête for 15 feet and traverse left to a corner, which is followed on good holds to a ledge just below the faultline. Traverse 15 feet left along the ledge and break through to a belay in a short corner.
2 60 feet 4c. Climb up over an awkward bulge to a narrow roof and a peg runner before traversing left with difficulty to where the roof diminishes. Pull onto the wall above (crux) and step back right into the corner (the corner can be gained direct but this is harder). Follow the corner to the top with extreme care and belay at a stake.

⋆ **Asp**   110 feet   Very Severe   (24.6.73)
A devious yet worthwhile line which starts as for *Viper*.
1 50 feet 4b. Climb the short, rounded arête. Move across rightwards and follow a corner to the faultline. Belay a few feet to the right in a niche.
2 60 feet 4c. Move back left and climb a corner to a bulge; then traverse out right and go up to a ledge on the arête. Come back left and gain a second ledge above the bulge. Climb the shallow groove above past a peg runner to a steep finish on solid rock. Scramble over grass and blocks to a stake belay slightly right.

Enos   140 feet   Very Severe   (1963)
A tricky route with a steep, earthy finish. Start 15 feet right of a distinctive pointed boulder midway between the *Thunderball* bay and the pedestal

block of *Hard Day's Night*.
1 60 feet 4b. Climb discontinuous cracks to the faultline ledge.
2 80 feet 4c. From the left-hand end of the ledge, make some difficult moves across to a ragged crack, and climb this to a resting-spot after 10 feet. Move back right and climb up with difficulty over sloping ledges to the final corner and an exit on the left. Stake belay.
Variation
Little Brown Mouse   Hard Very Severe †   (15.11.75)
2a 60 feet 5a. Surprisingly difficult. Follow *Enos* up the ragged crack before continuing straight up the wall above. Move left into a corner and climb this to the top. Stake belay.

Mr Punch   140 feet   E1   (30.5.92)
Start at a small cave below a rightward-facing corner.
1 60 feet 4c. From the back of the cave, follow the jamming crack around the overhang, and then the corner above to the faultline.
2 80 feet 4c. From the centre of the ledge, climb the wall until it is possible to step right onto an obvious prow. Climb the groove above to a ledge 15 feet from the top. Finish up the corner on the left or, harder, the wall right of the corner. Stake belay.

★★ Cloud Nine   150 feet   E1 †   (21.3.76/6.7.91)
A wild expedition with exciting positions which is high in its grade. Start 15 feet right of *Enos* at a corner which has an obvious ledge at 30 feet, and beneath a huge alcove at the faultline, formed by a recent rockfall which has altered the route.
1 70 feet 5a. Climb the corner to the ledge at 30 feet and the awkward crack above to the faultline. Traverse 15 feet left to belay above the initial pitch of *Enos*.
2 80 feet 5b. Climb diagonally right to the top left-hand corner of the large alcove. Pull up to a roof and traverse rightwards to a foot-ledge in space. Move left and up over a bulge on large holds. Keep going up leftwards to a shallow groove and then a prow, and continue up to the top roof (two peg runners). Climb through the roof and finish up to the left. Stake belay on the right-hand side of some thorn bushes: hard to spot.
Variation
High Cirrus   130 feet   E1 5a †   (23.5.92)
Climb the corner and the awkward crack as for *Cloud Nine*. Traverse 8 feet left along the faultline and climb a flake to a slab beneath a large roof. Pull over the roof on good holds to a second large roof. Traverse right a few feet and climb up into the shallow groove of the parent route. Climb up left to a prow and follow it to the top roof (two peg runners). Pull though the roof and finish leftwards.

Hard Day's Night   100 feet   Hard Very Severe 4c   (8.11.75)
Start 25 feet further east at a conspicuous pedestal block abutting the cliff. Bold.
Climb the chockstone-filled corner behind the pedestal past the faultline to

a roof. Move left across the wall and around the rib to a resting-place. Surmount the bulge above to gain a recessed corner (optional belay). Traverse out right and finish up a steep crack on good holds. Stake belay.

The Cat Skinner   140 feet   Hard Very Severe   (28.10.75)
A steep and loose top pitch makes this a serious route.
1 60 feet 4b. As for *Hard Day's Night*, climb the chockstone-filled corner to the faultline. Traverse right for 20 feet to a good ledge shared with *Ulysses*.
2 40 feet 4b. From the left end of the ledge, move up and left below an overhang, and make a rising traverse left across the steep wall to a crack and corner.
3 40 feet 4c. Climb the corner for a few feet and traverse right across a steep and exposed wall. Move awkwardly around the arête into a groove and climb this very carefully to the top. Stake belay.

Ulysses   140 feet   E1   (7.5.78)
Bold, strenuous, and very exposed on its second pitch. Start 20 feet right of the high pedestal block.
1 50 feet 4c. Climb the groove to the faultline, surmounting the bulge at 20 feet on good holds. Make an awkward step left to a peg and nut belay on a good ledge.
2 90 feet 5a/b. Pull up rightwards onto the wall above the belay and go right for 15 feet on poor rock past a small but prominent block. Climb up a few feet to a roof, and traverse right until it is possible to gain a niche at its right-hand end. Move right again to a downward-pointing flake below a bulge and climb directly over this to a second niche. Traverse back left for 10 feet and follow a short, broken groove to the top. Double-stake belay.

BOULDER RUCKLE CENTRAL

Boulder Ruckle Central (along with the area eastwards from *Marmolata* to *Strophanthin*) attracts the majority of visitors to the Ruckle, the entry points being simple to find and the routes accessible under most conditions. The abseil from two yellow stakes situated 200 yards west of the *Marmolata* buttress leads down to the foot of *Ulysses*. The traverse along the boulders from here, past the *Marmolata* buttress abseil, and along as far as *Strophanthin* usually presents no problems. The one exception to this is a short section below the seaward face of the *Marmolata* buttress which becomes impassable when the sea is at all rough.

To the east of the abseil over the large roofs of *Ulysses* lies Pillar Bay. Here the low-level roofs are bounded on the western side by *Scythe's* enormous, orange-coloured corner and on the other side by the detached column of *Little Matterhorn*. Scrambling eastwards over boulders leads to *Rattler*, a steep groove running the full height of the cliff. The next main feature is the impressive line of *Buccaneer*, a towering yellow groove that narrows towards the top, ending below a series of roofs. The large, undercut prow hanging below the faultline is just next to *Sheerline*, while *Koo-Koo* starts up an east-facing corner beyond. *Finale Groove* provides another reference point, an overhanging groove which soars the full height of the cliff. One hundred feet further on is a big sentry-box from which *Tatra* finds its way up the seaward face of the *Marmolata* buttress. Continuing across some low boulders which are occasionally wave washed brings one to the huge east-facing corner formed by the *Marmolata* buttress. The recommended abseil entry down the eastern face of the buttress is entirely free-hanging.

The most amenable exit from this section of the Ruckle is the line of *Larus*, which climbs a corner midway between the western side of Pillar Bay and *Rattler*. *Gimcrack* (east of the *Marmolata* buttress) is handy for anyone climbing nearby, but unless the sea is calm it should not be relied upon as a means of escape.

★ **Prayers for Rain**   130 feet   E3 5c   (29.10.89)
Enjoyable climbing with good rock and protection. Start 25 feet right of the high pedestal block.
Climb the juggy wall, trending slightly right, and follow a thin crack in the centre of a smooth wall to the faultline (large *Friend* and nut). Pull onto the wall and continue to a junction with *Ulysses* and *The Grim Reaper* at a strip roof. Cross this using a good block to reach a short flake, and swing 5 feet leftwards beneath a second overhang. The crux: extend up a shallow groove in the bulge to a projecting jug and pull steeply into the exit corner of *Ulysses*. Twin stake belay.

★★ **The Grim Reaper**   140 feet   E1   (6.6.84)
Sustained and absorbing climbing. Start just before the left arête of the big groove of *Scythe* (a few feet left of a short, upright column of rock sticking out from the boulders).
1 70 feet 5a. Climb up to a small ledge below a bulge at 20 feet (mediocre peg runner). Surmount the bulge and follow a bulging crackline to a minute stance 10 feet above the faultline. Multiple belay on nuts and *Friends*.
2 70 feet 5a. Traverse left under the overhangs to where they lessen, and pull over using a good block (junction with *Ulysses*). Move up and skirt the roofs above to the right before going back left a few feet to get established in a short corner. Traverse right, go up to the final set of roofs, and make a hand-traverse right to easier ground. A safe exit leads to a stake belay.

★ **Alas, Poor Yorick**   130 feet   E3   (5.6.87)
The arête left of *Scythe*. Bold, exposed climbing with some good moves. Loose on the second pitch.
1 70 feet 6a. Climb to a small roof right of *The Grim Reaper* and go rightwards to a steep flake. Use this to reach jugs leading rightwards to the arête. Follow the arête to the faultline, and move left and up to belay on *The Grim Reaper*.

2 60 feet 5c. Climb rightwards to a roof on the arête, pull over leftwards, and finish up the exposed headwall. Stake belay.

✶ Scythe 140 feet E3 5b (19.4.80)

A very impressive and intimidating outing up the enormous orange corner. Start just right of the short upright column sticking up from the boulders at the western end of Pillar Bay.

Climb the corner past the faultline to the first roof. Turn this and two more roofs on their right, and follow a dusty groove to an exit on the left. Stake belay.

Talking to the Angel 145 feet E4 † (11.8.91)

An initial rightward traverse from *Scythe* allows the more appetizing parts of the loose-looking yellow wall to be sampled. The traverse pitch feels committing and demanding despite most of the climbing being in balance.

1 50 feet 5c/6a. Climb a short overhanging corner to a ledge on *Scythe*. Traverse right between roofs to a shallow roof-capped niche (*Friend 1* in pocket). Move up and right out of this to a downward-pointing flake above another roof. Continue the traverse to the arête and go up easily to a small ledge.

2 95 feet 6a. Climb the crack on the left to the faultline. Move up and then right to small ledges beneath the lowest of the roofs above. Follow the roofs leftwards and climb the crack at their end. Continue straight up, avoiding the temptation of a rest on the right, to a sound finish. Stake belay.

Razor Blade Smile 25 feet E5 6c † (16.10.89)

A breach of the big long roof in Pillar Bay gives the highest E-grade per foot in the Ruckle! Start from the tip of a boulder 15 feet left of the square-cut recess of *Blow the House Down*, beneath a blind crack.

Pull onto the 10-foot ceiling using juggy pockets. Cross it using an intriguing footlock and a vital 'pint glass handle'. On reaching the lip, layback with haste to the break. *In-situ* thread lower-off point.

✶ Blow the House Down 170 feet E3 † (10.11.85)

An imposing climb up the corner and hanging arête to the left of *Gold Fever*, reached by a long traverse above the lip of the large roofs. Start below a square-cut recess at the right-hand end of the low-level roofs of Pillar Bay.

1 80 feet 5c. Climb up into and around the square-cut recess, and traverse leftwards above the long horizontal crack. Move up into the corner and belay on a small stance below the faultline.

2 90 feet 5b. Climb the corner until just above the faultline, and break left past an *in-situ* thread to gain an exposed position on the undercut arête. Sustained climbing on good holds up the flake-line above leads to a reasonably solid finish and a stake belay.

Gold Fever 140 feet E4 (23.10.83)
An awkward start coupled with a sustained and unrelenting second pitch. Start as for *Blow the House Down*.
1 40 feet 5c. Climb up into and around the square-cut recess to reach good jams in the prominent horizontal crack, and pull up. Climb diagonally left for 15 feet to a stance in the centre of the wall.
2 100 feet 5b. Move up onto a small flat ledge above the belay and continue up the wall moving slightly left (poorly protected) to gain the faultline. Step right and climb up on small holds to a strange metal spike. Step left and pull over into a very steep corner, which is followed to the top. Stake belay.

Little Matterhorn 115 feet Very Severe (4.10.75)
The route sees considerably fewer ascents than its namesake, although the rock is similar, being very loose and unstable. Hire a guide and send him or her up first! On the right-hand side of Pillar Bay is a prominent detached column of rock; (don't!) start here.
1 55 feet 4a. Climb easily up the right-hand side of the column and belay on its top.
2 60 feet 4c. Climb the crack on the left, make a committing move to the right, and continue up on good holds into the corner. Move out right below the roof and continue to the top, exercising great care. Stake belay.

Love Comes Tumbling 120 feet E3 (1.5.86)
Start just right of *Little Matterhorn*. The roofs on pitch 2 are hollow and scary.
1 60 feet 5a. Climb to a ledge at 10 feet and continue up a steep crack to the faultline. Belay on nuts and a peg over the roof.
2 60 feet 5b. Pull over and up to the first roof, which is passed by moving right and then left. Climb up right to the second roof and swing left over it. Follow a finger-crack in the headwall and then step right to its continuation, which leads to a stake belay.

Ilium 120 feet E1 5b (8.9.68/5.11.77)
Start on the eastern edge of Pillar Bay at a curving corner leading to a vertical crack. Some difficult climbing on the crux.
Climb up easily to a wedged block and move out right on large but doubtful holds. Step right, pull into the corner with difficulty, and follow the crack to the faultline. Pull onto the face on the left and climb to a deep groove that leads to the top. Stake belay.

Little Yellow Jug 125 feet Hard Very Severe (14.5.78)
Start beneath the corner of *Larus*, 40 feet right of Pillar Bay. The leftward traverse across the shallow undercut groove to the left of the corner is strenuous and hard.
1 60 feet 5a. Traverse across the groove onto the seaward wall and a peg runner. Climb straight up and then diagonally right to the top of the groove. Follow the corner to the faultline.

2 65 feet 4b. Follow *Larus* to its second roof; then swing around and traverse left on good holds into the centre of the buttress. Move up and right to an arête after 20 feet, and finish up the corner to the left. Stake belay.

Variations

Broken Crockery E3 † (1987)
1a 60 feet 5c. From 10 feet right of *Ilium*, pull over a bulge and traverse right to the peg runner on *Little Yellow Jug*. Go straight up as for *Little Yellow Jug*, but continue to the roof above. Surmount this and carry on up to the faultline.

No Yellow Jug E1 (16.4.83)
1b 45 feet 5b. A sustained and serious first pitch with some bold moves to get started. Fairly high in its grade. Start as for *Little Yellow Jug*. Launch up into the bottomless groove and follow this until pushed out onto the left wall. Go up a few feet, regain the groove, and continue to a belay at the faultline.

Larus 140 feet Hard Severe (8.5.64)
The easiest exit from this part of the Ruckle, frequently climbed. Some doubtful rock on the second pitch makes it a fairly serious route. Start below the obvious corner 40 feet east of Pillar Bay.
1 75 feet 4b. Move up to an overhang, step left, and follow a crack to a ledge. Climb the corner to the faultline, and traverse left across a gap to a good belay ledge.
2 65 feet 4a. Climb over a flake and pass two roofs on their right. Move back left and follow a corner to a stake belay at the top.

Joe 90 120 feet E5 6a (4.89)
A repetitive description but an excellent pitch tackling the bulging wall to the right of *Larus*. Sustained, strenuous, and committing in places. Climb easily to a roof at 20 feet. Pull over this and trend left to the faultline. Press on up the wall above to another roof, pull over, and step right to a short flake leading to a further roof. Climb up to a long flake which leads to the top.

Flying Finish 115 feet E2 (31.3.79/28.3.85)
A technically absorbing initial pitch leads to exciting moves over the roof high above. Start below the left-hand end of a long roof at 35 feet.
1 50 feet 5b. Climb up to the roof, swing left, and continue up a crack to a hanging stance on nuts and a chicken-head.
2 65 feet 5b. Follow the groove above with care to the roof. Traverse right for 5 feet, pull leftwards through the roof, and continue up an easy crack to the top. Stake belay.

Billy Pigg 110 feet E1 (28.7.68/11.3.78)
A popular route giving a good introduction to the mysteries of the Swanage roof. Start beneath the cracks in the middle of the strip roof at 35 feet.

1 50 feet 5b. Climb the wall to the cracks in the roof. Pull directly over, and continue up, stepping right to belay to the right on a large ledge.
2 60 feet 4c. From above the first pitch, move up onto the wall and climb the groove to a small roof. Step left and back right, and follow the corner to the top. Stake belay to the left.

★ **Rattler**   120 feet   E1   (27.7.68)
A powerful, compulsive line giving strenuous jamming and bridging up the towering groove that runs the full height of the cliff to the right of the strip roof. In the lower section there is a distinctive flake of rock accompanied by a big block on its right. Near the top, a large suspect block provides (only, one hopes) the psychological crux.
1 60 feet 5b. Climb the groove to the top of the large overhanging flake, step right to a sloping ledge, and climb a break in the bulge above. Belay on a good ledge at the faultline.
2 60 feet 5a. Step back into the groove again and follow it to a very dubious block. Gain the top of this from the right and continue up to a stake belay.

★ **Fish Supper**   130 feet   E2   (8.12.84)
Some good climbing and exposed on the second pitch. Start 15 feet right of *Rattler* on a boulder below a left-facing corner-crack.
1 60 feet 5a. Pull over a roof into the crack and climb it until it is possible to step right and move up a short corner. Step back left onto the large hanging boulder. Move up a few feet, step right, and follow a crack to the faultline.
2 70 feet 5b. Move up left onto the wall and climb to a small corner below a roof. Surmount the roof on jugs and climb past a peg runner to another overhang. Cross this and traverse right to a groove, which is followed to the top and a stake belay.

★ **Sinbad**   130 feet   E1   (11.5.69)
Two hearty pitches of varied and enjoyable climbing. Start below a short V-groove on the front of the buttress that separates the big grooves of *Buccaneer* and *Rattler*.
1 60 feet 5b. The initial V-groove proves problematic, but succumbs to an old-fashioned approach and leads to a crack and a thread runner. Move left over the roof and step out right onto the smooth face. Continue up and follow a deep jagged crack to the faultline.
2 70 feet 5a. Pull onto the wall above the first pitch and follow a crack on the left to a bulge. Surmount this and cross some smooth slabs to a small exit corner, which is climbed to a move right at the top. Stake belay.

★★★ **Mickey Mouse**   150 feet   E3   (8.2.75/1.79)
A remarkable and intimidating route of great character that climbs the overhanging cracks on the left side of a huge yellow corner before heading up into the roofs above.
1 70 feet 5b. Climb the cracks in the left wall of the corner and the

wider crack above to a large hanging block. Surmount this with difficulty to reach the faultline. Belay on a good ledge to the left.

2 80 feet 5c. Climb the curving crack on the left to the niche above and move up to the roof. Traverse out left across the roof and make some hard moves to pull over onto the exposed wall above (peg runner). Step up and left into the exit corner of *Sinbad* and follow this to a stake belay.

★ **Buccaneer**   140 feet   E2   (7.6.69/2.78)
A magnificent line up the huge yellow corner that narrows towards the top and ends below a series of daunting overhangs. Steep, strenuous and very exposed on the crux. Take long slings to thread a strange hole in the main roof. Start at the foot of the continuous corner-crack (350 feet west of the *Marmolata* buttress).

1 70 feet 4c. Climb the crack to a slight bulge at 30 feet, move right to a layback crack, and follow this for a short way before regaining the corner-crack. Continue to a restricted belay in the corner above.

2 70 feet 5b. Climb the corner past a peg runner to the roof and squeeze up inside for a rest and a superb thread runner. Drop back down and pull directly over the roofs to a steep crack, which is followed to an exit on the left. Stake belay.

Ishmael   120 feet   E3   (14.4.84)
An interesting though wandering route up the steep face right of *Buccaneer*. Start 10 feet right of *Buccaneer* below a thin crack.

1 70 feet 5b. Climb the crack until it closes and move diagonally right to gain the prominent ledge on *Bosun's Wall*. Continue with difficulty straight up the wall (immediately left of the cracks of *Bosun's Wall*) past a peg runner to the faultline. Belay up and to the right.

2 50 feet 5b. Follow the crackline leading to the right-hand end of the large *Buccaneer* roof. At the roof continue up for 5 steep feet, where an awkward swing right gains a short groove leading to the top. Stake belay.

Cutlass   130 feet   E5 6a/b †   (4.6.87)
A direct line with bold climbing to gain the faultline. Start 25 feet right of *Buccaneer*.
Climb straight up to a blind flake in a very shallow groove, and then go for it! Step left at the faultline to a crack, before trending right to the large roof. Pull over between *Buccaneer* and *Ishmael* and step right to finish.

Bosun's Wall   120 feet   Hard Very Severe   (24.9.73)
An exhilarating route, well protected but with some bold wall-climbing on the second pitch. Start 30 feet east of *Buccaneer* at the foot of a crack.

1 60 feet 4c. Climb the crack to an obvious ledge and follow the cracks above to a small stance just below the faultline. Good nut belays above.

2 60 feet 5a. Pull up into the niche above and step left around the arête onto the face. Continue up the bulging wall and move right to reach a corner. Climb the corner and exit right before continuing up to a stake belay.

Coxswain's Route   130 feet   Very Severe   (24.9.73)
It is a bit of a gamble with the blocks on pitch 2, but many have had a flutter here and won. Start at the first, short corner right of *Buccaneer*.
1 60 feet 4b/c. Make a difficult traverse left to reach the arête which is climbed to a large ledge. Traverse right across blocks to a groove and follow this to the big ledge atop the prow. Thread belays.
2 70 feet 4c. Climb a groove up and to the left (as for *Sheerline*) and continue directly up to a roof and peg runner. Step left around piled blocks onto the wall, and move up into an open groove, which leads to the top and a stake belay.

An eliminate, **Yield Point** (E1 5b 4c 21.10.84), pulls around the left-hand side of the prominent square-cut prow to meet with *Coxswain's Route*, before following pitch 2 of *Sheerline* as directly as possible. Interesting but with little independent climbing.

Sheerline   110 feet   Very Severe   (20.11.66)
Start at a crack beneath a large square-cut prow suspended beneath the faultline. The route is high in its grade, being serious on the second pitch and steep at the top.
1 50 feet 4a. Follow the crack in the wall and move up into the corner on the right of the prow. Climb up, step left, and go on up to thread belays on the large ledge.
2 60 feet 4c. Climb a groove up and to the left, where a step right gains a peg runner and the steep corner above. The corner leads to a stake belay at the top.

Kittiwake   110 feet   Very Severe   (31.7.76)
Some blocks on the second pitch give cause for concern. Start at a small corner on the rib to the left of *Diagonal*.
1 50 feet 4b. Climb the corner and follow large holds up left to gain the corner of *Sheerline*. Continue to a thread belay on the large ledge above the prow.
2 60 feet 4b. Climb an awkward short corner at the right-hand end of the ledge, step right, and move up to some suspect blocks. Pull over these with care and climb the final corner formed by a large flake to blocks and earth. Stake belay.

Diagonal   135 feet   Hard Very Severe   (13.6.76)
A good route, steep and exposed near the top. The suspect blocks on the second pitch should not present much difficulty for the seasoned Ruckle climber. Start in a corner 20 feet right of the hanging prow of *Sheerline*, below a line of stepped roofs that lead out rightwards across the face to meet the faultline.
1 80 feet 5a. Climb up the corner to the first of the three stepped roofs.

Traverse right to the far end of a good ledge and go up through a slot on the right of the third roof. Belay at the faultline.
2 55 feet 4c. Move up left to a blunt arête which is followed for a few feet until a steep smooth corner can be gained on the right. Climb the corner and bridge up some suspect overhanging blocks to reach the top. Stake belay.

High Tide and Green Grass   120 feet   Very Severe   (5.2.84)
Start below a triangular niche 10 feet east of the corner of *Diagonal*.
1 50 feet 5a. Climb the niche and go straight up into a short corner. Continue over the roof above and step up to a belay on the faultline.
2 70 feet 4b. Climb up for 6 feet and traverse right to the arête. Climb to a flake on the left and use it to swing left into a groove. Follow this to the top and a stake belay.

Dandruff   130 feet   Hard Very Severe   ††   (13.6.76)
Start 20 feet right of *Diagonal*, just left of the steep arête. The top pitch has collapsed and is in a dangerous condition. It has **not yet been reclimbed**; the original description is given.
1 75 feet 4b. Climb the wall on good holds, trending right until the arête is gained at a horizontal crack. Climb up until just below the steep groove of *Diagonal* and traverse right under a flat roof to a bottomless corner-crack. Follow the corner to the faultline.
2 55 feet 4b ††. 'Climb up onto the huge detached block on the right. Move up and follow a steep loose groove with difficulty to a trying exit on the left. Stake belay.'
Direct Start   E2 †   (31.8.86)
1a 60 feet 6a. Climb the corner and 6-foot roof before following the bottomless corner of the original route.

Smokestack Lightning   130 feet   E1   (10.9.84/21.10.84)
Start beneath the east-facing wall immediately left of the start of *Koo-Koo*.
1 70 feet 5b. An undercut start leads to a flake crack; climb this, step left, and follow a corner to the faultline. Traverse left and belay on top of the large detached block.
2 60 feet 5a. Exposed. Move up and delicately rightwards above the huge roof capping *Koo-Koo*'s first pitch to reach a short corner. Continue up this (peg runner) and exit to the right as for *Koo-Koo*. Stake belays to the left and right.

✳ Koo-Koo   135 feet   E2   (2.9.73/12.8.78)
An amenable route once the hard start has been overcome. It climbs the huge corner capped by a large roof just above the faultline. Start beneath a roof at the foot of the corner, some 60 feet right of *Sheerline*. The loose, overhanging corner above the traverse on pitch 2 has been climbed, but the unwitting first ascensionist 'wouldn't wish it on anyone'.
1 70 feet 5c. Surmount the roof with difficulty, taking care not to leave a foot behind, and follow the corner above to easier ground. Traverse

across the wall on the right to a pillar and climb it to the faultline. Take a stance a few feet to the right.
2 65 feet 5a. Climb up above the belay to a ledge over the bulge. Traverse left around the arête to a shallow corner and continue up this (peg runner), exiting rightwards at the top. Stake belays to the left and right.

RIP   120 feet   Hard Very Severe   (3.11.68)
A compelling line that is worth investigating. Start 20 feet east of *Koo-Koo*, below a line of overhanging corners and grooves.
1 60 feet 4c. Climb up into the corner, surmount the slight bulge on good holds, and continue to the roof. Traverse right and go up to a belay at the faultline.
2 60 feet 4c. Enter the overhanging groove with difficulty and follow it to a small roof and a small ledge on its left arête. Move left again and climb another groove to its end, from where a traverse back to the original groove leads to a finish directly above. Stake belay. (Climbing straight up the groove raises the standard to E1 5b.)

★ **Headstone**   125 feet   E3 †   (10.8.85)
This tackles the centre of a steep wall and is similar in nature to its neighbour. Start at a small roof above a drop to the boulders.
1 60 feet 5b. Surmount the roof on an enormous jug. Move up and right to follow a crack through a steep bulge to reach a semi rest. Climb the perfect hand-crack above to a belay at the faultline.
2 65 feet 6a. Gain a ledge up to the right, move left, and pull onto the headwall at a short crack (about 5 feet right of *RIP*). Climb back right and continue directly up the headwall to easier ground and stake belays beyond.

★★ **Wide Awake in America**   140 feet   E5   (11.12.84/7.11.88)
Two good pitches of contrasting character climbing an impending crack and smooth headwall. A fine climb despite dubious rock and a poor peg runner at the start of pitch 2. Start 25 feet right of *RIP* below a short, deep groove.
1 65 feet 6a. Climb the groove and exit right to a resting-position on a short slab (thread runner). Extend through the large bulge to reach a jammed flake on the lip (crux). Follow the crack above strenuously but on good holds to the faultline. Belay to the right as for *Sweet and Sour*.
2 75 feet 6b. Move 5 feet left and climb straight up past two peg runners to a small foot-ledge in the middle of the smooth grey wall. Make some difficult moves to a sloping hold, swing up left to a jug (small wire placements just to the left), and pull over onto easier ground. Climb the slab above to a firm finish and a belay stake.

Sweet and Sour   120 feet   Very Severe   (1.6.69)
An unbalanced route: pitch 1 is enjoyable and well protected whereas pitch 2 is rather poor and sparsely protected. Start beneath the next corner.

1 60 feet 4c. Climb the corner until 15 feet below the big roof. Traverse left to a crack and follow it to a belay at the faultline.
2 60 feet 4b. Surmount the bulge and move up to a corner that leads to a roof. Step left around this and continue to the top. Stake belay.

★**Boatpusher's Arête** 110 feet E4 6a † (4.11.84)
Good, exposed climbing on solid rock up the stepped arête to the left of *Finale Groove*. Graded for its serious start.
Climb directly up the bulging arête for 20 feet (difficult, committing, and unprotected) to a step right by a shallow scoop on the arête. Continue up the arête past a resting-ledge to the faultline, and pull over the overhang as for *Finale Groove*. Move up 10 feet, traverse out left to a small ledge on the arête, and climb up the seaward face just left of the arête straight to the top. Stake belay.
A variation start (E5 6a † 7.6.92) climbs the left-hand side of the arête via a thin crack before following the parent route.

★**Finale Groove** 110 feet Hard Very Severe 4c (12.4.66)
An outstanding route, which gives an immaculate piece of climbing up a steep and impressive line. Ample holds and plentiful protection make this one of the most popular routes of the cliff. Start 100 feet east of the prominent faultline boulder of *Dandruff* (160 feet west of the *Marmolata* buttress) beneath a soaring groove-line that tapers towards the top.
Climb the rightward-facing corner for 40 feet to a bulge. Surmount this awkwardly to gain a niche and then the faultline (optional belay). Pull around an overhang onto the wall above and follow the groove, stepping left at its very top. Scramble up to a stake belay.

Rif-Raf 120 feet Hard Very Severe [R] (10.4.77/1.79)
A nice first pitch leads to an awkward roof followed by a steep, worrying finish. Start 15 feet right of *Finale Groove*.
1 60 feet 4c/5a. Climb up slightly rightwards to reach the left end of a roof. Continue up a crack, undercling out right, and move up to belay at the faultline.
2 60 feet 5b. Pull over the roof a few feet to the left of the belay (peg runner). Continue up, moving first to the right and then back left until below a small roof. Turn this on its right and climb the groove above to exit steeply left on dubious holds to a stake belay.

'B' Line 110 feet Very Severe [R] (10.4.66)
Start below the rightward-leading flake right of *Finale Groove*. A serious top pitch.
1 60 feet 4b. Climb the flake and the deep continuation crack on superb holds to the faultline. Belay to the right.
2 50 feet 4c/5a. Climb the grey wall above past a peg runner to a shallow groove that leads to the top. Stake belay.

⋆ **Sweet S A** 120 feet Very Severe [R] (1963)
The top pitch is serious and the route high in its grade. Start below the
bottomless corner 35 feet to the east of *Finale Groove*.
1 70 feet 4c. Climb up the corner to a bulge and pull over this strenuously
to a ledge. Continue to the faultline and traverse left to a stance.
2 50 feet 4c/5a. *'B' Line* pitch 2.

⋆ **All Guns Blazing** 120 feet E3 [R] (29.8.86)
A beautifully sculptured roof-climb but a poor, loose, and vegetated top
pitch. Start as for *Sweet S A*.
1 70 feet 6a. Four *in-situ* thread runners. Climb up the corner to a bulge
and then traverse 10 feet right (as for *Sea Lion* so far). Cross the 5-foot
roof and continue up a crack to the faultline. Nut and thread belay.
2 50 feet 5c. Strenuously climb over the bulge just right of the belay
and continue more easily to a detached overhang. Pass this on the right
(spike and *in-situ* thread) to gain a ledge. Finish up the wall above.
Stake belay.

Sea Lion 150 feet Hard Very Severe [R] (19.5.68/18.11.79)
A fine traverse beneath the long roof to the right of *Sweet S A* leads to a
loosish top pitch. A large block has fallen at the end of the traverse; it is
not known whether the grade is affected.
1 80 feet 5a. Follow *Sweet S A* to its bulge, traverse out right beneath
the roof, and pull around to reach the faultline, Belay on nuts and a thread
beneath a loose undercut groove.
2 70 feet 4b. Traverse right for 15 feet, climb up for the same distance,
and return left into the groove. Climb the groove to a steep finish. Stake
belay.
Direct Start E1 [R] † (10.8.85)
1a 60 feet 5b. Start 30 feet right of the original. Climb up to a hanging
boulder, which is apparently solid, and swing right using a jug on its outer
edge. Move up to the roof above, step left, and follow a crack to the belay
at the faultline.

⋆ **The Heidelberg Creature** 140 feet Very Severe [R] (18.9.66)
A splendid first pitch, tempered by some dubious-looking flakes wedged
in the initial corner. Start midway between the corner of *Sweet S A* and the
sentry-box of *Tatra*, below a slightly overhanging corner.
1 70 feet 4c. Climb the corner and turn the first bulge on its left to gain a
small ledge on the arête. Follow the overhanging crack to pull up over a
second bulge, and trend left to belay on a ledge.
2 70 feet 4b. Surmount the overhang and climb the wall and groove
above to a ledge near the top. Exit to the right over loose blocks and grass
to a stake belay.

⋆ **The Tool** 130 feet E2 [R] (6.7.74/9.10.77)
Some tricky moves and exposed situations. Start at parallel cracks below
a hanging block.

1 80 feet 5a. Climb directly up for 15 feet to the block, turn it on its left, and continue up the corner above to a large overhang. Pass this also on its left and follow the corner to a small roof. Belay on nuts and a peg.
2 50 feet 5b. Step left around the arête and go straight up the wall above via a thin crack. Gain a shallow groove and follow it to the top. Stake belay.

★ **Promotion to Glory**   130 feet   E3   [R]   †   (10.12.84)
A rightward diagonal line from *The Tool* to *Teenage Wasteland*. Possibly affected by rockfall on pitch 2.
1 70 feet 5c. Follow the cracks of *The Tool*, and then move out right to follow the obvious rightwards-slanting overlap. Make a layback move up the continuation flake in order to gain a ledge on the right. Continue easily to the chimney of *Tatra Direct* and belay using large nuts at the faultline.
2 60 feet 6a. Pull around the right arête onto the wall and climb the short groove to an embedded flake below the bulge. Traverse six feet right to a weakness in the bulge and move up on hidden holds past a peg to the groove of *Teenage Wasteland*. Finish up that route.

Conan the Vegetarian   120 feet   E3   [R]   †   (10.11.84)
A thuggish first pitch. Start as for *Tatra*.
1 60 feet 5b. Climb up the centre of the sentry-box to a ledge at 15 feet. Traverse left to below the overhanging hand-cracks and fight these to a niche on the lip of the roof. Launch around the lip, step right very quickly, and continue easily to the chimney of *Tatra Direct*. Large nut and thread belay.
2 60 feet 5a. *Tatra Direct* pitch 2.

★ **Tatra**   160 feet   Very Severe   [R]   (Pre-1963)
An early classic of the Ruckle that continues to prove highly popular. Though a wandering line, *Tatra* has good positions and rock and is at the top of its grade. Start beneath the huge sentry-box 35 feet west of *Marmolata Arête*.
1 65 feet 5a. Enter the sentry-box and traverse across its right-hand wall, via a move up a vertical crack, to gain the outside rib at the overhang. Surmount this and follow a steep crack more easily to the chimney. Large nut and thread belay.
2 40 feet 4b. Traverse horizontally right to a small corner in the centre of the face. Pull up to the break above and hand-traverse right to a good ledge on the prow of the buttress.
3 55 feet 4b. Follow the two corners to the top and belay on the abseil point.

Tatra Direct   110 feet   E2   [R]   †   (25.11.66/3.12.67/30.11.91)
A strenuous first pitch up to the cave stance of *Tatra* is followed by very exposed bridging. Surprisingly, a rockfall in the upper section has created an enjoyable, clean, and well-protected finish. Start just right

of *Tatra* below the left-hand of two roof-cracks.
1 50 feet 5c. Climb the crack direct to the cave. Large nut and thread belay.
2 60 feet 5a. Follow the overhanging chimney to a small ledge. Climb twin cracks to the top and belay on the abseil stake.

★ **Teenage Wasteland**   125 feet   E4 [R]   (9.78)
A hard climb up the seaward face of the *Marmolata* buttress. A badly-protected crux makes this a serious route. Start below a crack in the roof 8 feet left of the arête. Belay pegs are required and the peg runner on pitch 3 may need replacement on abseil.
1 45 feet 5b. Pull over the roof and follow the crack and wall above to a large ledge in the centre of the face.
2 25 feet 5b. Move up to a bulge split by twin cracks. Surmount the bulge and continue to a sloping ledge on the right. Place pegs to belay.
3 55 feet 5c. Climb the slight arête on the left for a few feet, and traverse left past a very poor peg runner to reach the foot of a slim groove. Climb this to a large flake, step left, and finish up cracks. Belay on the abseil point.

★ **Marmolata Arête**   120 feet   E4 [R]   (31.3.79)
A proud line in a prime position, the line up the discontinuous prow of the *Marmolata* buttress has now been straightened out. Some serious climbing, though escapable in a number of places. Start just right of the prominent arête of the *Marmolata* buttress.
1 60 feet 6a. Climb up to a horizontal break, step left, and follow a hanging groove to a short slab and optional stance. Continue up the sharp arête for 25 feet to easy ground and a belay on *Tatra*.
2 60 feet 6a. Climb the arête to a peg runner and continue straight up over two bulges with a diagonal ramp between them. Finish more easily and belay on the abseil point.

★★ **Marmolata Buttress**   125 feet   E3 [R]   (2.6.73/20.11.77)
A strenuous and fairly serious first pitch gives way to slightly less taxing climbing in an exposed position. Low in its grade. Start as for *Marmolata Arête*.
1 35 feet 5c. Climb up the wall to a thin crack, which is followed with difficulty to a large ledge on the seaward face.
2 50 feet 5b. Traverse back around the corner (peg runner) to a groove, which leads to the faultline. Traverse right again and climb another groove to the stance of *Marmolata*.
3 40 feet 5b. Step left onto the wall and climb the flakes above to a ledge near the top. Finish up the crack or the arête to the left. Belay on the abseil point.
Direct Start   E4 †   (7.2.88)
1a 70 feet 6a. Very strenuous. Climb the thin crack on pitch 1. Continue steeply over a difficult bulge to another crack leading to the groove on

pitch 2. At the top of the groove traverse rightwards along the faultline and climb up to the stance of *Marmolata*.

Marmolata   100 feet   E2   (Pre-1963/9.4.69)
The huge overhanging corner that bounds the east-facing wall of the *Marmolata* buttress yields well-protected and poorly-protected pitches, though both of them are strenuous. (The top crack can be avoided by climbing up and right to follow the final delicate wall of *Ashes and Diamonds*; this reduces the overall standard to E1.)
1 60 feet 5b. Climb the corner and any of the various cracks above to gain a sloping ledge in the deep corner. Thread and nut belays.
2 40 feet 5b. Struggle up the overhanging crack to the top. It is as difficult as it looks! A *Friend 4* helps the nerves even if it appears to be walking out of its placement as you climb! Belay on the abseil point.

★ **Marmolata Combination** (E2). The linking of the first pitch of *Marmolata* with the top pitch of *Marmolata Buttress*, makes a superb, well-protected outing that is a popular choice.

BOULDER RUCKLE EAST
The free-hanging abseil down *Marmolata* is the recommended entry point for this area except for the routes from *Agincourt* onwards, for which the *Old Faithful* abseil is best. Just to the east of the landing-spot is a cluster of groove-lines such as *Director's Groove*. The large half-height roof further east provides considerable exposure for *Lightning Wall*. From here, smooth walls, with a discontinuous yet easily crossed rock platform beneath, extend to the corner of *Strophanthin*, where a hanging flake forms a roof at 30 feet. Here an awkward hand-traverse can be made just above the boulders if the sea is calm; otherwise a low tide is needed to boulder-hop across to a ledge. Sixty feet further on is the large diamond-shaped roof of *Gimcrack*. A low tide is required to pass by the chimney of *Victoria* and continue via a steep and greasy hand-traverse to an impressive, overhung bay. This bay has a series of four stepped roofs; *Agincourt* finds its way up the rock to the left of these overhangs. Further east is the projecting rib of *October Lady* with a roof high above. Then the start of *Jasper* is marked by a huge block in its own tailor-made alcove. A fin-backed boulder beneath a wide crack which extends up to the faultline is the landing place for the next entry point, the abseil down *Old Faithful*.

The section of cliff between *Marmolata* and *Strophanthin* is well defended from the sea and is often climbable when other parts of the Ruckle are inaccessible. However, the routes from *Strophanthin* all the way to Subluminal have some difficult access problems and should be avoided unless conditions are favourable. Also, attempts to traverse westwards along the boulders from the *Marmolata* abseil are sometimes frustrated by a short section below the seaward face of the *Marmolata* buttress when the sea is a bit rough; an important point to remember before committing yourself to the abseil down *Marmolata*.

Director's Groove   130 feet   Hard Very Severe   (10.4.66)
An enjoyable main pitch. The difficulties are short-lived, but they just bump
up the grade to HVS. Start beneath the wide, open groove just right of the
big corner of *Marmolata*.
1 90 feet 5a. Follow the groove to a roof at 60 feet and turn it on its
right. Tiptoe back left with difficulty just above the roof and traverse out to
the left arête. Step up to a bulge and fix protection for the second before
making a rightward rising traverse (some loose blocks) to a stance a few
feet below a wide crack.
2 40 feet 4b. Climb the wide crack to a stake belay.

Freddy   110 feet   E2 5c †   (23.11.91)
Start just right of *Director's Groove*.
Climb up easily before crossing the wall diagonally rightwards to the
faultline. Move left and then up to the bulge, which is crossed by using a
hold up to the right. Follow a crack in a lichenous wall to some large
flakes. Finish up a vague rib just right of the final wall of *Ashes and
Diamonds*. Stake belay.

Ashes and Diamonds   100 feet   E1 5b   (Pre-1963)
Start 25 feet east of *Marmolata* behind a large boulder.
Climb the crack and groove past a jammed block at 30 feet to the
faultline. Step right and climb the bulge strenuously on dubious holds to a
small ledge. Continue up to a chockstone runner in the large crack above
and traverse left for 10 feet to the base of a pedestal. From the ledge on
top of this, climb delicately up the wall, trending left to a ledge just below
the top. Step right and finish over blocks to a stake belay.

Windy City   125 feet   E1   (9.10.77)
Start 40 feet east of *Marmolata*, below a sizeable ledge at 10 feet which
is formed by a suspended block. Some loose rock.
1 110 feet 5a. Climb up to the ledge at 10 feet and follow a groove at
its left-hand end to the faultline. Pull up into a niche and surmount the
bulge with difficulty. Continue steeply and with poor protection to a small
resting-place where the angle eases. Finish easily up over broken rock
and belay at the right-hand end of a large recess.
2 15 feet. A short scramble leads to the top. Stake belay.

Canned Heat   140 feet   E1   (18.7.71)
Poor rock on the upper section makes this a serious proposition. Start as
for *Windy City*.
1 50 feet 4b. Climb up to the ledge and follow a groove on the right for
20 feet. Traverse right to the arête and go up to an awkward stance.
2 90 feet 5a. Climb the groove on the left with difficulty to a peg runner
after 6 feet. Traverse back to the arête and continue up to loose
impending rock and an optional peg belay beyond. Go diagonally right
and follow a groove until it is possible to step left to better holds. Continue
up to the top.

∗∗ Lightning Wall   125 feet   Hard Very Severe   4c   (10.4.66)
A classic Swanage experience savouring the exhilaration of steep,
exposed positions from the comfort of positive holds. It also carries an *On
the Edge* seal of approval! Start below a groove to the left of a
conspicuous corner.
Climb the groove to an overhang at the faultline and traverse right to an
optional belay in a niche on old pegs (and more besides!). Climb the wall
above for 6 feet to the start of an obvious traverse. (Alternatively, at 5a,
move right onto the wall and then up.) Traverse rightwards to the arête
and climb up to a niche and peg runner. Leave the niche diagonally
rightwards and climb a corner to a stake belay.
Variation
1a 60 feet 4c (1984). Climb the obvious corner on the right to the
faultline and swing left to the optional belay.

Melancholy Lane   130 feet   E3   †   (30.5.87)
Start 8 feet right of the corner.
1 70 feet 5c. Climb the wall just to the left of *Elysium* to a ledge and go
right to the faultline. Enter the first of two short corners on *Elysium* and
break left immediately onto the lip of the huge roof. Move up to a hanging
belay on the traverse of *Lightning Wall*.
2 60 feet 5c. Traverse left and go up a large hanging groove to finish
on the right (*in-situ* thread) up another groove. Stake belay.

∗∗ Elysium   120 feet   E1   5b   (7.1.68)
One of the trade routes of the Ruckle at this grade. Varied climbing with
ample protection on good rock throughout ensures its continued acclaim.
About 60 feet east of the *Marmolata* buttress is a distinctive corner
bounding the left side of a wall capped by a large roof. (*Lightning Wall*
traverses out above this roof.) Start 15 feet east of the prominent corner.
Climb a ragged crack to a ledge at 20 feet. Step left and climb a thin
crack to where hard moves gain a tiny ledge on the left under the large
roof. Traverse right to the end of the roof and enter a short corner. Go
right again and pull up into a second corner. Move left around the arête
(joining the end of the *Lightning Wall* traverse) and climb up to a niche
containing a peg runner. Leave the niche diagonally rightwards and climb
a corner to a stake belay.
Variation (5b 28.6.86): instead of moving left to join *Lightning Wall*,
continue straight up over a bulge to the exit corner of the original.

∗ The Adventures of Portland Bill   250 feet   E2   (9.8.86)
High-quality climbing, which is well protected and low in its grade.
1 90 feet 5b. Follow the ragged crack of *Elysium* and then traverse
rightwards along twin horizontal cracks until a step down gains a ledge
on *Gypsy*.
2 60 feet 5b. Regain the breaks and traverse past a peg runner to spike
belays at the right edge of the wall.
3 30 feet 5b. The crux: climb the flake crack on the right to the faultline;

the *Strophanthin* belay is 10 feet to the right.

4 70 feet 4c. A pitch shared with *Strophanthin* gives the easiest but also the most serious climbing of the expedition. Climb the obvious weakness up right and follow the steep wall leftwards to a small roof. Move into the groove and continue to the top. Stake belay.

★★ **Singing Winds**   130 feet   E4 6a   (24.7.83)
A difficult and fingery pitch up the full-height wall just right of *Elysium*. Protection above the faultline is rather sparse. Start as for *Elysium*. Climb the ragged crack of *Elysium* for 15 feet before moving right to a large spike on the lip of an overhang. Go up to flat holds and step right to a very shallow groove. Step up again onto a square foothold and continue (bold and fingery) to gain the faultline and a peg runner. Climb the wall for 10 feet to another peg runner and then trend leftwards to reach good wire placements in a thin crack. Move right to good holds and continue up to meet an easy exit corner. Stake belay.

Dune Dust   120 feet   E3   (5.9.86)
An enjoyable eliminate with a good first pitch.
1 80 feet 6a. Follow *Thunder Groove* for 20 feet to chert jugs and climb straight up over a bulge to a horizontal break. Continue up the black streak above, past two peg runners, to the faultline. Go rightwards through a bulge and up a corner to the belay ledge of *Thunder Groove*.
2 40 feet 4c. Climb up and leftwards around the arête to an exit corner. Stake belay.

★ **Thunder Groove**   120 feet   Hard Very Severe   (16.9.67)
The most amenable of the routes in this imposing neighbourhood. Difficulties are short but taxing, and the climbing high in its grade. Start in a small corner, directly behind the highest boulder in the vicinity.
1 80 feet 5a/b. Traverse up right for 15 feet with poor protection and make an awkward move up to some good holds. Move up past a pinnacle block to a ledge below a shallow groove. Climb this difficult groove to the faultline. Fix good runners and continue up another groove to a large ledge on the left.
2 40 feet 4c. Step right and continue up the now much shallower groove to a ledge in a corner. Climb this more easily to a stake belay at the top.

Echoes from the Dead   130 feet   E3   (30.8.86)
Start 15 feet right of *Thunder Groove*.
1 80 feet 5c. Commencing with a thin crack, climb the leaning wall to the break. Move left for the crux of *Thunder Groove*. (Alternatively but harder, go up the wall just to its right.) From the faultline, move right past two *in-situ* threads and then diagonally right (peg runner) to a peg belay below a rock shield.
2 50 feet 5b. Either move out left (peg runner) and then back right or pull straight over the bulge. Continue directly up to the final groove and a stake belay beyond.

★ Gypsy 110 feet E1   (29.10.67)

Steep, strenuous, and sustained; a superb route, which is high in its
grade. Some care is required to find a safe belay at the faultline. Start
below a vertical break in the wall below the faultline.

1 50 feet 5b. Pull steeply up to a ledge below a short corner. Move up
to a roof and continue up past a smaller roof to the faultline. The multiple
belay includes two threaded wires.

2 60 feet 5b. Traverse right for 5 feet and pull up into an open groove.
Climb this past a peg runner to a small corner below a roof and another
peg runner. Step right and continue straight up to a stake belay.

★ Strongbow 150 feet E1   (19.5.74)

A steep and satisfying route. Start at a short rightward-facing corner.

1 50 feet 5a. Climb the corner and pull left around the arête to a ledge.
Move up and across to a ledge on the right and belay at the foot of some
cracks.

2 100 feet 5b. Climb the difficult cracks to where a committing move
above the faultline enables some good holds to be reached. Traverse right
to a shallow corner with a peg runner. Climb up to a more pronounced
corner, which leads to a stake belay.

Variation

1a 50 feet XS 6a † (1988). Climb the bulging arête just left of the
corner. Continue up and across to the right as for the parent route.

★ Vortices 140 feet E2   (21.4.85)

A strenuous first pitch gives way to easier climbing, though both pitches
are well protected. Start 5 feet right of *Strongbow*.

1 70 feet 5c. Climb the wall, moving right at the overhang to reach a
hanging flake. Climb up the groove to a horizontal break, rightwards for
15 feet to a thin crack, and up to the faultline. Nut and peg belay.

2 70 feet 5a/b. Pull onto the wall above and step left to join *Strongbow*.
Surmount a bulge and climb directly to the top via a rightward-facing
corner.

★ The Mace 130 feet E5   (30.11.86)

Intricate climbing. Start below a triangular niche.

1 60 feet 6a. Climb up past the niche to a thread on the right, and then
trend leftwards to the break. Climb the shallow groove - which forms the
bold crux - to the faultline. Belay on wires placed over the roof and a large
Friend.

2 70 feet 5c. Step left and pull over the roof to join *Strongbow* before it
moves right beneath a second roof. Swing left around the rib and climb
up the face with poor gear, before moving back right to the base of a
hanging groove. Finish up this more easily. Stake belay.

Aquarius 140 feet E2   (19.5.79)

Some bold and difficult climbing, which is very poorly protected on the
top pitch. Start next to an obvious hole at waist height.

1 50 feet 5b. Climb past the hole and continue up a crack for 15 feet. Make a rising traverse right on black, juggy rock to gain a ledge below two thin cracks in a smooth wall. Climb these to the faultline. Peg and nut belay.

2 90 feet 5b. Climb up to the right-hand end of the rather loose overhang above the stance. Surmount this and move left into the bottom of a shallow groove. Follow the groove on its right-hand side to reach easy-angled rock and a fairly sound finish. Stake and block belays.

** **Acapulco**   120 feet   E4   (5.4.87)
An excellent steep line with a bold and strenuous start. Start 10 feet left of *Strophanthin*.
1 60 feet 6a. Climb the overhanging buttress just left of the arête to easier ground and twin spikes. Continue directly up cracks to the faultline.
2 60 feet 5c. Climb rightwards over the bulge into a curving groove which leads to a roof. Cross this carefully to reach easier ground and exit slightly leftwards. Stake belay.

Strophanthin   140 feet   Very Severe   (11.12.66)
Whilst strophanthin (a heart stimulant) may have been required in the 1960s, a rack of modern gear is an adequate substitute, despite the relatively serious second pitch. Start where the flat boulder-pavement gives way to low boulders, below a corner leading to a roof at 30 feet (180 feet east of the *Marmolata* buttress).
1 70 feet 4a. Climb the corner-crack to a good spike runner below a roof formed by a large hanging flake. Step out right and continue up to belay on the faultline.
2 70 feet 4c. Climb the flakes on the right and then move up left across a steep wall to a small roof in a corner. Cross the roof and continue up the steep corner above. Stake belay just behind a pointed block.

** **The Planet**   170 feet   E3   (31.7.85)
An impressive and superbly positioned top pitch that follows the very steep prow clearly outlined when looking east from the *Marmolata* buttress. An overhanging version of *Lightning Wall*, it is sparsely protected on pitch 2; several leaders have turned back before reaching the spike. Start 15 feet right of *Strophanthin*, at an overhung ledge.
1 80 feet 5b. Pull over the roof and follow an arête to join *Strophanthin* at the spikes. Move left under a square-cut roof and climb the steep crack up above to gain the faultline. Belay on the right as for *Strophanthin*.
2 90 feet 5c. Follow *Strophanthin* until it is possible to traverse rightwards above the big roof to ledges on the arête. Climb up the wall just left of the arête past a spike to a break. Finish up a short groove. Block belay.

*** **Ximenes**   120 feet   E2   (4.9.71/1977)
An excellent route, strenuous and sustained throughout, with an unusual crux that is harder for the tall. The route climbs the striking crackline 35

feet east of *Strophanthin* which pierces the right edge of the huge double-stepped roof .

1 60 feet 5b/c. Climb the crack in the wall to a niche below an overhanging corner. Gain this corner with difficulty and continue to a cramped belay at the faultline.

2 60 feet 5b. Surmount the roof directly above the belay and climb the steep wall to a rest beneath another roof. Step up right, pull over the roof, and continue up the right-hand of two vertical grooves. At the top of this, step left and scramble up to belay on stakes to the left and to the right (below the seasonal restriction boundary post).

Tiger Moth 140 feet E1 (1.5.77)
The very top of the grade, having a steep and thin crux, which can be avoided by finishing up *Gimcrack* (giving an HVS 4c).

1 50 feet 4c. Follow *Ximenes* to the overhang, move right, and climb a diagonal crack to the faultline.

2 90 feet 5b. Surmount a small overhang above the stance. Move up and follow a long, diagonal crack to a ledge on the arête just left of *Gimcrack*. Make a strenuous series of moves up left across the impending wall to reach a cave-like recess for a tense 'rest'. Continue up to a good ledge from which a few easier moves over loose rock lead to the stake belay.

★ Death's Head Hawk Moth 120 feet E3 † (5.4.87)
Start 10 feet right of *Ximenes*.

1 60 feet 6a. Turn a small roof on its right and continue over large bulges to the faultline. Belay below a crack just left of *Tiger Moth*.

2 60 feet 5c. Climb the crack to a ledge and go steeply up to reach a finger-crack. Follow this to undercuts leading right around a prow to a final easy corner.

The Mutiny 130 feet E1 (31.7.85)
An eliminate based upon the line of *Gimcrack*. Low in its grade. Start from the island boulder situated beneath a large diamond-shaped roof.

1 60 feet 4b. Climb the obvious chimney past spikes to the roof. Traverse out right and continue as for *Gimcrack* to the large ledge.

2 70 feet 5b. Follow *Gimcrack* to the first ledge above the faultline. Continue up slightly right to the prominent large roof. Climb leftwards around this roof and left again around the next (smaller) roof. A sound finish on the right leads to a stake belay.

Variation

★ Skulduggery E5 † (8.94)
An interesting pitch, possibly E6, which feels quite bold.

1a 50 feet 6b. Climb the chimney to the diamond-shaped roof and arrange good gear - the last for a while. Step down and traverse across the left wall on 'slopers' to the arête. Climb this to jugs and continue more easily to the faultline.

Gimcrack   120 feet   Very Severe   (Pre-1963)
The easiest route on this part of the cliff, and a good introduction to the
atmosphere of the Ruckle. Start 100 feet east of *Strophanthin* where a
short, easy-angled buttress protrudes from the face, just east of a large,
diamond-shaped roof.
1 50 feet 4a. Climb the rib for 20 feet, traverse left to a corner, and
climb it to a large ledge protected by a roof.
2 70 feet 4b. Surmount the overhang and follow the groove above to a
large ledge. A short corner on the left leads to a stake belay by the
seasonal-restriction boundary-post.

★ **Quasimodo**   125 feet   Hard Very Severe [R]   (24.8.74/11.3.78)
Worth doing for its fine second pitch. Low in its grade. Start as for
Gimcrack. (A harder start can be made up the corner to the right.)
1 45 feet 4c. Climb the rib for 20 feet, and then the groove on the right
to where it steepens. Make a delicate move right and pull up to the
faultline. Belay to the right of the prow.
2 40 feet 5a. Move back left and follow the leftward-sloping crack
easily to the first overhang. Step right and go up steeply to the big roof
before hand-traversing strenuously leftwards to a ledge.
3 40 feet 4b. Climb up to a loose-looking overhang, traverse right, and
then go up right and back left to belay far back on a stake.

Leave It to the Birds   120 feet   E3 5c [R] †   (27.2.93)
The crux traverse has some dubious rock but leads to a fine, hanging exit
corner.
Climb the initial rib of *Gimcrack* to a roof, and the corner above to the
faultline. Traverse leftwards just above the roof to a hanging flake and a
rest above. Finish up the corner. Stake belay.

The section of cliff from *Fury 161* to *Agincourt* can be approached only at low
tide and when the sea is calm.

Fury 161   120 feet   E1 [R] †   (19.9.92)
1 60 feet 5a. Climb a thin crack in an east-facing wall to easier ground.
Move up right and make an exposed traverse beneath a roof to a corner.
Belay in this corner on a ledge.
2 60 feet 5b. Traverse 5 feet right and climb up past the faultline to a
roof. Step leftwards and pull up the wall using three big flat holds.
Continue up and right to a narrowing of the strip roof, joining *The Navajo
Wars*. Pull over and climb diagonally leftwards across a slab with care.
Stake belay far back to the right.

★★ **The Navajo Wars**   120 feet   E4 [R]   (28.10.88)
A tremendous route on good rock, which has some blind moves and none
too obvious gear on the sustained first pitch. Start 20 feet right of
Gimcrack at the back of a bay.
1 60 feet 6a. Climb a short cracked groove and move diagonally

rightwards across the overhanging wall to a small roof at 30 feet. Step right and go up a blank-looking, slabby groove to the faultline (*in-situ* thread). Belay on the left.
2 60 feet 6a. Climb up and pull over the large roofs at their widest point (*in-situ* thread). Make thin moves onto a slab, which is followed to another roof band (*in-situ* thread). Surmount this and finish leftwards up a slab with care. Stake belay far back to the right.

★ **West of the Pecos**   120 feet   E1 5b [R] †   (1.11.88)
Start 50 feet right of *Gimcrack*, on the right-hand side of a large roof at 12 feet.
Climb up to the large roof and pass to the right of it. Follow the open groove above to the faultline and continue up a short crack on the right to a slabby ledge. Climb a vague groove to a small overhang near the top, whence good holds lead diagonally leftwards into a deep, easy groove. Stake belay.

Apache   150 feet   E3 [R] †   (6.8.85)
Low in its grade but poorly protected in parts. Start at the blunt arête midway between *West of the Pecos* and the chimney of *Victoria*. Pegs required.
1 50 feet 5b. Climb to a ledge at 10 feet and follow the groove above to a bulge. Pull straight over this and continue up grooves and a slab to the faultline. Place pegs to belay at the right-hand end of a good ledge.
2 100 feet 5c. Step right, move up, and climb across leftwards to a large ledge directly above the belay. Trend rightwards up a compact slab to a break below the line of roofs; traverse right to cracks and pull over. Traverse back left above the lip on stepped slabs, move up onto a slab above the lip of another roof, and finish to the right. Stake belay a long way back on the right and a block belay to the left.

The huge boulder out to sea is all that remains of The Arch, once a useful point of reference in this area.

Victoria   140 feet   Very Severe [R]   (2.6.73)
The obvious, east-facing chimney behind the huge boulder. Pegs required.
1 50 feet 4c. From the back of the cave, climb the chimney and crack to the faultline. Move left and place pegs to belay on a good ledge.
2 90 feet 4a. Climb easily to an overlap above the left end of the belay ledge, step down right, and continue under blocks to a break. Pull through the break and gain a short corner up to the left via an obvious flake crack. Go up the corner and exit left at the top to a nut belay.

★ **Fallen from Grace**   130 feet   E4 [R] †   (21.8.89)
An outstanding climb tackling the face and roofs to the right of *Victoria*. Start 25 feet east of *Victoria* at a pointed boulder.
1 80 feet 6b. Climb steeply up and then boldly rightwards to good holds. Continue direct (*in-situ* thread) to the faultline (large *Hex*). Cross the

5-foot ceiling to good flakes around the lip. Trend right to gain a large
scoop and belay using nuts and a high peg.
2 50 feet 5b. Step up to the large roof and swing out right onto the
seaward wall (two old peg runners). Follow a big flake and finish straight
up (thread runner) through solid overhangs. Belay on nuts and *Friends* in a
block as well as a stake.

To the right, a large pillar of rock known as The Arch met with the main
cliff near the faultline, until it succumbed to the strength of the sea in the
late 80s. The bottom pitches of three climbs were lost by this collapse. The
bulk of the second pitch of **Geronimo** (4.9.71) was subsequently
incorporated into *Fallen from Grace*. The top pitches of **Giraffe** (80 feet
Very Severe 5a [R] †† 14.4.71) and **Nasal Symphony** (60 feet Hard
Very Severe 5a †† [R] 9.10.77) are now hanging in space above the
faultline, and have yet to be reascended. The second pitch of *Giraffe*
climbed a rib and made a tenuous and very memorable rightward
traverse across an overhang, before following a leftward-facing corner to
the top. Pitch 2 of *Nasal Symphony* climbed a small chimney, crossed two
overhangs, and finished up a steep crack.

To the right of *Fallen from Grace* is an unclimbed block-filled crack in a corner.

* **Blood, Sugar, Sex and Magic**   50 feet   E4 6a [R] †   (8.94)
Start below the corner-crack. A good pitch. Hard moves left lead to a semi
rest at the right-hand end of a strip roof. Pull steeply up and right, and then
continue up cracks to the faultline.

To the right again is a bay overhung by a series of four roofs.

Agincourt   120 feet   E2 5c [R] †   (3.2.79)
Start below the left end of the quadruple overhangs, on a small, flat-
topped boulder exposed at low tide. If the tide is high, start on a tiny
ledge on the arête at the end of the hand-traverse from the west. The
climbing matches its appearance; it is a serious undertaking, particularly
on the traverse.
Climb up on juggy rock and follow an overhanging groove to an optional
belay at the faultline. From an undercut hold for the left hand, surmount
the overhang and gain a good ledge under another overhang. Traverse
left across a bottomless corner on dubious rock and move up to a
shattered resting-place. Trend leftwards to a wide, shallow groove and
follow it until diagonal moves left gain a shattered rib. Climb the groove
on the left of this to an awkward finish. Stake and thread belay.

The Curse of Testosterone   120 feet   E3 5c [R] †   (31.10.92)
Start as for *Agincourt*. The bottom groove is excellent and the two
overhangs exciting, but the climbing eases thereafter.
Move up and right boldly to gain the overhanging groove right of
Agincourt and follow this to the faultline. Traverse left a few feet and use a

left-hand undercut to surmount the overhang (as for *Agincourt*). Climb up to good *Friend* placements at the next overhang before passing it on its left-hand side by a committing series of moves. The angle now eases and pleasant climbing leads to a safe exit. Stake belay.

Corollary 120 feet E2 [R] † (30.1.77)
About 25 feet east of the quadruple overhangs is a wall, split by a crack, with a corner on its left and a roof to the right. The initial section of pitch 2 is not obvious; it is also steep, on poor rock, and unprotected!
1 30 feet 4c. Climb the crack, and belay at the faultline.
2 80 feet 5b. Climb the wall above the belay, step left, and continue up to a triangular roof. Follow the arête on the left (strenuous) to where the angle eases. A move right onto a slab leads to a corner; go up the corner and over some large blocks to the top. Stake belay.

Winter's Tale 110 feet E2 [R] (7.1.78)
Start 50 feet right of the quadruple overhangs beneath a square roof. Quite a serious top pitch.
1 40 feet 5b. Climb to the roof and traverse left to reach a groove. Follow this groove with difficulty to the faultline and belay on a wide ledge.
2 70 feet 5a/b. At the right-hand end of the ledge is a hanging rib with a crack to its left. Climb the crack for 25 feet to a small ledge (peg runner). Move up to the roof above and traverse out left for 8 feet on friable undercut holds. Layback past the roof to a horizontal break beneath another, smaller roof; traverse left and cross the roof at its narrowest point. Finish diagonally right over slabby rock to a stake belay.

★ **October Lady** 120 feet E1 [R] (25.10.75)
Recommended for its superb second pitch. Midway between the quadruple overhangs and *Old Faithful* is a projecting rib with a roof to its left (and a long roof high above). Start in the corner to the right of the rib.
1 50 feet 4c. Climb steeply up, make a tricky move to gain the corner, and follow this to a large ledge at the faultline.
2 70 feet 5a/b. Directly above the stance is a hanging rib. Climb a crack to its right to the long roof, and traverse right on jams and undercuts. An exposed layback around the end of the roof gains a shallow groove leading to the top. Stake belay.
Variation
Merlin 50 feet 5b [R] † (1991)
More in keeping with pitch 2. Start left of the normal setting-off point, as for *Winter's Tale*. Follow *Winter's Tale* to the roof and traverse right on underclings to an overhanging groove. Climb this, difficult to start, to reach the large faultline ledge.

★ **Ice Queen** 120 feet E4 6a [R] (29.12.85)
A quality pitch rising straight up to meet the final groove of *October Lady*.

Difficulties are both technical and strenuous. Start about 20 feet right of *October Lady* beneath a bulging arête.
Climb the undercut, cracked arête with difficulty to a resting-ledge at 15 feet (peg runner). Further taxing moves up rightwards lead to a second peg runner. Continue more easily up past the faultline and move rightwards over a bulge. Move back left to an *in-situ* thread just above the right-hand end of a long roof. Finish up the shallow groove as for *October Lady*. Stake belay.

★ **Sun King**   110 feet   E4 6a [R] †   (29.11.90)
A contrived yet exciting start is combined with a direct line up the wall above. Start on the left-hand side of a massive block which resides in an alcove at the base of the cliff.
Climb straight up the block to meet *Jasper* at its crack. Swing left immediately to a projecting hold on the lip of the roof (crux) and left again into a thin crack (peg runner). Go straight up to the faultline. Step up rightwards and continue up, with good holds but poor protection, to large flake holds and good runners. Climb boldly up the white headwall on sloping holds to a good horizontal crack. Pull rightwards around the edge of a strip roof before going straight for the top. Stake belays.

★ **Jasper**   110 feet   Hard Very Severe [R]   (4.5.69)
A refreshing contrast to the usual Swanage HVS. However, the protection on pitch 2 is sparse and awkward to arrange. Start at the massive block 30 feet west of *Old Faithful*.
1 50 feet 4c. Climb the block and move left to reach the start of an unmistakable crack. Follow the crack to a belay at the faultline on the right.
2 60 feet 4c. Step back left, surmount a bulge on good holds, and continue to a ledge on the right. Move right until below a slight corner and climb this for a few feet. Move right again to another smaller ledge, and exit to the left of a small roof just below the top. Stake belay.

Nunentity   120 feet   Hard Very Severe [R]   (30.8.75/1.78)
A good first pitch. Start just right of the massive block, below an obvious break leading up to the faultline.
1 40 feet 4c. Climb the wall to a bulge, pull steeply over this, and follow the break to a belay at the faultline.
2 80 feet 5a. Enter the recess above, swing around the left arête, and continue up to a large ledge. Follow the corner above to a narrow roof, traverse left, and finish straight up. Stake belay.

★ **Big Bertha**   100 feet   E1 [R] †   (9.12.89)
The roof makes this high in its grade. Start 5 feet left of *Old Faithful*.
1 40 feet 5a. Climb the wall to the faultline, passing good *Friend* placements half-way.
2 60 feet 5b. Cross the roof 4 feet left of *Old Faithful*. Step left and climb straight up to a solid finish. Double-stake belay.

BOULDER RUCKLE FAR EAST

The line of the recommended entry abseil for the area, down *Old Faithful*, is recognizable from below by a prominent, fin-backed boulder; *Old Faithful* is also the safest exit from this area. Immediately east is the large square-cut groove of *Black Crack*, with the two sides of the bay beyond being climbed by *Dragon's Teeth* and *White Horse* respectively. Progress past the zawn beneath *White Horse* involves a fingery traverse across a steep wall, which is possible only at low tide; at very low tide it is just possible also to boulder-hop across. *Prudence*, in the bay of the same name, takes the right-hand of two parallel cracks running up from a small cave to the faultline. On the opposite, eastern side of the *Prudence* bay is a steep crack, the start of *Ganymede*. Low tide is needed to continue across ledges to the next bay, where *Airy Legs* is found. From here, boulders lead to the corner of *War*. This point marks the start of *The Nutcracker Traverse*, which follows the obvious faultline across a steep bare wall to Subliminal. The lines of *Hermes* and *Insectitude* are alternative entry abseils; they avoid some of the tidal complications but may be hard to locate from above.

★ **Old Faithful**   100 feet   Very Severe   [R]   (4.5.69)
Nice climbing, good runners, and solid rock. The line of the usual abseil entry to this area, this route also provides a useful exit. The start of the route is marked by a conspicuous, fin-backed boulder that must be surmounted when traversing along the bottom.
1 40 feet 4b. Climb the crack above the boulder (awkward in places) and belay on the large faultline ledge beneath a roof.
2 60 feet 4b/c. Follow the crack boldly around the roof and continue up to a ledge on the left. Pull up right into a corner and climb this to a double-stake belay at the top.

Baker's Dozen   110 feet   Very Severe   [R]   (13.9.75)
Start just right of *Old Faithful*. An unlucky number and a wandering line but well worth doing.
1 40 feet 4c. Fingery! Pull up to a thin crack and follow it with difficulty to the faultline.
2 70 feet 4b. Move rightwards along the faultline and around the arête. Climb a crack, difficult to start, to a good ledge. Traverse left for 20 feet and make a delicate step up before following the corner of *Old Faithful* to finish. Double-stake belay.
Variations
Nineteen to the Dozen   Hard Very Severe   [R]   (25.10.75)
2a 60 feet 5a. Climb the crack in the bulge above the first pitch and continue straight up to the good ledge (some loose rock). Traverse left, step up delicately, and finish up the corner of *Old Faithful*. Double-stake belay.
Direct Finish   Hard Very Severe   [R]   (1987)
2b 70 feet 4c. Not recommended. Follow pitch 2 to the good ledge and then step right. Bridge past a detached flake (as for *Black Crack*) and continue up the loose groove to the top. Double-stake belay.

Black Crack   155 feet   Hard Very Severe [R]   (3.65)
Amenable but poor climbing. Immediately east of *Old Faithful* is a large
square-cut groove with an undercut buttress to its right. Start at the foot of
the groove.
1 60 feet 4a. The left side of the groove and the cracks above lead
pleasantly to the faultline. Belay to the left below an overhanging corner.
2 95 feet 4c. Climb the steep corner to a loosish overhang. Make an
awkward move left and pull over the nose with difficulty (stance possible
above). Bridge up past the detached flake on the right, move right, and
finish directly up to a double-stake belay.

★ **Argo**   110 feet   Hard Very Severe [R]   (6.9.75)
A poorly-protected and fingery start, but an enjoyable top pitch. Start
below a small roof 8 feet above a ledge (midway between *Black Crack*
and *The Golden Fleece*).
1 40 feet 5a. Climb up over the roof and move left to a ledge at the foot
of a groove; follow this to a belay at the faultline.
2 70 feet 4c. Climb the west-facing wall above the belay to a niche
beneath a large bulge. Continue up overhanging cracks and the corner
above to the top of a detached block. Traverse right for 10 feet and climb
a groove to the top. Stake belay.

★★ **The Golden Fleece**   120 feet   Hard Very Severe [R]   (2.8.75)
A splendid climb and justifiably popular. The main difficulties are amply
protected. East of *Black Crack* is an undercut buttress; start in a short
corner on the right-hand side of the seaward face.
1 50 feet 5a. Climb the steep corner to a ledge on the left. Continue up
the wall above with difficulty, and move right at the top to belay at the
faultline on the obvious prow.
2 70 feet 5a. An intimidating series of moves up and rightwards gains a
foothold on the edge above. Pull around into a slight groove, and
continue up on large but doubtful-looking holds to a good ledge on the
left. The corner above leads to a safe exit on the left. Stake belay.

★★ **Moose's Tooth**   120 feet   E3 [R]   (28.2.86/29.9.86)
Two fine pitches.
1 50 feet 5a. From the initial corner of *The Golden Fleece*, gain a
sloping ledge on the right. Climb trending right to a huge hold on the
arête and thereby gain the faultline.
2 70 feet 6a. Pull over the bulge left of *The Golden Fleece* and go up to
an overhang. Climb over this (crux) and follow the left side of the arête to
a sound finish. Stake belay.
Variation
★ **Decay 9**   E5 (R) †   (1.10.94)
Start on a boulder just right of the foot of the undercut buttress. Strenuous
and spectacular.
1a 50 feet 6b. Contort out of a black niche to reach good flake holds.
Swing left to a diagonal crack leading to hand-ledges on the prow. Now

climb the right-hand side and finally the tip of the arête (peg runner on the right) to the faultline.

Dragon's Teeth   120 feet   E3   [R]   †   (1.8.85)
A good climb with two contrasting pitches, although slightly contrived at the top. Start at a short chimney next to a cave in a big corner on the west side of a wide bay.
1 50 feet 5b. From the top of the chimney, stretch out left to a wide jamming-crack that leads up to a large niche. Move left onto the wall and follow cracks to the belay of *The Golden Fleece*.
2 70 feet 5c. Pull over the bulge directly above the initial corner of *The Golden Fleece* and continue up to some ledges. Climb straight up the centre of the wall above, using small pockets and discontinuous cracks, until it is possible to step left into a wide crack (feet level with the *Argo* overhang). Climb the crack and then finish up a shallow groove as for *Argo*. Stake belay.

Symplegades   120 feet   E2   [R]   †   (6.8.85)
Airy climbing up the steep ground between *The Golden Fleece* and *Behemoth*. Start just right of *Dragon's Teeth* at a cracked groove situated beneath a slender finger of rock projecting from the faultline.
1 50 feet 5b. Climb the groove, surmount a bulge, and continue on to gain the rock finger from the left. Bridge across to the left and belay on the prow as for *The Golden Fleece*.
2 70 feet 5b. Pull into the niche above the finger and break out left onto *The Golden Fleece*. Traverse steeply right above the roof to the arête and move up, stepping left onto a large, perched block. Continue up rightwards to reach a corner to the left of *Behemoth*. Climb this corner and step left to finish. Stake belays to the left and the right.

Behemoth   120 feet   Hard Very Severe   [R]   (14.11.71/1.75)
An especially fine route with an exhilarating top pitch that climbs the steep corner 50 feet east of *Old Faithful*. Well protected throughout. Start at the foot of a crack which leads into the corner-line at 20 feet.
1 50 feet 5a. Follow the crack and the corner up to the roof. An insecure move around the arête leads past a peg runner to a belay on a small ledge at the foot of an overhanging corner.
2 70 feet 5a. Climb the corner and surmount a bulge to gain a good resting-spot. Follow steep cracks on the right and exit rightwards across the wall to a solid ledge and a stake belay beyond.

Soul Sacrifice   120 feet   E3   5b   [R]   (2.2.83)
Bold and strenuous climbing with good protection, a classic.
Climb the initial crack of *Behemoth* to a ledge. Traverse right and follow a line of thin cracks up rightwards to the faultline. To the left is a short chimney bisecting the overhang above; follow this and the rib above it (peg runner) to small ledges below the smooth wall. Make a difficult move

to reach pockets and follow these steeply up right to a resting-place on *White Horse*. Step back left and climb the centre of the wall to a ledge. Stake belay over the top. (A more direct start can be made up the bulging wall 10 feet right of *Behemoth* at 6a.)

* **On Life's Edge**   120 feet   E4   [R]   (12.4.87)
Start on the left-hand side of the zawn containing *White Horse*, the old starting-place (and aid point) of that route. High in the grade.
1 50 feet 6a. Make hard moves over a bulge (peg runner) to gain a jug on the arête. Climb the front face of the arête boldly past a poor peg runner to the faultline.
2 70 feet 5b. Traverse right using an undercut flake to the front face of the buttress. Climb straight up the wall on good holds to an *in-situ* thread runner on the final flake. Stake belay.

* **White Horse**   125 feet   E1   [R]   (3.10.71/1979)
A powerful line on good rock. Start on the left-hand side of the small, deep zawn situated on the right side of the bay. Unfortunately, the start is often wet; the initial section of *Soul Sacrifice* offers an equally good though contrasting alternative.
1 55 feet 5b. Move round into the back of the zawn and climb upwards and outwards to reach the corner above. Continue steeply to the faultline.
2 70 feet 5a. Climb the crack above (peg runner) and make a tricky move to reach a smooth roof. Follow the crackline around the roof and climb the steep wall above (peg runner). Continue up cracks to a solid ledge at the top. Stake belay above.

Dublin Packet   120 feet   Hard Very Severe   [R]   (13.11.71)
Start as for *White Horse*. Cracking good climbing on pitch 2.
1 50 feet 4c. Pull across onto the opposite wall of the zawn and traverse right to a niche at the entrance to the zawn. Follow a crackline in the wall above and move back left at its top to belay on a ledge. (If the sea obstructs the start, an alternative at 4c/5a is possible climbing diagonally left from a ledge on the eastern end of the traverse.)
2 70 feet 4c. Climb the deep groove above the left end of the belay ledge and continue up to a sound finish. Stake belay.
Variation
Down in Ruckly Ruckly Land   E4   [R]   †   (8.89)
1a 50 feet 6a. From the initial niche of *Dublin Packet*, climb a fingery wall to a bulge with a crack beneath it. Follow the crack rightwards and upwards to the faultline.

Anger Is an Energy   100 feet   E5   [R]   (4.7.87)
Bold face-climbing which starts 30 feet east of the *White Horse* zawn.
1 40 feet 6a. Climb the centre of the smooth wall past a poor peg runner to the faultline.
2 60 feet 6a. Layback around an overhang 6 feet left of the belay groove. Make strenuous moves diagonally left on poor rock and then up

to a strip roof. Pull over on good holds and go up slabs more easily to the top. Stake belay.

To the right is a slight buttress bounded on its left by *Poseidon* and on its right by *Let the Punka Burn*.

Poseidon   100 feet   Hard Very Severe [R]   (26.5.68)
Start below a corner-crack 40 feet east of *White Horse*.
1 40 feet 4b. Climb the crack to a belay at the faultline.
2 60 feet 5a. Crawl left under a rib and step back onto it. Move up and make some strenuous moves up and left to a foot-ledge. Step across to another good ledge on the right and continue up to the top. Stake belay.
Variation
Hermes   Very Severe [R]   (25.5.69)
2a 65 feet 4c. Climb diagonally right to the end of the roof above and step left onto a short wall. Move straight up (crux) to a short easy crack, which leads to a stake belay at the top.

Let the Punka Burn   100 feet   E3 [R] †   (31.8.86)
Poseidon forms the left-hand side of a slight buttress; this route is on its right-hand side.
1 40 feet 6a. Climb a thin crack in a shallow groove to the faultline. Belay to the left.
2 60 feet 5b. Pull over the roof with difficulty and go up to a niche on *Hermes*. Continue straight up a crack and wall to finish. Stake belay.
Variation
Sparky   E5 [R] †   (1.10.94)
A fall from the crux of the pillar between *Poseidon* and *Let the Punka Burn* could prove a lengthy flight. Start just left of the latter route.
1a 40 feet 6b. Surmount an intitial bulge and continue on big holds to a horizontal break. Climb straight up the face on finger-flakes (*in-situ* thread low on the right) until a crucial reach gains better holds and the faultline.

Too Precious   100 feet   E6 6b [R]   (14.8.87)
A fine but serious wall-climb, on which there is the chance of a deckout from above the faultline! Start 15 feet right of *Let the Punka Burn*.
Climb easily up for 20 feet; then move left to runners in a short crack. Step right and climb the centre of the pock-marked wall boldly to the faultline. Step right again and pull over the roof at a tiny corner. Come back left above and go directly up past an alcove to an obvious finishing-crack. Stake belay.

Sinking Feeling   100 feet   E5 6a [R] †   (1.10.94)
A good start and finish. The bold central section can be avoided by the not-so-bold; after the ledge, a detour via *Prudence* drops the grade to E3 5c. Start 10 feet left of *Laurence*.
Climb easily to a rightward-slanting crack and follow this, with little gear,

until committing moves up the rib lead to the faultline ledge (junction with the aforementioned climbs). Step left and pull boldly through the roof (5 feet left of the *Prudence* crack) to reach a break. Now climb straight up the left-hand side of the arête, using the arête at times, to a solid exit.

* **Laurence**   120 feet   E2 [R] †   (10.10.82/6.11.83)
One hundred and fifty feet east of *Old Faithful* are two very large boulders opposite a smooth-walled bay. On the left-hand side of this bay is a small cave below two parallel cracks running up to the faultline. Start here.
1 40 feet 5a. Climb the left-hand crack above the cave to the faultline (strenuous). Move right to a nut and thread belay.
2 25 feet 4b. Traverse right past the corner to a crack. Follow this up to a ledge and step right to small foot-ledges.
3 55 feet 5b. Go up the crack to the roof and step left to a break. Climb past the roof and finish up the groove above. Stake belay.

** **Prudence**   100 feet   Hard Very Severe [R]   (26.11.67)
Two really good pitches on solid rock throughout. Low in its grade. Start as for *Laurence* in the small cave.
1 40 feet 4b. Climb the right-hand crack and move left to a nut and chockstone belay at the faultline.
2 60 feet 5a. Move back right, climb awkwardly over the overhang above, and follow the crack to a second overhang. Pull around this and continue more easily to a sound finish and stake belay.

> The smooth-walled bay between *Prudence* and *Ganymede* has been breached by two bolt routes, **King of Strain** (35 feet E5 6b/c [R] † 26.5.87) and **Medician Star** (100 feet E5 6c 6b [R] † 7.1.89). These were climbed before Boulder Ruckle was designated a bolt-free area; consequently the bolts may have been removed.

* **Ganymede**   120 feet   E1 [R]   (13.8.77)
Start beneath a steep crack on the right-hand side of the shallow, smooth-walled bay.
1 60 feet 5a. Climb the crack to the faultline, traverse left for a few feet, and use a large flake to gain a belay above (poor peg but good nuts).
2 60 feet 5b. Traverse easily right for 20 feet and move up to the right-hand end of the roof above. Make a difficult move diagonally left onto the lip of the roof and follow the groove above to the top.

In the Heat of the Night   85 feet   Hard Very Severe [R]   (27.9.84)
Start from a hanging belay beneath the bulge left of the initial crack of *Callisto*. Alternatively, at low tide, traverse in from *Callisto*.
1 30 feet 5a/b. Climb via the wide crack in the bulge at 15 feet to a large faultline ledge (junction with *Insectitude*).
2 55 feet. Climb straight up the corner and easier ground above to a right-facing corner. Follow this to a stake belay high up to the left.

Callisto   90 feet   Hard Very Severe   5b [R]   (27.9.84)
The crux is just above an easily-spotted short diagonal crack on the left
side of the next bay.
Move up and left before climbing the thin crack to a slab and the faultline.
Pull up a crack on the right and climb a groove to a ledge. Step right and
go up another groove to the top. Stake belays to the left and right.

Insectitude   100 feet   Hard Severe [R]   (1963)
Also on the left-hand side of the bay is a short, wide crack which splits
near the faultline to form a Y.
1   25 feet 4b/c. Climb up onto a narrow foot-ledge on the left wall of the
big crack. Good runners protect a long reach to jugs. Belay on the large
ledge above.
2   20 feet. Traverse left along the faultline beneath an overhang and
belay on a large ledge.
3   55 feet 4a. Step onto the wall and move right above the overhang.
Continue up for about 25 feet to where the angle relents and finish up the
flakes above. Stake belays far to the right and left.

Airy Legs   80 feet   Hard Severe [R]   (1963/1984)
Although sometimes climbed as an escape from the Ruckle, it is
nonetheless a pleasant climb in its own right.
1   25 feet 4b/c. *Insectitude* pitch 1.
2   55 feet 4a. Climb the chimney above before moving left just below the
top to avoid some loose blocks. Stake belay a long way up on the right.

Insecticide   80 feet   Hard Very Severe   5b [R] †   (16.11.91)
Start as for *Nutcracker Exit II*.
Climb the thin crack just left of *Nutcracker Exit II* to the faultline. Head
straight upwards and follow the rightward-curving crackline. Step right to
avoid the final bulge and continue to the top. Stake belay.

Nutcracker Exit II   80 feet   Hard Very Severe   4c [R]   (30.9.79)
Start at the flake crack in the middle of the bay.
Climb the main flake crack to the faultline, and continue up until a ledge
can be reached on the left. Trend leftwards up the wall above and finish
straight up over loose rock. Stake belay.
Variation (*80 feet Hard Very Severe 4c [R] † 11.9.88). Follow the parent
route to the ledge on the left. From the left end of this, climb up past two
peg runners, trending right on good holds to a safe, solid exit.

Warriors   90 feet   E1   5b [R]   (2.80)
A good route taking an appealing series of flakes above a faultline
overhang. Start from large boulders on the right-hand side of the bay.
Step up onto a small ledge and follow a shallow groove to the faultline.
Traverse left for 10 feet and surmount the overhang to reach a thin crack;
climb this and the flakes above to the top. Stake belay.

War   70 feet   Hard Very Severe [R]   (7.7.75)
Well protected but high in its grade, with some awkward steep bridging.
Start at the easternmost limit of the boulders.
1 20 feet. *The Nutcracker Traverse* pitch 1.
2 50 feet 5a. Climb the overhanging corner and wall above to the top.
Stake belay.

Purple Heart   80 feet   E3 5c [R] †   (4.8.87)
A medal awarded to those wounded in action, but do not think of that
when you are on the poorly-protected bulging crux! Start where the
boulders end.
Traverse at low level for 10 feet and follow flakes to the faultline. From here,
the bottom crack of *Intersection*, climb flakes diagonally leftwards before
strenuously surmounting a bulge and finishing up a corner. Stake belay.

The Nutcracker Traverse   80 feet   Severe [R]
A fairly serious and intimidating traverse to escape Boulder Ruckle. For
those in distress, *Intersection* provides the easiest way out from this area.
Start at the eastern limit of the boulders at the base of the cliff.
1 20 feet. From the boulders, step across a short steep wall and follow an
easy corner to the faultline. Belay on a good ledge at the foot of the
overhanging corner of *War*.
2 60 feet 4a. Traverse rightwards along the faultline to the ledges of
Subluminal. Belay next to *Greasy Chimney*.
Variation
Intersection   Severe [R]
2a 50 feet. Traverse right from the belay and climb the obvious stepped
crack to a stake belay.

An interesting low-level traverse, **Subnutcracker** (80 feet Severe [R]),
leads across into Subluminal; possible only when the sea is calm.

The last four climbs in Boulder Ruckle are approached from Subluminal. Traverse leftwards past *Greasy Chimney* and descend the slab to ledges just
above sea-level.

★ **The Long Goodbye**   45 feet   Hard Very Severe 4c [R]   (8.84)
An absorbing piece of wall-climbing with spaced-out protection. Start on
the leftmost ledge.
Move up for 10 feet to a smaller ledge and from its left-hand end take a
direct line up to the faultline. Climb the steep wall above until 12 feet from
the top. Now go slightly right and diagonally back left to an airy exit at a
notch. Stake belay.

★ **Seventh Wave**   45 feet   Very Severe 4c/5a [R]   (4.8.84)
Enjoyable, open climbing. Start at a thread belay on the rightmost ledge,
beneath a prominent flake in the upper wall. The technical grade depends
on height.

Climb up leftwards to the faultline and pull over the bulge to a resting-position below the roof. Move left and climb the wall above to finish beside a thin crack. Stake belay.

Second Sight   50 feet   Very Severe   4c/5a   [R]   (1.7.84)
Follow *Seventh Wave* over the bulge to the resting-spot beneath the roof. Step right, pull up into the flake crack, and follow it to the top. Stake belay.

Loony on the Loose   40 feet   E2   5c   [R]   †   (20.2.88)
Start as for *Seventh Wave*.
Climb straight up to the faultline and surmount the roof at a crack. After three strenuous pulls, easier but less-well-protected climbing leads straight to the top. Stake belay back to the left.

The Lighthouse Cliffs   OS Ref 028 768 to 031 769

These are the cliffs that stretch from Subluminal (immediately west of the Swanage lighthouse, and known locally as Anvil Point) eastwards towards Tilly Whim Caves.

Approach. From the car-park at Durlston Country Park (parking fee charged), follow the tarmac road that leads down across a wooded valley to the lighthouse. From here, a path on the right leads past some tamarisk bushes down to the rocky ledge at the top of Subluminal.

From Subluminal, boulders and ledges lead eastwards past the narrow cleft of *Avernus* and an overhung bay to the inlet of the Black Zawn. The cliff to the east is split at half height by the faultline followed by *Traverse of the Gods*. The western section of this traverse has many vertical routes above it, but east of the midway point of *Scotsman Chimney* the cliff is capped by a large, loose slope of earth and rubble which denies escape. The ledge sandwiched between *Traverse of the Gods* and Tilly Whim Caves has some strange speleological routes beneath it. Tilly Whim Caves themselves, situated further to the east, are a restricted area and should not be climbed upon, as is Durlston Castle Cliff beyond.

SUBLUMINAL
Subluminal is the most popular (and populated!) of all the Swanage cliffs. It gives probably the best introduction for the lower-grade climber to the characteristic steepness of Dorset limestone, although beginners may prefer the gentler angle of Cattle Troughs. Subluminal lies below the open grassy slopes immediately west of the lighthouse. It is endowed with worthwhile climbing in all but the highest grades. The cliff here is short, composed of excellent rock, and conveniently situated above large ledges

which are clear of the waves except in the roughest of seas. The top is clean-cut and stake belays are always within reach. Subluminal should not be taken for granted, however; there have been a number of accidents here, including several fatalities. (There are also two cars rusting beneath the waves.)

Access to the ledge at the foot of the climbs is usually by abseil from the metal stake with an eye in it located 25 feet west of a cliff-top alcove; this is the line of *High Street*. Reversing *High Street* or *Pedestal Crack* are good alternatives once they are familiar.

The distinctive *Greasy Chimney* can be easily seen at the western end of the ledge. The flat wall to the right is taken by the *'Face'* climbs and is bounded by the rightward-facing overhanging corner of *Transcript Direct*. Above a narrow section of the ledge, *Stroof* seeks out a thin crack in a smooth headwall. *High Street* follows juggy ribs and grooves above a wider part of the ledge just before a buttress. Around the corner, somewhat isolated between two easily-negotiated breaks in the ledge, is *Botany Bay*. To the right, above a zawn, is the corner of *Double Chockstone*. *First Corner* is the undercut rightward-facing corner beyond, and *Second Corner* a fairly open climb above The Bad Step, another break in the ledge. This gap is best jumped across, although a rope may be preferred for a first attempt! The Pedestal bounds the ledge on its eastern side. Directly below The Pedestal is an isolated cube of rock which gives the local name for the area, Anvil Point. To the east of this is the deep cave of *Avernus* followed by a large, overhung bay just before the Black Zawn.

Subluminal Traverse   280 feet   Hard Very Severe   5b   [R]
An ideal route for creating chaos and confusion on a busy day, the high-level girdle of Subluminal starts from *Intersection* and finishes at The Pedestal. The crux consists of a series of fingery moves to gain *Baboon*, while the final wall of *Grandma's Groove* provides further difficulty. The initial section of the traverse from *Intersection* to *Greasy Chimney* is situated within Boulder Ruckle and is affected by seasonal restrictions.

★ **Via Christina**   30 feet   Hard Very Severe   4c   (1.4.66)
A strenuous and demanding route. Start just past the extreme western end of the ledge, beneath the overhanging buttress.
Climb the overhanging buttress starting from the left and take the overhangs direct.

Dead Good   30 feet   E5   6b   †   (19.4.92)
The steep and smooth left wall of *Greasy Chimney* gives the hardest route on the main cliff. Easier for the tall, but it is bold and requires an alert belayer should a slip occur near the top. Start as for *Greasy Chimney*. Step left onto the wall and climb steeply on small holds to below the short left-facing corner (good large *Rock* on the right). Gain the top by a combination of hard moves and long reaches (and long falls?).

Greasy Chimney   30 feet   Very Difficult
At the western end of the main ledge is a large, black, and sometimes greasy chimney.
An awkward start using the flake leads to easier climbing up the wide chimney.

Suspension   30 feet   Severe 4a
Start 6 feet right of *Greasy Chimney*.
Climb a short corner for 10 feet, swing left, and continue up to a broad ledge. Finish to the right.

Whynot   30 feet   Hard Severe 4b   (13.5.90)
Start at the thin, vertical crack just right of *Suspension*.
Climb the crack and surmount the right side of a small overhang to reach a ledge. Move left up a ramp, pull over a bulge, and continue more easily to the top.

Dolphin   30 feet   Hard Severe 4a
Start at the foot of a rib 8 feet right of *Suspension*. Very poorly protected.
Climb the rib keeping close to the edge. From a small, sloping ledge, pull over a bulge and continue more easily to the top.

Curving Crack   30 feet   Severe 4a
A good tough test of bridging technique; especially hard for the hesitant. Large *Hex* required.
Climb the obvious, overhanging corner-crack. Much easier climbing then leads to the top.

Face   30 feet   Severe 4a
Start at the right arête of the corner enclosing *Curving Crack* and follow the easiest line up the wall above. Well protected.

Face Central   30 feet   Very Severe 4c
Poorly protected. Start to the right of the break in the ledge.
Climb in a direct line up the wall past a hole at 10 feet.

Face Away   30 feet   Very Severe 4b
Fingery and poorly protected. Start at a groove 4 feet right of *Face Central*.
Move up rightwards out of the groove and up to the horizontal crack at two-thirds height. Continue up and slightly right before gaining a slab and the top.

Tittsworth   30 feet   Hard Very Severe 5a   (18.4.76)
An eliminate giving sustained climbing up the wall immediately right of *Face Away*. Protected by small *Friend* placements half-way. Start at a diagonal flake on the right-hand side of the flat wall.

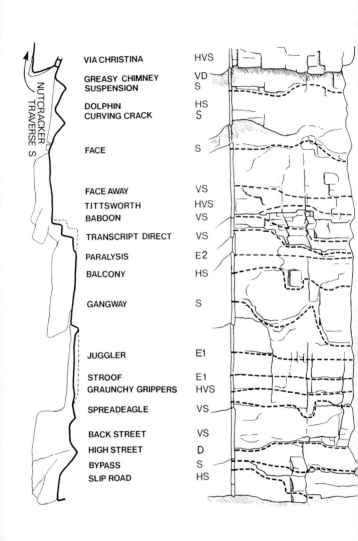

NUTCRACKER TRAVERSE S

VIA CHRISTINA	HVS
GREASY CHIMNEY	VD
SUSPENSION	S
DOLPHIN	HS
CURVING CRACK	S
FACE	S
FACE AWAY	VS
TITTSWORTH	HVS
BABOON	VS
TRANSCRIPT DIRECT	VS
PARALYSIS	E2
BALCONY	HS
GANGWAY	S
JUGGLER	E1
STROOF	E1
GRAUNCHY GRIPPERS	HVS
SPREADEAGLE	VS
BACK STREET	VS
HIGH STREET	D
BYPASS	S
SLIP ROAD	HS

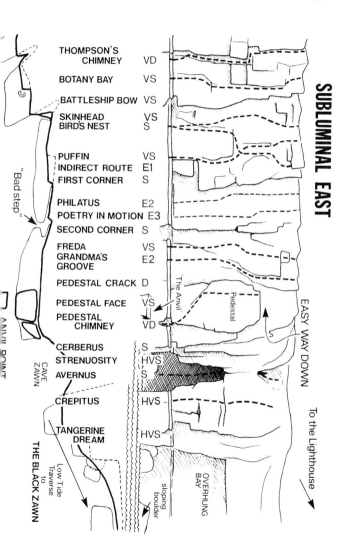

SUBLUMINAL EAST

THOMPSON'S CHIMNEY	VD
BOTANY BAY	VS
BATTLESHIP BOW	VS
SKINHEAD	VS
BIRD'S NEST	S
PUFFIN	VS
INDIRECT ROUTE	E1
FIRST CORNER	S
PHILATUS	E2
POETRY IN MOTION	E3
SECOND CORNER	S
FREDA	VS
GRANDMA'S GROOVE	E2
PEDESTAL CRACK	D
PEDESTAL FACE	VS
PEDESTAL CHIMNEY	VD
CERBERUS	S
STRENUOSITY	HVS
AVERNUS	S
CREPITUS	HVS
TANGERINE DREAM	HVS

"Bad step"

ANVIL POINT

CAVE ZAWN

THE BLACK ZAWN

Low Tide Traverse to

'The Anvil

Pedestal

EASY WAY DOWN

To the Lighthouse

OVERHUNG BAY

sloping boulder

Pull up to a small roof and step left onto the wall. Climb directly up to a smooth left-facing corner, which is followed to the top.

Dead Man Hunt   30 feet   E1   5b   (7.5.76)
Start as for *Tittsworth* and climb up easily to a resting-position and good runners below the main roof. Move up and left to gain a small hanging groove; pull up the groove to a good hold and finish direct: the crux!

★**Baboon**   30 feet   Very Severe   4c   (7.65)
A highly entertaining route that is well worth the required effort. Start as for *Tittsworth*.
Follow good holds to a resting-place below the main roof (as for *Dead Man Hunt*). Swing out right under the roof and gain the corner above; this usually requires a violent struggle! Finish more easily.

The Grobbler   30 feet   E1   5b   (7.65)
A very strenuous eliminate up the overhanging left side of the rightward-facing corner.
A series of very thin cracks traces a line up through the bulges; follow these to join the final corner of *Baboon*.

★**Transcript Direct**   30 feet   Very Severe   4c/5a
This climbs the overhanging corner to the right of the jutting overhangs.

Paralysis   30 feet   E2   5c   (7.65)
An insecure and difficult problem which is not over-protected. Start midway between *Transcript Direct* and *Balcony* and take a direct line up the wall.

Balcony   30 feet   Hard Severe   4b
Start below a jutting block, The Balcony.
Climb up to The Balcony, step rightwards beneath it, and gain the ledge on its top. Move up into a slight corner and climb the layback-flake above.

Gangway   30 feet   Severe
An unusual start for this grade. Climb the steep, rightward-leading layback flakes to a short corner and resting-place. Move up, tip-toe along a 'gangway' on the right, and from its end finish straight up.

Joker   30 feet   Very Severe   4c   (1988)
Start just right of *Gangway*.
Climb the bulging groove on good holds. Move 5 feet right and continue up a thin crack to join the top of *Gangway*.

Juggler   30 feet   E1   5b   (1970)
Start beneath a thin crack in the low-level roof, near its right-hand end. Some bold moves both to start and to finish.

Pull over the large overhang to a resting-ledge below a smooth wall. Three small finger-ledges lead to the top.

★ **Stroof**   30 feet   E1 5c   (12.65)
An inspiring and well-protected test-piece. Start on the right-hand side of the low-level roof, below a hairline crack splitting the smooth headwall.
Pull up through the bulge to a good resting-ledge. Gain the thin crack above and continue straight up to finish.

Graunchy Grippers   30 feet   Hard Very Severe 5b   (1977)
A technically demanding and, yes, graunchy eliminate. Start below the slim groove on the right-hand side of the smooth upper wall.
Climb straight up to a bulge beneath the slim groove. Pull over the bulge and move right to a rest and runners on *Spreadeagle*. Step back left into the shallow groove and follow it to the top.

★ **Spreadeagle**   30 feet   Very Severe 5a
A good route with some technically interesting climbing in its upper section. Start 10 feet left of *High Street*.
Climb easily to a roof under a V-groove. Step right and enter the groove with difficulty. Continue with interest to the top.

Back Street   30 feet   Very Severe 4c
Start immediately left of *High Street*.
Climb a shallow groove for 20 feet, followed by a smooth slab leading leftwards. Finish straight over the roof.

High Street   30 feet   Difficult
A popular beginners' route giving steep, well-protected climbing up the shallow, juggy groove that bounds the right-hand side of a distinctive, smooth headwall. One of the few polished routes in the area.

Station Road   30 feet   Hard Severe 4b   (22.5.76)
Fingery climbing to start.
Climb the wall 3 feet right of *High Street* to a short vertical crack and the ledge above. Continue up thin cracks to the top.

By-Pass   30 feet   Severe 4a
Start on the blunt arête 5 feet right of *High Street*.
Climb the wall to a bulge and surmount this on its right to gain the ledge above. Climb a crack past a large, jammed flake to the top.

Slip Road   30 feet   Hard Severe 4b   (16.12.71)
Start below a flake crack in the wall before the break in the ledge.
Climb the flake crack and step right to a crack in a bulge. Pull steeply over the bulge and move right to gain a corner, which leads to the top.

Republic   30 feet   E2 6a   (8.2.92)
A hard struggle for independence, which has large holds and reasonable
protection, but some quick thinking is required on the top section.
Climb up just right of *Slip Road* and fix a runner in the crack of that route
before pulling over the bulge. Step left and slap up the front of the final
block with difficulty.

Thompson's Chimney   30 feet   Very Difficult
High in its grade. Start by the break in the ledge to the right of *High Street*.
Climb the overhanging chimney above the cleft and finish direct.

Straits of Hormuz   30 feet   E3 6a   (23.8.87)
High in the grade.
Boulder up just right of *Thompson's Chimney* to wire placements at the
roof. Pull over the centre, reaching rightwards (crux) to a jug on the
arête. Finish *à cheval* up the arête.

Botany Bay   30 feet   Very Severe 4c
A problematical and strenuous start to pull over the bulge. The classic
dilemma: stopping for runners on the crux could lead to failure, whereas
far worse could result from missing them out!
Climb the wide bay to easier ground and finish up the corner above.

Battleship Bow   30 feet   Very Severe 4b
A serious, unprotected route. Start to the right of *Botany Bay* by a rib
above a cleft in the ledge.
Climb the rib from the left and finish leftwards at the top.

★ **Double Chockstone**   30 feet   Very Difficult
High in its grade. Start at the foot of the big corner above the cleft.
Climb the corner, passing two large chockstones near the top.

Skinhead   30 feet   Very Severe 5a   (28.8.77)
An interesting eliminate, high in its grade, with the crux right at the top.
Right of *Double Chockstone* are two small overhangs, offset in height,
which appear from beneath to form a square-cut slot. Climb up between
these and then in a direct line to the top, keeping 5 feet right of *Double
Chockstone*.

Bird's Nest   30 feet   Severe
Low in its grade. Start as for *Skinhead*.
Trend slightly right up the wall to a big ledge. Continue up right through
an odd gap to finish on the arête.

Puffin   30 feet   Very Severe 5a   (4.65)
Start under the low roof right of *Bird's Nest*. High in its grade.
Pull up to the left and continue up the overhanging groove above to the

ledge on *Bird's Nest*. From the left end of the ledge, move straight up to a steep groove, which is climbed with difficulty to the top.

The Indirect Route 30 feet E1 5b (14.11.76)
Start under the low roof right of *Bird's Nest*. Poorly protected.
Pull strenuously over the roof before traversing delicately rightwards to the arête. Continue up and over the next roof and finish as for *Bird's Nest*. Alternatively, finish over the roof to the left (harder).

✦✦ First Corner 30 feet Severe 4b
The obvious, bottomless corner gives a well-protected classic. Tricky for its grade, but it can be laced with runners.
Pull directly up into the corner or traverse in under the roof from the left. Climb the corner past an awkward bulge to the top.

✦✦ Philatus 30 feet E2 5b (7.65)
An enjoyable pitch on reasonable holds, although protection can be fiddly to arrange. Start in the centre of the smooth wall.
Climb up the wall and move slightly left at 15 feet. Continue in a direct line to the top.

✦✦ Poetry in Motion 30 feet E3 6a (19.2.84)
A hard and sustained eliminate up the wall between *Philatus* and the left arête of *Second Corner*. However, using wires, and a hard-to-place *Friend 1* at the overlap, it is better protected than *Philatus*. (Stepping right to a small ledge on the arête at two-thirds height avoids the crux and reduces the standard to E2.)

✦ Second Corner 30 feet Severe 4a
A popular route with some nice climbing. Start by the Bad Step where a cleft splits the ledge.
Climb directly up the groove above the Bad Step past a bulge, and finish either left or right.

✦ Freda 30 feet Very Severe 4c/5a
A superb, sustained pitch which is fairly high in its grade on account of its lower half. Start just right of the Bad Step at the foot of a thin crack.
Follow the thin crack on small holds past a peg runner. Continue more easily up the wall above.

✦ Grandma's Groove 30 feet E2 5b/c (7.65)
A hard-to-protect, fingery lower section. Start 5 feet left of *Pedestal Crack*.
Climb straight up the bare wall for 15 feet before moving left, up, and back right to the base of a shallow groove. Climb the groove to a ledge and the top.

Grandpa's Grope 30 feet Very Severe 4c (14.7.71)
Start as for *Pedestal Crack* and climb the crack for 15 feet. Step left onto the

wall and move up to a flake, which leads to the top. Some good climbing.

Pedestal Crack   30 feet   Difficult
A useful descent route. In ascent, start in the corner at the eastern end of the main ledges.
An awkward start up the polished corner-crack leads to an easier chimney and the top of The Pedestal. Step onto the main cliff and scramble up to the right to finish.

The short western face of The Pedestal gives a poor variant at Hard Severe. Described only in Annette's guide, **Interlude** has been regularly claimed ever since!

Below *Pedestal Crack*, a flake and good jugs lead down a steep wall to the tidal ledge on which sits The Anvil.

Pedestal Face   40 feet   Very Severe   4b
Not over-protected but worthwhile nevertheless. Start from The Anvil, the block on the low-level ledge below The Pedestal.
Climb a crack and then, once above the faultline, go diagonally left across the seaward face of The Pedestal. Finish upwards near its left-hand edge.

Pedestal Chimney   30 feet   Very Difficult
A small corner, although chimneying moves may be found useful. Start as for *Pedestal Face*.
Climb the crack in the seaward face of The Pedestal and continue up the shallow corner above.

Styx   40 feet   Severe
Just to the right of *Pedestal Chimney* is a corner in an east-facing wall. Climb the corner to the faultline and continue up the corner above to reach the top of The Pedestal. Stake belay above.

Cerberus   40 feet   Severe   4a   (28.12.74)
Start just right of *Styx*.
Climb the short wall to the faultline, and the steep corner above to a loose finish. Stake belay.

The cave to the east of the main ledge is the home of a Swanage favourite, *Avernus*, as well as two less-well-frequented routes.

Strenuosity   100 feet   Hard Very Severe   4b   (28.7.75/31.3.79)
On the left wall of the *Avernus* cave are a crack and a chimney with an overhung niche above. Start at the foot of the crack.
Climb up via the chimney to gain the niche. Traverse left across the wall of the cave to an overhanging prow; pull up and around this on loose blocks. Follow the final few feet of *Cerberus* to the top.

⋆ **Graduation Day**   60 feet   E2 5c   (24.6.89/27.6.89)
A well-protected and strenuous route with an exceedingly odd crux. Start
at a corner in the left wall of the *Avernus* cave, just seaward of the start of
Avernus itself.
Climb flakes to the lower strip roof and traverse left to its end. Use
undercuts to cross the roofs and attain a 'full-body' bridge. Strange and
constricted moves now allow the stance of *Avernus* to be gained. A
thread belay immediately above enables full participation in the
second's plight!

⋆ **Avernus**   70 feet   Severe 4a   (22.8.71)
A highly unusual and entertaining route which climbs through the roof of
the cave east of The Pedestal. Well worth doing. Start near the back of the
cave.
Climb large steps on the left wall until it is possible to chimney up the back
of the cave to a ledge on the right. Bridge up through a slot to the roof,
and traverse out on good holds to a window at the seaward end of the
cave. Belay here. Easy scrambling then leads to the top.

The overhung bay between the cave of *Avernus* and The Black Zawn provides some steep lines, most of which are best approached from Subliminal.

Crepitus   50 feet   Hard Very Severe 4c   (16.7.78)
Start at a groove on the east side of the buttress separating the *Avernus*
cave from the overhung bay. The creaking blocks which inspired the name
were removed by a leader who accompanied them part way down the
climb!
Pull over a bulge and climb the groove above to the top. (It is possible to
escape leftwards just below the final short corner.) Stake belay far back.

⋆ **Rainy Day Dream Away**   70 feet   E2 5c †   (7.7.91)
Good protection and two interesting overhangs should make this a
popular route. Start just right of *Crepitus*.
Climb into the niche and then rightwards through the overhang. Continue
straight up through the next set of overhangs, up a short corner, and left
onto a ledge. Stake belay far back.

⋆ **All the Shakespearoes**   70 feet   E2 5c   (11.12.88)
A well-protected pump. Start at the boulder-choked zawn.
Climb the roof-capped groove above the zawn, finishing rightwards at the
top to exit as for the next route. Stake belay far back.

⋆ **The Great Rock 'n' Dole Swindle**   70 feet   E3 6a †   (27.11.88)
The overhanging buttress before the end of the ledge.
Climb an overhanging scoop to a large roof at one-third height.
Overcome this with difficulty using a projecting jug, and gain a V-groove.
Follow this to the top and a stake belay far back.

★ **Tangerine Dream**   90 feet   Hard Very Severe   5a/b   (8.4.78)
Further right the ledge ends, necessitating a descent to the boulders. Start
from these boulders below the left end of a squarish roof at 15 feet.
Climb the crack in the east-facing wall and surmount the overhang.
Continue strenuously up the obvious line above to a roof 15 feet from the
top. Move left onto the arête and finish straight up. Stake belay.

★ **A Subtle Shade of Emptiness**   90 feet   E5 6b †   (11.5.88)
Very strenuous. Start near the back of the overhung bay.
Climb a short arête on the left wall and traverse left across a hanging
wall. Climb straight over a large bulge (hard) and go up a shallow groove
to the final roof (*in-situ* thread). Pull out left to an easier finish. Stake belay.

The remaining routes in the overhung bay are best approached by abseil to
seaward from a pair of stakes on the west side of The Black Zawn. This abseil
leads to a large flat boulder at sea-level. Calm seas required.

Close to the Sun   90 feet   E4 6b †   (27.11.88)
A line through the right-hand side of the overhung bay.
Climb leftwards above an overlap to the faultline and follow a shallow
groove to a horizontal break (*in-situ* thread). Cross the roofs (three *in-situ*
threads) and finish up a slight groove. Stake belay.

Gentle Touch   80 feet   Hard Very Severe   4c †   (21.8.84)
Start as for *Close to the Sun*. Some loose holds that could be dangerous in
the wrong hands!
Climb up to the ledge on the arête. Continue up the wall 10 feet left of the
arête to a roof, swing left around a block, and enter the groove above.
Climb this very carefully and scramble up to stake belays.

Vaseline   80 feet   Very Severe   5a †   (8.8.84)
Start as for *Close to the Sun*, climb up to the ledge, and pull onto the wall
5 feet left of the arête. Continue up to a roof, step right almost to the arête,
and climb up into the groove above. Follow this and easy ground beyond
to reach the stake belays.

Grooved Arête   80 feet   Very Severe   4b   (29.6.75)
The overhanging groove bounding the west face of The Black Zawn is a
worthwhile climb. Start as for *Close to the Sun*.
Climb the short wall to a good ledge on the left arête of the overhanging
groove (optional stance). Step right and climb the groove to a ledge on
the right. Pull back into the groove and climb this to a rocky slope.
Continue carefully up the slope to stake belays at the top. (A harder
alternative from the ledge on the right is to follow the steep crack right
again to the rocky slope.)

THE BLACK ZAWN
A unique attraction at Swanage. Situated below some tamarisk bushes just

BLACK ZAWN and final pitches of TRAVERSE OF THE GODS

MELPOMENE E4
MARS E1
TRITON E3
ASTRID VS
THE PECCARY E2
GROOVED ARÊTE VS
MELLOW YELLOW VS
RAY OF SUNSHINE E2
MAGIC MOUNTAIN E4
HARVEST GOLD VS
ZOË VS — ROUT VS
T.O.T.G.

west of the lighthouse, The Black Zawn gives dramatic and committing climbing amidst unusual surroundings. The rock here is particularly solid and the finishes are clean-cut and safe.

The conspicuous crack that splits the west face is the unmistakable line of *Astrid*. Just to the right of this lies the showpiece of the zawn, *Mars*, which tackles an overhanging corner partially hidden from view. To the right again, a jutting square-cut groove sports an insecure-looking block at its base; this is the original finish to *Melpomene*, a route which now finishes up a series of cracks in the wall to the right. At the back of the zawn a further hidden corner is the venue for *Triton*. The distinctive crack in the middle of the east face is climbed by *Io*.

The **approach** to the routes on the west face is by abseil down the line of *Astrid*. This can prove problematical as the wall overhangs and requires runners to be placed for the climber to keep in contact with the rock. Two good stakes are in place on the ledge above *Astrid* and the abseil rope should be positioned well to the right (facing out). It is advisable to carry prusik devices and to ensure that the ropes are kept out of the water; several parties have lost ropes amongst submerged boulders. If conditions in the zawn are damp, the routes here will be found much harder than their grades suggest as the rock becomes exceptionally greasy. Needless to say The Black Zawn is a very serious environment if the sea is at all rough.

THE WEST FACE
The two traverses of The Black Zawn can be approached at low tide by scrambling east from Subluminal. Alternatively, a ledge on the arête may be reached by abseil to seaward from the pair of stakes on the west side of the zawn.

Aquaphillia (VS+A2 †† 7.6.69) is a low-level girdle of the zawn traversing from west to east. The aided crossing of the west face has been superseded by the higher and finer *Deaf Boy Hug*, while the climbing on the east face has been affected by rockfall and has **not yet been reclimbed**. From the large sea-level platform, the route followed a crack in the left-hand side of the wall before traversing right (using more aid) to reach the crack of *Io*.

⋆ **Deaf Boy Hug**   270 feet   E3   (12.8.84)
A superb, varied route, comprising a series of well-protected boulder-problems in inspired positions. The final section of pitch 2 suffered a rockfall but has been reclimbed. Start from a flat sea-level boulder.
1 130 feet 5c. Climb the short wall to a ledge and then the overhanging groove to a ledge on the right (all as for *Grooved Arête*). From here, traverse right to a ledge on *Astrid* (optional stance). Continue with difficulty past a square-cut pocket to gain the corner of *Mars*. Bridge out onto the arête and climb to the top of the perched block at the base of the distinctive square-cut groove. Belay here on good nuts in an exposed position.

2 140 feet 5b. Cross the steep wall on the right to a ledge on *Triton*, move right again, and go up across a rib to a small green 'field' below a green streak. Bridge out onto the lip of the roof and follow good holds to the big ledge above. Grovel across to the right and finish up a short rubble corner. Belay on the stakes above *Mellow Yellow*.

Just Seventeen 85 feet E4 6a † (23.9.84)
An eliminate with a poorly-protected lower section which appears to be unrepeated; perhaps the previous guidebook's photograph of a 'surfing' second is to blame! Start from the hanging stance of *Astrid*.
Traverse 15 feet left and follow the crack of *The Peccary* for 5 feet. Make a series of thin moves diagonally left to a low (rusty) peg runner; then move up for 10 feet to the arête. Step back right and finish up a thin crack. Stake belays.

★ **The Peccary** 80 feet E2 5b (31.5.76)
A strenuous but enjoyable route up the thin, ragged crack some 15 feet left of *Astrid*. Start from *Astrid*'s hanging stance.
Traverse left and follow the thin crack on small but positive holds to a niche at 40 feet. Continue to the top and belay on the abseil stakes.

★ **Astrid** 70 feet Very Severe 5a (11.8.74)
The obvious crackline up the centre of the west face provides a splendid route, high in its grade though well protected. The first 15 feet give a hard crux, especially if the wall is greasy. Start from a hanging stance on a spike and various nuts 15 feet above the sea, reached by abseil. The wall is overhanging, so it is necessary to fix runners in the crack to hold in the abseil rope for the first man.
Climb up to a small roof and follow the short corner on its left to a small ledge on the right. Climb the crack to the top and belay on the abseil stakes.

Morbid Orbit (70 feet E2 5b † 1987) is an eliminate starting as for *Astrid*. Follow *Astrid* to its ledge. From the right-hand side of this, climb a bulge and step right into *Mars*. Follow *Mars* until a large flake leads back left to the top.

★ **Mars** 100 feet E1 (11.8.74)
A remarkable climb giving sustained and intimidating climbing on excellent rock with a perfect blend of position, commitment, and bombproof protection. Start from the hanging stance of *Astrid*.
1 20 feet 5a. Traverse rightwards along the faultline and belay on a sloping ledge beneath the roofs (very hard if wet). Alternatively, descend a crack on the right to a sea-level ledge, move right, and climb a greasy crack to the stance; this is the easier approach.
2 80 feet 5a. Climb the overhanging corner above past several roofs to a steep groove and the top. Belay on the abseil stakes.

The Damp Link (100 feet E2 5c † 1987) follows *Melpomene, Mars,* and then *Deaf Boy Hug* to the belay of the latter, before finishing up the square-cut groove above.

** **Melpomene**   100 feet   E4 5c   (1.1.78)
A particularly fine pitch, technically difficult and on very steep rock. Well endowed with protection. Start as for *Astrid.*
Make a rising traverse across the smooth wall above the faultline into *Mars.* Move up and traverse right beneath the overhang to a sharp arête; then gain a projecting foothold above. Follow leftward-slanting cracks to a tiny, sloping ledge and finish up the face above keeping to the right of the square-cut groove. Belay on the abseil stakes.

Triton   110 feet   E3 5c †   (5.6.76/22.7.78)
Very steep and strenuous climbing in a serious position. Unfortunately, the route is often wet even in the summer months and is sometimes affected by effluent discharged from the lighthouse toilets! Follow the low-level start for *Mars* but continue across into the next corner and climb this to a stance below a roof.
Traverse out rightwards below the roof to the arête. Move around this and climb the wall above to gain the corner. Follow the corner to a cramped niche and pull over the bulge above (optional stance). Continue up the deceptively steep corner to a ledge, traverse out left, and go up to reach the main ledge. Belay on the abseil stakes.

* **Achelous**   110 feet   E5 6a †   (11.12.88)
Very calm seas and a low tide required. Very sustained but with good protection. Abseil to the platform as for *Io* and boulder-hop across to the back of the zawn.
Climb the arête right of *Triton* to the faultline and power up a rib to a thin crack on *Triton.* Before reaching the main roof, swing left with difficulty to a good knob (*in-situ* thread). Follow a thin crack leftwards to the projecting hold on *Melpomene* and finish as for that route. Belay on the abseil stakes.

THE EAST FACE
* **Io**   90 feet   Very Severe 4c/5a   (12.8.84)
A good introduction to the steep walls of The Black Zawn. Well protected, but strenuous and high in its grade, this climbs the prominent crack in the east face of the zawn. From stakes, abseil down the line of the route and tension out from the wall to gain a large platform in the middle of the zawn. If the platform is awash, a belay can be taken on the obvious ledge just above sea-level.
Pull across onto the wall and move right until the good ledge can be reached just above. Climb the corner to the faultline and step left to a good rest and runners. Regain the crack and follow it to a niche beneath a small overhang. Step across to the right and pull up a tiny groove to a big ledge. Easy climbing up the juggy slab leads to the abseil stakes.

TRAVERSE OF THE GODS AREA

The first route to appear on the cliff east of The Black Zawn was *Traverse of the Gods (TotG)*. Since then, twenty or so routes have been climbed above the western half of this traverse. They are ideal if you require solitude without too great a walk. Although the climbs here lack the commitment of the neighbouring Black Zawn, they do have a serious aspect due to their situation.

The routes that lie between *Mellow Yellow* and *Yellow Brick Road* are best approached by abseiling to seaward from stakes on the east side of The Black Zawn. This takes one down the line of *Ray of Sunshine*, which is easily identified when viewed from the west side of the zawn. The starts of the climbs in the middle section (from *Shakin' Off the Ghosts* along to *Mother Duck*) are more difficult to locate from above, so it is probably better to follow *TotG* westwards from *Scotsman Chimney* on a first visit. This chimney is the preferred descent for the remaining routes, from *Drop in the Ocean* to *ZANU*.

The pinnacle at the top of *Scotsman Chimney* is situated directly below the east wall of the Lighthouse, but it can be seen only from the very edge of the cliff. Although it is a relatively straightforward climb to reverse, it is best to use a rope the first time.

Nesting-season restrictions apply eastwards from *Scotsman Chimney* to the start of *Traverse of the Gods* (see Introduction).

Mellow Yellow   70 feet   Very Severe 4c   (18.8.74)
A pleasant route on secure rock, despite appearances when viewed from the top. Low in its grade if the right-hand start is taken. Start at the end of pitch 14 of *TotG* on a good flat ledge situated 15 feet above the sea.
Move up left to a small square-cut ledge below a bulging crack. Climb this strenuous crack to the faultline, step right, and follow a break to a sloping grassy ledge. Exit up the slab on the right to stake belays. (The initial crack can be avoided at 4b by climbing directly up above the stance and stepping left).

Catch the Wind   70 feet   E3 5c †   (20.6.92)
Low in its grade. Take the variation start to *Mellow Yellow* and continue straight up the rib above to the top.

★ **Ray of Sunshine**   70 feet   E2 5c   (25.5.83)
A fine route on excellent rock, sparsely protected. Start as for *Mellow Yellow*.
From the left-hand end of the ledge, climb easily to the faultline. Move left and back right into the shallow groove above, and follow this to the top. Stake belays.

★ **Magic Mountain**   80 feet   E4 6a   (6.11.83)
Quality climbing which is initially very strenuous and sustained. The rock

is solid throughout. An additional set of small wires is required for
protection. Start as for *Mellow Yellow*.
From the right-hand end of the ledge, climb cracks immediately right of a
smooth, rounded pillar. At the faultline proceed steeply up to an obvious
undercut block and then swing up and left onto the face to good
fingerholds. Reach left and climb straight up the wall above to an
excavated ledge. Exit right to a stake belay.

★ **Fraggle Rock**   80 feet   Hard Very Severe 5a   (20.5.84)
Start below and to the left of the prominent jutting overhang at the
faultline. A varied route on good rock with a strenuous start.
Climb up to the corner-crack in the overhang. Swing left and move up until
a traverse right on jugs leads around onto the seaward face. Climb up just
left of two overhangs and then up rightwards to an arête. Step left and
continue to the top. Belay using stakes to the left and right.

★ **Live at the Witch Trials**   80 feet   E1 5b †   (7.84)
Start from the ledge on the right of the prominent jutting faultline overhang
(at the end of pitch 13 of *TotG*).
Step up onto the arête by the stance and climb diagonally left to good
runners. Traverse steeply left to gain a flake above. Move up and left onto
a sloping ledge; then traverse left to finish up the short groove of *Magic
Mountain*. Stake belay.

★ **Hard Nose the Highway**   70 feet   Very Severe 4c   (7.4.84)
Start as for *Live at the Witch Trials*.
Step up onto the arête by the stance and climb diagonally left to good
runners (as for *Live at the Witch Trials* so far). Step up with difficulty in
order to traverse back right, using handholds just above the upper roof.
Follow the groove above to the top. Stake belay.

Harvest Gold   60 feet   Very Severe 4c   (17.5.75)
Start as for *Live at the Witch Trials*.
Climb the corner using the rude cracks, trending up right to the overhang
above. Move around the right-hand end of the overhang and on up to a
stake belay.

Yellow Brick Road   60 feet   Very Severe 5a   (7.4.84)
A worthwhile and well-protected upper section. Start as for *Live at the
Witch Trials*.
Climb diagonally right to an obvious half-way ledge and continue straight
up the wall above via a thin crack. Stake belay.

Shakin' Off the Ghosts   70 feet   Hard Very Severe 5a †   (27.10.84)
High in the grade, this takes the wall between a zawn (scene of the 'fall
across the zawn' pitch on *TotG*) and the arête left of *Zoë*.
Climb the wall above the belay, trending right to a small niche on the
arête. Move out left (avoiding some doubtful blocks) to gain the steep

headwall above the stance and follow it to its top. Step right to good holds and a safe finish just left of *Zoë*. Stake belay.

⋆ Zoë 75 feet   Very Severe 5a   (13.9.75)
Some unusual moves. High in its grade, but on firm rock. Start 15 feet east of the zawn which provides a heart-stopping moment on pitch 13 of *TotG*. Climb a faint groove for 10 feet, step right to a ledge, and gain a second ledge above. Move awkwardly left into a groove and continue up left across a wall to a prominent prow. Climb the groove on the right and exit left at the top to a stake belay.

Rout 70 feet   Very Severe 4c   (9.4.77)
Start on a good ledge 15 feet east of *Zoë* at a wobbly flake on the wall. Climb leftwards past the flake and up into a corner. Follow the corner (solid and well protected) to belay on a stake as for *Zoë*.

Under Toad 50 feet   Severe 4a †   (21.7.85)
Start on the front of the buttress just west of the huge boulder at the end of pitch 11 of *TotG*.
Climb into a niche before moving left and up to gain a shallow groove. Exit to the right at the top of the groove and belay using stakes situated to the left and right.

Stone Doubt 50 feet   Very Difficult †   (21.7.85)
Start on a small ledge a few feet west of the huge boulder at the end of pitch 11 of *TotG*.
After climbing the crack in the east-facing wall, continue up over ledges and loose rock to the top. Stake belays both to the left and the right.

Mother Duck 70 feet   Hard Very Severe 5a †   (21.4.85)
Indifferent climbing on loose rock which may get worse with traffic.
Thread belay (in the faultline crack) at the end of pitch 10 of *TotG*.
Make a committing move up onto the front of the buttress and climb to the roof. Swing out left, surmount some overhanging boulders with care, and finish up a loose corner. Stake belay.

⋆ Drop in the Ocean 70 feet   Hard Very Severe 4c   (2.6.85)
The initial 12-foot crack between the wall and roof is strenuous and exciting... and safe if large nuts are carried. High in the grade. Start on the right-hand side of a zawn, at the end of pitch 8 of *TotG*.
Traverse left into the back of the zawn and then out on the opposite side just under the roof. Pull around the end of the roof to a well-earned rest in a chimney. Follow this to a stake belay at the top.

Heathcliffe 50 feet   E1 5b †   (7.7.91)
Just right of *Drop in the Ocean* is a good ledge with a strip roof above it. Start at an arête on the left-hand side of the ledge.
Pull up the arête into a steep groove. Step out right and go up more easily

to the base of a double groove-system. Climb the right-hand groove and exit from it with difficulty. Stake belay.

Withering Heights   50 feet   E1 5b †   (25.5.91)
Twenty feet right of *Drop in the Ocean* the ledge with a roof above it ends at an arête. Start here.
Pull into the groove above the arête and continue steeply to a good ledge shared with *No Great Shakes*. Climb the cracks above with increasing difficulty. Stake belay.

No Great Shakes   75 feet   Very Severe 4c   (19.7.84)
Start as for *Accidents Never Happen*.
Step up from the belay ledge and traverse left for 15 feet to an undercut slab. Climb into the scoop above and pull out over a bulge. Follow a ramp on the right and scramble up the earth slope to a stake belay.

Accidents Never Happen   70 feet   Very Severe 4c   (8.7.84)
Start 20 feet left of *Scotsman Chimney* at a crack leading through an overhang to a second overhang. A good route.
Climb the crack to the second overhang, step left, and pull over. Traverse right across a bottomless corner and continue up slabs to a short arête and the final earth slope. Stake belay.

Dreamboat Annie   70 feet   Very Severe 4c   (30.10.79)
Start 10 feet left of *Scotsman Chimney* by the second of two parallel grooves.
Climb the groove and a bulge to reach a small roof. Pull over this on to a slab and continue up a groove to the top. Stake belay.

Scotsman Chimney   70 feet   Very Difficult   (15.9.63)
This, the easiest escape from *TotG*, finishes below the east wall of the lighthouse. Start from the good ledge at the end of its pitch 7.
The block-filled, west-facing chimney is steep to start and takes one to the top of a pinnacle. The short wall and earth slope above lead to a stake belay on the left.

Three more climbs join at the top of the pinnacle.

Rhodesian's Retreat   65 feet   Very Difficult [R]   (7.64)
Start from a small ledge at the end of pitch 6 of *TotG*.
Follow the crackline above the ledge for some 40 feet to join *Scotsman Chimney* on top of the pinnacle. Go up a short wall and earth slopes to a stake belay on the left.

The slab and groove immediately right of *Rhodesian's Retreat* is **UDI** (Severe [R] † 4.9.84).

ZAPU   70 feet   Very Difficult [R] †   (4.9.84)
Start on the ledge 10 feet east of *Rhodesian's Retreat* just before a zawn.
Climb a crack past several chockstones to the pinnacle of *Scotsman Chimney*. Go up a short wall and earth slopes to a stake belay on the left.

ZANU   70 feet   Severe [R] †   (4.9.84)
'Protected' by a single micronut. Start at the foot of an obvious groove 20 feet east of *Rhodesian's Retreat*.
Climb the groove and the continuation corner to earth slopes. No belay.

★ Traverse of the Gods

2000 feet approx.   Very Severe (E1) [R]   (15.9.63/5.9.88)
A really tremendous expedition at its standard which girdles the cliffs from Tilly Whim to Subliminal. Although a number of routes exist above the traverse-line this remains a serious outing and should not be undertaken lightly. Well endowed with entertainment (pendulums, tyroleans, falling across a zawn, and even a swim to finish), it is a classic that should not be missed by any competent team. The route has now been climbed completely free, following the original line and avoiding the easier, generally lower, options. The original style is described here, however, since it makes a more consistent outing. **Nesting-season restrictions** affect the climb to the east of Scotsman Chimney (an easy midway escape route). Start to the west of the Tilly Whim Caves where it is possible to descend easily.
1 4b (5a/b free). A cave of deep water bars the way. Hand-traverse steeply across to a protruding beak of rock above the cave and rope down diagonally left from a peg. The second pendulums across from the peg.
2 150 feet of scrambling across three caves leads to a big flat ledge with a corner behind containing a large block.
3 Climb the corner to a ledge and traverse left for some 30 feet.
4 4c. Descend to an overhung slab and cross this to a corner-crack. Go up the crack and work out left to gain a narrow, undercut and overhung ledge, which is liberally coated in guano.
5 (5a free). Either hand-traverse through the deep guano or else abseil over the ledge and tension across to the greasy corner at the back of the zawn. From here, belly and hand-traverse the obvious ledge to gain a niche, and secure the ropes to a bollard so that the second can tyrolean across.
6 Step around the corner and scramble along a large ledge for some 50 feet to a zawn. Traverse across this on good holds to a small ledge below the crackline of *Rhodesian's Retreat*.
7 4b. Twenty feet of hand-traverse (awkward if wet) leads to a good ledge at the bottom of *Scotsman Chimney*.
8 4a. A few feet of scrambling leads to some awkward moves and a ledge before a zawn.
9 5a. A thin traverse and a wide step around a corner leads into the back of the zawn. Cross a steep wall with difficulty to the top of a crack. Pull over

onto a tiny ledge with a thread belay, perched atop a 'battleship-bow'.

10 4c. Traverse the next slab under an overhang into yet another corner and step across onto a ledge above a second 'battleship-bow'.

11 4b. Continue across another zawn and swing around a corner into a cave zawn choked with an enormous boulder.

12 Further scrambling and a smooth flat wall lead eventually into a niche above a narrow, bottomless zawn.

13 5a. Fall across the zawn onto awkward handholds and swing around onto the seaward wall. Hand-traverse quickly until footholds present themselves and eventually lead to a decent ledge. A superb but intimidating pitch which is even more frightening for the second!

14 4b. Step around the corner and climb down a slab (easier than it looks) to a series of wide steps and a good ledge 15 feet above the sea. This ledge is situated at the mouth of The Black Zawn.

15 Those with an aversion to getting wet can now escape by following *Mellow Yellow*. The less faint-hearted jump into the sea and swim to the far side of the zawn (about 75 feet). Climb up steep, rough rock to the obvious faultline running across the wall and haul across the clothes and extra equipment. The second either swims or tyroleans across.

16 A series of short scrambles and boulder-hops leads eventually to Subluminal.

The Cormorant   5 miles approximately   (1971)

The continuous barrier of cliffs stretching from Durlston Head all the way to St Aldhelm's Head present a worthy challenge for the 'coasteer'. The complete traverse is rarely done (and still awaits a continuous non-stop crossing). Exploring these traverses, preferably with as many friends and as few clothes as possible, can provide good sport on a hot summer's day and an excellent way of gaining familiarity with the area.

A long and interesting expedition open to most able climbers as the difficult sections can be avoided by either swimming or semi-buoyant traversing. The climb is divided into ten sections, each between convenient escape points. Calm seas required.

★ **1** Tilly Whim to Subluminal [R]

Low tide essential. The traverse below *Traverse of the Gods* (Very Severe) requires some semi-buoyant. Crossing The Black Zawn is hard (5c) but easily avoided by swimming. Boulder-hopping leads to Subluminal and an easy escape up *Pedestal Crack* (Difficult).

2 Subluminal to Cattle Troughs [R]

Low tide essential. *Subnutcracker* (Severe) leads in to the boulders of Boulder Ruckle and a lengthy boulder-hop to the start of *Paradise Street* (Hard Severe). This is best taken low down (harder but less serious).

3 Cattle Troughs to Fisherman's Ledge

Mostly easy scrambling along ledges interspersed with the occasional problem. The crossing from the Promenade to Fisherman's Ledge is best swum. Escape up *Helix* (Difficult).

★ **4 The Skua** Fisherman's to Blackers Hole

Swim the cave of Conner Cove and continue with some semi-buoyant to a second swim. Easier climbing leads to boulder-hopping and Blackers Hole. (When the tide is low a hard traverse of the Conner Cove cave is possible.)

5 The Easter Pathway Blackers Hole to Guillemot Ledge [R]
Low tide essential. Some impressive cave scenery and futuristic-looking walls lead to the boulders of Cormorant. Boulder-hopping leads to Guillemot and an exit up *Ledgend* (Hard Severe).

6 The Swim Guillemot Ledge to Dancing Ledge [R]
A long swim and some semi-buoyant usually leads to a crowd of tourists at Dancing Ledge.

7 The Dungeon Dancing Ledge to Hedbury Quarry [R]
Strenuous with much semi-buoyant and some swimming. A swim across the impressive Hedbury Big Cove leads to easier ground and an escape up *Rear Entry* (Difficult).

8 The Gannet Hedbury Quarry to Seacombe
A difficult and interesting traverse with some good climbing at half height.

9 The Seal Seacombe to Winspit [R]
Swim the large cave and then mostly boulder-hopping to Winspit.

10 Purbeck Perambulation Winspit to St Aldhelm's Head [R]
Low tide essential. Mostly easy going except for a fine half-immersed hand-traverse.

TILLY WHIM WEST
The low ledges west of Tilly Whim Caves are often frequented by tourists and fishermen, and one could be forgiven for dismissing this small area as a climbing venue. However, beneath the other visitors' feet are some short, interesting problems. All the routes here require calm seas. (Remember that in the Tilly Whim Caves area and on the sea walls beneath them climbing is prohibited.)

Climb down rock steps to a square-cut zawn in the centre of the easily accessible ledges. This small zawn has leaning, undercut walls, and fissures lead back from it to give two of the climbs. The climbs all start from the east side of the zawn.

Turkish Delight　60 feet　XS 5c [R] †　　　　　(24.8.89)
Drop down the steep sidewall and traverse left around the zawn to the arête. Continue across a wildly leaning wall and finish up a crack.

Numb Bum　25 feet　E1 6a [R] †　　　　　(6.88)
Follow *Turkish Delight* by traversing around the zawn and turning the arête. Finish up the wildly leaning wall.

Slap Ya Dromedary　30 feet　E1 5b [R]　　　　　(8.88)
Easier for cavers!
Drop down and traverse across the back wall of the zawn. Enter the cave with difficulty before chimneying further back and then up to the top.

The Hump   20 feet   E3 6a [R] †   (6.88)
Drop down, step across, and climb the steep wall to the top.

★ **Camel Filter**   40 feet   E1 5c [R]   (28.4.88)
A weird cave gives an unusual climb. Before setting off, check that the exit
has not been used as a toilet!
Drop down the steep wall and enter the cave strenuously. Continue into
the cliff by back-and-footing just above the water, finally to emerge
through a blowhole.
Variation
Llama Roundabout   60 feet   XS 5c [R] †   (14.8.94)
This odd little detour breaks away from the parent route at the blowhole.
Traverse the right wall of the cave to the north, dropping down towards a
boulder in the water. After a problematic jump onto the boulder, traverse
the other wall with difficulty before escaping up the blowhole.

Outlying Areas

Old Harry Rocks OS Ref 056 825

Old Harry Rocks situated on Handfast Point near Studland are a well-known Dorset feature, easily spotted from Swanage sea-front, or from Poole Harbour if approached via the ferry crossing. Although only one of these chalk sea stacks rises above the 70-foot contour they provide a worthy challenge for the more adventurous sea-cliff climber.

Old Harry is the slender and seductive pinnacle farthest out to sea from the headland. Old Harry's Wife, once of equal stature to her husband, is the short, dumpy stack nearby. Lying between Old Harry and the headland are two very large stacks sporting several arches and almost linked by a narrow ridge running down from the outer of the two.

A short distance towards Swanage from the headland are two imposing stacks; their authoritative but unimaginative names of The Pinnacle and The Little Pinnacle are often replaced by The Parson, The Clerk, The Wine Bottle, or The Haystack. The Pinnacle is an especially attractive feature endowed with a razor-sharp summit ridge.

All the climbing in the Old Harry area is on chalk, a medium foreign to most climbers but one that is has gained a measure of acceptance as progressively looser cliffs are explored. The routes are similar in nature to those found at Beachy Head in Sussex and on the Isle of Wight; the chalk is relatively solid, and protection is from pegs and nuts. Ice screws are useful to secure the belays.

Approach from the *Banks Arms Hotel* in Studland village, some two and a half miles north of Swanage. Walk fifty yards down a small hill and follow a track on the left signposted to South Beach. Continue south along the foreshore for about half a mile to the base of the stacks. A low tide is essential to traverse the foreshore and to avoid getting too wet. To view the stacks from the headland, follow a large signposted track that starts 80 yards down the hill from the *Banks Arms Hotel*. The Pinnacle, The Little Pinnacle, and Old Harry are best approached by boat.

La Traversée Intégrale de la Pointe Ballarde à la Pointe Handfaste   4000 feet   Very Difficult   (1977)
Calm seas and an aptitude for both swimming and the French language are required.

THE PINNACLES

Between Swanage Bay and Handfast Point are two stacks. The southernmost of the pair, The Pinnacle, is a superb, slender structure and has two memorable routes.

*** **The Tusk** 120 feet   XS   (9.5.87)
Start beneath a groove on the narrow south face. Peg runners used throughout.
1 40 feet 5b. Climb to overhangs at 15 feet and a foot-ledge on the left. Pull over a small overhang into a groove and climb the wall above to the left-hand end of the prominent ledge.
2 80 feet 5b. Climb the right-hand side of the mainland face to a small ledge overlooking the stance. Move 15 feet left to the centre of the face and follow a leftward-trending crack to the knife-edge summit. Abseil descent from peg belays placed on the far side.

*** **The Plunge** 120 feet   E4   (16.7.88)
The second route on this excellent stack takes the groove on the north side of the seaward face. Start directly beneath the groove.
1 100 feet 5b. Surmount the initial overhangs either directly or by climbing the groove just to the right and stepping back left. Follow the groove for 30 feet until it is possible to traverse 10 feet right to a ledge. Continue more easily to a good stance on the arête.
2 20 feet 4c. Follow the arête to the top, surmounting the overhang on the left. Abseil descent from peg belays placed on the far side.

The northernmost pinnacle is the shorter of the two and also has two routes. The curious small holes near its base are the result of gunnery practice during the war!

* **Press Gang Pinnacle** 75 feet   Hard Very Severe 4c   (22.9.85)
Start at a sheltered stance on the left side of the slabby north face. Peg runners needed throughout.
Climb rightwards to a wide, shallow depression. Step left out of it and climb straight up on loose rock to the summit. Place pegs on the far side for the belay and abseil anchors.

Testing 75 feet   Hard Very Severe 4c   (25.4.92)
Similar climbing to the original route on the stack. Belay near the landward side of the north face.
Climb more or less straight up to finish 6 feet from the landward end of the summit crest. Abseil off, using pegs placed on the far side.

OLD HARRY AREA

Wading to Old Harry (up to the neck to reach the east face!) requires a low spring-tide, so a boat may be preferable.

The Witch's Tit 75 feet Grade V † (5.86)
The west face of Old Harry has been climbed using rock, ice, aid, and building-site techniques. Hammered-in reinforcing rods were used for protection and removed afterwards. Although undoubtedly an impressive ascent, this famous landmark deserves better treatment! Start from a hanging stance on the right-hand side of the landward face.
Climb up leftwards and follow a very shallow depression straight up to a loose finish. Belay using ice screws, or lower off down the far side and place pegs. Simultaneous abseil descent.

Old Harry East Face 80 feet XS † (14.5.87)
Peg runners required throughout. Aid was used to place ice screw protection on a short section of pitch 2 before the pitch was free-climbed.
1 40 feet 5a. Climb rightwards to skirt overhangs and then come back left to a fault leading to an obvious belay ledge.
2 40 feet 5c. Climb up the leaning wall on the right to a resting-niche before going rightwards over bulges to a loose, character-building finish. Belay as for *The Witch's Tit*. Simultaneous abseil descent.

Old Harry's Wife 25 feet Very Difficult
The short, stubby thumb of rock alongside Old Harry is all that remains of a once much larger pinnacle which succumbed to storms in 1898.

The Outer Main Stack provides two contrasting routes:

Northern Bay 70 feet Severe † (4.7.76)
Start at a shallow bay near the northern corner of the stack. Hammers required for hold clearance.
Climb the loose bay, placing an ice-screw *en route*. Stake belay.

The Ridge 70 feet Severe (4.7.76)
More solid than its companion route. Start between the inner and outer main stacks.
Starting from its outer edge climb the attractive slim ridge. Stake belay.

The Inner Main Stack also has two routes.

Original Route 60 feet Hard Very Severe 4a † (1979)
Start from the right-hand side of the small bay which is out of sight of the headland. The route climbs 30 feet to a faultline before moving horizontally left along it and up to the top via some large, loose blocks. Descend using a retrievable ice-axe technique. Good practice for the greater ranges!

Team Teva 60 feet Severe † (9.92)
The scoop in the middle of the north face.

The Agglestone

OS Ref 024 828

Also known as The Devil's Night Cap, The Agglestone is an unlikely sandstone formation perched on its own amidst the bare Dorset heathland. Reaching nearly 25 feet at its highest point, this huge boulder has a coarse texture almost like gritstone.

The Stone is ideal for an evening's bouldering session, overhanging for most of its girth and surrounded by soft, sandy landings. Problems of all standards have been worked out on the boulder, the hardest being 7a. For the maximum benefit, start from a sitting position!

The Agglestone is situated about half a mile due west of Studland. On the B3351 between Corfe Castle and Studland is a parking-place situated one quarter of a mile east of the golf club. From here, follow a footpath for three quarters of a mile to the north-east across a golf course and Godlingston Heath to reach the boulder. (The shorter walk, from Studland itself, is often boggy.)

Isle of Wight

OS Ref 294 849

'...bound for the Isle of Wight. Mick Fowler and chalk. The kind of combination that brings a flutter to the stoutest heart. I wasn't sure how many return tickets to buy for the ferry over. The old joke about the four Japanese alpinists only buying two didn't seem very funny any more.' (Bill Birkett)

Climbing interest in the Isle of Wight is focused on the extreme western tip of the island. Here, at the end of a headland are The Needles, three chalk sea-stacks, with a lighthouse situated at the base of the outermost one. On the northern side of the headland is Alum Bay while to the south lies Scratchell's Bay, an impressive area of cliff accessible only by a 300-foot abseil. The climbing is on the same beds of chalk as on Old Harry Rocks to the west across the Solent. Here too, protection is from pegs and nuts, with ice screws used to make the belays more relaxed affairs.

The Needles headland is the site of the Old Battery, a Palmerstonian fort owned by The National Trust. A large number of tourists are attracted to the headland for its view of the island's best-known landmark, The Needles themselves. Difficulties in the approach to certain climbs, together with rare plants and birds which are sensitive to disturbance, has led The Trust to impose some restrictions on climbing.

The Old Battery is defended on its landward side by walls and a moat, and surrounded on its other sides by a safety fence designed to keep the public away from the cliff edge. One of the approaches is by abseil from a stake in the moat, and the finish of *Skeleton Ridge* leaves one outside the safety fence. As the approach to the abseil stake is complicated and the gate in the fence is normally locked, The Trust require climbers wishing to use this way down and way off to notify them in advance. This is for three reasons: so that they can supply a leaflet showing the approach and explaining the ecological importance of the site; so that they can charge admission to climbers, just as they do to all other visitors; and so that arrangements can be made regarding the gate in the fence. Access to the Old Battery is possible for climbers whenever there are staff at the site: any day of the week in July or August, and Sunday to Thursday inclusive for the remainder of the year. (This is more often than for normal visitors.)

To notify The Trust of your intention to climb the routes requiring access to the Old Battery (*Wrinklie's Retreat, Strapped to the Wing with the Engine Running, Skeleton Ridge*, and its variation *Hot and Cold*) or to use the *Wrinklie's Retreat* abseil, phone the administrator of the Old Battery on 01983 754772. Alternatively, write to The Administrator, Old Battery, c/o 35, St James Street, Newport, Isle of Wight, PO30 1LB. On arrival at the Old Battery, make yourself known at the Guardroom.

The National Trust do not allow the 'gardening' of climbs and would not encourage the climbing of new routes. Neither do they allow climbing east of Sun Corner; this has resulted in the loss of one route, **Ship of Fools** (7.11.92). However, the long traverse, *Albatross*, is not included in this year-round ban as there is a degree of sea-level disturbance from yachts and other craft anyway. A **nesting-season restriction** exists at Sun Corner (see Introduction). The coastguard should be informed before climbing here so that a rescue is not mounted unnecessarily (01983 753451).

Approach. The nearest car-park is at Alum Bay (parking fee charged). The Needles are a mile's walk away. The abseil down the line of *Wrinklie's Retreat* (used to approach *Skeleton Ridge, Hot and Cold, Wrinklie's Retreat* itself, and *Learning to Fly*) is about 300 feet long. All other approach details are included in the main text.

ALUM BAY
Albatross   4 miles   Severe [R] †   (20.6.87)
A sea-level traverse from Alum Bay to Freshwater Bay via The Needles. A serious expedition with no easy escape routes; calm seas are essential. The route consists of three sections of sustained climbing, each of which feature several swimming and semi-buoyant sections. The Sun Corner and Highdown Cliffs section is subject to a **nesting-season restriction**.

The walls between Alum Bay and The Needles have only one route. This is best approached by descending the top two pitches of *Skeleton Ridge* to the horizontal section below the final tower, and then abseiling 160 feet down a steep slab to sea-level. At low tide the belay will be dry, otherwise a hanging stance is necessary.

Strapped to the Wing with the Engine Running
200 feet   E1   † (4.11.84)
A fine climb up a huge, clean slab reminiscent of The Promontory at Baggy Point. The slab is cut by an obvious, narrow ramp-line, access to which is guarded by a series of roofs. Start at the roofs below the end of the ramp.
1 120 feet 5a. Climb a corner, traverse rightwards along roofs, and pull over onto the bottom of the ramp. Follow this easily to its end.
2 80 feet 4c. Climb a series of three short walls to arrive back on the crest of *Skeleton Ridge*.

THE NEEDLES
Three sea-stacks stand offshore, the outer two of which can be reached only by boat; the inner one, however, is just accessible at low tide. Dangerously strong currents flow around these stacks and it would seem prudent to use a powered vessel if venturing onto the outer Needles.

The outer Needle has two routes to its summit.

Lighthouse Arête   200 feet   Difficult   (c.1858)
From the lighthouse platform, follow in the footsteps of history up the seaward arête. Many cut steps and lots of *in-situ* ironmongery: highly unethical!

★ South East Arête   120 feet   Severe †   (21.5.88)
Start just west of the true south-east arête and trend right up to the arête. Make an awkward move up a slab and eventually gain easier ground leading to the top.

South Face   80 feet   Severe †   (21.5.88)
The middle Needle has frequently been lowered onto during RAF training sessions but appears not to have been climbed previously. Start just left of the centre of the south face in a shallow bay with a left-trending line leaving its left-hand side.
Climb steeply up left and continue in the same line before moving right to a steep concluding 10 feet and the summit ridge. Traverse the ridge to the top.

The inner Needle is reached by walking to the western extremity of the beach at Scratchell's Bay and continuing (dead low tide essential) to an exposed promontory that stops just short of the pinnacle.

★**The Crisp** 70 feet Hard Very Severe 5a † (4.11.84)
Make an awkward step across a gap onto the south face and traverse for 30 feet to a ledge situated 25 feet above sea-level.
Leave the ledge by its left-hand end and climb the crack past a dubious block to its end. Trend left to reach the crest 15 feet left of the highest point. From here, the top is easily gained.

The inner Needle is also climbable by its west face (the one facing the second Needle). The standard of the climb is only Moderate but the base of the route can be reached only by boat or by a very dangerous swim.

SCRATCHELL'S BAY
★**Skeleton Ridge** 390 feet Hard Very Severe (3.11.84)
This unique classic tackles the main ridge of the headland. A very impressive and committing climb up one of Britain's finest coastal features. Start below the col after the first pinnacle of the ridge on the south (Scratchell's Bay) side. Low tide is required for the approach.
1 40 feet. Climb a shallow groove and then trend left to the col.
2 40 feet. Traverse around the left-hand side of the pinnacle ahead.
3 40 feet 4c. Cross the knife-edge and follow the very sharp crest to a surprisingly good ledge.
4 50 feet. A very narrow knife-edge leads to a ledge on the left.
5 20 feet. Continue on ledges left of the crest to a stance below the prominent steep tower.
6 40 feet. Traverse left and climb a chimney/crack to the col behind the tower.
7 60 feet. The shattered ridge leads easily to a final steep step and the top.
Variation
Hot and Cold 260 feet Hard Very Severe † (2.12.89)
An alternative start up the south side of the ridge; useful when the original entry pitch is wave-swept. Start 50 yards right of the starting-point of *Skeleton Ridge* at a projecting prow with a line of holds leading leftwards into a shallow groove.
1a 80 feet 5a. Climb leftwards into the groove and follow this to the base of a prominent straight crack in a rightward-leaning corner. Climb the corner to ledges.
2a 80 feet 4b. Continue easily in the same line for 40 feet and then go straight up over looser material to gain the ridge. Belay below the prominent steep tower. Finish up pitches 6 and 7 of the parent route.

Wrinklie's Retreat 300 feet Hard Very Severe † (22.9.84)
This follows the line of the recommended abseil descent. The ground is loose and serious, ice-axes having been used, though with rock boots, on the first ascent. The line of the climb is variable. Two pitches (the first is the crux) climb up to the base of the prominent groove/gully. This groove/gully gives the final pitch, which leads rightwards to the abseil stake.

** **Learning to Fly**   340 feet   XS †   (9.7.88)
The challenging middle pitch of this route takes the prominent left-trending groove directly beneath the coastguard lookout, and features exciting climbing on flints bolstered by dubious protection. An intermittent line of grass ledges leads diagonally rightwards towards the groove; start beneath the leftmost ledge.
1 120 feet 5b. Climb an overhanging, right-trending line and gain the vegetated ledge with difficulty. Trend up right past various vegetated ledges and belay up and right of the farthest one.
2 120 feet 5c. Climb very steeply to enter the groove from directly beneath. Follow it to a point 20 feet below the capping overhang, where it contains a dubious block and becomes very smooth. Traverse left for 10 feet, move up, and trend diagonally back rightwards to rejoin the groove just below the overhang. Cross the overhang via the prominent jamming crack and go up 15 feet to belay.
3 100 feet 5a. Follow the obvious right-trending ramp past an ancient *in-situ* stake until after 60 feet it is possible to climb straight up, finishing at a short crack.

The following three routes are on Sun Corner, the headland at the southeast end of Scratchell's Bay, and are reached by abseiling from stakes to a sloping area about 100 feet above the sea. The routes take the steep upper wall.

* **Blood Sweat and Bullets**   150 feet   XS †   (12.10.85)
The impressive left-hand crackline on the face gives a fine yet serious climb. Start at the extreme left-hand edge of the wall overlooking Scratchell's Bay.
1 70 feet 5c. Climb the scooped, overhanging crack for 25 feet to where the angle eases. Continue in the slanting crack (passing the indistinct junction with a crack which could give a variation start) to belay where the crack goes straight up.
2 80 feet 5b. Climb the crack, stepping right to finish.

* **Negotiator**   120 feet   MXS 5b †   (12.10.85)
A good introduction to harder chalk-climbing, taking the crack just before the right arête of the headland's frontal facet.
Start just left of the crack and climb diagonally rightwards to gain it 10 feet below the overhang. Follow the crack/chimney to the top.

Gateway to Heaven   110 feet   Very Severe 4b [R] †   (12.10.85)
Start just right of *Negotiator*.
Move rightwards around the corner and follow a rightward trending ramp to the foot of a chimney, which leads past a wedged gate to the top of a pinnacle. Step easily onto the top.

Albatross excepted, climbing is not permitted on the cliff east of Sun Corner.

FRESHWATER BAY
Stag Rock   60 feet   Severe   (22.5.88)
The most westerly stack. Climb up the left (east) side of the landward face.

Nearby, Arch Rock gave a climb until this stack fell down late in 1992.

Bear Rock   85 feet   Very Severe †   (22.5.88)
This is the easterly and most enticing stack in the bay. Start on the south-west corner, which is approached by boat or by a 5b traverse. Climb the edge and trend right at 25 feet to gain steep grass and the top. Simultaneous abseil descent.

First Ascents

(AL) or (VL) indicate alternate or varied leads respectively. Please refer also to the note at the end of this list on page 288.

SWANAGE
Richard Holt, Harland Holt, Paul Wallace, and Paul French were responsible for most of the lines on the sea walls at Dancing Ledge.

c.1957   **The Ramp**   J S Cleare, A G Smythe, S A Clark
           The final wall was climbed with several points of aid.

Pre-1963   **Ashes and Diamonds**   F J Clarke, P A Bell (2 pts aid)
Pre-1963   **Gimcrack**   B Annette, W Hill
Pre-1963   **Jericho Groove**   J F Clarke, A G Smythe
Pre-1963   **Marmolata**   J F Clarke, J Histed (3 pts aid)
           The first ascensionists originally finished up to the left of the top pitch of Ashes and Diamonds. The direct finish was climbed with two slings for aid by G Smith, D D Whillans on 9 April 1969.

Pre-1963   **Tatra**   B Annette, P Kemp (7 pts aid)
Pre-1963   **Blood Gully, East Milton Wall**   M J Stephenson and party
Pre-1963   **Crack of Dawn**   B Annette, W Hill
           Reclimbed after the rockfall by P Finklaire, G Hounsome on 1 April 1979, but now completely destroyed by a second rockfall.

1963 May 5   **Mañana**   J S Cleare, A G Smythe (1 pt aid)
1963 July 10   **Granny Smith**   T A Goodfellow, J Mustoe
           Variation climbed by I Howell, A Rowe. Destroyed by rockfall.

1963 July 11   **Thunderball**   P A Bell, T A Goodfellow
           Pitch 2 has been interchanged with pitch 2 of Thor in the main text.

1963 July 12   **Apex Corner**   J Mustoe, T A Goodfellow, P A Bell
1963 Sept 15   **Traverse of the Gods**   R Baillie, J S Cleare
           First free ascent J Williams, J Biddle on 5 September 1988.

1963 Sept 15   **Scotsman Chimney**   I Martin
1963 Sept   **Hell's Teeth**   R C White, R J Black, A Monnery
1963 Sept   **Poof**   R J Black, R C White, A Monnery
1963 Oct   **Grottle**   R C White, G T Davis
1963 Nov   **Clov**   R J Black, A Monnery
1963   **DWM**   B Thomas, S Lowe (1 pt aid)
           First free ascent G Hounsome on 15 May 1977.

1963   **Isis**   D Rowlands
1963   **Airy Legs**   D Oldroyd, D Burrin, D Eastwood
           The large boulder which formed the first pitch has

	disappeared. Reclimbed by K Turner, G A Jenkin in 1984.
1963	**Enos** A Alvaraz, A G Smythe, S A Clark, J F Clarke (1 pt aid)
	Little Brown Mouse variation climbed by B Snell, K Knight on 15 November 1975.
1963	**Sweet S A** F Clarke, A Alvaraz
1964 May 8	**Larus** A Hartley, R Snell, I Howell
1964 June 16	**Bottomless Buttress** I Howell, A Hartley, A Rowe
	Pitch 3 has been affected by rockfall.
1964 July	**Rhodesian's Retreat** I McMorrin
1964 Aug 29	**Aventura** P Crew, P A Bell
1964 Aug 29	**Viper** P A Bell, T A Goodfellow
1964 Sept 14	**Moonraker** P A Bell, T A Goodfellow
	Affected by rockfall.
1965 March	**Black Crack** D Burgess, J R Allen
1965 April	**Puffin** R C White
1965 May 15	**Paradise Street** P A Bell, T A Goodfellow
1965 May	*H Evans and partner climbed a line on the quarried wall at Dancing Ledge, resorting to a top-rope for the final desperate 20 feet.*
1965 June	**Due Care and Attention** A C Willmott, J Browne
1965 July	**Paralysis, The Grobbler, Baboon, Grandma's Groove, Philatus** A C Willmott
	Philatus was originally climbed as an A2 pitch by an unknown party.
1965 Dec	**Stroof** A C Willmott
1966 Jan	**Flyover** R C White, G T Davis
1966 April 1	**Via Christina** K A V Cartwright
1966 April 10	**'B' Line** D Boone, M Talbot, D Hadlum, P Grainger
	The top pitch originally traversed left from the peg runner into the upper section of Finale Groove.
1966 April 10	**Director's Groove** D Hadlum, P Grainger
1966 April 10	**Lightning Wall** G Smith, A Webster (1 pt aid)
	Variation start climbed by D Walker in 1984.
1966 April 11	**Valkyrie** D Hadlum, G Smith, P Grainger, J Midgley, A Webster
1966 April 11	**Summit Route** R Leeming, D Horne, R J Cummerford
1966 April 11	**Ledgend** D Burgess, J R Allen, R Colledge
1966 April 12	**Finale Groove** G Smith, D Hadlum
1966 July 17	**Perversion** K A V Cartwright, D C Unwin
1966 Aug 28	**Springbok Route** T Kerrick, R Sugden
1966 Sept 18	**The Heidelberg Creature** A C Willmott, A Heppenstall
1966 Nov 20	**Sheerline** P Neame, M R Forrest, A B Monnery
	Affected by rockfall.
1966 Nov 25	**Tatra Direct** A C Willmott, A Heppenstall (2 pts aid)
	Pitch 2 added by R J Crewe, R Kent, J Yaldren on 3 December 1967 and reclimbed after the rockfall by N A Coe, T Dunsby on 30 November 1991.

1966 Dec 11   **Strophanthin**   A C Willmott, W H Church
The route originally finished up a loose groove to the left. Pitch 2 as described was climbed by P Grainger, D Hadlum, A Webster, G Reynolds on 27 March 1967.

1966 Dec 16   **Solitude**   W H Church, A J Young

1967 Feb 12   **Smutti**   R C White, R James
Direct finish climbed by S Tomlin, R J Crewe, D Sargeant on 1 February 1975.

1967 Feb 12   **Ledgend Direct**   P Neame, A B Monnery

1967 Feb 12   **Aquascrotum**   R Snell, I Howell
Reclimbed after the rockfall as Aquascrotum II by G Hounsome, P Finklaire on 1 April 1979.

1967 March 5   **Noddy**   R Smith (1 pt aid)
First free ascent S L Titt, J L Titt on 17 November 1977.

1967 March 5   **Squeeze Chimney**   D Norton, A Hartley, J S Cleare, I Howell
Affected by rockfall.

1967 March 21   **Ndizi**   R Smith, B Cliff

1967 March 25   **Batt Crack**   D Hadlum, G Reynolds

1967 March 25   **The Cleft**   D Boone, R Smith
Destroyed by rockfall.

1967 March 25   **Cleft Buttress**   R Smith, D Boone
Destroyed by rockfall.

1967 March 26   **Rainbow**   B Metcalfe, J R Allen

1967 March 26   **Robud**   R Wood, B Metcalfe

1967 March 27   **Strapiombo**   A Webster, D Hadlum

1967 March 28   **The Crevice**   B Metcalfe, R Wood

1967 May 21   **Valkyrie Buttress Direct**   R C White, B Wood

1967 July 30   **Mystery Bonus**   R J Crewe, J Yaldren (aid)
The first new route from the 'genial giant'. Superseded by free climbs.

1967 Aug 6   **Squid**   R J Crewe, J Yaldren (3 pts aid)
First free ascent F Rech, H Lancashire in 1975.

1967 Sept 9   **Cheroot**   R J Crewe, P Charman, K Winkworth (2 pts aid)
First free ascent D Ivory, E Hart c.1974.

1967 Sept 16   **Thunder Groove**   R J Crewe, K Winkworth (6 pts aid)
First free ascent P R Littlejohn and partner.

1967 Sept 24   **Mushroom**   J Armitage, R J Crewe, R Kent (aid)
Superseded by free routes.

1967 Sept 24   **Eskimo Nell**   D H Lister, D F Lewis, D C Montague
The main groove was avoided on the first ascent. The groove was climbed on 16 February 1969 by H Evans, P Deketelaere, who then finished to the left using two pegs for aid.

1967 Oct 8   **Tilt**   R J Crewe, J Yaldren, R Kent (aid)
First free ascent (renamed Swimming in Jugs) by P Oxley, J Biddle, J Williams on 6 February 1988.

1967 Oct 29   **Gypsy**   R J Crewe, K Winkworth (4 pts aid)

1967 Nov 26   **Prudence**   K A V Cartwright

1968 Jan 7   **Elysium** R J Crewe, K Winkworth (2 pts aid)
Variation climbed by A Blakely, J Blyde on 28 June 1986.

1968 Feb 3   **Pippin Crack** K A V Cartwright, Ms P L Serby
Destroyed by rockfall.

1968 May 19   **Sea Lion** D M Roberts, R M Wilson
Originally a variation finish to Sweet S A, reached by a traverse along the faultline. Pitch 1 added by G Hounsome, S L Titt on 18 November 1979. Direct Start climbed by C Waddy, A Ford on 10 August 1985.

1968 May 26   **Poseidon** K A V Cartwright, J C Wilkinson

1968 June 16   **Gaston** J D Griffiths, M E Nunn

1968 June 16   **Jo** R J Crewe, R C White, K Winkworth, J Yalden
Originally Thunderball variation start. Pitch 2 added by H Lancashire, P Holden on 31 March 1975.

1968 June 29   **Higgins** M E Nunn, J D Griffiths

1968 June 30   **Cascara** B Metcalfe, J R Allen

1968 July 27   **Rattler** M E Nunn, R J Crewe (AL) (2 pts aid)
First free ascent B Snell, W Lyons.

1968 July 28   **Billy Pigg** R J Crewe, K Winkworth (4 pts aid)
First free ascent G Hounsome on 11 March 1978.

1968 Sept 8   **Ilium** R J Crewe, J Armitage, R Kent (1 pt aid)
First free ascent G Hounsome on 5 November 1977.

1968 Nov 3   **RIP** R J Crewe, P Charman
Direct Finish climbed by C Crowther, E Sinclair on 27 March 1989.

1968   **Steep** First free ascent K Topping

1968   **Long John's** W H Church, R J Houston

1968   **Little Red Watering Can** M Milner, W H Church
Affected by rockfall.

1968   **Sue's Route** W H Church, R J Houston

1968   **Varina** (and variation) R Heigh, W H Church

1969 March 30   **Sea View** A Grainger, P Broadley, J Marchant, R Fleet (aid)
Thirty-five pegs and thirteen hours of climbing were put in for the first route on the Ocean Boulevard wall. Superseded by free climbs.

1969 April 6   **Chamberwall** G Smith, J Midgley, B Metcalfe
This route originally finished up the top pitch of Chamberwall II.

1969 April 19   **Chasm Groove** M Boater, D Fell
The climb originally surmounted the initial overhang direct using a shoulder and two pegs for aid. Direct start climbed by P Oxley in 1987.

1969 April 26   **Boulder Ruckle Girdle** R J Crewe, K Winkworth (9 pts aid)
Completed on this date, the route having been climbed in stages through the winter. G Hounsome and D Gumn reduced the aid to one point in 1978, climbing from east to west. The climb has since been affected by rockfall.

1969 May 4   **Old Faithful** R Kent, R J Crewe, K Winkworth

1969 May 4	**Jasper** R J Crewe, K Winkworth, R Kent
1969 May 11	**Blinking Crack** G Smith, J R Allen (3 pts aid)
	Destroyed by rockfall.
1969 May 11	**Sinbad** R J Crewe, K Winkworth (1 pt aid)
1969 May 25	**Hermes** I W Bayman, K A V Cartwright
1969 May 31	**Romu, Searide** M Boater, R Shergold (1 pt aid)
1969 June 1	**Sweet and Sour** R J Crewe, P Charman
1969 June 7	**Buccaneer** R J Crewe, K Winkworth (7 pts aid)

First free ascent G A Jenkin, R Harrison in February 1978, climbing the top roofs direct. Difficult communication, rope drag, and the speed with which Harrison followed on the top pitch meant that he took a monster lob when a flake gave way.

| 1969 June 7 | **Aquaphillia** M Collison, T H Angus (aid) |

After successfully retreating to the cliff-top on a previous attempt the pair were surprised to find the lifeboat had been called out. They were even more astonished to read later in the Evening Standard that they had been rescued from a 200-foot cliff!

| 1969 June 29 | **Mongoose** R J Crewe, K Winkworth (1 pt aid) |

First free ascent H Lancashire, F Rech in Oct 1975.

| 1969 Sept 7 | **The Conger** R J Crewe (2 pts aid) |

First free ascent F Farrell in September 1979. Jellied variation soloed on-sight by J Biddle on 3 August 1990. Snap Crackle and Plop variation soloed by D M Cook on 11 September 1990. His on-sight solo attempt ended in the water when a hold snapped.

1969 Sept 14	**The Razor's Edge** B Metcalfe, R Withers (2 pts aid)
1969 Oct 11	**Cormorant Buttress West** J Yaldren, R J Crewe
1969 Oct 11	**Cormorant Buttress East** R J Crewe, J Yaldren, P Charman

Reclimbed after the rockfall by A Yeend, Ms T Gronlund.

| 1969 Oct 12 | **Stretch** R J Crewe, J Yaldren, P Charman |
| 1969 Oct 18 | **Serpent** R J Crewe, K Winkworth |

The route originally traversed across right to finish up what is now Flake Crack. Pitch 2 as described climbed by R J Crewe, D D Gray on 12 April 1974.

| 1969 Oct 18 | **Middle Buttress** K Winkworth, R J Crewe (AL) |
| 1969 Oct 19 | **Sea Cow** R J Crewe, K Winkworth, P Charman (1 pt aid) |

Direct Start (the pitch described) climbed by K Turner, G Stace in August 1979.

| 1969 | **Synergy** J Winthorpe, S Smith (1 pt aid) |

First free ascent J Godding in 1977. Reclimbed after the disappearance of the boulder by P Oxley (solo after top-rope practice) on 22 July 1986.

1970 March 1	**Aubergine** R Kent, K Winkworth, P Charman, R J Crewe
1970 March 27	**Oran** K Winkworth, R J Crewe
1970 March 29	**Wall Street** R J Crewe, K Winkworth (AL)
1970 June 3	**Eavesdropper** D J Armitage, M L Bransby

1970 July 5	**Cormorant Buttress Central** R J Crewe, E Butt, K Winkworth	

The original upper corner was destroyed by rockfall.

1970 Aug 6	**Blackers Hole Traverse** M Boater, P Deketelaere
1970 Aug 6-8	**Laughing Arthur** M Boater, P Deketelaere (aid)

First free ascent P Oxley: pitch 1 on 3 December 1988 (yo-yo); pitch 2 on 27 August 1989 (redpoint); pitch 3 on 28 August 1989 (redpoint). Coma II variation climbed by P Oxley, M Ford (yo-yo).

1970 Oct 11	**Jupiter** K Winkworth, P Charman (1 pt aid)

First free ascent J Worthington. Variation start climbed by N A Coe, F Farrell, G A Jenkin on 13 August 1984.

1970 Oct 18	**Early Bird** R J Crewe, K Winkworth

Destroyed by rockfall.

1970 Oct 23	**Vicissitude** J L Titt, J Green (AL)
1970	**Juggler** S Evans
1971 Feb 7	**Neptune's Wall** R J Crewe, E Butt

Destroyed by rockfall.

1971 March 24	**Wallcreeper** D Armitage, C Campbell
1971 April 11	**Easter Egg** P B Scott, M K Freeman
1971 April 14	**Giraffe** D Fell, A Hall

Pitch 1 destroyed by rockfall.

1971 April 18	**Ricochet** R J Crewe , J Yaldren

Pitch 1 has been affected by rockfall.

1971 June 13	**Ambler Gambler** R J Crewe, P Charman, K Winkworth
1971 June 15	**The Corner, Lunar** D J Armitage, A Moon
1971 June 15	**Cuboid, Nautilus, Query** J S Green, A Slingo
1971 June 27	**Talus** J L Titt, A Hall, C Bristow
1971 July 14	**Grandpa's Grope** T Dunsby
1971 July 18	**Canned Heat** E Grindley, R J Crewe (AL)
1971 July 22	**Thunder Wall** J L Titt, S L Titt

Destroyed by rockfall.

1971 July 25	**Cheat** P Hollington, R Bosdet (aid)

First free ascent G A Jenkin, F Farrell on 30 June 1984.

1971 Aug 22	**Avernus** M Hurn, Ms F Higgins, D W Partridge
1971 Aug 22	**Flake Crack** R J Crewe, K Winkworth (3 pts aid)

First free ascent G A Jenkin, D Wiggin on 24 April 1982.

1971 Sept 4	**Ximenes** G Smith, R J Crewe (AL) (5 pts aid)

First free ascent K Turner, N Buckley, D Over in 1977.

1971 Sept 5	**Zimbalist** R J Crewe, G Smith, K Winkworth (2 pts aid)

Destroyed by rockfall.

1971 Sept 13	**Geronimo** J L Titt, D Fell, J Pycroft (2 pts aid)

First free ascent G A Jenkin, F Farrell on 31 December 1977. Pitch 1 has since been destroyed by rockfall and part of pitch 2 incorporated into Fallen from Grace.

1971 Oct 3	**White Horse** G Smith, R J Crewe (AL) (3 pts aid)

Climbed using only the initial aid peg by F Rech, H Lancashire in October 1975. This was avoided by Lancashire in 1979 by climbing up the back of the zawn.

1971 Oct 24	**Black Sunshine**	J L Titt, J Thornby
1971 Nov 13	**Dublin Packet**	R J Crewe, G Smith, R Kent

Variation start climbed by C Waddy, C Mallen on 11 September 1984.

1971 Nov 14 **Behemoth** R J Crewe, G Smith (AL) (1 pt aid)
First free ascent H Lancashire, F Rech in January 1975.

1971 Dec 16 **Slip Road** D Hope, E Hart

1971 Dec 30 **Balrog** T P Cripps, C Evered (1 pt aid)
First free ascent G Hounsome, S L Titt on 31 August 1981.

1971 Dec 30 **Billy** T P Cripps, C Evered

1971 **Jim's Jam** D Sargeant, J Winthorpe

1971 **Wessex Hangover** A Hall and partner

1971 **The Cormorant** H R Cripps, P J Cripps, T P Cripps
This incorporated the 1000-foot Combsea Traverse (pre-1963), the description of which included 'The descent from the other side of this ledge has been made once, and was achieved by falling.' The Black Zawn was traversed in 1977 by G A Jenkin, N Buckley, R Dalgleish.

1972 Jan 22 **Bilbo** T P Cripps, P J Cripps

1972 Feb 19 **The Last Hurrah of the Golden Horde** J L Titt (1 pt aid)
First free ascent G Hounsome in 1976. An impressive ascent on which he employed only three runners!

1972 March 31 **Petrification** P J Cripps, T P Cripps (AL) (3 pts aid)
First free ascent G Hounsome, S L Titt on 12 January 1980.

1972 March 31 **Brass Monkey** R J Crewe, J Worthington, P G Crewe

1972 April 1 **Dogwatch** R J Crewe, K Butler, P G Crewe (4 pts aid)
First free ascent N Buckley, S Bartlett in 1980. Reclimbed after the rockfall by T Dunsby, S L Titt, N A Coe on 9 June 1990.

1972 April 3 **Sapphire** G Smith, K Winkworth (1 pt aid)

1972 April 3 **Yellow Wall** R J Crewe, A Wilde, P G Crewe
Pitch 2 added by G Smith, R J Crewe on 23 September 1973.

1972 April 3 **Bachelor Boy** P B Scott, G Smith, K Winkworth
The route has been affected by rockfall. Fledglings' Flight variation climbed by S Keates, M Thompson on 10 July 1983.

1972 April 28 **Degradation, Pete's Corner** P J Cripps, T P Cripps

1972 April 30 **Powder Groove** R J Crewe, K Winkworth
Variation start climbed by T Dunsby, N A Coe on 8 September 1990.

1972 Aug 5 **Oceanid** P R Littlejohn, K S Goodman

1972 Aug 17 **Rusty Groove** R J Crewe, K Winkworth (1 pt aid)
First free ascent C King, G A Jenkin on 13 January 1980.

1972 Sept 23 **Codpiece** D Allwright, K J Wilkinson
The start of the route was destroyed by rockfall and the remainder superseded by Limited Edition.

1973 Feb 10 **Judy** P J Cripps, T P Cripps

1973 April 22 **Pandora** G Smith, A Wilde, R J Crewe

Pitch 3 added by G A Jenkin, F Farrell on 11 August 1984.

1973 May 12	**Caroline**	T P Cripps, P J Cripps
1973 May 12	**Gwen**	P J Cripps, T P Cripps
1973 June 2	**Victoria**	R J Crewe, G Smith
1973 June 2	**Marmolata Buttress**	G Smith, R J Crewe (2 pts aid)

First free ascent G Hounsome, S L Titt on 20 November 1977.
Direct start climbed by P Oxley, J Williams on 7 February 1988.

1973 June 24	**Asp**	R J Crewe, P Charman
1973 Sept 2	**Koo-Koo**	R J Crewe, P Charman (4 pts aid)

First free ascent A Strapcans, G A Jenkin on 12 August 1978.

1973 Sept 24	**Bosun's Wall**	G Smith, R J Crewe (AL)
1973 Sept 24	**Coxswain's Route**	R J Crewe, G Smith (AL)
1973 Oct 21	**Tomorrow's Grief**	R J Crewe, P Charman

Reclimbed after the rockfall by R J Crewe, R Ramsay.

1973 Oct 28	**August Angie**	B Snell, M Colson (1 pt aid)

First free ascent R J Crewe.

1973 Dec 8	**Tensor II**	B Snell, W Lyons
1973	**Shelob**	J Evans, D Sargeant
1974 Feb 10	**Quality Street**	R J Crewe, P Charman
1974 March 10	**Black Jack**	P Charman, R J Crewe (AL)
1974 March 24	**Alternative**	B Snell, W Lyons (4 pts aid)

First free ascent P Oxley, G A Jenkin on 11 November 1984.
Destroyed by rockfall.

1974 March 24	**Yo-Yo**	B Snell, W Lyons

Climbed via what is now described as the variation pitch 3.
Pitch 3 added by D Viggers, P Debbage on 1 February 1976.

1974 March 31	**The Spook**	R J Crewe, P Charman
1974 April 7	**The Heat**	B Snell, W Lyons (4 pts aid)

After top-rope practice. First free ascent G Hounsome,
G de Lacy (AL)

1974 April 8	**Rosemary**	T P Cripps, P J Cripps
1974 April 9	**Lasteen**	T P Cripps, P J Cripps (AL)

The first pitch, originally known as Jack Halliday, was climbed
by the same team.

1974 April 11	**Rubble Rouser**	R J Crewe, D D Gray
1974 April 13	**Dead Red**	P Holden, R J Crewe (AL)
1974 April 13	**Lichen Wall**	B Snell

The upper section had been climbed before with a peg for aid
by R J Crewe, J Yaldren on 6 September 1970 as part of a
route called Jaywalker.

1974 April 14	**Nemesis**	R J Crewe, G Smith (1 pt aid)

First free ascent G Hounsome, P Finklaire in 1979.

1974 April 14	**Redruth**	P Holden, C Radcliffe

Destroyed by rockfall.

1974 May 5	**Archangel**	S Evans, R Evans
1974 May 5	**Tudor Rose**	R J Crewe, P Charman

The route originally finished up the final pitch of Nemesis.

Pitch 2 was added several weeks later.

1974 May 11 **Electric Sheep** B Snell, W Lyons (1 pt aid)
The climb finished up Yo-Yo. *Pitch 2 (which also required a peg for aid) was added by F Rech, H Lancashire on 1 February 1975. First free ascent J Godding, C Mellor in August 1981.*

1974 May 19 **Strongbow** R J Crewe, P Charman
Variation start climbed by C Waddy, J Williams in 1988.

1974 June 2 **Trimeringue** J L Titt, D Gumn (aid)
Superseded by Mother Africa.

1974 June 15 **Myriotissa** N Porter, S Tomlin (1 pt aid)
First free ascent G Hounsome on 2 April 1978.

1974 June 16 **Edward's Effort** B J Heard

1974 June 29 **The Eastern Girdle** B Snell, I Bartlett
The original first two pitches (starting up Cleft Buttress*) have been destroyed by rockfall.*

1974 July 6 **The Tool** B Snell, W Lyons (3 pts aid)
First free ascent G Hounsome on 9 October 1977.

1974 July 28 **Sambapati** R J Crewe, G Mair (AL)

1974 Aug 4 **Lobster** N Porter, R J Crewe

1974 Aug 11 **Procrastinating Giant** D Fell and a cast of thousands (aid)
This was the completion date. First free ascent M J Crocker, J Robertson on 10 October 1983.

1974 Aug 11 **Astrid** R J Crewe, S Garner, T Dunsby

1974 Aug 11 **Mars** R J Crewe, T Dunsby

1974 Aug 11 **Dynamic Uno** T P Cripps, P J Cripps
Affected by rockfall.

1974 Aug 17 **Apathy** P J Cripps, T P Cripps

1974 Aug 18 **Mellow Yellow** R J Crewe, T Dunsby

1974 Aug 24 **Quasimodo** T Dunsby, A Yeend (2 pts aid)
First free ascent G Hounsome on 11 March 1978.

1974 Dec 28 **Cerberus** A Yeend, D N McFadyen

1974 **Jonah** R J Crewe, K Winkworth

1975 Feb 8 **Mickey Mouse** B Snell, R J Crewe, T Tanswell (VL) (4 pts aid)
First free ascent A Strapcans, G A Jenkin in January 1979.

1975 March 15 **Rhino** R J Crewe, K Winkworth
Reclimbed after the rockfall by D Gumn, D Close on 21 September 1975.

1975 March 29 **Spasm Chasm** P Holden, R Chambers

1975 March 30 **Fetish** P Holden, P Chambers

1975 March 31 **Snowdrop** P Holden, H Lancashire (AL)

1975 April 20 **Excalibur** P Finklaire, R Nelson
Pitch 2 added by B Snell, K Knight on 22 August 1979.

1975 May 10 **Crystal Wall** R J Crewe, I Wright (2 pts aid)
First free ascent G Hounsome.

1975 May 17 **Harvest Gold** A Parker, S Allen

1975 May 25	**Tenuicollis** G De Lacy, P Jackson
1975 June 7	**Thor** D Snell, W Lyons
	Pitch 2 has been swapped with pitch 2 of Thunderball *in the main text.*
1975 June 29	**Grooved Arête** R J Crewe, D Little
1975 July 7	**War** B Snell, W Lyons
1975 July 12	**The Corpse** B Snell, K Knight
	Stiff Start variation climbed by G A Jenkin, S Briggs on 29 November 1981.
1975 July 16	**Nassty Spider** B Snell, K Knight (2 pts aid)
	Rockfall has changed the nature of the initial roof. Climbed free in the fashion described by G A Jenkin, T Dunsby on 10 June 1984.
1975 July 26	**Luke** D Little, W H Church
1975 July 27	**Grockles' Passage** P B Scott, R J Crewe
1975 July 28	**Strenuosity** R Stead (1 pt aid)
	First free ascent P Finclaire, G Hounsome on 31 March 1979.
1975 July 29	**Friends of the Earth** S L Titt, P B Scott
1975 Aug 2	**The Golden Fleece** R J Crewe, S L Titt
1975 Aug 30	**Nunentity** R J Crewe, J Cross (1 pt aid)
	First free ascent G A Jenkin, G Forward in January 1978.
1975 Sept 6	**Argo** R J Crewe, D Close
1975 Sept 13	**Baker's Dozen** T Baker, R J Crewe (AL)
	Nineteen to the Dozen variation climbed by F Rech, H Lancashire on 25 October 1975. Direct finish climbed by R Collings, Mrs S Collings in 1987.
1975 Sept 13	**Zoë** B Jefferies, J Cross
1975 Oct 4	**Little Matterhorn** B Snell, K Knight (AL)
1975 Oct 4	**Parson's Pleasure** S L Titt, R J Crewe, G Seymour
1975 Oct 11	**Snout** R J Crewe, D Marshall
	Pitch 2 was added later by G Hounsome, S L Titt on 1 June 1980.
1975 Oct 12	**Black Shag** S L Titt, M Hunt
	Destroyed by rockfall.
1975 Oct 25	**October Lady** D Gumn, G Hounsome
	Merlin variation climbed by A Davies, Ms S Arnold in 1991.
1975 Oct 27	**Scarface** S Evans, D Sargeant, N Porter
	Mostly superseded by Coercri *and* Cosa Nostra.
1975 Oct 28	**The Cat Skinner** N Porter, D Sargeant
1975 Nov 1	**Hazhard** N Porter, T Baker, D Sargeant (1 pt aid plus a short abseil part way up)
	Climbed free in the manner described by G Hounsome, S L Titt on 17 April 1982.
1975 Nov 8	**Hard Day's Night** B Snell, J MacPartlin
1975 Nov 16	**Peaceful Peel** B Snell, K Knight
	The large boulder which provided the first pitch has disappeared.
1975	**Epidemic** R J Crewe, S L Titt (AL)

1976 Feb 14	**Valentino** S L Titt, G Seymour, P Warren
	Destroyed by rockfall.
1976 Feb 21	**Warlord** B Snell, K Knight (aid)
	The original first pitch is now part of Vikings. *Climbed with just one point of aid by R Harrison, A Hall in 1978. First free ascent S Monks, S Findlay on 28 November 1981.*
1976 March 23	**Cloud Nine** B Snell
	Reclimbed after the rockfall by T Dunsby, N A Coe on 6 July 1991. High Cirrus variation climbed by P Finklaire, R Phillips on 23 May 1992.
1976 March 28	**Revelation Chimney** G Hounsome, S L Titt
1976 April 3	**Buttend** T Tanswell, R J Crewe
	Pitch 2 had been climbed before by R J Crewe, D Marshall on 12 October 1975.
1976 April 18	**Tittsworth** J L Titt, W Wheeler
1976 April 24	**Benny** S L Titt, D Gumn, R J Crewe (aid)
	Named after a four-legged friend which counted the Mupe Bay Traverse *amongst its achievements.*
1976 April 24	**Rock Widow** D Gumn, S L Titt
1976 April 25	**Concubine** B Jefferies, J Cross
1976 April 25	**Harlot** J Cross, B Jefferies (AL)
1976 May 7	**Dead Man Hunt** J L Titt
1976 May 22	**Station Road** J L Titt, F Farrell
1976 May 30	**Paternoster** M Barnicott, R Henderson
1976 May 31	**The Peccary** G Hounsome, M Barnicott
1976 June 5	**Triton** R J Crewe, S L Titt (6 pts aid)
	First free ascent G Hounsome on 22 July 1978.
1976 June 13	**Dandruff** P R Debbage, J Hodges
	Direct start climbed by C Waddy, P Oxley on 31 August 1986.
1976 June 13	**Diagonal** P R Debbage, J Hodges
1976 July 25	*D Gumn made the first recorded jump from the top of* The Conger.
1976 July 31	**Kittiwake** T Tanswell, R J Crewe
1976 Sept 19	**Sardine Special** B Snell, K Knight (aid)
	Climbed with just two points of aid by N Buckley, P Jarvis on 11 August 1984. A nut was preplaced from abseil prior to the ascent and left in situ. First free ascent P Oxley, S Williams on 7 June 1987, before the boulder at the start shifted (dogged).
1976 Oct 24	**Shadow People** G Hounsome
	Destroyed by rockfall. So named because the four other members of the party prusiked up the rope in the dark!
1976 Nov 13	**Moonstone** G Hounsome, R J Crewe
1976 Nov 14	**Crystal Voyager** G A Jenkin, R Dalgleish (aid)
	Jenkin's first contribution was an aid extravaganza whilst many of his later offerings were aid eliminations. First free ascent K Turner, P Dawson on 20 April 1980.
1976 Nov 14	**The Indirect Route** J L Titt, S L Titt
1976 Nov 21	**Aguas Verdes, Damson** J L Titt, S L Titt

1976 Dec 4	**A Torrent of Faces** G Hounsome, J L Titt
	Destroyed by rockfall.
1976 Dec 5	**The God Slot** J L Titt, S L Titt
1976	**Mistaken Identity** P Finklaire, B Etheridge
	Probably climbed before.
1977 Jan 9	**Moebius** G Hounsome, S L Titt
1977 Jan 30	**Corollary** S L Titt, G Hounsome (AL)
1977 Feb 20	**Ratmate** G Hounsome, D Gumn
	Destroyed by rockfall.
1977 Feb 27	**Valhalla** S L Titt, D Sargeant
	Pitch 2 (Scotch Corner Finish) had been climbed previously by R C White, N MacAllister on 12 March 1967.
1977 March 10	**Scorpion** G Hounsome, D Gumn (1 pt aid)
	First free ascent K Turner, N Buckley in 1980. Superseded by Sting in the Tail.
1977 April 9	**Rout** J L Titt, S L Titt
1977 April 10	**Winking Wall** G Smith, M Schalkwijk, K Winkworth (1 pt aid)
	First free ascent G A Jenkin, N A Coe on 6 June 1984.
1977 April 10	**Rif-Raf** P Holden, P Scott (1 pt aid)
	First free ascent G A Jenkin, A Strapcans in January 1979.
1977 April 30	**The Orange-Throated Gronk** F Farrell, G A Jenkin (AL)
1977 April 30	**Tim** B Snell, K Knight, M Colson
1977 April 30	**Forty** G De Lacy, G Hounsome (1 pt aid)
	First free ascent S Lewis, J Godding in October 1983.
1977 May 1	**Tiger Moth** G De Lacy, G Hounsome (AL)
1977 June 12	**Raindrop** G Hounsome, D Gumn
1977 June 19	**Happy David** B Snell, K Knight
1977 June	**The Ram** P R Littlejohn, C Ward-Tetley
1977 July 2	**Andycap, Midge** B Snell, K Knight
1977 July 10	**Ringworm** G Hounsome, D Gumn
1977 Aug 7	**Indigo** R J Crewe, K Winkworth
1977 Aug 7	**Frank's Little Secret** V Dennis, N Buckley
1977 Aug 13	**Ganymede** G Hounsome, T Daniells
1977 Aug 13	**Nasal Symphony** G Hounsome, T Daniells
	Squeeze variation climbed by C Waddy, C Mallen on 9 September 1984. Both now destroyed by rockfall.
1977 Aug 28	**Skinhead** M Hunt, A Gilbert
1977 Sept 4	**Dougal the Great** B Snell, K Knight
	Completed after four sessions.
	First free ascent P Oxley, J Biddle on 12 February 1988.
1977 Oct 9	**Windy City** G Hounsome, D Gumn
	The upper part had previously been climbed by A G Cram in 1965 as a variation to Ashes and Diamonds.
1977 Oct 27	**Slipshod** S L Titt, D Sargeant
1977 Nov 6	**Cima Petite** B Snell, N Porter (6 pts aid)
	First free ascent S Monks, S Findlay on 29 November 1981.
1977 Nov 10	**Spout** S L Titt, J L Titt

1977	**Black Wall Avoidance** K Turner, S L Titt (AL)
1977	**Graunchy Grippers** K Turner
	Turner's first ever route on rock.
1978 Jan 1	**Melpomene** G Hounsome (2 pts aid)
	On the first ascent the route started out from Mars and finished up the large square-cut groove. Climbed free in the fashion described by P R Littlejohn, C King in 1978.
1978 Jan 7	**Winter's Tale** G Hounsome, B Tilley
1978 Jan 13	**Abysmal** G Hounsome, R J Crewe
1978 Feb 13	**Boongary** S L Titt, B Tilley
1978 Feb	**Death Is a Gift** K Turner, N Buckley, M Barrett
	Pitch 2 was added by N Buckley, P Jarvis in November 1983.
1978 April 8	**Tangerine Dream** G Hounsome, K Turner
1978 May 7	**Ulysses** G Hounsome, T Daniells, R J Crewe
1978 May 14	**Little Yellow Jug** B Snell, K Knight
	No Yellow Jug variation added by M Priestman, D Ivory on 16 April 1983. Broken Crockery variation added by C Waddy, J Alcock in 1987.
1978 May 14	**Silhouette Arête** B Snell, K Knight
1978 July 16	**Crepitus** G Hounsome, S L Titt
1978 Aug 13	**Polaris** A Strapcans, G A Jenkin, F Farrell
	Pitch 1 had been climbed before by G A Jenkin, F Farrell on 7 August 1977. Ruptured Raspberry K Turner, F Farrell 1979; Nuke D Ivory, E Hart (1 rest pt) 1 March 1980 (First free ascent C Waddy, A Ford October 1987); Bolt the Blue Sea? M J Crocker, J Harwood (yo-yo) 15 October 1994; Weapons of Sound (flashed) and Enter the Void M J Crocker, J Harwood on 2 October 1994.
1978 Sept	**Teenage Wasteland** K Turner, N Buckley, P Dawson (VL)
	Pitch 1 had been climbed previously by H Lancashire, P Holden c. 1975 as a variation to Tatra Direct.
1978 Nov	**The Ritz** N Buckley, K Turner (AL)
1979 Feb 3	**Agincourt** G Hounsome, S L Titt
1979 Feb 18	**Dysentry** G Hounsome, P Finklaire
1979 March 1	**Quo Vadis Direct** C King, P R Litlejohn
	The original route traversed in as for The Wey of All Men. The start described was climbed by N Buckley, R Dalgleish in 1981.
1979 March 31	**Marmolata Arête** G Hounsome, P Finklaire
1979 March 31	**Flying Finish** A Strapcans, G A Jenkin
	Pitch 2 added by C Waddy, J Vlasto on 28 March 1985.
1979 March	**Ocean Boulevard** K Turner, N Buckley, S Bartlett
	Climbed without the hanging stance by S Monks, G A Jenkin on 21 November 1981.
1979 April 1	**Barracuda** A Strapcans, G A Jenkin (1 pt aid)
	Climbed without the rest-point and the hanging stance by D Ivory, P Preston on 1 April 1983.
1979 May 19	**Aquarius** G Hounsome, F Berwick

1979 July 6	**Thermidor** F Farrell, C Ruaé
1979 July 13	**Primrose Hill** G Hounsome, S L Titt
1979 July 14	**Coral Slabs** B Snell, K Knight (1 pt aid)

First free ascent S Bartlett, N Buckley, K Turner in 1980. Reclimbed after the rockfall by T Dunsby, N A Coe on 28 April 1995.

1979 July 15	**Captain Cat** G Hounsome, S L Titt
1979 Aug 26	**Snap Crack** B Snell, K Knight
1979 Aug 27	**The Rise and Dear Demise of the Funky Nomadic Tribes, The Friendly Ranger From Clontarf Castle** K Turner, F Farrell
1979 Aug	**Freeborn Man** N Buckley, K Turner

A sparsely-protected pitch which was led after failure on a top-rope!

| 1979 Sept 7 | **Ace of Spades** B Snell, K Knight |

The route originally finished out left up what is now described as Pandora. Pitch 2 climbed by G A Jenkin, F Farrell in August 1980.

| 1979 Sept 7 | **Lunatic Fringe** B Snell, K Knight |
| 1979 Sept 22 | **Pendulum** G Hounsome, S L Titt |

Variation finish climbed by S L Titt, P Finklaire on 30 September 1979.

| 1979 Sept 22 | **Caiaphas** G Hounsome, S L Titt |

The top section had previously been climbed as a direct finish to Valkyrie Buttress by K Turner, D Over in 1977.

| 1979 Sept 30 | **Jackal** R J Crewe, K Winkworth |

The last of Crewe's harvest of new routes, the majority of which were climbed on-sight, and all of which were climbed without a leader fall.

| 1979 Sept 30 | **Nutcracker Exit II** B Snell, K Knight |

Variation climbed by A Davis, Ms S Arnold on 11 September 1988.

1979 Sept	**Halcyon Days** G A Jenkin, F Farrell
1979 Sept	**A Bridge Too Far** N Buckley, P Dawson
1979 Sept	**Crackers** K Turner, N Buckley

Pitch 1 had been climbed previously by N Buckley, M Barrett in May 1979.

1979 Oct 7	**Solifluction** S L Titt, D Sargeant
1979 Oct 30	**Dreamboat Annie** G Willgress, A Monument
1979 Dec 31	**Angel Pavement** G Hounsome, S L Titt
1979	**Think about It** K Turner, P Williams [-]
1980 Jan 1	**Decayed** N Buckley, P Dawson
1980 Jan 1	**Cold Comfort** G A Jenkin, K Greenald (AL)
1980 Jan 12	**Random Enterprise** C King, G A Jenkin (AL)
1980 Feb 9	**Triaxiality** G Hounsome, S L Titt
1980 Feb 10	**D Sharp** G Hounsome, T Daniells
1980 Feb	**Warriors** K Turner, N Buckley
1980 March 2	**Parallel Lines** (Slippery Ledge) F Farrell, N A Coe

1980 March 2   **Cosmic Cabbage** N A Coe, F Farrell
1980 March 15   **Delicatessen** K Turner, G Stace
1980 April 6   **Suicide** K Turner, P Boyland
                Superseded by Charge of the Wild Horsemen *and* The Lusty,
                Decadent Delights of Imperial Pompeii.
1980 April 19   **Scythe** G Hounsome, S L Titt
                *Climbed less than three months after this huge corner was
                formed by the collapse of* Blinking Crack.
1980 April 20   **All Square** G Hounsome, S L Titt
1980 April 26   **Squeez It Pleez It** G A Jenkin, F Farrell, N A Coe
1980 April 27   **Cruel Passions** G A Jenkin, F Farrell (1 pt aid)
                *First free ascent G A Jenkin, D Wiggin on 24 April 1982. The
                Adults Only start was added by F Farrell, G A Jenkin (VL) on
                19 August 1984.*
1980 May 10   **Sirius** G Hounsome, S L Titt (on-sight)
                *Hounsome had sufficient in reserve to stop half-way up to do a
                'Harry Worth'.*
1980 May 11   **High Noon** G Hounsome, S L Titt
1980 May 16   **The Law** N Buckley, P Dawson
1980 May 17   **Limited Edition** G A Jenkin, F Farrell
                *The initial unprotected wall was practised on a top-rope.
                Altered by rockfall.*
1980 Aug 3   **Rhythm** G Hounsome, S L Titt
1980 Aug 16   **Brainless and Nameless** G Hounsome, S L Titt
1980   **Coercri** K Turner, N Buckley
                *A rope was used to finish over the top bulge. Pitch 2 cleaned
                and free-climbed by M J Crocker, J Robertson on 20 August
                1983.*
1981 June 10   **Luxury Liner** G A Jenkin, A Hall
1982 May 2   **Swingtime** G Hounsome, S L Titt
1982 May 11   **Jackie** N A Coe, T Dunsby
1982 May 11   **Magic** R Parker, T Dunsby
1982 May 22   **Alternate Angle** T Dunsby, N A Coe
1982 May 22   **Ruth** T Dunsby, N A Coe (AL)
1982 June 27   **Vampire** T Dunsby, N A Coe
                Direct start climbed by S Lewis, J Bentley in 1982.
1982 Sept 30   **Moonshine** N A Coe, T Dunsby
1982 Oct 10   **The Mary Rose** S Cardy, A Orton
1982 Oct 10   **Laurence** T Dunsby, N A Coe (1 rest pt)
                First free ascent by the same pair on 6 November 1983.
1982 Nov 27   **Race for the Oasis** M J Crocker, J Robertson
                *Pitch 1 had been climbed previously by the same pair on
                13 November 1982 using a nut for resting.*
1983 Jan 8   **Facedancin'** M J Crocker, J Robertson
1983 Feb 2   **Soul Sacrifice** M J Crocker, J Robertson
                *The first part of the route had been previously climbed by
                D Ivory, P Hamilton in 1973 as a variation start to* White

Horse. *Direct start climbed solo by P Oxley on 14 March 1987.*

1983 March 27	**The Vapour Edge** M J Crocker, J Robertson	
1983 May 25	**Ray of Sunshine** T Dunsby, R Parker	
1983 June 4	**Frontiersman** M J Crocker, J Robertson	
1983 June 4	**Personality Clash** M J Crocker, J Robertson	

Destroyed by rockfall.

1983 June 5 **Mother Africa** M J Crocker, J Robertson
Superseded Trimeringue.

1983 June 11 **The Lean Machine** M J Crocker, J Robertson (flashed)
Green Machine *variation climbed by M Atkinson on 5 March 1987 (yo-yo).*

1983 June 12 **Wall of the Worlds** M J Crocker, J Robertson

1983 June 25 **Third World** N Buckley, G Stace (VL), G A Jenkin
This supersedes End of November, *which traversed in from above the roof of* Dogwatch, *and was climbed with four points of aid by B Snell, W Lyons on 30 November 1974,*

1983 July 23 **The First Och-Aye of the Tartan Army** M J Crocker, J Robertson
Pitch 1 added by K Turner, G A Jenkin in February 1984.

1983 July 23 **Relax and Swing** M J Crocker, J Robertson
Climbed with an in-situ nut at the lip of the main roof.

1983 July 24 **The Fin, Singing Winds** M J Crocker, J Robertson

1983 July **Dorset Non-Rhyming Slang** C Waddy, G Banks

1983 Aug 2 **Len's Rule of the Sea** D Ivory, A Ivory

1983 Aug 20 **Credit in the Straight World** M J Crocker, J Robertson

1983 Aug 21 **Vikings** M J Crocker, J Robertson
Pitch 1 had been climbed previously by B Snell, K Knight on 21 February 1967. The Horny Hat Finish was added by A Donson, M Silcox on 24 August 1989. 'The obvious line if you didn't read the route description properly.'

1983 Sept 17 **Black September** C Flewitt, P Jarvis

1983 Sept 24 **Giantslayer** M J Crocker, D Light

1983 Sept 26 **Fly Crazy but Free** M J Crocker, D Light (yo-yo)

1983 Oct 23 **Gold Fever** M J Crocker, J Robertson
This superseded A Touch of Black Magic, *which took an easier line and had been affected by rockfall; it was climbed with three points of aid by B Snell, K Knight on 18 October 1975.*

1983 Oct 23 **The Great Hunter House Milk Robbery** B Moon
(1 rest pt)
Long before 6b was a rest; in fact, when 6a was a rest-point! First free ascent P Oxley on 16 October 1985.

1983 Nov 5 **Future Primitive, Road to Ruin** M J Crocker, D Light

1983 Nov 6 **Magic Mountain** M J Crocker, D Light

1983 Dec 6 **Be-Bop-Deluxe** P Jarvis, C Flewitt (AL)

1983 **The Impending Gleam** N Buckley, N Stein

1984 Feb 5 **High Tide and Green Grass** T Dunsby, N A Coe (AL), R Lovett, P Oxley

1984 Feb 19   **Poetry in Motion** P Oxley, N A Coe (redpoint)
The first of a multitude of new routes from Pete Oxley.

1984 April 7   **Hardnose the Highway, Yellow Brick Road**
T Dunsby, P Oxley

1984 April 14   **Ishmael** N Buckley, P Jarvis (AL)

1984 April 15   **Armed Insurgence** G Stace, S Cook

1984 May 6   **Aerial Pursuit** C J Inns, J O'Dowd

1984 May 20   **Fraggle Rock** N A Coe, T Dunsby

1984 June 6   **The Grim Reaper** T Dunsby, R Lovett

1984 June 9   **Wall Street Crash** N A Coe, G A Jenkin (AL)
*Pitch 1 (via the Direct Start) had been climbed previously by
M Redman, J Walmsley using one point of aid. This was
eliminated by B R Wilkinson, J Stewart on 31 July 1982.*

1984 July 1   **Second Sight** G A Jenkin, F Farrell

1984 July 8   **Accidents Never Happen** N A Coe, T Dunsby

1984 July 19   **No Great Shakes** T Dunsby, N A Coe

1984 July   **Live at the Witch Trials** C Waddy, G Banks
'We had climbed this far on Traverse of the Gods *but the sea
became rough and, being only VS leaders, we wouldn't do the
VS above as the guidebook said "No belay". So I set off for
the belay above* Io *and ended up taking a huge fall onto a
homemade nut. I was then hit by waves about 40 feet up the
cliff. Someone saw this and gave us a rope. We learnt how to
prusik. The milestone we prusiked on fell over afterwards.
Second attempt: similar fall. Third time lucky.'*

1984 Aug 4   **Rough Boys** N A Coe, F Farrell

1984 Aug 4   **Seventh Wave** N A Coe, F Farrell

1984 Aug 8   **Vaseline** T Dunsby, N A Coe

1984 Aug 11   **French Lessons** G A Jenkin, F Farrell

1984 Aug 12   **Deaf Boy Hug** N Buckley, P Jarvis (AL)

1984 Aug 12   **Io** G A Jenkin, F Farrell
*The upper section of the route had been climbed previously
with some aid as part of* Aquaphilia.

1984 Aug 13   **Stern Mistress** F Farrell, G A Jenkin (AL)
*Disaster nearly struck when Jenkin pulled off a block; hitting
the cliff on its downward path, it broke in two, and Farrell
missed decapitation by inches as the halves whistled past
either side of his head. [The Editor survived a similar
experience with GAJ elsewhere, though the latter was less
fortunate on that occasion!].*

1984 Aug 13   **Old Lag's Corner** F Farrell, G A Jenkin

1984 Aug 21   **Gentle Touch** T Dunsby, N A Coe

1984 Aug   **The Long Goodbye** T Dunsby, M Higgins

1984 Sept 1   **Isolation Ward** P Oxley, C Ciumei

1984 Sept 4   **ZANU** T Dunsby, N A Coe

1984 Sept 4   **ZAPU, UDI** N A Coe, T Dunsby

1984 Sept 10   **Smokestack Lightning** C Waddy, C Mallen
Pitch 2 added by S Cook, K Turner on 21 October 1984.

1984 Sept 23	**Just Seventeen** S Briggs, R Neath	
1984 Sept 27	**Callisto, In the Heat of the Night** C Waddy, G Percival	
1984 Oct 6	**Blockbuster** T Dunsby, M Higgins (1 pt aid)	

First free ascent T Dunsby, P Oxley on 13 October 1984. Dunsby received a black eye on the first attempt after pulling off an undercut hold. The only rewards the second time were torn knee ligaments, a hand swollen to twice its size, and an aid point left to free. Third time lucky, however!

1984 Oct 21	**Displacement Activity** N A Coe, T Dunsby

Pitch 2 was practised on a top-rope.

1984 Oct 21	**Yield Point** P Oxley, D Sharman
1984 Oct 27	**Shakin' Off the Ghosts** P Oxley, T Dunsby
1984 Nov 4	**Boatpusher's Arête** P Oxley, T Dunsby

Originally given E2 by Oxley: undergrading in the time-honoured Swanage tradition! Variation start climbed by M J Crocker, J Harwood on 7 June 1992.

1984 Nov 10	**Conan the Vegetarian** N Buckley, P Jarvis (AL)
1984 Dec 8	**Fish Supper** N A Coe, T Dunsby (AL)

Pitch 1 had been climbed previously by C Waddy, G Percival on 28 September 1984. Coe was still trembling after nearly being throttled when his helmet strap was pulled into his descender on the free-hanging abseil. On the route, Dunsby performed a spectacular backward dive from the top overhang, accompanied by several undercut holds.

1984 Dec 10	**Promotion to Glory** N Buckley, P Jarvis, P Perkins
1984 Dec 11	**Wide Awake in America** P Oxley, A Blakely

Pitch 2, starting up Sheerline, added by P Oxley, E Hart on 31 August 1985. Climbed as described by P Oxley on 7 November 1988.

1985 April 21	**Vortices** P Finklaire, D Glover
1985 April 21	**Mother Duck** N A Coe, S L Titt
1985 May 29	**The Flail Trail** P Oxley, I Freeman
1985 May 29	**Stakk Attakk** P Oxley
1985 June 2	**Drop in the Ocean** N A Coe, T Dunsby
1985 June 16	**Mr Gymnasia, Ocean of Violence** P Oxley, T Dunsby
1985 June 30	**Pogor** C Waddy, N Radcliffe
1985 July 7	**The Coral Prison** P Oxley, D Sharman
1985 July 7	**Howling Stone** P Oxley
1985 July 9	**Ape Crap, Doppler Shift, Revolt into Style** P Oxley, J Biddle
1985 July 15	**Troubled Waters** P Oxley (solo)
1985 July 18	**Surge Control** P Oxley (yo-yo)
1985 July 21	**Stone Doubt** N A Coe, T Dunsby
1985 July 21	**Under Toed** T Dunsby, N A Coe
1985 July 31	**The Planet** C Waddy, A Ford

Pitch 1 had been climbed before by C Waddy, G Banks on 26 June 1985.

1985 July 31	**The Mutiny** C Waddy, A Ford

1985 Aug 1	**Dragon's Teeth** C Waddy, A Ford
1985 Aug 1	**Bold for the Old, Heart of the Matter, Got to Go**
	T Dunsby, R Mardon
1985 Aug 1	**Mardon's Hard 'Un** R Mardon, T Dunsby
1985 Aug 3	**Jude the Obscure** T Dunsby, N A Coe
1985 Aug 3	**Yankee Doddle** N A Coe, T Dunsby
1985 Aug 3	**Symbolic Stack Dump** N A Coe, T Dunsby (AL)
1985 Aug 6	**Apache** A Ford, C Waddy (AL)
1985 Aug 6	**Symplegades** C Waddy, A Ford (AL)
1985 Aug 10	**Headstone** C Waddy, A Ford

Pitch 1 had been climbed previously by S Cook, K Turner, M Hall on 18 November 1984.

1985 Aug 16	**Figurehead** C Waddy, A Ford
1985 Aug 17	**Aquamarine** C Waddy (solo)
1985 Aug 17	**Gimme Gimme Shock Treatment** G Yardley, I Handel, M Hopkins
1985 Aug 17	**Zircon** C Waddy (solo)

The top pitch was originally the same as for Aquamarine. Pitch 2 as described was climbed solo (as Big Trouble) by P Windall in September 1986.

1985 Aug 18	**Sea of Tranquillity** C Waddy, A Ford (aid)
1985 Aug 18	**Spanish Harlem** A Ford, C Waddy
1985 Sept 1	**Harry Seacombe, Ship of Fools** (Seacombe) N A Coe, G A Jenkin
1985 Sept 15	**Divine Decadence** N A Coe, S Portnoi
1985 Sept 15	**Punks in Power** P Oxley (dogged)
1985 Sept	**Jam Up Jelly Tight** D Simpson, M Able
1985 Nov 10	**Blow the House Down** P Oxley, N A Coe

Pitch 1 had been climbed before by A Strapcans, F Farrell in 1980.

1985 Dec 29	**Ice Queen** P Oxley
1985	**Joyride** T Dunsby, N A Coe
1986 Jan 26	**Battle of the Bulge** S L Titt, N A Coe
1986 Jan 26	**Difficult Descent** N A Coe (solo)
1986 Jan 26	**Little Corner, Quick Chimney** S L Titt (solo)
1986 Feb 23	**Absence Makes the Heart...** M J Crocker, N A Coe
1986 Feb 28	**Moose's Tooth** C Waddy, C Mullen (on-sight with 1 rest pt)

Climbed in a snowstorm. First free ascent C Waddy, P Oxley, 29 September 1986.

| 1986 March 15 | **Indian Pacific** P Oxley (yo-yo) |

He also reversed this traverse pitch by 'abseiling sideways', in order to retrieve the gear.

1986 March 23	**Space Threshold** P Oxley
1986 April 5	**Arapiles Syndrome** P Oxley, N A Coe
1986 April 26	**Cool and the Gang, Magnesian Days** P Oxley, B Tilley
1986 April 27	**One Nut Crack, Slimline** N A Coe, S L Titt
1986 April 27	**Weight Watchers** S L Titt, N A Coe
1986 May 1	**Love Comes Tumbling** P Oxley, B Tilley

Pitch 1 climbed 1 September 1985 by P Oxley, E Hart.

1986 May 18	**Screaming Blue Messiah** P Oxley, B Tilley
1986 June 7	**Land of the Leaning** P Oxley, J Biddle
1986 June 8	**In a Big Sky** P Oxley, G A Jenkin
1986 June 21	**Le Jaune Mecanique** P Oxley, C Waddy (AL)
1986 July 10	**Tessellations** P Oxley, C Waddy. (yo-yo)
1986 July 10	**Test Department** P Oxley, C Waddy
1986 July 11	**Sargasso** C Waddy (solo)
1986 July 11	**Calcitron, Damage Case** P Oxley, C Waddy
1986 July 11	**Sting in the Tail** C Waddy, P Oxley

Superseded Scorpion.

1986 July 12	**Zeitgeist** C Waddy, P Oxley (VL) (yo-yo)
1986 July 12	**Berserka** P Oxley, C Waddy (yo-yo)

Climbed with an in-situ wire at the roof.

1986 July 13	**St Elmo's Firé** C Waddy, P Oxley
1986 July 22	**The Gangster Lean** P Oxley
1986 Aug 8	**Zoolookologie** P Oxley (redpoint)
1986 Aug 9	**The Adventures of Portland Bill** P Oxley, J Biddle. (on-sight)
1986 Aug 17	**Form a Queue** J Biddle, J Blyde, M Higgins, D Simpson
1986 Aug 29	**All Guns Blazing** P Oxley, C Waddy

Pitch 1 by P Oxley, J Biddle on 14 August 1986.

1986 Aug 30	**Echoes from the Dead** P Oxley, C Waddy

Variations by C Waddy, J Williams, later in 1986.

1986 Aug 31	**Let the Punka Burn** P Oxley, C Waddy (AL) (on-sight)

*On a previous roped solo attempt, Waddy's self-belay system
failed, nearly depositing him in the sea! Sparky variation
climbed by M J Crocker, J Harwood on 1 October 1994. Part
of this pitch had been climbed two months earlier by
C Waddy, N Craine before they moved very close to the
parent route to gain the faultline.*

1986 Aug 31	**Sun Streets** P Oxley, C Waddy
1986 Sept 5	**Dune Dust** P Oxley, J Preston (AL)
1986 Sept 5	**Not Forgotten, No Fade Away** M J Crocker, M Ward (flashed)
1986 Sept 5	**Centrepiece** M J Crocker, M Ward (dogged)
1986 Sept 6	**That Disillusioned Feeling When You See Your Jumper Disappear Beneath the Waves** P Windall (solo)
1986 Sept 6	**Fat Necrosis** M J Crocker, M Ward
1986 Sept 6	**To Fever Pitch** M J Crocker, M Ward

Climbed with an in-situ thread.

1986 Sept 6	**Distant Early Warning** M Ward, M J Crocker
1986 Sept 6	**The Friendly Landlord of Durlston Castle** C Waddy (on-sight solo)
1986 Sept 6	**Wessex Way** A Blakely
1986 Sept 7	**Rufty Tufty** J Preston, J Biddle
1986 Sept 8	**Totally Insignificant and of Unparalleled Mediocrity** C Waddy (on-sight solo)

Destroyed by rockfall.

1986 Sept 8	**Rufty Tufty Vivisects His Mummy, Fathoms, Donald, Where's Your Trousers?, Whack Your Porcupine, Zawn Yawn** C Waddy (on-sight solo)
1986 Sept 8	**On the Third Day, Ruurd Ruum** C Waddy, T Foord-Kelsey
1986 Sept 8	**Alien Hum** P Oxley, J Preston (AL)
1986 Sept 9	**Tempting Truancy** C Waddy, P Windall, T Foord-Kelsey
	The holidays were over and the schoolboys couldn't stay; Waddy stole the route and then rubbed salt into the wound by informing them they wouldn't have succeeded anyway!
1986 Sept 18	**German New Order** P Oxley (yo-yo)
1986 Sept 27	**Chalkfree** A Blakely, N Weymouth
1986 Sept 27	**Swingtime Direct** P Oxley (solo)
1986 Sept 27	**Up on the Catwalk** P Oxley (solo with a hanging rope)
1986 Sept 28	**Jesus and Mary Chain** P Oxley, J Biddle
1986 Oct 4	**Load It for Me** P Oxley, G Gibson (yo-yo)
	The first peg runner was preclipped.
1986 Oct 8	**Blast Suburbia** P Oxley, C Lane (on sight)
1986 Oct 8	**Birth Pains of New Nations** P Oxley (yo-yo)
1986 Oct 11	**Tensile Groove Test** P Oxley, S Williams
	Started at 7.30 a.m. in order to beat the imagined competition!
1986 Oct 18	**Strangled in Black** P Oxley
1986 Oct 18	**Grossville** P Oxley (yo-yo)
1986 Nov 2	**Volts Discharge** P Oxley, J Biddle
1986 Nov 4	**The Futurist** P Oxley (flashed)
1986 Nov 12	**Lunatic** C Waddy, A Donson (on-sight)
1986 Nov 30	**The Mace** C Waddy, P Windall
1986 Dec 14	**Atomic Road Hero** P Oxley (dogged)
1986 Dec 14	**Blitzkrieg** P Oxley
1986 Dec 20	**Return of the Native** T Dunsby, B Wyvill, N A Coe
	Two natives in fact: Dunsby was back on the loose stuff after a year in Yosemite, and Blob Wyvill was on a flying visit from Calgary.
1986 Dec 20	**Calamity Jane** N A Coe, B Wyvill, T Dunsby
1986 Dec 20	**Graffiti Bombers of New York City** P Oxley, R Newey
1987 Jan 14	**Coccyx** S Winder
1987 Jan 31	**Chicago Peace** P Oxley
1987 Feb 21	**Coming in a R-U-S-H** P Oxley
1987 March 14	**Big Brother Is Watching** P Oxley
1987 April 5	**Acapulco** C Waddy, P Windall (AL) (yo-yoed)
1987 April 5	**Death's Head Hawk Moth** C Waddy, J Vlasto
1987 April 11	**World in Action** P Oxley, S Williams
	Splashed and then flashed; the week before the same pair had barely touched rock when they were 'glubbed' by a large wave.
1987 April 12	**Genetix** P Oxley, S Williams
1987 April 12	**On Life's Edge** P Oxley, S Williams (flashed)

1987 April 14	**Northern Sky, Claire's Brother** C Deacon	
1987 April 14	**Distortion Plan** P Oxley	
1987 April 25	**Dreamtime** P Oxley, S Williams	
1987 April 26	*The Guillemot abseil ledge, approximately 500 tons of rock, felt the call of the wild and fell to the boulders below, leaving several nearby climbers unscathed. Two trashed abseil ropes were the only casualties!*	

1987 May 6	**Friends from the Deep** T Dunsby, N A Coe
1987 May 6	**Funeral Pyre** P Oxley, S Williams (AL)
1987 May 10	**Michelle** N A Coe, T Dunsby
1987 May 19	**Crazy Fingers** P Oxley (on-sight solo)
1987 May 23	**Down in the Sewer** P Oxley, A Perkins (dogged)
1987 May 23	**Nuclear Sunset** P Oxley, A Perkins
1987 May 26	**King of Strain** P Oxley (redpoint)
1987 May 30	**Melancholy Lane** C Waddy, J.Vlasto
	'In-situ dead seagull at the faultline.'
1987 May 31	**The Equalizer** P Oxley (flashed)
1987 May	**Tina** Reclimbed after the rockfall by S Rogers
1987 May	**Helen's Return** D Coley
1987 June 4	**Cutlass** C Waddy, J Alcock
1987 June 5	**Alas, Poor Yorick** C Waddy, J Alcock
1987 June 6	**The Big Heat** P Oxley, J Williams
1987 June 6	**Toiler on the Sea** P Oxley, G Anstey (yo-yo)
	Pitch 2 had been climbed before as a variation to August Angie by H Lancashire, C Radcliffe on 26 October 1975.
1987 June 6	**Younger Days** M Saunders and party
1987 June 14	**The Roaring Forties** T Dunsby, N A Coe
1987 June 20	**All Quiet on the Southern Front** P Oxley, S Williams
1987 June 27	**Rambling Moses Weetabix and the Secona Park Seven** P Oxley, G Anstey [2P;1N]
1987 July 4	**Anger Is an Energy** P Oxley, G Anstey
1987 July 4	**Made in Britain** P Oxley, S Williams
	Affected by rockfall.
1987 July 22	**It Sank the Ship, Now Eat the Lettuce** N A Coe, T Dunsby
1987 July 24	**Armed and Dangerous** P Oxley, D Sharman (redpoint)
1987 July	**Mayhem on the Terraces** T Dunsby, N A Coe (1 rest pt)
	Pitches 1 to 3 on 6 July; pitches 4 and 5 on 16 July; pitches 6 to 9 on 18 July. First free ascent T Dunsby, N A Coe on 25 October 1987.
1987 Aug 1	**The Roaring Boys** P Oxley, S Williams (yo-yoed)
1987 Aug 4	**Purple Heart** P Oxley (roped solo)
	The self-belay system jammed on the crux!
1987 Aug 14	**Too Precious** P Oxley, R Mardon (flashed)
1987 Aug 23	**Straits of Hormuz** P Oxley, B Tilley, S Williams
1987 Sept 27	**Who Needs Friends?, Insectitude** (Winspit), **Praying Mantle, Emmy's Roof, Dream Topping** M Ripley, R Rogers

1987 Sept 27	**Swordfish Trombones** C Waddy, A Ford (1 pt aid)	
	First free ascent C Waddy in 1989.	
1987 Oct 4	**Tuna Lick** P Oxley, B Tilley	
1987 Oct 4	**The Tide's Coming In** M Ripley, R Rogers	
	Destroyed by rockfall.	
1987 Oct 11	**Three little Pigs** R Rogers, M Ripley	
	Destroyed by rockfall.	
1987 Oct 11	**Christine** M Ripley (solo)	
1987 Oct 12	**Herem Roof** P Oxley, J Williams	
1987 Oct 13	**Sexaphone** P Oxley, J Williams (yo-yo)	
1987 Oct 24	**Sunset Finish** P Kidd, P Hiscouk	
1987 Oct	**Jockanesse** M Higgins, S Hathaway	
	Probably climbed before.	
1987 Oct	**Toby's Revenge** S Hathaway, M Higgins	
1987 Nov 7	**Yellow-Bellied Fink** P Oxley, T Dunsby	
1987 Nov 13	**The Ancient Order of Free-Marblers** P Oxley, T Dunsby [1T]	
1987 Nov 14	**Wingwalker Extraordinaire, Cave Rave** P Oxley, T Dunsby	
1987 Nov 26	**A Quantum Jump for Apekind** P Oxley	
1987 Nov 28	**Seizure** P Oxley (redpoint)	
	On day three. A straightened-out but shorter version, Total Seizure, was climbed by P Oxley on 11 June 1994.	
1987 Nov 29	**Rock around the Block** T Dunsby, N A Coe	
1987 Nov 29	**Jug Index** P Oxley, J Williams	
1987 Nov	**Golden Oldie** S Hathaway, I Belcher	
	Probably climbed before.	
1987 Dec 5	**Exit Chimney II the Sequel** P Oxley, J Williams	
1987 Dec 20	**Stonemason** T Dunsby, N A Coe (flashed) [-]	
1987 Dec 20	**Jargon Eater** N A Coe, T Dunsby	
1987 Dec 22	**Mental as Anything** P Oxley	
1987 Dec 23	**Peppercorn Rate** P Oxley, T Dunsby [1P]	
1987 Dec 31	**Queen Anne's Men** P Oxley, N A Coe (yo-yo) [1P]	
1987 Dec 31	**Unseen Ripples of the Pebble** N A Coe, P Oxley	
1987 Dec	**The Cat That Ate Marrowbone** C Appleby	
1987	**Percy the Palm** S Hathaway, M Higgins	
	Probably climbed before.	
1987	**The Eastern Traverse** First free ascent C Waddy	
1987	**Morbid Orbit** C Waddy	
1987	**The Damp Link** C Waddy (solo)	
1988 Jan 3	**Gallows Gore** P Oxley, T Dunsby [-]	
1988 Jan 3	**Red Rain** T Dunsby, N A Coe (2 rest pts) [-]	
	First free ascent P Oxley, B Tilley on 7 January 1988.	
1988 Jan 7	**Ideal World** B Tilley, P Oxley	
1988 Jan 10	**China in Your Hands** N A Coe, T Dunsby (flashed)	
1988 Jan 17	**Wet, Wet, Wet** N A Coe, T Dunsby	
1988 Jan 21	**The Nolans Meet Impulse Manslaughter** P Oxley	
1988 Jan 31	**Divine Wind, Cabbage Patch Kids** N A Coe, T Dunsby	

1988 Jan 31	**Sigmoid Direct** T Dunsby, N A Coe
1988 Feb 3	**Les Hommes en Noir, Freedom Fighter** P Oxley, J Biddle
1988 Feb 6	**Sunyata** P Oxley (redpoint)
1988 Feb 15	**Rock around the Block Direct** P Oxley
1988 Feb 17	**Paparazzi News** P Oxley, B Tilley (yo-yo)
1988 Feb 20	**Loony on the Loose** T Dunsby, N A Coe
1988 Feb 20	**Stress Analysis of a Strapless Evening Gown** N A Coe, T Dunsby (on-sight)

An unwitting first ascent; the chalk seen on the start was from the first ascent of Les Hommes en Noir.

| 1988 Feb 24 | **Inspector Clouseau** P Oxley |
| 1988 Feb 27 | **Boys Keep Swinging** P Oxley, B Tilley |

Destroyed by rockfall.

| 1988 Feb 27 | **Everybody's Downfall** B Tilley, P Oxley |

Destroyed by rockfall.

1988 Feb 28	**Ozark Mountain Daredevils** T Dunsby, N A Coe, G A Jenkin
1988 Feb 28	**Squalid Walid and the Druze Blues** G A Jenkin, N A Coe, T Dunsby [3P]
1988 Feb 28	**Commander Cody and the Lost Planet Airmen** N A Coe, G A Jenkin, T Dunsby [1P]

Subsequently bolted, against the first ascensionist's wishes.

1988 March 12	**The Energy, The Faith, The Devotion** P Oxley (redpoint)
1988 March 17	**Haunted by a Million Screams** P Oxley
1988 March 22	**Mexican Wave** P Oxley (redpoint)
1988 April 3	**Girl from the Snow Country** P Oxley, T Hughes
1988 April 3	**Vigilante** P Oxley, T Hughes, S Williams (flashed)
1988 April 3	**My Wildest Dreams** P Oxley, S Williams
1988 April 19	**Violent Breed** P Oxley, J Williams (yo-yo)

Climbed with an in-situ wire.

1988 April 20	**Fat Chance Hotel** P Oxley (yo-yo) [2P;1T]
1988 April 21	**Cosa Nostra** J Williams, P Oxley
1988 April 28	**Camel Filter** J Williams (on-sight solo)

Llama Roundabout variation climbed by M Robertson, M Williams, M Arnall, all on-sight solo, on 14 August 1994.

1988 May 11	**A Subtle Shade of Emptiness** P Oxley, J Williams (yo-yo)
1988 May 21	**The Mind Cathedral** P Oxley, S Williams (flashed)
1988 May 22	**Spaghetti Western** K Kiessling, J Rihan (aid)
1988 May 22	**Any Which Way but Loose, The Good, the Bad and the Ugly** K Smith, G Foster, R Meyor
1988 May 28	**Bad Young Brother** P Oxley
1988 May	**Knobcrook Road** S Hathaway, M Higgins

Probably climbed before.

1988 June 11	**Roof Supreme** P Oxley (dogged)
1988 June 12	**The Beautiful and the Damned** P Oxley
1988 June	**The Hump** J Williams (on-sight solo)

1988 June	**Numb Bum** J Williams
1988 July 30	**Avenging the Halsewell** P Oxley (flashed) [1B;1P]
1988 Aug 1	**The Musharagi Tree** (formerly *The Great Durlston Prawn Robbery*) J Biddle, J Williams (on-sight)
1988 Aug 29	**Charge of the Wild Horsemen** P Oxley (roped solo)
1988 Aug	**Slap Ya Dromedary** J Williams (on-sight solo)
1988 Oct 28	**The Navajo Wars** P Oxley
1988 Oct	**Spiderman** S Hathaway, M Higgins
1988 Oct	**Wolverhampton Wanderer** M Higgins, S Hathaway *Probably climbed before.*
1988 Nov 1	**West of the Pecos** P Oxley (roped solo)
1988 Nov 5	**JCB** A Davies, Ms S Arnold
1988 Nov 18	**Crack Gang Killing** P Oxley *Direct start added by P Oxley (solo) in April 1989.*
1988 Nov 27	**Close to the Sun** P Oxley
1988 Nov 27	**The Great Rock 'n' Dole Swindle** P Oxley
1988 Nov	**California Here I Come** M Higgins, S Downes
1988 Dec 11	**All the Shakespearoes** P Oxley
1988 Dec 11	**Achelous** P Oxley (flashed)
1988 Dec 27	**Guano on My Face** S Bartram, G Bennett, C Waddy, P Oxley
1988	**Plasma Stream** P Oxley (1 pt aid) *First free ascent P Oxley on 13 April 1989.*
1988	**Tightrope** S Dore, K Smith
1988	**Rawhide** K Smith, S Dore
1988	**Come On Arms, Totally Gone Now** P Oxley (solo)
1988	**Moving Away from Rufty Tufty** C Waddy (on-sight solo)
1988	**Joker** A Blakely *Probably climbed before.*
1989 Jan 7	**Medician Star** P Oxley (redpoint in one pitch)
1989 Feb 8	**Peacemaker** P Oxley
1989 March 25	**The Wey of All Men** D Thomas, C Waddy *Pitch 1 had previously been climbed as part of* Quo Vadis.
1989 March	**Seppukku** P Oxley
1989 March	**The Great Shark Hunt** C Waddy, D Thomas
1989 March	**Furious Pig** C Waddy (on-sight solo)
1989 March	**Suntrap** Mrs A Keates, J Keates
1989 April 7	**J J Burnel, King of the Bass** P Oxley
1989 April 8	**Crimes against the Soul** P Oxley
1989 April 18	**The Lusty, Decadent Delights of Imperial Pompeii** P Oxley *Led in one pitch.*
1989 April	**Joe 90** C Waddy, D Thomas
1989 April	**Bon Firé** C Waddy, D Thomas (on-sight)
1989 June 24	**Graduation Day** S L Titt, N A Coe (1 rest pt) *First free ascent S L Titt, N A Coe on 27 June 1989.*
1989 July 23	**Finger Cwack, Benny's Apprentice** G Foster, A Cousins (aid on the latter)

1989 July 23	**Rubble Trubble**	A Cousins, G Foster
	Destroyed by rockfall.	
1989 July 30	**Pale Rider** K Smith, J Dallimore	
1989 Aug 21	**Fallen from Grace** P Oxley, B Tilley (AL)	
1989 Aug 22	**Street Fighting Years** P Oxley (pitch 1 redpoint, pitches 2 and 3 flashed)	
1989 Aug 24	**Turkish Delight** A Donson (solo)	
1989 Aug 28	**Clever Dick** A Donson (solo)	
1989 Aug 29	**End of the Innocence** P Oxley	
1989 Aug 29	**Hallucinating Freely** P Oxley	
	The Rock 2 was preplaced prior to the ascent.	
1989 Aug	**Down in Ruckly Ruckly Land** C Waddy (on-sight solo)	
1989 Aug	**Bloodlust** C Waddy, R Struke	
1989 Sept 3	**Monsters of Rock** P Oxley, J Biddle (flashed)	
1989 Sept 5	**Gnarly Scar Tissue** P Oxley	
1989 Oct 9	**Barney Rubble** K Smith, M Greenway	
	Destroyed by rockfall.	
1989 Oct 9	**Internal Examination** G Foster, A Cousins	
	Destroyed by rockfall.	
1989 Oct 9	**Gary** G Foster, A Cousins	
1989 Oct 16	**Razor Blade Smile** P Oxley (redpoint)	
1989 Oct 24	**Whispers Deep** P Oxley	
1989 Oct 25	**True Nature's Son** P Oxley, J Williams	
1989 Oct 25	**Loneshark** P Oxley	
1989 Oct 27	**I Am Stone, Melancholia, Another Youth Explodes** P Oxley	
1989 Oct 29	**Prayers for Rain** P Oxley	
	Climbed in a downpour.	
1989 Dec 3	**Shatterbox** G Foster, M Greenway	
1989 Dec 3	**Gardeners' Question Time** M Greenway, G Foster, K Smith	
1989 Dec 3	**Pineapple Edge** M Greenway, G Foster	
1989 Dec 9	**Big Bertha** N A Coe, T Dunsby (AL), N Holley	
1989 Dec	**Flasheart, Rubic's Hex** G Jefferies, M Dutson	
	The former has since been superseded by Born To Be Free climbed by M Robertson, S Taylor on 7 August 1993.	
1989	**The Men They Couldn't Hang** N Gresham, S Kincaid	
1989	**William McGonigall** C Waddy, A Popp	
1989	**Celibacy Screws You Up** P Oxley, S Taylor, D Kilburn	
	Affected by rockfall.	
1990 March 10	**The Last Corner** S L Titt, N A Coe	
1990 March 10	**The Other Gully** N A Coe, S L Titt	
	Probably climbed before.	
1990 March 22	**I Got the Spirit** P Oxley (redpoint)	
1990 March 22	**Buzz Cocked** P Oxley (flashed)	
1990 March 23	**The Earth's at Flashpoint** P Oxley	
1990 March 23	**Theory of Everything** P Oxley (redpoint)	
1990 April	**Titter Ye Not, Mrs!** P Oxley, M Hamblin	

1990 May 7	**Every Whichway...** R Curry, Ms P Longland
1990 May 7	**Prophets of Rage** P Oxley (redpoint) [2B;1P]
1990 May 7	**A Short Story about Power** P Oxley (flashed)
	Reclimbed after the rockfall by P Oxley on 19 June 1991.
1990 May 13	**Seven Years Solitary, Day of the Lords** P Oxley [1B]
	& [2B] respectively.
1990 May 13	**Whynot** G Foster, J Ross
	Probably climbed before.
1990 June 9	**The Dead Can't Judge** S L Titt, N A Coe, T Dunsby
1990 June 23	**Only Thisbig** P Frost, C Tym, M Vaiceities
	The top section had been climbed before as a variation to The Hobbit.
1990 July 1	**Absent Friend** S Taylor M Ford
	Destroyed by rockfall four months later. Probably the shortest-lived climb in Dorset!
1990 July 6	**Ceri's Route** M Grover, Ms C Hanson
1990 July 6	**Uncertain Smile** S Taylor, M Grover
1990 July 7	**Can't Touch This** S Taylor, Ms C Hanson, S Kerr, M Grover
1990 July 7	**Sunday Joint** S Kerr, S Taylor
1990 July 7	**Cup Final Day** S Taylor, M Grover, S Kerr
1990 July 7	**Mark's Route** M Grover (solo)
1990 July 9	**Cosmic Swing** S Kerr, S Taylor
1990 July 9	**East of Eden** S Taylor, S Kerr (redpoint)
1990 July 11	**Make Like a Bird** S L Titt, N A Coe
1990 Aug 5	**The Garden of Earthly Delights** T Dunsby, G A Jenkin (AL), N A Coe
1990 Aug 7	**A Dose of the Malhams** P Oxley (redpoint)
1990 Aug 8	**...And Captain Blood's Cavern** J M Cook
	On-sight solo. A previous on-sight solo attempt by D B Cook ended with an involuntary swim after failure on the final moves. Davey Jones' Lock-off variation climbed on sight by C Waddy, J Vlasto in August 1994.
1990 Aug 11	**Necromancy** P Oxley
1990 Aug 23	**Naked and Savage** P Oxley, J Williams (redpoint)
	On day two.
1990 Sept 8	**Supergrass** P Oxley
1990 Sept 10	**Vicky the Viking** D M Cook, J M Cook
	The second pitch was climbed in January 1978 (as Bumbly) by N Buckley, K Turner, P Dawson.
1990 Sept 16	**Volx with Friction** G Jefferies, P Oxley
	The first sport climb at Swanage. Subsequently debolted to comply with the Dancing Ledge access agreement.
1990 Sept 16	**Atrocity Exhibition, This Should Move Ya!** P Oxley, G Jefferies
1990 Sept 16	**Birth, School, Work, Death** P Oxley (on-sight solo)
1990 Sept 26	**Fear of a Black Planet** P Oxley
1990 Sept 26	**The Glue Krux Klan** P Oxley [1B]

1990 Sept 30	**Lucretia, My Reflection** P Oxley [2T]
1990 Oct 7	**The Pump Will Tear Us Apart** P Oxley, M Ford (flashed)
1990 Oct 8	**Sheffield über Alles** P Oxley (redpoint)
1990 Oct 8	**Sure Shot** P Oxley
1990 Oct 13	**Moves for the Masses** P Oxley, M Ford [1B;1T]
1990 Oct 19	**Mariner's Graveyard** P Oxley [2P;3T]
	He also reversed the first pitch and seconded the second!
1990 Nov 11	**Daylight Robbery, All Fall Down** S Taylor, S Kerr
1990 Nov 29	**Sun King** P Oxley
1990 Nov	**Aboriginal Script** P Oxley
1990 Dec 1	**Diving for Pearls** P Oxley, M Ford
1990 Dec 2	**The Wonders of Wallkraft** P Oxley, M Ford [2B;1T]
1990 Dec 13	**Vapour Trail** P Oxley (yo-yo)
1990 Dec 15	**Hieronymus GBH** P Oxley, M Ford
1990 Dec 15	**Taylor Made Tracking Damage** M Ford, S Taylor, P Oxley
1990 Dec 22	**Corona Envelope, Slap, Bang, On A Hang** P Oxley [1b] for the first
1990 Dec 22	**Cold Steal** M Ford, P Oxley [1B]
1991 Jan 20	**Transparent Birthday Suit** M Robertson (redpoint) [-]
1991 Feb 17	**Disco's Out - Murder's In** D B Cook (redpoint) [3B]
1991 March 3	**Marianas Trenchcoat** P Oxley, S Taylor (flashed)
1991 March 7	**Hangs Like a Dead Man** P Oxley [2B]
1991 March 7	**Jumping the Gun** P Oxley [-]
1991 March 23	**Today Forever** P Oxley, B Tilley (flashed)
1991 March 24	**The Jesus Lizard** P Oxley (redpoint)
1991 April 8	**Names Is for Tombstones (Baby)** D M Cook [3P;1T]
1991 April 13	**Date with a Frog** M Robertson
1991 April 14	**A Boschboy, a Trad, and a Funky Dredd** P Oxley (flashed)
1991 April 26	**Gymslip, Octopus** S L Titt, N A Coe
1991 May 6	**Ken Wilson's Last Stand** P Oxley, D B Cook (flashed)
1991 May 6	**Cinderella's Big Score** P Oxley (redpoint)
1991 May 9	**Mouth Breather** P Oxley (redpoint)
1991 May 11	**For Your Arms Only** M Robertson
	Subsequently debolted by the first ascensionist to comply with the Dancing Ledge access agreement.
1991 May 11	**Hiccup** M Robertson, D B Cook
1991 May 12	**Solid State Logic** P Oxley (redpoint)
1991 May 14	**Mr Choo Choo** D M Cook, J M Cook [3B]
1991 May 19	**Dark Millenium, Idiot Joy Showland** P Oxley (flashed)
1991 May 19	**Frisbee** N A Coe, S L Titt
1991 May 19	**Charge of the Light Brigade** T Dunsby, N A Coe, S L Titt
1991 May 25	**Withering Heights** S L Titt, S Murphy (yo-yo)
1991 May 27	**Godfodder** P Oxley (redpoint)
1991 June 6	**A Brutal Equation** P Oxley (flashed)
1991 June 9	**Bad Day** S Taylor, M Robertson (redpoint) [2B;1T]
1991 June 9	**Rescue Corner, Spider Ledge** S L Titt, N A Coe

1991 June 19	**Shinhead Clash** M Robertson	

Robertson fell 20 feet onto his second's head!

1991 June 29	**Produced by Fred Quimby** M Robertson, S Taylor [3B]
1991 June 29	**Mindless Optimism** M Robertson [2B]
1991 July 7	**Rainy Day Dream Away** T Dunsby, S L Titt (flashed)
1991 July 7	**Heathcliffe** S L Titt, T Dunsby (redpoint)
1991 July 14	**Calm, Calm** T Dunsby, S L Titt (AL) (on sight)
1991 July 14	**Rage, Rage** T Dunsby, S L Titt (flashed)

Pitch 2 added by the same pair on 27 October 1991.

1991 July 24	**Tekneeque** A Blakely, D Ashley
1991 July 31	**Rocket USA, Slow Dive, Waiting for the Death Blow** P Oxley (redpoint)
1991 July	**Double or Quits** P Oxley (redpoint)

Mike Robertson ended up five pounds poorer after betting that the line he had cleaned could not be climbed.

1991 Aug 11	**Talking to the Angel** T Dunsby, R Mardon, N A Coe (flashed)
1991 Aug 18	**Ciao Pupa** J M Cook, D B Cook
1991 Aug 18	**Ozymandias** D B Cook, J M Cook (flashed)
1991 Aug 18	**La Rue sans Issue** D M Cook, P McKenna
1991 Sept 21	**Palace of the Brine** P Oxley (redpoint)

On day four.

1991 Sept 22	**Things That Make You Go Hmmm** P Oxley (redpoint)
1991 Oct 27	**Tape and Ape** T Dunsby, S L Titt

Success was achieved on the sixth visit, when a nut was preplaced near the lip of the roof.

1991 Oct 30	**Song to the Siren** P Oxley (flashed)
1991 Oct	**Gold Mother** D M Cook, J M Cook
1991 Oct	**Fifteen to One** P McKenna (on-sight solo)
1991 Nov 9	**Pump Me Tenderly** M Robertson
1991 Nov 16	**Insecticide** T Dunsby, Miss P Holt, N A Coe, R Elder
1991 Nov 23	**Freddy** T Dunsby, B Tilley, N A Coe (VL)

On the first ascent the lichenous wall was avoided on the left; subsequently straightened out by B Tilley.

1991	**One Move Wonder** N A Coe, S L Titt
1992 Jan 11	**Internal Exile** S L Titt, N A Coe
1992 Jan 11	**Seriously Short** S L Titt, N A Coe (redpoint)
1992 Feb 8	**Republic** S L Titt, N A Coe (redpoint)
1992 Feb 22	**Here Comes the Hizbollah** M Ford [-]
1992 Feb 29	**Other Times** S L Titt, N A Coe (flashed)
1992 April 4	**Other Places** S L Titt, N A Coe (redpoint)
1992 April 4	**Elm Street** N A Coe, S L Titt (yo-yo)
1992 April 5	**Landslide Victory** P J Osborne, J Homewood
1992 April 8	**Sugar Ray, Negative Creep** P Oxley (redpoint)
1992 April 10	**Judgement Day** T Dunsby, N A Coe

Brightened us up after the dismal election results the day before.

1992 April 11	**Eye Am the Sky** P Oxley, M Ford
1992 April 19	**Dead Good** S Taylor, M Robertson (yo-yo)

1992 April 20	**Don's Long Gone** T Dunsby, S L Titt, N A Coe, S Taylor, G A Jenkin (yo-yo) [-]
1992 April 20	**Strange Devices** N A Coe, T Dunsby, G A Jenkin, S L Titt (VL)
1992 April 20	**Bop Ceroc** G A Jenkin, S L Titt, T Dunsby, N A Coe (redpoint)
1992 May 3	**Hell's Darker Chambers** P Oxley (redpoint)
1992 May 3	**Fiddler on the Roof** N A Coe, S L Titt (VL)
1992 May 3	**Libertine** S L Titt, N A Coe (flashed)
1992 May 30	**Mr Punch** P Finklaire, N Withers
1992 May 31	**The Safety Rail** T Dunsby, S L Titt, N A Coe (VL)
1992 June 20	**Catch the Wind** T Dunsby, N A Coe, S L Titt (flashed)
1992 July 21	**The Ghost of Ian Curtis** P Oxley (redpoint)
1992 Aug 11	**Rufty's Roll Up** D Simpson, A Hedger
1992 Aug 11	**Parallel Lines** (Blackers Hole) A Hedger, D Simpson
1992 Aug	**Infinite Gravity** P Oxley (redpoint)
	Six days spread over two years.
1992 Aug	**John Craven's Willy Warmer** M King (solo)
1992 Sept 19	**Fury 161** T Dunsby, N A Coe (AL), S L Titt
1992 Sept 19	**Wild at Heart** T Dunsby, N A Coe (redpoint)
1992 Oct 31	**The Curse of Testosterone** T Dunsby, S L Titt (flashed)
1992	**Hard Tackle** M King, A Snow
	This line was improved by S Taylor, M Bateman as The Honeymonster on 21 August 1993.
1993 Feb 21	**Temple Redneck** P Oxley (redpoint)
1993 Feb 23	**The Schwarzechild Radius** P Oxley (aid)
1993 Feb 27	**Leave It to the Birds** T Dunsby, N A Coe
1993 March 25	**Drunken Butterfly** P Oxley (redpoint)
1993 March	**Juggernaut, Jack-knife, Techno Sketching, Puddle Jumper, Ride the Lightning** P Oxley (solo)
	Ride the Lightning was climbed in three stages.
1993 April 10	**Old Ghosts (Scare Me Most)** S L Titt, N A Coe (redpoint)
1993 May 10	**The Garage Mechanic** P Oxley (redpoint)
1993 May	**Left-Hand Route** S L Titt, N A Coe (on-sight)
1993 June 4	**Amazonia** J M Cook (solo)
1993 June	**Crime Wave, Tsunami** D B Cook
1993 June	**Leap of Faith** D B Cook (on-sight solo)
1993 July 31	**The Vixen, Chrissy** M Robertson, J Boyle
1993 Aug 5	**Exuberance, Insect Graveyard** M Robertson, S Taylor
1993 Aug 11	**Any Old Time** M Robertson, G Fitch
1993 Aug 25	**White Rave** M Robertson (redpoint)
1993 Aug 26	**Carol's Little Injection** M Robertson, Ms C Robertson
1993 Aug 26	**Perpetual State of Confusion, Sloping and Hoping** M Robertson, J M Cook
1993 Aug 29	**Marble Halls, Cold Empty Cross** P Oxley (redpoint)
	Predatory bolting which has spoilt an existing route.
1993 Sept 1	**Nine Years' Absence** M Robertson, T Huisman
1993 Sept 5	**Chicago Pipe Dream** Ms J Wylie

1993 Sept 6	**Option B** D B Cook, J M Cook	
1993 Oct 17	**Ammonitemare** S Taylor, J Boyle	
1993 Oct 17	**Bust Ya Boiler** P Oxley, J Picalli	
1993 Nov 5	**Gorilla Tactics, Know What I Mean, Pal?** M Robertson, M Williams	
1993 Nov 12	**Rampant Love Jugs, Nosey** M Robertson, M Williams	
1993 Nov 27	**Corridors of Power** M Robertson, M Williams (redpoint)	
1993 Nov 28	**The Damnation Game** M Robertson (redpoint)	
	After three hours of aborted start sequences.	
1993 Nov 29	**Billy Winspit** S Taylor	
1993 Dec 4	**Restless Heart, Lips of a Stranger, Knickerless Crutches** M Robertson, M Williams	
1993 Dec 5	**Dick Dastardly** M Robertson (redpoint)	
1993 Dec 5	**So Naughty** Ms C Robertson, M Robertson, M Williams, Ms V Robinson	
1993 Dec 11	**Idiot Village** M Robertson, D B Cook	
1993	**Herman Borg's Basic Pulley Slippage** P Oxley	
1994 March 4	**Agonies of a Dying Mind** M Robertson	
1994 March 12	**Goddamn Sexual Tyrannosaurus** M Williams, G Fitch, M Robertson	
1994 March 12	**Tethered by Gravity** S Taylor, Miss M Huisman	
1994 March 18	**Of Mice and Men** M Robertson, G Fitch	
1994 March 18	**Into the Realm of Radical Cool** M Robertson	
1994 March 18	**Post-Coital Snooze** M Robertson, M Williams	
1994 March 20	**Insanely Yours** M Robertson	
1994 May 13	**Resin Devotion, The Genius of SK** M Robertson, M Williams	
1994 May 17	**War of the Wardens** M Williams	
1994 May 22	**Empty Promises** S Taylor, Miss M Huisman, M Williams	
1994 June 5	**Revhead's Hi-Roller** P Oxley, M Higgs (flashed)	
	Climbed before the car-crash of the same name.	
1994 June 5	**Lunacy Booth** P Oxley (redpoint)	
1994 June 10	**Just Another Victim** P Oxley (redpoint)	
1994 June 18	**Knee and a Tall Man** M Robertson, M Williams	
1994 June 19	**Waves Become Wings** P Oxley, M Higgs (flashed)	
1994 June 19	**Hot to Trot** P Oxley (redpoint)	
	Hot Flush Down Under variation climbed by P Oxley on 24 September 1993.	
1994 June 29	**All Apologies** P Oxley	
1994 July 13	**Liquid Steel** P Oxley (redpoint)	
	An act of bad faith by the first ascensionist, who was party to the Dorset bolt agreement.	
1994 July 30	**Playtime with Playtex** P Oxley (flashed)	
1994 Aug 25	**Sea of Holes** M Williams, B Lewis	
1994 Aug 28	**Empowerless** B Tilley	
1994 Aug 28	**Norseman, Deaf Mosaic, Sons of Pioneers** M J Crocker, N A Coe	
	Coe followed the first route, was winched up the crux of the	

second, and had trouble aiding parts of the third, finishing in the dark with a cramped-up arm!

1994 Aug	**Davy Jones' Lock-Off** C Waddy, J Vlasto (on-sight)
1994 Aug	**Blood, Sugar, Sex and Magic, Skulduggery** C Waddy, N Craine (on-sight)
1994 Oct 1	**Decay 9** M J Crocker, J Harwood
1994 Oct 1	**Sinking Feeling** M J Crocker, J Harwood

Pitch 1 had been climbed by C Waddy, N Craine in August 1994.

1994 Oct 9	**True Identity** P Finclaire, N Withers
1994 Oct 15	**Once it's Gotcha** M J Crocker, J Harwood (flashed)
1994 Oct 15	**Havana** M J Crocker, J Harwood
1994 Oct 16	**Get outta Your Armchair and into This** M J Crocker, J Harwood
1994 Oct 22	**It Can't Be Denied** M Robertson, M Williams
1995 Feb 25	**Mammotholian** M Robertson, Ms T Mockford, M Williams

TILLY WHIM AND DURLSTON CASTLE CLIFF

These two cliffs now form part of a bird sanctuary and climbing is not permitted. The details below are included for their historical interest only. The few climbs recorded since the establishment of the sanctuary are not included.

1960 Feb	**Poem Wall** A G Smythe, J S Cleare (aid)
Pre-1963	**Poem Corner** I McMorrin (4 pts aid)

First free ascent K Topping in 1968.

Pre-1963	**Rendezvous Manque** S A Clark, A G Smythe
1963 May 8	**Steeple** P A Bell, J Mustoe

Variation climbed by P A Bell, J F G Clarke on 12 July 1963.

1963	**Siesta** R Baillie, J S Cleare
1964 July	**Ghost Line, Fairy Exit** M Image, K Stubbs
1964 Dec 26	**Tempus, Brutus** A M Green, J E Crew
1964	**Pinewood, Madness, Scrotonomy, HMC, Stardust, Florence** M Image, K Stubbs
1966 Dec 17	**Megan** A J Young, W H Church
1968	**Lion's Mane Direct** First free ascent K Topping

OLD HARRY ROCKS and ISLE OF WIGHT

Surprisingly, chalk has attracted a high proportion of female first ascensionists.

c.1858	**Lighthouse Arête** Lighthouse construction workers
1971	**Outer Main Stack** I Howell, J S Cleare, J Fowler, R Collomb

The exact line of the climb remains unknown.

1976 July 4	**Northern Bay** S L Titt, D Gumn
1976 July 4	**The Ridge** R J Crewe, T Tanswell

After these two ascents an attempt was made to cast a line over Old Harry in order to jumar up to the summit. The attempt was foiled by air turbulence.

1977	**La Traversée Intégrale de la Pointe Ballarde à la Pointe Handfaste** S L Titt, T Tanswell
1979	**Original Route** A Strapcans, Ms L Heinemann, A Henderson

Louise performed handstands on top of the stack for the benefit of the tourists watching from the mainland.

1984 Sept 22	**Wrinklie's Retreat** H Todd, B Craig (AL), Ms L Allen
1984 Nov 3	**Skeleton Ridge** M Fowler, Ms L Smyth (VL)
1984 Nov 4	**The Crisp** M Fowler, Ms L Smyth
1984 Nov 4	**Strapped to the Wing with the Engine Running** C Jones, P Thornhill (AL)
1985 Sept 22	**Press Gang Pinnacle** M Fowler, C Newcombe
1985 Oct 12	**Gateway to Heaven** A Meyers, M Fowler
1985 Oct 12	**Blood Sweat and Bullets, Negotiator** M Fowler, A Meyers
1986 May	**The Witch's Tit** S Ballantine, J Henderson

Climbed at night, wearing wetsuits. 'Have you ever tried coiling a rope whilst treading water encumbered with helmet, axes and a harness?'

1987 May 9	**The Tusk** M Fowler, A Meyers (AL), Ms S Vietoris (on-sight)
1987 May 14	**Old Harry East Face** M Fowler, C Newcombe, M Lynden, A Meyers

Aid was used to place peg protection on a short section of pitch 2 before the pitch was free-climbed.

1987 June 20	**Albatross** R Hoare, G Haines
1988 May 21	**South East Arête** M Fowler, J Lincoln (both solo)
1988 May 21	**South Face** M Fowler, Ms N Dugan, J Lincoln, R Hoare
1988 May 22	**Stag Rock** R Hoare, J Lincoln, Ms N Dugan, M Fowler

Probably climbed before.

1988 May 22	**Arch Rock** R Hoare, J Lincoln, Ms N Dugan, M Fowler

The whole stack has now fallen down.

1988 May 22	**Bear Rock** M Fowler, Ms N Dugan, J Lincoln, R Hoare
1988 July 9	**Learning to Fly** M Fowler, A Meyers
1988 July 16	**The Plunge** M Fowler, D Tunstall, Ms N Dugan
1988 Dec 2	**Hot and Cold** M Fowler, M Morrison (AL), B Birkett

Birkett does his homework for his book.

1992 April 25	**Testing** M Fowler, J Lincoln, A Meyers, Ms C Delgardo
1992 Sept	**Team Teva** D Hornby, D Barlow
1992 Nov 7	**Ship of Fools** (Isle of Wight) C Jones, D Hornby

Details of the fixed protection (if any) employed on first ascents have been included for routes that have been retrobolted. B indicates bolt runner; D drilled peg runner; P peg runner; T *in-situ* thread runner; N *in-situ* nut runner; [-] that no fixed protection was used.

Index

Accident Procedure

FIRST AID
If spinal or head injuries are suspected, do not move the patient without skilled help, except to maintain breathing.

If breathing has stopped, clear the airways and start artificial respiration. Do not stop until expert opinion has diagnosed death.

Stop bleeding by applying direct pressure.

Summon help.

RESCUE
In the event of an accident where further assistance is required, DIAL 999 and ask for the COASTGUARD. The Coastguards are responsible for the co-ordination of all sea-cliff rescues, and will co-ordinate the other services such as helicopters, lifeboats, cliff rescue teams, etc.

It is important to report the exact location and details of the accident and also to have someone meet the rescue team to guide them to the spot.

NEAREST PHONE POINTS
Portland & Lulworth Cove - Both within easy reach of a phone.

Durdle Door - At the top of the hill behind the arch is a phone box by a caravan park; this is closer than Lulworth Cove itself.

St Aldhelm's Head - There is a 999-only phone on the landward wall of the Coastguard lookout.

Winspit & Seacombe - There is a public phone box on the green at Worth Matravers.

Hedbury Quarry, Dancing Ledge, Guillemot Ledge, Cormorant Ledge & Blackers Hole - Spyway Barn (on the track leading from the normal parking spot towards Dancing Ledge).

Cattle Troughs Area, Boulder Ruckle, The Lighthouse Cliffs - There is a 999-only phone by the entrance to the Lighthouse.

Old Harry Rocks, Isle Of Wight - Easiest by contacting a nearby boat.

HELICOPTER
In the event of a Helicopter evacuation **all** climbers on or off the cliff should take heed. A helicopter flying close to the cliff will make verbal communication very difficult and small stones will be dislodged by the rotor downdraught. All loose equipment should be secured and climbers in precarious positions should try to make themselves safe.

The people with the injured person should try to identify their location. **No** attempt should be made to throw a rope at the helicopter, but assistance should be given to the helicopter crew if requested. **Do not** touch the lowered crew member or his winch wire until the trailing wire has earthed the helicopter's static electricity.

LOCAL HOSPITALS
The walking wounded can receive treatment in the casualty departments of the following hospitals:

Weymouth & District Hospital, Melcombe Avenue, Weymouth. Phone number (01305) 772211.

Swanage Hospital, Queens Road, Swanage. Phone number (01929) 422282.

Poole General Hospital, Longfleet Road, Poole. Phone number (01202) 675100.

FOLLOW-UP
After an accident a written report should be sent to the Mountain Rescue Committee Statistics Officer, Mr David Noott, Gorsefield, Springbank, New Mills, Stockport, SK12 4BH, giving details of: date, extent of injuries, and name, age, and address of the casualty. Normally this will be done by the police or local rescue team involved, who will also require the names and addresses of those climbing with the injured party.

If unreasonable equipment failure is suspected then the British Mountaineering Council's technical committee may wish to investigate; contact the BMC at 177-179 Burton Road, West Didsbury, Manchester, M20 2BB.

Addendum - New Climbs

HEDBURY QUARRY
The Living Dead   100 feet   E3 5c †   (25.3.95)
Medium wires are required to supplement the bolts of the routes crossed by
this girdle of The Cannon Quarry.
Climb *Jumping the Gun* to its final bolt runner. Traverse leftwards under the
roof of *Moves for the Masses* and with difficulty across a ramp to reach *Of
Mice and Men*. Continue left to the lower-off bolts of *Tethered by Gravity* at
the blunt arête.
M Robertson, S Taylor

On the Hedbury Quarry Sea Walls, between *Finger Cwack* and *East Milton
Wall* is an overhung bay. Two climbs take advantage of the horizontal
breaks between the stepped roofs of the bay.

Juvenile Product of the Working Class   40 feet   E2 5b †   (25.3.95)
Start from the ledge on the west side of the bay.
Move up and traverse rightwards along the short half-height wall to a
prow and move up to the next break. Continue rightwards to a huge
blocky flake; climb this and cross a roof to reach the top.
M Robertson, S Taylor (on sight)

∗**Rebel without a Clue**   60 feet   E2 5b †   (25.3.95)
Start on the east side of the bay and traverse leftwards along the short wall
at half height. Committing!
M Robertson, S Taylor (on sight)

GUILLEMOT LEDGE
The second ascent of *Funeral Pyre* has prompted a regrade from E3 to E5
on account of the risk of a ground fall from poor holds high on pitch 1.

FISHERMAN'S LEDGE
The start of *That Disillusioned Feeling...* has fallen down.

BOULDER RUCKLE
I Just Wanna Be Free   120 feet   E6 †   (29.5.95)
A gruellingly strenuous battle with the hanging crack in the leaning wall just
left of *I Got the Spirit*. Adequate gear, but very strenuous to place.
1 80 feet 6b. Pull up onto the arête left of *I Got the Spirit* and follow it to
a hollow spike beneath the crack. Launch up the crack, and make a very
difficult move to reach a break. Surmount the bulge slightly to the left and
pull up into the vertical for a rest. Move up and right to a jammed jug,
climb carefully direct, and exit left to a belay in the corner of *High Noon*.
2 40 feet 5a. Follow *High Noon* to the top.
M J Crocker, R Chappell

*Jugs in Space   140 feet   E4 6a †   (24.6.95)
A strenuous route, run out in places, which starts as for *Yellow-Bellied Fink*.
Traverse 15 feet left and climb a shallow groove to the overhang. Move
diagonally right and then follow the obvious traverse back leftwards to a
resting-place. Climb a crack and a difficult groove to the faultline. Use a
diagonal flake to cross the bulge and head up a steep wall to a niche and a
small slab above. Move up past an undercut to better holds and rightwards
with difficulty to easier ground. Pull out on a rope preplaced on a stake.
T Dunsby, C Dunsby, N A Coe

In Triplicate (130 feet Hard Very Severe 5b † 11.6.95) is a rightward
diagonal linking three walls. Climb the flat wall left of *Due Care and
Attention* before crossing that route. Move up onto blocks and climb a
second wall up past the faultline to the base of a corner. Finish up the wall
on the right.
N A Coe, T Dunsby

Bunch of Weirdos   110 feet   E4 †   (14.5.95)
Start as for *The Cat Skinner*. A spectacular top pitch which forces the roofs
left of *Ulysses*.
1 50 feet 4c. Climb diagonally rightwards and follow the crack left of
the arête to the faultline. Swing right to a corner.
2 60 feet 6a. Climb the corner and surmount the bulge. A fingery and
pumping traverse leads rightwards beneath a roof to an obvious exit
groove.
M J Crocker, R Chappell

*Waiting for God   120 feet   E6 †   (14.5.95)
A significant addition which combines a run-out first pitch with a strenuous
but protectable top. Start as for *Little Matterhorn*.
1 60 feet 6b. Climb the centre of the wall to a horizontal break (peg
runner) and link calcite edges (poor tied-off peg runner slightly left) to
reach the faultline. The final move is delicate, and the inevitably peg-
ripping plummet would need a sprinting second if a ground fall is to be
avoided. Good wire belay on the left.
2 60 feet 6a. Climb up just right of the right-facing corner, and surmount
the first roof with difficulty. Pull over the second roof using a good block
and finish up a thin crack in the headwall.
M J Crocker (on sight)

Additional Information (2002)

GUILLEMOT LEDGE
Graffiti Bombers of New York City considered E3 5c. The poorly-protected section is the middle.

CORMORANT LEDGE
The Triple Arch has collapsed and the following routes are no more:
Easter Egg
Calm, Calm
Rage, Rage
Indigo

Their immediate neighbours should be treated with suspicion. However, the fall has not affected *Quality Street*.

Cormorant Ledge Routes with natural (i.e. unquarried) tops receive so little traffic that in essence you will be doing a second ascent, with all that that implies in terms of looseness.

THE CATTLE TROUGHS AREA
Amazonia considered E3 5c

BOULDER RUCKLE
Judgement Day Affected by rockfall, making the the big roof even larger. Not yet reclimbed.

The Earth's at Flashpoint considered E4 6a – run out.

West of the Pecos considered hard E2 5c.

Corollary considered E3 4b 5b.

Ice Queen considered E5 6a. There are two bold sections with groundfall potential. The peg on the second of these is all but impossible to clip if you are of normal stature.

Purple Heart considered E4 5c.

THE LIGHTHOUSE CLIFFS
All the Shakespearoes considered E3 6a

THE ISLE OF WIGHT
Albatross is a very serious proposition, and plenty of time should be allowed.

Skeleton Ridge pitch 5 is 120 feet, not 20.

The Dorset Bolt Agreement

The issue of bolting was debated at length at a BMC area meeting held locally in 1993 and the agreement reached was amended in 1996. It identified certain sections of cliff where, and under what conditions, bolting was permissible:

Winspit Quarried Walls Bolts acceptable.

Hedbury quarried walls Bolts acceptable.

Dancing Ledge Bolts acceptable (and also *required* for lower-off points on the back wall by the owners).

Blackers Hole Far West Existing bolt belays only.

Blackers Hole Cave Area Bolts acceptable.

Blackers Hole quarried wall Bolts acceptable.

Blackers Hole East Bolt belays for a small number of the harder routes.

Fisherman's Ledge cave (the large cave on the east side of Fisherman's) Bolts acceptable.

The Promenade Bolts acceptable.

All other cliffs described in this guidebook are designated bolt free.

It was agreed that if retrobolting were considered necessary, the permission of the first ascensionist would always be sought. If permission were not forthcoming then no retrobolting would take place.

It was also agreed that in the development of new cliffs it should be left to first ascensionists' discretion to assess the style of climbing appropriate to the venue; this would then be confirmed or otherwise at the next appropriate meeting.

Acknowledgements

I should like to thank the following, who have all contributed in some way to this guidebook: Richard Alldread, Barrie Annette, Sally Arnold, Peter Bain, Colin Beechey, Jon Biddle, Bill Birkett, Andy Blakely, Dick Burt, Martin Cade, Jackie Coe, Michelle Coe, Rick Collings, Sally Collings, Damian Cook, Dominic Cook, Jon 'Joff' Cook, Victoria Copley, Richard Crewe, Martin Crocker, Alan Davies, Andy Donson, John Drummond, Tim Dunsby, Bob Elder, Anthony Felton, Mike Ford, Geoff Foster, Mick Fowler, Gary Gibson, Mark Glaister, André Hedger, David Hope, Phil 'Flip' James, Gordon Jenkin, John Keates, Steve Kerr, Mick MacInnan, Gary McAvoy, Chris Mellor, Bob Moulton, Simon Nadin, Phillipe Osbourne, Pete Oxley, Rod Pirie, Kath Pyke, Doug Reid, Mike Robertson, Ian Robertson, Keith Robichaud, Mike Rosser, Mark Ryle, Don Sargeant, Steve Scott, Ian Smith, Tom Snape, Ian Surface, Ian Taylor, Steve Taylor, Andy Tims, Scott Titt, Kevin Turner, Crispin Waddy, Pete Watkins, Chas White, Brian Wilkinson, Emma Williams, Mark Williams, John Willson, and Bill Wright.

NAC 1995/2002

Climbers' Club Guides

THE CLIMBERS' CLUB

The publisher of this guidebook is The Climbers' Club, which was founded in 1898 from origins in Snowdonia and is now one of the foremost mountaineering clubs in Great Britain. Its objects are to encourage mountaineering and rock-climbing, and to promote the general interest of mountaineers and the mountain environment.

It is a truly national club with widespread membership, and currently owns huts in Cornwall, Pembrokeshire, Derbyshire, Snowdonia, and Argyll. Besides managing seven huts, The Climbers' Club produces an annual Journal and runs a full programme of climbing meets, dinners, and social events. Club members may also use the huts of other clubs through reciprocal arrangements. The club publishes climbing guidebooks (currently 20 in number) to cover most of Wales and Southern England. The club is a founder-member of, and is affiliated to, the British Mountaineering Council; it makes annual contributions to the Access and Conservation Trust, as well as to volunteer cliff and mountain rescue organizations. In 1999, the Climbers' Club Colin Kirkus Guidebook Fund was established as a means of distributing some of the profits earned from guidebooks to assist climbing-related projects that are in keeping with the aims of the club, though they need not be confined to the club's guidebook areas.

Membership fluctuates around 1,200, and at present there are no limits on growth. Members of two years' standing may propose a competent candidate for membership and, provided that adequate support is obtained from other members, the Committee may elect him or her to full membership; there is no probationary period.

CLIMBING STYLE

The following policy statement on climbing style was agreed in principle at The Climbers' Club Annual General Meeting on 25th February 1990:

The Climbers' Club supports the tradition of using natural protection and is opposed to actions which are against the best interest of climbers and users of the crags. This applies particularly to irreversible acts which could affect the crags and their environs.

Such acts could include: the placing of bolts on mountain and natural crags; retrospective placing of bolts; chiselling, hammering, or altering the rock appearance or structure; excessive removal of vegetation and interference with trees, flowers, and fauna.

The Climbers' Club policy is that guidebooks are written to reflect the best style matched to the ethos and traditions of British climbing.

GUIDEBOOK DISCLAIMER

This guide attempts to provide a definitive record of all existing climbs and is compiled from information from a variety of sources. The inclusion of any route does not imply that it remains in the condition described. Climbs can change unpredictably: rock can deteriorate and the existence and condition of *in-situ* protection can alter. All climbers must rely on their own ability and experience to gauge the difficulty and seriousness of any climb. Climbing is an inherently dangerous activity.

Neither The Climbers' Club nor the author and editor of this guidebook accept any liability whatsoever for any injury or damage caused to climbers, third parties, or property arising from the use of it. Whilst the content of the guide is believed to be accurate, no responsibility is accepted for any error, omission, or mis-statement. Users must rely on their own judgement and are recommended to insure against injury to person and property and third party risks.

The inclusion in this guidebook of a crag or routes upon it does not mean that any member of the public has a right of access to the crag or the right to climb upon it. Before climbing on any crag in this guidebook, please read the relevant access and conservation notes.

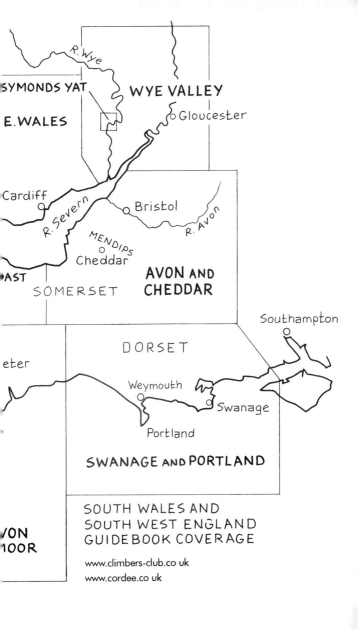

SYMONDS YAT

R. Wye

WYE VALLEY

o Gloucester

E. WALES

Cardiff o

R. Severn

o Bristol

R. Avon

MENDIPS
o
Cheddar

AVON AND
CHEDDAR

AST

SOMERSET

Southampton

DORSET

eter

Weymouth
o

Swanage
o

Portland

SWANAGE AND PORTLAND

VON
100R

SOUTH WALES AND
SOUTH WEST ENGLAND
GUIDEBOOK COVERAGE

www.climbers-club.co uk
www.cordee.co uk